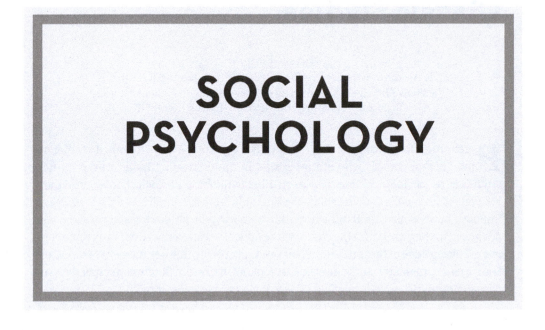

SOCIAL PSYCHOLOGY

Psychology: Revisiting the Classic Studies

Series Editors:
S. Alexander Haslam[1], Alan M. Slater[2] and Joanne R. Smith[2]
[1]School of Psychology, University of Queensland, Brisbane, Australia
[2]School of Psychology, University of Exeter, Exeter, UK

Psychology: Revisiting the Classic Studies is a new series of texts aimed at students and general readers who are interested in understanding issues raised by key studies in psychology. Volumes centre on 12–15 studies, with each chapter providing a detailed account of a particular classic study and its empirical and theoretical impact. Chapters also discuss the important ways in which thinking and research has advanced in the years since the study was conducted. They are written by researchers at the cutting edge of these developments and, as a result, these texts serve as an excellent resource for instructors and students looking to explore different perspectives on core material that defines the field of psychology as we know it today.

Also available:
Brain and Behaviour: Revisiting the Classic Studies
Bryan Kolb and Ian Wishaw

Cognitive Psychology: Revisiting the Classic Studies
Michael W. Eysenck and David Groome

Developmental Psychology: Revisiting the Classic Studies
Alan M. Slater and Paul C. Quinn

2ND EDITION

SOCIAL PSYCHOLOGY
REVISITING
THE CLASSIC STUDIES

EDITED BY:
JOANNE R. SMITH &
S. ALEXANDER HASLAM

SAGE

Los Angeles | London | New Delhi
Singapore | Washington DC | Melbourne

Los Angeles | London | New Delhi
Singapore | Washington DC | Melbourne

SAGE Publications Ltd
1 Oliver's Yard
55 City Road
London EC1Y 1SP

SAGE Publications Inc.
2455 Teller Road
Thousand Oaks, California 91320

SAGE Publications India Pvt Ltd
B 1/I 1 Mohan Cooperative Industrial Area
Mathura Road
New Delhi 110 044

SAGE Publications Asia-Pacific Pte Ltd
3 Church Street
#10-04 Samsung Hub
Singapore 049483

Editor: Luke Block
Editorial assistant: Lucy Dang
Production editor: Imogen Roome
Marketing manager: Lucia Sweet
Cover design: Wendy Scott
Typeset by: C&M Digitals (P) Ltd, Chennai, India
Printed by CPI Group (UK) Ltd, Croydon, CR0 4YY

First published 2017
First edition published 2013
Reprinted 2013, 2014, 2015 (twice), 2016

Library of Congress Control Number: 2016962465

British Library Cataloguing in Publication data

A catalogue record for this book is available from the British Library

ISBN 978-1-4739-7865-2
ISBN 978-1-4739-7866-9 (pbk)

At SAGE we take sustainability seriously. Most of our products are printed in the UK using FSC papers and boards. When we print overseas we ensure sustainable papers are used as measured by the PREPS grading system. We undertake an annual audit to monitor our sustainability.

If I have seen a little further it is by standing on the shoulders of giants.

Isaac Newton in a letter to his scientific rival, Robert Hooke, 5 February 1676

Contents

Preface to the Second Edition   ix

Biographies of Contributors   xii

An Introduction to Classic Studies in Social Psychology   1
S. Alexander Haslam and Joanne R. Smith

1 **Social Facilitation and Social Loafing:
   Revisiting Triplett's competition studies**   11
   Steven J. Karau and Kipling D. Williams

2 **Attitudes and Behaviour: Revisiting LaPiere's hospitality study**   27
   Joanne R. Smith and Deborah J. Terry

3 **Cognitive Dissonance:
   Revisiting Festinger's End of the World study**   43
   Joel Cooper

4 **Norm Formation: Revisiting Sherif's autokinetic illusion study**   58
   Dominic Abrams and John M. Levine

5 **Conformity: Revisiting Asch's line-judgment studies**   77
   Jolanda Jetten and Matthew J. Hornsey

6 **Minority Influence:
   Revisiting Moscovici's blue-green afterimage studies**   93
   Robin Martin and Miles Hewstone

7 **Obedience: Revisiting Milgram's shock experiments**   108
   Stephen Reicher and S. Alexander Haslam

8 **Tyranny: Revisiting Zimbardo's Stanford Prison Experiment**   130
   S. Alexander Haslam and Stephen Reicher

9 **Intergroup Relations and Conflict:
   Revisiting Sherif's Boys' Camp studies**   146
   Michael J. Platow and John A. Hunter

10 **Discrimination: Revisiting Tajfel's minimal group studies**   164
    Russell Spears and Sabine Otten

11 **Group Decision-Making: Revisiting Janis' groupthink studies**   182
    Dominic J. Packer and Nick D. Ungson

12 **Helping in Emergencies:
    Revisiting Latané and Darley's bystander studies**   201
    Mark Levine

13 **Promoting Positive Intergroup Relations:
    Revisiting Aronson et al.'s jigsaw classroom**   217
    John F. Dovidio

14 **Stereotype Formation:
    Revisiting Hamilton and Gifford's illusory correlation studies**   231
    Craig McGarty

15 **Stereotypes and Performance:
    Revisiting Steele and Aronson's stereotype threat experiments**   245
    Toni Schmader and Chad Forbes

Author index   269
Subject index   277

Preface to the Second Edition

In 2012 when we published the first edition of *Social Psychology: Revisiting the Classic Studies*, it never occurred to us to write a preface, largely because we were happy for the book to speak for itself. We also had no thought of producing a second edition – especially not so soon after the first. Yet the success of the first edition far surpassed our expectations (and those of our publisher). So, although only five years have passed since the first edition was published, it is clear that there is demand for the volume to be updated. Not least, this is because there have been seismic shifts in the field of social psychology during this period that make the original ambition of the volume – and of the *Revisiting Psychology* series more broadly – even more relevant today. In particular, while the classic studies are no more 'classic' now than they were five years ago, the lessons to be learned from re-engaging with them seem to be much more pertinent as the discipline negotiates its way through the so-called 'replication crisis' and agonizes about how to define a pathway forward. In this context, having a clear sense of where we have come from seems imperative for understanding where we might want to go, and how we might get there.

Although we touch on some of the reasons for editing a volume on classic studies in social psychology in the introductory chapter, we can include a somewhat fuller account here. At the University of Exeter, a first-year module on 'Classic Studies in Psychology' has been taught since 2005. The module was developed by Alex and Alan Slater (our series co-editor) with a number of objectives in mind. First, we wanted to give students (not all of whom would go on to graduate with a degree in psychology) exposure to studies that are commonly seen as the building blocks of the discipline and about which every student should be expected to have some knowledge. Second, we knew that many students had already had some exposure to these studies in school, but we were keen for them to 'unlearn' some of the myths about those studies – and hence about social psychology – that had previously been drilled into them. Groups are not inherently bad; people do not always conform; resistance is not necessarily futile. Third, we wanted to give students not only a sense of how knowledge around particular studies and topics had evolved over time, but also insight into the *process* through which this had occurred. How does one set about critiquing established knowledge, and how does scientific understanding thereby progress (or not)? As the replication crisis has reaffirmed, these questions are among the most important in our discipline, and a course that gives students insights into how to answer them struck us as filling an important gap in the undergraduate curriculum.

In late 2007, Joanne joined the department at Exeter and took over delivery of the Classic Studies course. It was during an early handover meeting that we first mooted the idea of writing a book that would reflect the goals of the course and would satisfy the demands of students for a textbook to accompany it. It took a further five years for us to finally publish the first edition. In the intervening years we discussed various potential formats for the book. Initially we toyed with the idea of writing all the chapters ourselves, before arriving at the much more satisfactory conclusion that it would be far better to ask world-leading researchers to author chapters in which they revisited a classic study into which their own research had given them particular insight. To give the book coherence, however, we agreed that all chapters should have a common format: first describing the classic study itself, then considering its impact, before going on to explain how the field has advanced in the time since the study was conducted.

As we finessed these ideas more, it also quickly became clear that a single volume of classic studies in psychology would not do justice to the exciting and diverse nature of the discipline and so we developed the idea of a book series. In this, expert editors within a sub-discipline of psychology would identify classic studies in their field and commission internationally renowned researchers to revisit and update those classic studies. From the outset SAGE were as enthusiastic about the project as we were. In 2012, they published titles on *Social Psychology* and *Developmental Psychology* (edited by Alan Slater and Paul Quinn). Since then, volumes on classic studies in *Cognitive Psychology* (edited by Michael Eysenck and David Groome, 2015) and *Brain and Behaviour* (edited by Bryan Kolb and Ian Wishaw, 2016) have been published. And, with the series going from strength to strength, new titles on *Personality and Individual Differences* and *Clinical Psychology* are also now in the pipeline. More, we hope, will follow.

So why have we decided to revisit our original volume? One reason is simply to address some omissions from the first edition. For reasons of brevity, we were only able to include 12 classic studies in the first edition. Naturally, this meant that other worthy studies were excluded. In this second edition, we have been able to include a further three studies that clearly meet the criteria for a classic study, criteria that we outline in the introductory chapter. Their inclusion allows us to reflect more accurately the wide array of methods in social psychology, to highlight the broad impact of social psychology in the world at large, and to showcase some more 'modern classics'.

Another reason relates to the tectonic shifts within the field of psychology that have taken place in the last few years. As we noted above, these have seen unprecedented debate and controversy regarding the reproducibility of the discipline's findings, and social psychology in particular has come under heavy fire. It is beyond the scope of this Preface to discuss these issues in depth, but needless to say, there is now greater interest in revisiting apparently canonical findings in social psychology to consider not only how reliable they are, but also how valid. As suggested above, we feel that the goals of this volume – and indeed of the series as a whole – are particularly relevant to this endeavour in helping readers explore new ways of thinking about this established corpus while also modelling the process of critical thinking that is central to scientific advance. Importantly, this is a matter not just of engaging with empirical detail but also of developing sound theory. It is our belief that, even more than the first edition, this second edition showcases the capacity for social psychology to be both self-reflective and self-correcting – and that by showing how we can learn important lessons from the past it helps dispel some of the gloomier forecasts for our future.

Since publishing the first edition, we have also experienced some personal tectonic shifts. One of us has moved continents, while the other has produced a first edition of a different kind. When we worked on the first edition, we had offices directly opposite each other and so could edit chapters at the same time, shouting our ideas, thoughts, and comments across the hallway. For the second edition, we found ourselves on opposite sides of the world, supplementing occasional face-to-face visits in Brisbane and Exeter with emails and cloud-based computing services. However, despite this spatial dislocation, we can honestly say that we have had just as much fun putting together this second edition as we had in working on the first.

In expressing gratitude to those who made this volume possible, it is appropriate to start by thanking the chapter authors whose excellent contributions allowed our aspirations for the book to be comprehensively exceeded. We are extremely grateful too to the team at SAGE who put their faith in the initial project and who have motivated us to move it forward. Thanks especially to Michael Carmichael for his original excitement and unstinting support, and for putting up with our (at times) unreasonable demands to tweak the artwork for the cover just one more time. Thanks also to Luke Block for encouraging us to revisit *Revisiting* and for his ongoing encouragement, commitment and confidence. We are extremely appreciative too of the high-quality advice and support that our many colleagues at the Universities of Exeter and Queensland (and many other places besides) have given us along the way. And, finally, thanks – and praise – to Colin and Cath for sustaining us through the bad times and the good, and for ensuring that the latter have been pronounced and plentiful.

Joanne Smith and Alex Haslam
The University of Exeter
The University of Queensland
October 2016

Biographies of Contributors

Dominic Abrams is Professor of Social Psychology and Director of the Centre for the Study of Group Processes at the University of Kent. His research interests are in the areas of group processes and social inclusion, with particular interests in macrosocial intergroup relations, intergroup contact and social cohesion, ageism, responses to deviance and innovation, the development of prejudice and its implications for intragroup relationships. As well as publishing widely in social and developmental psychology, he is the co-editor of *Group Processes and Intergroup Relations*. He is past President of the Society for the Psychological Study of Social Issues and current Vice President (Social Sciences) of the British Academy.

Joel Cooper is Professor of Psychology at Princeton University. His research has focused on attitude formation and change, with special emphasis on cognitive dissonance. He is the author of the 2007 book *Cognitive Dissonance: 50 years of a classic theory*, and co-author of *The Science of Attitudes* (2016). He is also co-editor of the *Sage Handbook of Social Psychology*, and co-author of the book *Gender and Computers*. His additional research interests are in jury decision making and the use of technology. Cooper is former editor-in-chief of the *Journal of Experimental Social Psychology*.

John F. (Jack) Dovidio is Carl Iver Hovland Professor of Psychology, as well as Dean of Academic Affairs of the Faculty of Arts and Sciences, at Yale University. He has previously served as editor of the *Journal of Personality and Social Psychology – Interpersonal Relations and Group Processes* and of *Personality and Social Psychology Bulletin*, and co-editor of *Social Issues and Policy Review.* His research interests are in stereotyping, prejudice, and discrimination; social power and nonverbal communication; and altruism and helping.

Chad Forbes is an Assistant Professor in psychological and brain sciences at the University of Delaware. With a background ranging from molecular biology to complex social processes, Dr Forbes has received multiple grants from the National

Science Foundation to examine how and why negative stereotypes and neurobio-markers associated with stress prompt minorities and women to leave academic and STEM fields at disproportionate rates compared to non-stigmatized individuals. He was recently elected as a Fellow in the Society of Experimental Social Psychology and recognized as a 'Rising Star' by the American Psychological Association.

S. Alexander Haslam is Professor of Social Psychology and Australian Laureate Fellow at the University of Queensland. His research focuses on the study of social identity in social, organizational, and clinical contexts. He is a former editor of the *European Journal of Social Psychology*, a Fellow of the Canadian Institute for Advanced Research, and a recipient of the European Association of Social Psychology's Lewin Medal. In 2010 he was awarded a National Teaching Fellowship for his work with Steve Reicher on the BBC Prison Study.

Miles Hewstone is Professor of Social Psychology and Fellow of New College, Oxford University. He has published widely in social psychology, and his current research focus is intergroup contact and conflict. His awards include the Kurt Lewin Award for Distinguished Research Achievement (2005), from the European Association for Social Psychology, and the Gordon Allport Intergroup Relations Prize (2005). He was elected a Fellow of the British Academy (the National Academy for the Humanities and Social Sciences) in 2002.

Matthew J. Hornsey is a Professor of Social Psychology at the University of Queensland. His research interests are in the areas of group processes and inter-group relations, with particular interests in (a) how people respond to trust-challenging messages such as criticisms, recommendations for change, and gestures of remorse; and (b) the dynamic and sometimes tense relationship between individual and collective selves. He is co-editor of the 2011 book *Rebels in Groups: Dissent, Deviance, Difference, and Defiance* (2011, Wiley-Blackwell).

John A. Hunter is a Senior Lecturer at the University of Otago. His research is concerned with the theoretical and practical ramifications of group-based behaviour. Recent publications on these topics include intergroup discrimination (e.g., anti-fat bias, sectarianism, nationalism and sexism), health-related outcomes (e.g., alcohol consumption, resilience), motivation (e.g., self-esteem, belonging), socialization and contact experiences.

Jolanda Jetten is Professor of Social Psychology at the University of Queensland. Her research is concerned with social identity, group processes and intergroup relations. She has a special interest in marginal group membership and deviance within groups, and recently she has examined the way identity can protect health and well-being. She has co-edited two recent edited volumes on these lines of work: *Rebels in Groups: Dissent, Deviance, Difference, and Defiance* (2011, Wiley-Blackwell) and *The Social Cure: Identity, Health and Well-being* (2011, Psychology Press). In 2014 she received the Kurt Lewin Award for Distinguished Research Achievement from the European Association for Social Psychology.

Steven J. Karau is the Gregory A. Lee Professor of Management at Southern Illinois University, Carbondale. He conducts research on a range of group process and organizational behaviour issues, with a special focus on motivation within groups, time pressure and group performance, gender differences in leadership, personality influences in organizational contexts, and the ethics of managerial change initiatives. He is a frequent contributor to a variety of top management and psychology journals.

John M. Levine is Professor of Psychology and Senior Scientist, Learning Research and Development Center, at the University of Pittsburgh. His research focuses on small group processes including newcomer innovation in work teams, reaction to deviance and disloyalty, and the social dynamics of online groups. He has served as editor of the *Journal of Experimental Social Psychology* and Chair of the Society of Experimental Social Psychology. Dr Levine was co-recipient of the Joseph E. McGrath Award for Lifetime Achievement in the Study of Groups from the Interdisciplinary Network for Group Research in 2011, and received an Honorary Doctorate from the University of Lausanne in 2016. He is currently an Honorary Professor of Psychology at the University of Kent, Canterbury.

Mark Levine is a Professor of Social Psychology at the University of Exeter. His research focuses on the role of social identity in pro-social and anti-social behaviour. His recent work has examined the role of group processes in the regulation of perpetrator, victim and bystander behaviour during aggressive and violent events. He is co-editor of *Beyond the Prejudice Problematic: Extending the Social Psychology of Intergroup Conflict, Inequality and Social Change* (2011, Cambridge University Press).

Craig McGarty is Professor of Psychology at the University of Western Sydney. The focus of his research currently is on social change through collective action based on opinion-based group memberships. His (co-)authored and edited books include *The Message of Social Psychology* (1997, Blackwell), *Categorization in Social Psychology* (1999, Sage), *Stereotypes as Explanations* (2002, Cambridge University Press), and *Research Methods and Statistics in Psychology* (2003, Sage).

Robin Martin is Professor of Organisational Psychology at Alliance Manchester Business School, University of Manchester. He conducts research in a variety of areas including majority and minority influence, workplace leadership and workplace innovation. He has been a consultant for many organizations, working on a range of managerial issues but most specifically how to develop effective leadership. He recently co-edited *Minority Influence and Innovation: Antecedents, Processes and Consequences* (2010, Psychology Press).

Sabine Otten is Professor of Intergroup Relations and Social Integration at the University of Groningen. She is a former associate editor of the *European Journal of Social Psychology*, and co-edited *Intergroup Relations: The Role of*

Motivation and Emotion (2009, Psychology Press) and *Towards Inclusive Organizations: Determinants of Successful Diversity Management at Work* (2015, Psychology Press). In her research she focuses on basic processes underlying ingroup favouritism and group identification, the role of social categorization in social conflicts, and the psychological analysis of inclusion and diversity in the workplace.

Dominic J. Packer is Associate Professor of Psychology and Associate Dean for Research and Graduate Programs in the College of Arts and Sciences at Lehigh University. His research interests are in the areas of conformity and dissent, intergroup relations, and moral evaluation and decision-making, with particular attention to processes that may mitigate against some groups' more harmful proclivities, including blind conformity to social norms, intergroup prejudice and moralistic aggression.

Michael Platow is a Professor of Psychology at the Australian National University. He has published research in leading journals on the social psychology of justice, leadership, social influence, helping, trust, interdependence, and education. He was President of the Society of Australasian Social Psychologists, and an associate editor of *Social Psychology and Personality Science*. His teaching has been recognized by an Australian Commonwealth Office of Learning and Teaching Carrick Citation, while his contributions to research have been recognized through his election as a Fellow of the Academy of Social Sciences in Australia. His (co-) authored and edited books include *Self and Social Identity in Educational Contexts* (2017, Routledge), *The New Psychology of Leadership: Identity, Influence and Power* (2011, Psychology Press), *Social Identity at Work: Developing Theory for Organizational Practice* (2003, Psychology Press), and *Self and Identity: Personal, Social and Symbolic* (2002, Routledge).

Stephen Reicher is Professor of Social Psychology at the University of St Andrews. He is also co-author of *Self and Nation* (2001, Sage) and *The New Psychology of Leadership: Identity, Influence and Power* (2011, Psychology Press). In 2010 he received the British Psychology Society's annual award for excellence in teaching for his work on the BBC Prison Study. He is former editor of the *British Journal of Social Psychology* and a Fellow of the Royal Society of Edinburgh.

Toni Schmader holds the Canada Research Chair in Social Psychology at the University of British Columbia. Her research examines the interplay between self and social identity, particularly when one's social identity is targeted by negative stereotypes. In 2013, she was the recipient of the Killam Faculty Research Prize. She has served as an associate editor at the *Journal of Personality and Social Psychology* and *Personality and Social Psychology Bulletin,* and on the executive committees of both the Society for Personality and Social Psychology and the Society of Experimental Social Psychology, where she is also an elected Fellow.

Joanne R. Smith is an Associate Professor in Social Psychology at the University of Exeter. Her research interests are in the areas of social influence, norms, behaviour change, and social identity. Her most recent research focuses on the way in which normative messages are used in campaigns, why campaigns often fail, and how we can better harness the power of norms to change behaviour. She is a Senior Fellow of the Higher Education Academy.

Russell Spears is a Professor of Psychology recently appointed to an endowed chair at the University of Groningen. His research focuses on social identity and intergroup relations, social stereotyping, prejudice and discrimination, resistance and social action, and the role of intergroup emotions in these processes. He has also researched the role of social identity, influence and power in the new communications technologies. A Fellow of the Society for Personality and Social Psychology, he is a former editor of the *British Journal of Social Psychology* and the *European Journal of Social Psychology.*

Deborah J. Terry was appointed Curtin University's Vice-Chancellor in February 2014 and is the immediate past President of the Academy of Social Sciences in Australia (ASSA) and member of the Board of Universities Australia. She is also past Chair of the Australian Council of Learned Academies and the Australian Research Council's College of Experts in the Social, Behavioural and Economic Sciences. Professor Terry completed her PhD in Social Psychology at the Australian National University. She had a distinguished career at the University of Queensland, initially as an internationally recognized scholar in psychology, before progressing through a number of senior leadership roles, including Senior Deputy Vice-Chancellor. She is a Fellow of the Academy of Social Sciences in Australia and was made an Officer in the General Division (AO) in June 2015 for distinguished service to education in the tertiary sector.

Nick D. Ungson is a doctoral student in Social Psychology at Lehigh University. His research focuses on the role of social identity in intragroup and intergroup evaluation – for example, he examines how individuals react, both behaviourally and attitudinally, to disloyal group members. He also examines situational factors that influence intergroup cooperation. His other research interests include the social cognitive processes moderating harsh blame reactions in response to moral transgressions.

Kipling D. Williams is a Professor of Psychological Sciences at Purdue University. His research interests are in the areas of group processes and social influence, with particular interests in ostracism, social loafing and social compensation, internet research, stealing thunder, and psychology and law. A frequent contributor to a variety of top social psychology journals, he is author of *Ostracism: The Power of Silence* (2001, Guilford Press), and co-editor of *The Social Outcast* (2005, Psychology Press), *The Oxford Handbook of Social Influence* (2016, Oxford University Press), and *Ostracism, Exclusion, and Rejection* (2016, Psychology Press). He is also editor of the journal *Social Influence.*

An Introduction to Classic Studies in Social Psychology

S. Alexander Haslam
and Joanne R. Smith

Social psychology emerged as a discipline in the late nineteenth century centred on a core concern to understand the psychological underpinnings of society and social life. What is it that makes people feel love or hate, display pride or prejudice, or choose to fight or flee? And what determines who they do these things with, and how they engage and interact with other people more generally? Answering such questions has involved thousands of researchers conducting many hundreds of thousands of studies. Yet which of these are worthy of being identified as true 'classics'? As it turns out, this is both an easy and a difficult question to answer: easy, because there is a reasonable amount of consensus among social psychologists as to what the classic studies are, but difficult, because in creating this volume we wanted to be extremely choosy. Indeed, although the second edition of this book contains three more studies than the first edition, it still restricts its attention to just 15 studies. In the chapters that follow, quite a few more studies are discussed – either as elaborations or as extensions of the focal studies – but nevertheless those that are included constitute a highly selective sample.

Unsurprisingly, then, the studies that are examined in the chapters that follow are very well-known within social psychology. They are described in almost every introductory textbook (and in many advanced texts as well) and they serve as common points of reference for researchers, teachers and students alike. As Christian Jarrett, author of *The Rough Guide to Psychology*, has noted, 'while other sciences have their cardinal theories ... psychology's foundations are built not of theory, but with the rock of classic experiments' (2008: 756). A key reason for this is that the studies speak powerfully to the goals of social psychology as a discipline that is concerned with providing a scientific analysis of the relationship between mind and society (Asch, 1952; McDougall, 1910; Turner and Oakes, 1997). As a result, they have played an important role in setting the research agenda for the field as it has progressed over time.

However, one quality that makes these studies genuine classics is that their details are well-known not just inside but also *outside* social psychology – not only by researchers in other academic disciplines (e.g., sociology, politics, economics, history), but also by journalists, social commentators, policy makers and other interested members of the general public. In this respect, a central feature of the studies is their capacity to captivate those who read about them. Indeed, this has meant that as well as arousing intellectual curiosity they have also impacted upon our culture in a diverse array of forms – including music, art, theatre and film. These studies, then, do not just belong to social psychology. Rather, they have widespread currency in society (or, at least, western society) and have played an important role in shaping everyday understandings of the behaviour within it. In Serge Moscovici's (1984) terms, they have become central to people's *social representations* of social psychology in the sense that they both anchor and objectify understanding – serving as concrete reference points for ongoing dialogue and debate.

THE INGREDIENTS OF A CLASSIC STUDY

As noted by Patricia Devine and Amanda Brodish (2003), there is a difference between knowing what the classic studies in social psychology are and knowing *why* they have become classics. Moreover, there are no fixed criteria to decide whether a study can be raised to this status. To adapt Tolstoy's observation about the nature of unhappy families in the first line of *Anna Karenina*, each classic study is classic in its own way. Nevertheless, as Tolstoy noted of happy families, there are some features that most of the classic studies in social psychology share.

BIG QUESTIONS

The single most important feature of the classic studies in social psychology is that they address fundamental questions about human sociality. Why do we conform and obey? Why do we fight and oppress? Why do we help and support? In this regard, many of the classic studies were inspired by large-scale world events that demanded, but seemed to defy, comprehension. And the scale of these events often motivated the researchers to be equally ambitious in their quest for answers.

In this regard, nothing in the last century played a greater role in shaping the sensibilities of social psychologists than the Second World War and the Holocaust. It is therefore unsurprising to discover that although many of the classic studies were conducted before 1945, most of those classic studies that came afterwards were motivated by a desire to understand the behaviour of those who participated in these events (both as perpetrators and victims), and that they were conducted by researchers who had first-hand experience of their devastating consequences. Dissatisfied with tinkering at the edges, these researchers wanted their research to engage powerfully with the stuff of fear and loathing, and the dynamics of war and peace. And as a result of these intense motivations they sought to conduct studies that captured the spirit of the times and that were not only novel and intriguing, but also forceful and compelling. Their point was to conduct research that *demanded* attention and could not be brushed idly aside.

Accordingly, while a criticism of contemporary social psychological research is that it has sometimes become bogged down in statistical sophistication and methodological minutiae (what Iain Walker, 1997, has referred to as 'impeccable trivia'; see also Baumeister et al., 2007; Rozin, 2009), this was never true of the studies included in this volume. Thus, although much of the research that has come after them has been concerned with homing in forensically on the processes they uncover, the classic studies themselves were often conspicuously deficient in their concern for the niceties of methodological and statistical nuance. It is almost certainly unreasonable to judge them by today's standards (and to do so rather misses their point), but nevertheless many were single studies that had limited experimental control, limited theoretical grounding, limited hypotheses and limited insight into the internal processes responsible for the effects they uncover. Somewhat ironically, then, this almost certainly means that the majority of these studies would struggle to be accepted for publication in leading journals today (Diener, 2006; Haslam and McGarty, 2001). Nevertheless, this lack of sophistication is one further feature of their enduring appeal: for this means that you don't need to have specialized training in order to understand the points they make.

CHALLENGING FINDINGS

Yet while the classic studies are of interest to, and can be understood by, the proverbial man or woman in the street, another of their important features is that they do not simply tell them what they already know. On the contrary, their findings are often unexpected and counterintuitive, and in this way they often *challenge* received ideas about human nature. For example, most people would imagine that a large incentive should produce greater change in someone's opinions than a small incentive. However, work on cognitive dissonance by Leon Festinger and Merrill Carlsmith (1959) showed that, in fact, the opposite was true (see Chapter 3). Similarly, if you asked people whether they behaved in line with their attitudes, most people would probably respond that, generally speaking, they practise what they preach. However, when Richard LaPiere (1934) looked into this question systematically he found that people's attitudes and behaviour were largely unrelated (see Chapter 2). Or, to take another example, when Stanley Milgram (1963) asked students, psychiatrists and members of the general public what percentage of people would be prepared to deliver a lethal electric shock to another person when asked to do so by an experimenter, the typical response was 1%. In fact, though, this form of destructive behaviour was displayed by 65% – not 1% – of the participants in Milgram's classic study of obedience to authority (see Chapter 7).

In this way, all the studies led to significant changes in research focus and thinking. For the power of their findings was such that they made it hard – and in many cases impossible – to return to the forms of understanding that had previously been dominant (McGarty and Haslam, 1997). This is not to say, however, that the studies *closed down* enquiry into particular topics. As we have already noted, more investigation was always needed in order to replicate the effects, to clarify *when* they occurred, and to understand *why* they occurred. Indeed, a further element of the studies' influence was that they opened up exciting new lines of enquiry. Rather, than reducing or eliminating scientific uncertainty, then, their success lay in the fact that they *created* uncertainty that the broad scientific community then set about trying to resolve (see Haslam and McGarty, 2001). And, in this sense, rather than being part of what the philosopher of science Thomas Kuhn (1962) refers to as normal science, they proved to be the stuff of scientific *revolution*.

DEMANDING METHODS

The methods that the studies employed are also an important aspect of their classic status. Like much other research in social psychology these were ingenious and innovative, sometimes even drawing on established physiological or visual effects to study social phenomena (e.g., see Chapters 4 and 6), but more than most other studies they were typically very realistic and high in drama. Often this resulted from creating well-crafted and elaborate cover stories that required input from trained confederates (i.e., accomplices of the researcher). Usually they also placed the individual in some form of intense predicament in which he or she had to resolve a moral or practical dilemma – for example, conflict between attitudes and action, between one's moral code and the demands of the situation, between one's perception of reality and the influence of one's peers, or between a desire to be fair and a desire to advance one's group (Devine and Brodish, 2003). Furthermore, the nature of these methods lent itself to dramatic images that were often captured on film and that survive (as in the pages below) to provide students with powerful and provocative materials that engage them in the specifics of the research process (Millard, 2014). In particular, they invite onlookers to reflect on the choices they would make in the same situation: Would I modify my judgments to bring them into line with those of my peers? Would I press the lever to deliver a lethal electric shock? Would I abuse a prisoner if I were a prison guard? Would you?

Here too it is important to recognize that the classic studies are generally focused on explaining and understanding actual behaviour, rather than ticks on a questionnaire, reaction times on a computer, or blood flow to various regions of the brain (see Baumeister et al., 2007). The latter are all interesting and important aspects of science, but few things capture our imagination as powerfully as real people engaging in real behaviour in real situations (even if those situations have been artificially created).

One further consequence of this desire to study behaviour that centres on moral and practical struggles is that classic studies raise more than their fair share of *ethical issues*. Indeed, two of the studies that are discussed below (those conducted by Milgram and Zimbardo; see Chapters 7 and 8) are routinely taken as starting points for consideration of the ethical dimensions of psychological research (and other forms of research with human participants). Interestingly too, the difficulty of overcoming these issues has meant that it is very unlikely that many of the classic studies would still be conducted today, at least in their full original form. One reason for this is that the *cost* of addressing these ethical challenges (in terms of both time and money) is immense.

Indeed, more generally, the scale of the classic studies was often such that cost is a factor that would preclude many of them being conducted today. It is expensive to study interacting individuals and groups (especially over an extended period), to employ confederates, to measure and analyse actual behaviour, and to conduct the pilot work that establishes the viability of novel paradigms. Moreover, not only is the funding for such research harder to come by today, but also it is far harder for researchers to justify investing the time that projects of this form demand – especially in a world where employment and promotion are often based on the number of one's publications in leading journals and where, as we have noted, those journals' appetite for such research is not what it once was (Baumeister et al., 2007; Devine and Brodish, 2003; Haslam and McGarty, 2001).

Ultimately, though, while ingenious, dramatic and demanding methods certainly help, in our minds these are not sufficient to imbue a study with classic status. Instead, to develop our initial point, what marks the studies in this volume out from the vast majority of other studies is their capacity to address meaningful social psychological questions in powerful ways. As Paul Rozin observes, 'the great experiments capture a truth about the world, but it is the problem selection, not the elegance, that primarily determines the greatness' (2009: 439). In short, to find out about these studies is to find out something essential about the psychological dimensions of the social world around us. And in this, they satisfy a fundamental need for insight into what it means to be human.

REVISITING THE CLASSIC STUDIES

ASKING BETTER QUESTIONS

But big questions, challenging findings and demanding methods are not the only features that the classic studies have in common. Thus, we can observe that all the studies selected for this volume were conducted by men (mostly with male participants) and that most were conducted in leading American institutions (e.g., Yale, Stanford, Columbia). These features reflect the nature of the field at the time that most of the classic studies were being conducted (i.e., at least 30 years ago) – a time before the emergence of strong social psychology in Europe (see Tajfel et al., 1981) and a time in which female participation was very limited, either as researchers or as participants.

Although seemingly trivial, these shared demographic features are usually quite salient to students and other readers of the classic studies. One unfortunate consequence of this is that, when it comes to reflecting on their findings, people are often led to ask specific types of question – and not necessarily those that are most interesting. In particular, students commonly ask whether one would obtain the same effects if the classic studies were conducted today (in an age where people are assumed to be less conformist, more questioning of authority and less prejudiced than participants of yesteryear), with female (rather than male) participants and in other countries (e.g., Australia, Britain or China rather than the United States). As many of the chapters that follow testify, these questions typically turn out not to be especially interesting, for the simple reason that the short answer is usually 'Yes'. At the same time it is interesting to note – especially in light of what has come to be known as the 'replication crisis' in social psychology (Pashler and Wagenmakers, 2012) – that not all of the studies have proved easy to replicate and that in some cases doubts linger over whether the original findings are as reliable as most textbooks suggest (e.g., see Chapters 3, 6, 8 and 11). Nevertheless, core findings from most of these classic studies have been replicated many times, using a diverse range of participants, from different cultural backgrounds and over different time periods.

But if we are not just interested in matters of replication, what other sorts of questions might it be important to ask? As we see it, one key issue is whether political, ideological and other social contextual features influenced the types of problems that the researchers were interested in and the way they set about addressing them. For example, as we have already noted, many of the classic studies were conducted in the wake of the Holocaust, and it was the scale of this and other atrocities that led researchers to eschew individual-level explanations (e.g., in terms of personality) and instead seek to develop analyses that focused on the capacity for groups to promote conformity, obedience and oppression. However, because such work was (understandably) focused on the dynamics of tyranny, it is interesting to ask whether it tended to neglect countervailing forces of resistance (e.g., see Chapters 5 to 9). Similarly, researchers were drawn to social issues such as prejudice and failure to help in emergencies, because these were seen to constitute widespread social problems, but it is intriguing to ask whether this led to an over-emphasis on the prevalence and inevitability of these processes (e.g., see Chapters 10 to 15). And where our understanding of particular studies has changed over time (e.g., through simplification of their findings, or changes of emphasis), what has brought this change about? Why do misunderstandings and myths about the studies persist? Why do they take the particular form they do? And are these myths harmful to social psychology's ultimate goal of understanding the relationship between mind and society, because they stop researchers from asking certain types of question and close down potentially fruitful lines of interrogation (see Jarrett, 2008)?

In addition to answering basic questions (e.g., concerning replication), the chapters in this volume home in on questions of this more challenging form that have been prompted by work in the years since the classic studies were conducted. In particular, they do this by encouraging a deeper level of engagement both with the details of the studies themselves and with the nature of their contribution to the field of social psychology. This process is also facilitated by the fact that all the chapters have a similar structure. This starts by carefully laying each study out, but then goes on surgically to penetrate beneath its surface.

STRUCTURE OF THE CHAPTERS

The chapters that follow all start by seeking to locate and understand the classic studies they discuss within their social and historical *context* – identifying the concerns that motivated researchers and the particular perspective that informed their scientific thinking. The studies' *methods and results* are then presented. Here careful attention is paid to details that are routinely overlooked in standard textbook treatments, but which turn out to provide important insights into the phenomenon under investigation (e.g., evidence that the experimenter or specific methods encouraged particular outcomes, or that forgotten variants produced different results).

This is followed by a discussion of the studies' *impact*, which looks at the way in which ideas were taken up and developed by other researchers and the way in which they influenced both the field of social psychology and general understanding of the topic in question. There are two recurring themes here. First, while the impact of all the studies has been immense, they have often led researchers in unexpected directions and certainly have not always had the impact that those who conducted them intended. Second, it is apparent that accounts of the studies that are commonly provided in secondary sources (and hence the understandings that people take away from them) are often very simplified, and typically fail to capture important dimensions of richness and nuance. Sometimes such simplifications were encouraged by the researchers themselves, but more often they were a source of considerable frustration.

All of the chapters explore these themes but also build upon them by concluding with a consideration of the way in which, from the time that they were conducted, the field has *moved beyond* the classic studies. The key point here – and one that provides a central motivation for this volume – is that in the decades since they were published, the field of social psychology has not stood still. As we have observed, a key feature of the studies was that they proved to be catalysts for further research. Yet while further work has always built on the methods and insights that the studies provided, this has rarely provided straightforward confirmation of the authors' original claims. In all cases this advance has therefore involved at least some revision in thinking, and in some it has shaken the researchers' conclusions to their very core.

PURPOSE AND STRUCTURE OF THE VOLUME

Our goal in this volume is two-fold. As the foregoing discussion and the book's title suggests, we want to revisit the classic studies with a view to showing, first, how they shaped the field of social psychology, but also, second, how the field has itself moved on through engagement with the issues these studies raise. Rather than engaging superficially and merely reproducing standard accounts, we thus seek to engage critically with the studies in order to reveal new ways of thinking both about them and about the ideas they explore. In effect, then, we want to show how social psychology can be – and has been – taken forward in interesting and exciting ways through a careful re-examination of the 'sacred texts' that lie at its heart. In short, we want to respect and do justice to these texts, but the goal is not to fossilize or fetishize them.

In light of the sanctity of these texts and the mystique that surrounds them, this is no easy task, and it is certainly not one that we could undertake alone. Accordingly, in the process of planning this volume, our first priority was to assemble a team of contributors whose own work had shown that a project of this form was both viable and worth pursuing. This, it turned out, was far easier than we supposed – primarily because all of the people we approached were leading researchers who had been working for a considerable time on research programmes that were closely aligned with the book's goals. Happily for us, all agreed to participate and they did so with considerable enthusiasm.

As a result – and as their contributions and biographies attest – all of the authors are internationally renowned scholars who are working at the cutting edge of the areas mapped out by the particular classic study that their chapter addresses. In each case, their own work has been heavily influenced by a deep appreciation of the research and researchers that they write about, but this work has also moved the field on in new and exciting directions. In this respect, all give proof to Isaac Newton's famous dictum (handed down from the writings of Bernard of Chartres), which we have used as an epigram for the volume as a whole: that is, these contributors have been able to see further than others because they have stood on the shoulders of giants.

In writing their chapters, the authors were asked to stick closely to the structure and brief outlined in the previous section, and to write in a way that would make their contribution accessible not only to students of psychology (at many different levels), but also to readers from any walk of life who might be interested in the important issues to which these studies speak. Again happily for us, all did – using their chapters to give readers profound insights into the foundations of social psychology, but also showing how the discipline has advanced in important ways in the years since those studies were conducted. And while it is customary in a book's Introduction to provide a summary of the chapters that follow, our sense was that in the present case this would be superfluous. This is for the simple reason that the chapters all speak very clearly for themselves and certainly no gloss is required from us in order to explain how they fulfil the book's objectives and ambitions. Critically, then, they provide the strongest possible case for seeing social psychology as a discipline that is vibrant rather than moribund, and which is building in creative and insightful ways upon impressive historical foundations.

In organizing the chapters within the volume, our objective was to have an overall structure that provided a coherent sense of this advance. Because many of the classic studies built upon others that preceded them, the most obvious strategy was to arrange chapters in chronological order with reference to the date of each study's publication. Accordingly, as Figure 0.1 indicates, most of the chapters are arranged in this chronological sequence. Nevertheless, this principle is violated in several places in order to preserve the logical flow of ideas from one chapter to the next.

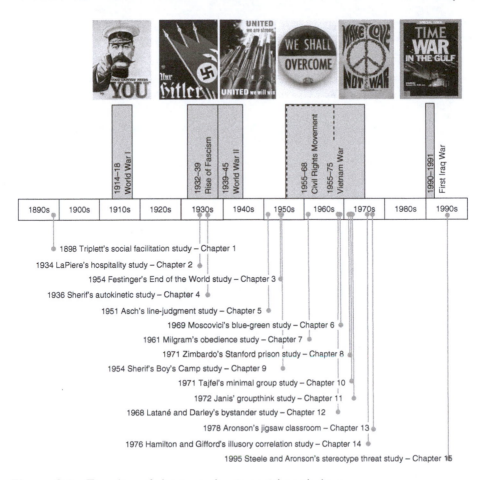

Figure 0.1   Time-line of classic studies in social psychology

The resulting sequence is one that we have found works best when teaching a course on 'Classic studies in social psychology' ourselves – a course that we have enjoyed delivering for the past ten years. Indeed, we would like to end by thanking not only our students, whose persistent demands for a suitable course textbook motivated us to develop this volume, but also the authors for their hard work in helping us achieve this goal. As editors, we have enjoyed our collaboration immensely and this has been a very positive experience from which we have learned a tremendous amount. This, we believe, is an experience that readers will share.

REFERENCES

Asch, S.E. (1952) *Social Psychology*. Englewood Cliffs, NJ: Prentice Hall.

Baumeister, R.F., Vohs, K.D. and Funder, D.C. (2007) 'Psychology as the science of self-reports and finger movements: Whatever happened to actual behavior?', *Perspectives on Psychological Science*, 2: 396–403.

Devine, P.G. and Brodish, A.B. (2003) 'Modern classics in social psychology', *Psychological Inquiry,* 14: 196–202.

Diener, E. (2006) 'Editorial', *Perspectives on Psychological Science,* 1: 1–4.

Ellemers, N. (2013) 'Connecting the dots: Mobilizing theory to reveal the big picture in social psychology (and why we should do this)', *European Journal of Social Psychology, 43*: 1–8.

Festinger, L. and Carlsmith, J.M. (1959) 'Cognitive consequences of forced compliance', *Journal of Abnormal and Social Psychology,* 58: 203–10.

Haslam, S.A. and McGarty, C. (2001) 'A 100 years of certitude? Social psychology, the experimental method and the management of scientific uncertainty', *British Journal of Social Psychology,* 40: 1–21.

Jarrett, C. (2008) 'Foundations of sand?', *The Psychologist,* 21: 756–9.

Kuhn, T. (1962) *The Structure of Scientific Revolutions.* Chicago: University of Chicago Press.

LaPiere, R.T. (1934) 'Attitudes vs. actions', *Social Forces,* 13: 230–7.

McDougall, W. (1910) *Introduction to Social Psychology* (3rd edn). London: Methuen.

McGarty, C. and Haslam, S.A. (1997) 'A short history of social psychology', in C. McGarty and S.A. Haslam (eds), *The Message of Social Psychology: Perspectives on Mind in Society.* Oxford, UK and Cambridge, MA, USA: Blackwell. pp. 1–19.

Milgram, S. (1963) 'Behavioral study of obedience', *Journal of Abnormal and Social Psychology,* 67: 371–8.

Millard, K. (2014) 'Revisioning obedience: Exploring the role of Milgram's skills as a film-maker in bringing his shocking narrative to life', *Journal of Social Issues, 70*: 439–55.

Moscovici, S. (1984) 'The phenomenon of social representations', in R.M. Farr and S. Moscovici (eds), *Social Representations.* Cambridge: Cambridge University Press. pp. 3–70.

Pashler, H. and Wagenmakers, E.-J. (2012) 'Editors' introduction to the special section on replicability in psychological science: A crisis of confidence?', *Perspectives on Psychological Science,* 7: 528–30.

Rozin, P. (2009) 'What kind of empirical research should we publish, fund, and reward?', *Perspectives on Psychological Science,* 4: 435–9.

Tajfel, H., Jaspars, J.M.F. and Fraser, C. (1981) 'The social dimension in European social psychology', in H. Tajfel (ed.), *The Social Dimension,* Vol. 1. Cambridge: Cambridge University Press. pp. 1–8.

Turner, J.C. and Oakes, P.J. (1997) 'The socially structured mind', in C. McGarty and S.A. Haslam (eds), *The Message of Social Psychology: Perspectives on Mind in Society.* Oxford: Blackwell. pp. 355–73.

Walker, I. (1997) 'The long past, short history, and uncertain future of social psychology', paper presented at the 4th meeting of the Society of Australasian Social Psychologists, Christchurch, New Zealand, April 16–19.

1

Social Facilitation and Social Loafing

Revisiting Triplett's competition studies

Steven J. Karau and Kipling D. Williams

BACKGROUND

More than 110 years ago, at the dawn of experimental psychology research, a promising master's-level graduate student and enthusiastic sportsman by the name of Norman Triplett decided to focus his thesis research on the topic of competition. A careful analysis of the records from competitive cycling events showed that riders were quicker when racing against other cyclists or when having a group of riders available as pacemakers than when they were simply racing against the clock alone. To study competition in the laboratory, Triplett asked children to work as hard as possible on a physical task that involved turning fishing reels, both alone and in competition with another child. Triplett found that competition seemed to have an energizing effect, leading many of the children to turn the reels more quickly. These results suggested that the presence of a competitor might lead most individuals to try harder and exert more effort than they would when working alone.

Triplett published his findings in the *American Journal of Psychology* in a thorough and engaging 1898 article entitled 'The dynamogenic factors in pacemaking and competition'. This article identifies a fundamental question at the very heart of the field: How does the presence of other people affect us as individuals? This general question eventually evolved into two large research literatures on phenomena that have come to be known as social facilitation and social loafing. *Social facilitation* refers to a tendency for the presence of other people (as co-actors or observers) to enhance our performance on simple or well-learned tasks, but to reduce it on complex or unfamiliar tasks (Geen, 1991; Zajonc, 1965). *Social loafing* refers to a tendency for individuals to reduce their efforts when working with others on group or collective tasks (Latané et al., 1979). Over time, many hundreds of studies have been conducted on social facilitation and social loafing, and a host of theories have been proposed to explain how and why various group and social factors affect individual effort and motivation (Bond and Titus, 1983; Karau and

Williams, 1993). Triplett's work is also frequently recognized as seminal to the development of sports psychology (Davis et al., 1995).

Triplett's famous competition study has therefore had a significant impact on both social and sports psychology, and was crucial to the development of research into social influence and group processes. But how and why did one relatively simple laboratory study involving children cranking fishing reels have such a profound impact? In this chapter, we seek to answer this question by providing an understanding of the historical context, methodological features and lasting impact of Triplett's classic study.

THE DAWN OF SOCIAL PSYCHOLOGY

D espite a long history of disciplined reasoning among philosophers about various psychological aspects of human affairs (going back at least as far as Plato and Aristotle), psychology as a scientific field was in its infancy when Triplett initiated his competition research. Scientific study of human perceptual processes had emerged earlier in the nineteenth century with pioneering work by researchers such as Hermann von Helmholtz and Gustav Fechner. In 1875, the first formal experimental psychology laboratory was established by Wilhelm Wundt at the University of Leipzig. In the United States, although William James had created a small, informal basement laboratory at Harvard University in 1875, the first formal American experimental psychology laboratory was established in 1883 by G. Stanley Hall at Johns Hopkins University, with additional labs being developed by various influential psychologists at a handful of other universities in the late 1880s. 1890 saw the publication of James's landmark two-volume treatise on the *Principles of Psychology*. Thus, with leadership from Wundt, James, Hall and others, at the end of the nineteenth century, psychology was really starting to flourish as a scientific discipline (Allport, 1954; Goethals, 2003; Hothersall, 2004).

Although much of the early psychological research examined basic perceptual processes and judgments, social issues soon entered into consideration. James speculated about a range of phenomena that might be influenced by social factors, including the self and human will, and Hall used questionnaires to examine social interaction among children (Goethals, 2003). A French agricultural engineer named Max Ringelmann had even conducted studies examining how group size affected individual effort in the 1880s. He found that, when groups of male volunteers were asked to pull as hard as possible on a rope in groups of various sizes, the increase in total force exerted was less than would be expected from the simple addition of individual scores. However, those results were not published until 1913 in a French agronomics journal (*Annales de l'Institut National Agronomique*) and lay largely undiscovered for many decades thereafter (Kravitz and Martin, 1986).

More prominently, Gustave Le Bon (1895/1960) used careful observations of a range of large groups and collectives to develop an influential theoretical analysis of crowd behaviour that emphasized emotional, irrational and unconscious influences. Le Bon's perspective on the potentially negative aspects of groups was highly influential, and can be seen as an intellectual precursor to modern research on deindividuation – the potential for an individual to lose his or her sense of self-awareness and accountability when submerged in a group (Zimbardo, 1969; see also Chapter 8). Thus, initial research clearly had directed some attention to group or crowd dynamics. However, Ringelmann's work was unknown to nearly all scholars at the time, and Le Bon's work was observational in nature. Therefore, as the end of the nineteenth century approached, the time was ripe for foundational experimental research on social and group influences on individuals.

The scientist who would rise to this challenge – Norman Triplett – was born on a farm near Perry, Illinois, in 1861. He graduated from Perry High School and later attended Illinois College in Jacksonville, Illinois, graduating as class valedictorian in 1889. Triplett was an enthusiastic player in a range of competitive sports. After completing his undergraduate degree, Triplett worked as a school system superintendent and later as a high-school science teacher, before pursuing his initial graduate degree at Indiana University. He worked in the laboratory of William Lowe Bryan, who later went on to serve as president of the American Psychological Association (Davis et al., 1995). And when Triplett arrived at Indiana University as a graduate student in 1895, the availability of one of the first experimental psychology laboratories in the country and his keen interest in athletic competition created the perfect situation for him to conduct research that would play a formative role in shaping the emerging discipline of social psychology and the field of group dynamics.

THE COMPETITION STUDIES

THE ARCHIVAL STUDY:
REVIEWING RECORDS FROM CYCLING COMPETITIONS

METHOD

Triplett starts his classic 1898 article with a detailed consideration of results from competitive cycling events. To this end, he reviewed official records provided by the Racing Board of the League of American Wheelmen through the close of the 1897 season to compare times across three types of races: (a) races against other riders, (b) paced races against time (in which a single rider is trying to beat a record but has the benefit of a group of other riders who run in tandem to provide a pace), and (c) unpaced races against time, in which a single rider tries to beat a record alone without the benefit of pacemakers.

RESULTS

What Triplett discovered was that average times per mile were faster for the actual races against other riders and the paced races against time than they were for the unpaced races against time. Specifically, relative to unpaced riding, there was a 23% improvement in times for paced competition, and a 26% improvement for actual races. In terms of average time, pacing reduced times by more than 34 seconds per mile, and racing reduced times by nearly 40 seconds per mile, from the average unpaced time of 2 minutes and 29 seconds per mile. Triplett notes that these results match nicely (and in fact exceed) the pattern that might have been predicted by polling the racers, stating that 'wheelmen themselves generally regard the value of a pace to be from 20 to 30 seconds in the mile' (1898: 508).

Triplett's analysis provides a very early and highly visible demonstration of the capacity for archival data from sporting competitions to have considerable value for understanding the dynamics of various social situations. The value of Triplett's findings was also enhanced by the fact that he drew together data from a large number of competitions with defined characteristics. As he states:

> In presenting these records, it is with the feeling that they have almost the force of a scientific experiment. There are, it is computed, over 2,000 racing wheelmen, all ambitious to make records. These figures as they stand to-day have been evolved from numberless contests, a few men making records which soon fall to some of the host who are pressing closely behind. (1898: 508)

At the same time, Triplett was also very astute in highlighting some limitations inherent to his analysis, including the fact that the records for each type of race were established by different sets of riders who may differ in skill level and other attributes:

> Regarding the faster time of the paced races, as derived from the records, it may be asked whether the difference is due to pacing or to the kind of men who take part ... Men fast at one kind of racing are found to be comparatively slow at another ... The racer finds by experience that race in which [he or she] is best fitted to excel and specializes in that. (1898: 508)

Triplett notes that comparisons involving the paced and unpaced times of the same riders would have allowed him to draw conclusions with greater confidence, had such comparisons been readily available. Nevertheless, as tentative information in this regard, he does locate and present the best one-mile times, both paced and unpaced, for two riders and notes that they reveal the same pattern as the larger pool of data.

THEORETICAL DISCUSSION

Yet Triplett's analysis didn't stop with a discussion of the cycling findings. Critically, he also identified a number of theories that might explain these results, and then reflected on the potential for testing one of these in a laboratory experiment.

As shown in Table 1.1, these theories ranged from physical (suction and shelter) to psychological (encouragement, brain worry and automatic theories) to somewhat fanciful (hypnotic suggestion). Triplett was especially interested in the 'dynamogenic

Table 1.1   Theories discussed by Triplett (1898) as possible explanations for the results of his archival study of cycling competitions

Theory	Explanation or relevant quote
Suction theory	'the vacuum left behind the pacing machine draws the rider following, along with it' (p. 514)
Shelter theory	Following behind another rider provides shelter from wind resistance
Encouragement theory	'The presence of a friend on the pacing machine to encourage and keep up the spirits of the rider' (p. 514)
Brain worry theory	Leading a race or keeping the pace requires a greater deal of concentration or worry than following the pace of another
Theory of hypnotic suggestions	'A curious theory, lately advanced, suggests the possibility that the strained attention given to the revolving wheel of the pacing machine in front produces a sort of hypnotism and that the accompanying muscular exaltation is the secret of endurance shown by some long distance riders in paced races' (p. 515)
Automatic theory	Compared to the leader, who must give careful attention to strategy and the movement of muscles, a follower can ride relatively automatically
Dynamogenic factors	'This theory of competition holds that the bodily presence of another rider is a stimulus to the racer in arousing the competitive instinct; that another can thus be the means of releasing or freeing nervous energy' (p. 516)

factors' involving competition. But how could he study these processes in a more controlled manner that would rule out factors such as wind patterns, slipstreaming or laying back in the pack and letting another rider take the lead?

THE EXPERIMENTAL STUDY: TESTING THEORY IN THE LAB

METHOD

To study competition in the laboratory, Triplett devised a clever apparatus – a 'competition machine' – whereby two individuals could compete with each other by turning fishing reels as quickly as possible. Two fishing reels were secured to the end of a Y-shaped apparatus that was clamped on top of a heavy table (see Figure 1.1). Bands of twisted silk cord were run over the axles of the reels and across two pulleys, such that turning the reel would cause a small flag sewed onto the silk cord to traverse the length of the four-metre circuit. The task was to turn the reel rapidly and complete the circuit four times as quickly as possible.

Using two reels and circuits of cord allowed Triplett to compare the performances of individuals working alone with their performances when competing with another person. The use of the visible flags also allowed for continuous comparison, allowing individuals to pace themselves just as cyclists could when riding in tandem. Times were measured with a stopwatch, and these times constituted the study's official data points. In addition, a kymograph was used to provide a graphical record of the rate at which participants turned the fishing reel over time within each trial (see Figure 1.2). As Triplett says:

Figure 1.1   A diagram of Triplett's 'competition machine' (Triplett, 1898: 519)

Figure 1.2   The kymograph used in Triplett's experiment, on display at the Indiana University Department of Psychological and Brain Sciences (photo courtesy of Robert Rydell and Jim Sherman)

> The records were taken from the course A D. The other course B C being used merely for pacing or competition purposes. The wheel on the side from which the records were taken communicated the movement made to a recorder, the stylus of which traced a curve on the drum of a kymograph. The direction of this curve corresponded to the rate of turning, as the greater the speed the shorter and straighter the resulting line. (1898: 518)

Although Triplett states that nearly 225 individuals of all ages participated in the study, his article focuses almost exclusively on the data from 40 children ranging from 8 to 17 years old. These children were allowed to practise turning the reel until they were familiar with the apparatus. They then participated in a series of six trials lasting on average around 30–40 seconds each, with five minutes of rest between trials. The first trial for all participants was alone, with the remaining five trials alternating between alone and competition with another child, with counterbalancing across the final five trials. In this way, children were assigned to one of two groups that followed different trial orders (Group A: alone, competition, alone, competition, alone, competition; Group B: alone, alone, competition, alone, competition, alone).

RESULTS

Based on trial times, as well as on his observations of the sessions, Triplett concluded that competition seemed to have an energizing effect on most of the children. As was customary for the time, prior to the advent of sophisticated statistical techniques, Triplett presented his results in a series of raw data tables and graphs. Of special interest were three tables, each divided into separate sections for participants in Group A and Group B. He placed participants' data into one of these tables and based his assessment of three general patterns of results that seemed present. Specifically, he concluded that 20 children were stimulated positively by competition, that ten were 'overstimulated', and that ten were little affected by competition.

Positively stimulated children generally had faster times on competition trials than on alone trials, and appeared to be motivated by competition. 'Overstimulated' children had slower times when working competitively rather than alone. However, Triplett did not attribute this reduced performance to reduced motivation, but instead to becoming too excited and losing mental or motor control as a result of trying to reel too hard. Finally, one quarter of the children showed relatively small differences between alone and competition trials, suggesting that they were relatively unaffected by competition.

In reference to the 'overstimulated' children, Triplett states:

> With them stimulation brought a loss of control. In one or more of the competition trials of each subject in this group the time is very much slower than that made in the preceding trial alone ... This seems to be brought about in large measure by the mental attitude of the subject. An intense desire to win, for instance, often resulting in over-stimulation. Accompanying phenomena were labored breathing, flushed faces and a stiffening or contraction of the muscles of the arm. (1898: 523)

Triplett provides a rather detailed consideration of how different reeling strategies could produce motor coordination, balance or muscular fatigue issues for some children. He then suggests that although most of the children who were stimulated by competition seemed able to use their increased energy to reel more quickly, others became too flustered to be consistently efficient when trying to reel more quickly.

Taken as a whole, the results presented in Triplett's classic 1898 article suggest that, for most of the children, competition led to higher effort and motivation levels than working alone. Reflecting on both the laboratory experiment and his archival study of competitive cycling results, he thus concluded:

> From the above facts regarding the laboratory races we infer that the bodily presence of another contestant participating simultaneously in the race serves to liberate latent energy not ordinarily available. This inference is further justified by the difference in time between the paced competition races and the paced races against time, amounting to an average of 5.15 seconds per mile up to 25 miles. (1898: 533)

However, it should also be recognized that there was notable variation in responses to competition across participants, both as reflected in Triplett's three categories and across the results of children within each of those categories.

STRENGTHS

Not surprisingly, Triplett's article is written in a style that is very different from that of most contemporary social psychology research articles. Because computer graphics and sophisticated statistical techniques were not yet developed, the article presents results in raw data tables accompanied by hand-drawn graphs and discussions of anecdotal information. Similarly, because extensive prior research had not yet been conducted, the article contains no formal reference list, though a handful of relevant prior works are discussed within the text.

However, these historical constraints were not entirely disadvantageous. It is refreshing to read an article free of the seemingly endless citations and statistically dense discussions that are characteristic of most current articles. It is also refreshing to read an article that includes open speculation about causal processes and detailed consideration of the responses of specific participants. These discussions give important insight into dynamics that might otherwise be overlooked. For example, careful consideration of the behaviour of some of the 'overstimulated' participants allowed Triplett to clarify why higher effort levels might actually lead to slower times on some competitive trials. Certainly, any later researchers who read Triplett's article would have gained insight into a range of factors that might influence competition.

Triplett's research also had several features that would later become hallmarks of high-quality social psychological research. First, he used multiple methodologies, grounding his hypotheses in a detailed archival analysis of competitive cycling results and then testing those hypotheses in a laboratory setting. Using multiple methods to provide converging evidence has become central to the development and advancement of social psychology (Cialdini, 1980).

Second, Triplett identified multiple theories that might account for the competition effects he noted in the cycling data. He then focused in on the 'dynamogenic factors' involving competition and designed a laboratory apparatus that would allow him to study those factors while controlling, at least to some extent, for others. Identifying competing hypotheses derived from multiple theories is crucial to the development of scientific knowledge (Platt, 1964) and has been a key to the advancement of social psychology over time (Ross et al., 2010).

Third, in designing and conducting his famous experiment, Triplett displayed a great deal of precision and attention to detail. For example, in describing the fine-tuning of his competition machine, he states:

Frequent trials of the machinery showed very small errors. In each regular trial the flag travelled 16 meters. For ten test trials the average number of turns of the reel necessary to send it over this course was found to be 149.87, with a mean variation of .15, showing that the silk band did not slip to any appreciable extent. If 40 seconds be taken as the average time of a trial (which is not far wrong), .15 of a turn will be made in .04 second. (1898: 518)

Similarly, although the kymograph was incidental to the experiment itself, given that trial times were measured with a stopwatch, Triplett also took great care to ensure that the kymograph maintained as consistent a rate of turning as possible to provide comparable visual records of the trials for each participant.

Fourth, Triplett's experiment showed ingenuity in modelling the dynamics of sporting competition in a more controlled setting. Using a small flag sewn to the silk cord meant that participants were able to gauge their progress throughout each trial and compare it with the progress of their competitor on the competition trials. The task itself was also rather simple and required a high degree of effort, with very fast reeling required for each brief trial. This helped increase the chances that results could be attributed to effort, although, as Triplett readily acknowledges, ability and strategy differences may still have played some role.

Finally, Triplett showed admirable attempts either to control for variables that were not of central interest, or to discuss their possible influence. In particular, he assigned children to one of two groups, with the order of alone versus competitive trials counterbalanced across these groups for Trials 2–6. This allowed for several useful comparisons of alone versus competition conditions at equal levels of practice and experience. Triplett also provided an insightful discussion of the possible influence of several variables that were not directly controlled. He discusses the potential impact of age, sex, motor skill, nervousness, reeling strategies, and muscular coordination levels. Although these discussions were speculative, Triplett did attempt to ground his conclusions on averages from various subgroups or on anecdotal information. For example, based on a consideration of the averages for boys and girls across various ages within a subset of trials, he suggested that times appeared to be slightly quicker for older children and that competition effects appeared to be slightly larger for girls than for boys. He also acknowledged that encouragement and trial time feedback were provided in some cases but not others, recognizing that this might have influenced results. And as a last detail, he also flagged the results of two left-handed participants in his data tables.

LIMITATIONS

Unsurprisingly too – given the historical context and the underdeveloped 'state of the art' – Triplett's landmark research also had limitations. Most notably, the unavailability of modern statistical techniques led Triplett to base his conclusions on careful inspection of raw data tables, averages for subgroups of interest, and graphs. His presentation of that data was detailed and compelling, and provides a wealth of insights into possible competition effects. It does not, however, allow readers to know which patterns were statistically significant or how they might change when including statistical control variables.

Fortunately, Triplett did present the raw data for all of the 40 children that his article focused on. Recently, a fascinating article by Michael Strube (2005) submitted this data to statistical analyses that were not available to Triplett in the late 1890s. After conducting a variety of analyses, Strube concluded that there was little consistent support for statistically significant competition effects within Triplett's data.

When considering Strube's (2005) analyses, it is important to recall that Triplett assigned children to one of two groups, with the order of the alone versus competition trials counterbalanced across the two groups on Trials 2–6. Therefore, on those trials, one group was working alone and the other group was working competitively, allowing for a measure of competition effects at equal levels of task experience. Strube notes that Trial 2 provided an especially promising performance comparison, because it was not subject to any carry-over effects from previous competitive trials. Such carry-over effects are a concern, because once children had engaged in a competitive trial, it was likely that later alone trials might still be influenced by this earlier experience of competition. Indeed, Triplett recognized this issue, stating:

> The competition element entered into the trials alone and it was found advisable in some cases to keep from the subject the time made, as there was a constant desire to beat his own or his friend's records, and thus make all the trials competitive. The competition feeling seemed present all the time. It is felt, therefore, that succeeding trials alone are not really non-competing trials. (1898: 530)

Comparing scores between the two groups on Trials 2–6, Strube found little evidence for competition effects. There was a very small tendency for children to reel more quickly competitively than alone on four out of the five trials, but these differences were not significant $(p > .42)$.[1] Noting that there were significant age and sex effects on the first trial (with older children and boys performing better), Strube then repeated the between-groups analyses for Trials 2–6, controlling for first trial performance. He still found no significant competition effects overall, even though the average across all five trials was slightly faster on the competition trials $(p = .24)$. There was, however, a significant competition effect for Trial 3.

Within-subjects analyses (i.e., comparing across trials for all of the participants) similarly failed to find a significant overall competition effect. However, when each participant's alone and competition trial scores were averaged, the

---

[1] p-values refer to the likelihood of an event occurring by chance. These values are expressed as a number between 0 and 1, where 0 indicates that an event will definitely not occur and 1 indicates that an event definitely will occur. Psychologists customarily take a p-value below .05 as a benchmark for statistical significance – indicating that a given effect is unlikely to have occurred by chance.

contrast between these scores did reveal a significant difference ($p = .048$), with faster average performance on competition trials (37.45 seconds) than on alone trials (38.14 seconds). Yet, even that difference was quite small, representing only a 1.81% reduction in trial times when working with a competitor rather than alone. Moreover, those differences disappeared in additional analyses that excluded the two left-handed participants in Triplett's sample. Finally, Strube failed to find any evidence that either age or gender affected responses to competition, despite Triplett's speculation that these factors may have played a role. All things considered, Strube's (2005) analysis suggests that the evidence for competition or social facilitation effects within Triplett's data was, at best, inconsistent and very small in magnitude.

One important reason for the lack of significant overall differences pertains to Triplett's distinction between 'positively stimulated' and 'overstimulated' participants. Here Triplett noted that although approximately three-quarters of the children seemed to be excited or energized by competition, only two-thirds of these energized children were able to translate their excitement into quicker reeling times. The remaining 'overstimulated' participants actually produced slower times as a result of not reeling in a consistently efficient manner due to a loss of mental or psychological control. This observation would anticipate, by many decades, the eventual realization that stimulation produced by the presence of others can actually interfere with performance under some conditions (Zajonc, 1965). Of course, the reduced performance of the overstimulated children works against the detection of an overall competition effect when averaging across all participants. It is also possible that more consistent or significant patterns were lurking within Triplett's larger pool of nearly 225 participants of all ages.

Yet despite the lack of consistent, statistically significant evidence for competition effects in Triplett's research, it nevertheless presents compelling information and rationale supportive of the general notion that the presence of other people can affect individual motivation. In addition, Triplett's identification of clear pacing and competition effects in competitive cycling results, along with his detailed analysis of how various participants responded to competition, certainly set the stage for later researchers to identify and test a host of hypotheses. Indeed, given the lasting impact of Triplett's work, it is really rather fortunate for the field of social psychology that the demonstration of statistical significance was not a criterion for publishing articles in the 1890s. As Strube states:

> The analyses presented here certainly make one wonder what would have happened had null hypothesis statistical testing been in fashion in Triplett's day ... It seems likely that social facilitation would have been demonstrated eventually, but one wonders how long that demonstration would have been delayed or how many creative minds would have been put off the trail ... Indeed, in all other respects, Triplett's study remains an admirable beginning to the field of social psychology ... His creative and prescient speculation about the conceptual underpinnings of social facilitation laid the groundwork for the important and statistically significant research that followed. (2005: 281)

IMPACT OF THE CLASSIC COMPETITION STUDIES

The impact of Triplett's classic research has been profound. It is often cited as the first published study in social psychology (e.g., Aiello and Douthitt, 2001; Strube, 2005), as well as in sports psychology (e.g., Iso-Ahola and Hatfield, 1986); and an influential review article on the early history of social psychology by Gordon Allport (1954) refers to it as the very first social psychological experiment (for a dissenting view, see Haines and Vaughan, 1979). As such, it is clear that Triplett's 1898 article represents a very early and vivid example of how social phenomena can be submitted to scientific scrutiny in an experimental laboratory.

Triplett's work also launched inquiry into the way in which the presence of other people affects individual motivation and effort. His evidence that the presence of competitors can enhance individual motivation stimulated a wealth of research into social facilitation (this term being coined by Floyd Allport in 1920). Eventually, researchers conducted hundreds of studies that examined the motivation and effort of individuals when working alone versus in the presence of other people who were observers, co-actors or audience members (Bond and Titus, 1983). Triplett's research also contributed indirectly to the eventual recognition that the presence of others can sometimes lead to social loafing (this term being coined by Bibb Latané and colleagues in 1979) by reducing individual motivation when those others are working together with the individual on a collective task as co-workers or teammates. Since the 1970s, more than 100 studies have been conducted too on social loafing (Karau and Williams, 2001). A host of theories have also been developed to explain both social facilitation and social loafing, and some of these echo Triplett's own speculative insights (i.e., as in Table 1.1).

CONCLUSION

Although Triplett's classic research made invaluable contributions to social psychology and sports psychology in general, and to the fields of social facilitation and social loafing in particular, research and theory on these issues has advanced immensely since the late 1890s. Indeed, if we take the publication of Triplett's article in 1898 as a key starting point for the field of social psychology, nearly all of the knowledge in the field has developed after Triplett's work. The other chapters in this book can be taken as clear testimony to the wide range of creative, influential and dynamic research that has been conducted by social psychologists throughout more than a century of research.

Regarding the specific issues of social facilitation and social loafing, both have evolved into mature and multifaceted mainstream research areas within social psychology. Triplett's article inspired a number of early studies showing that the presence of others seemed to have an energizing or motivating effect on individuals. These studies examined a wide range of tasks and also studied various animals in addition to humans. Although many early studies established performance gains in the presence of others (e.g., F. Allport, 1920), many were also starting to document situations in which the presence of others actually reduced performance (Dashiell, 1935).

This inconsistency in findings was somewhat stifling to research on social facilitation through the 1940s and 1950s until Robert Zajonc proposed an ingenious integration in 1965. He noted that a key idea from drive theory was that arousal tended to facilitate dominant responses (Hull, 1935; Spence, 1956). Dominant responses on simple or well-learned tasks are likely to be correct, whereas dominant responses on complex or unfamiliar tasks are likely to be either incorrect or inefficient. Zajonc reasoned that the presence of other people can serve as a source of arousal, and should thereby enhance performance on simple or well-learned tasks and reduce it on complex or unfamiliar tasks. This insight appeared to provide a neat explanation of the existing social facilitation research and stimulated a wealth of additional work. A number of later theories were then developed in an attempt to clarify what it is about the presence of others that creates drive or arousal, as well as to articulate additional process variables, moderators, or limiting conditions of social facilitation (for reviews, see Geen, 1991; Guerin, 1993).

The contrast between Triplett's findings (that the presence of others can enhance motivation) and those of Ringelmann (that working with others can reduce motivation) also helped stimulate the development of social loafing research. Although Triplett's research attracted a good deal of attention early in the twentieth century, it wasn't until 1974 that Alan Ingham and colleagues replicated Ringelmann's study in a more controlled setting (Ingham et al., 1974). A classic study by Latané and colleagues (1979) also nicely isolated some key dynamics of motivation losses and stimulated a flurry of additional research, with a number of theories being offered to explain the effect (for reviews, see Karau and Williams, 1993, 2001).

At first glance, social facilitation and social loafing might appear to be opposite effects because the presence of others typically stimulates effort in the case of facilitation but reduces it in the case of loafing. However, this inconsistency is readily resolved by noting the nature of the others present (Harkins, 1987). Specifically, in social facilitation research, the others who are present are observers, co-actors or audience members, creating the potential for increased arousal (Zajonc, 1965), evaluation (Cottrell, 1972) or distraction (Baron, 1986) relative to what would be experienced alone. On the other hand, in social loafing research, the others who are present are co-workers or teammates, creating an opportunity for individuals to reduce their efforts relative to what they might contribute when solely responsible for performing well at the task (Karau and Williams, 1993).

And what became of Norman Triplett? His early career saw him complete research projects on a range of issues. After finishing his master's thesis at Indiana University in 1898, he went to Clark University to work (with G. Stanley Hall) on his PhD work (Davis et al., 1995). His dissertation, which became a long article entitled

'On the conjuring of deceptions' in the *American Journal of Psychology* (Triplett, 1900), focused on the general issues of illusion and magic. It detailed a variety of techniques and tricks that could be used to create illusions, and traced them to their psychological underpinning, such as attention, perception, suggestion and concealment. Triplett (1901) also conducted a study on fish that had interesting social implications. He placed two perch in a tank that was separated by a glass barrier from minnows. Once the perch learned to ignore the minnows they later refrained from eating them when the barrier was removed, a result which speaks to the power of learning and experience in shaping seemingly innate behaviour (a thread later picked up by clinical researchers such as Seligman, 1975).

After these early notable empirical contributions, Triplett devoted much of his career to teaching and administration. In 1901, following a one-year appointment at Mt Holyoke College in Massachusetts, he joined the faculty at Kansas Normal School in Emporia (which later became Emporia State University). He served as the head of the Department of Child Study for 30 years, building a programme in psychology, before retiring in 1931. During this time, he developed a reputation as an outstanding teacher and mentor. Triplett also maintained his lifelong interest in competitive sports. He was an accomplished runner, a regular member of the faculty baseball team, and habitually attended practice sessions for a range of sports on campus. He even served as temporary track coach during the 1909 season (Davis et al., 1995).

Norman Triplett had a long and varied career not only as a great researcher but also as a teacher and administrator. But it was a single, timely master's thesis that would ultimately come to represent his greatest legacy. The clever and deceptively simple studies that he reported represent a foundational contribution to what would evolve into a rich and ever-growing body of research on the influence that the presence of other people has on individual arousal, motivation and performance. This work has left a lasting mark on the field of social psychology – not only because it unearthed a set of interesting social psychological phenomena, but also because it provided a powerful model for actually doing social psychological research. Compellingly, this was scientific, theory-rich, methodologically sophisticated and fun.

FURTHER READING

Triplett, N. (1898) 'The dynamogenic factors in pacemaking and competition', *American Journal of Psychology*, 9: 507–33.

For readers wanting a full appreciation of Triplett's inventive research, a careful review of this 1898 original article is a very rewarding experience.

Strube, M.J. (2005) 'What did Triplett really find? A contemporary analysis of the first experiment in social psychology', *American Journal of Psychology,* 118: 271–86.

This insightful piece provides a detailed statistical analysis of Triplett's original raw data.

Aiello, J.R. and Douthitt, E.A. (2001) 'Social facilitation from Triplett to electronic performance monitoring', *Group Dynamics: Theory, Research, and Practice,* 5: 163–80.

This paper presents an engaging historical overview of social facilitation research that, in part, traces the influence of Triplett's study on early research.

Bond, C.F. and Titus, T.J. (1983) 'Social facilitation: A meta-analysis of 241 studies', *Psychological Bulletin,* 94: 265–92.

This paper presents a detailed review and meta-analysis of social facilitation research and a discussion of its theoretical and practical implications.

Karau, S.J. and Williams, K.D. (1993) 'Social loafing: A meta-analytic review and theoretical integration', *Journal of Personality and Social Psychology,* 65: 681–706.

This paper presents a meta-analysis of social loafing research and offers an influential theoretical model that integrates the various findings in this area.

REFERENCES

Aiello, J.R. and Douthitt, E.A. (2001) 'Social facilitation from Triplett to electronic performance monitoring', *Group Dynamics: Theory, Research, and Practice,* 5: 163–80.

Allport, F.H. (1920) 'The influence of the group upon association and thought', *Journal of Experimental Psychology*, 3(3): 159–82.

Allport, G.W. (1954) 'The historical background of modern social psychology', in G. Lindzey (ed.), *Handbook of Social Psychology*, Vol. 1, 1st edn. Cambridge, MA: Addison-Wesley. pp. 3–56.

Baron, R.S. (1986) 'Distraction-conflict theory: Progress and problems', *Advances in Experimental Social Psychology,* 19: 1–36.

Bond, C.F. and Titus, T.J. (1983) 'Social facilitation: A meta-analysis of 241 studies', *Psychological Bulletin,* 94: 265–92.

Cialdini, R.B. (1980) 'Full-cycle social psychology', *Applied Social Psychology Annual*, 1: 21–47.

Cottrell, N.B. (1972) 'Social facilitation', in C.G. McClintock (ed.), *Experimental Social Psychology*. New York: Henry Holt & Co. pp. 185–236.

Dashiell, J. (1935) 'Experimental studies of the influence of social situations on the behavior of individual human adults', in C. Murchison (ed.), *A Handbook of Social Psychology*. Worcester, MA: Clark University Press. pp. 1097–158.

Davis, S.F., Huss, M.T. and Becker, A.H. (1995) 'Norman Triplett and the dawning of sport psychology', *The Sport Psychologist,* 9: 366–75.

Geen, R.G. (1991) 'Social motivation', *Annual Review of Psychology,* 42: 377–99.

Goethals, G.R. (2003) 'A century of social psychology: Individuals, ideas, and investigations', in M.A. Hogg and J. Cooper (eds), *The Sage Handbook of Social Psychology*. Thousand Oaks, CA: Sage. pp. 3–23.

Guerin, B. (1993) *Social Facilitation*. Cambridge, UK: Cambridge University Press.

Haines, H. and Vaughan, G.M. (1979) 'Was 1898 a "great date" in the history of social psychology?', *Journal of the History of the Behavioral Sciences,* 15: 323–32.

Harkins, S.G. (1987) 'Social loafing and social facilitation', *Journal of Experimental Social Psychology*, 23: 1–18.

Hothersall, D. (2004) *History of Psychology*, 4th edn. New York: McGraw-Hill.

Hull, C.L. (1935) 'The conflicting psychologies of learning: A way out', *Psychological Review*, 42: 491–516.

Ingham, A.G., Levinger, G., Graves, J. and Peckham, V. (1974) 'The Ringelmann effect: Studies of group size and group performance', *Journal of Personality and Social Psychology*, 10: 371–84.

Iso-Ahola, S.E. and Hatfield, B. (1986) *Psychology of Sports: A Social Psychological Approach.* Dubuque, IA: Brown.

James, W. (1890) *The Principles of Psychology.* New York: Henry Holt & Co.

Karau, S.J. and Williams, K.D. (1993) 'Social loafing: A meta-analytic review and theoretical integration', *Journal of Personality and Social Psychology*, 65: 681–706.

Karau, S.J. and Williams, K.D. (2001) 'Understanding individual motivation in groups: The collective effort model', in M.E. Turner (ed.), *Groups at Work: Theory and Research*. Mahwah, NJ: Erlbaum. pp. 113–41.

Kravitz, D.A. and Martin, B. (1986) 'Ringelmann rediscovered: The original article', *Journal of Personality and Social Psychology*, 50: 936–41.

Latané, B., Williams, K.D. and Harkins, S.G. (1979) 'Many hands make light the work: The causes and consequences of social loafing', *Journal of Personality and Social Psychology*, 37: 822–32.

Le Bon, G. (1895/1960) *The Crowd: A Study of the Popular Mind* (translation of La *Psychologie des foules*). New York: Viking Press.

Platt, J.R. (1964) 'Strong inference', *Science*, 146: 347–53.

Ringelmann, M. (1913) 'Recherches sur les moteurs animés: travail de l'homme', *Annales de l'Institut National Agronomique*, 12: 1–40.

Ross, L., Lepper, M. and Ward, A. (2010) 'History of social psychology: Insights, challenges, and contributions to theory and application', in S.T. Fiske, D.T. Gilbert and G. Lindzey (eds), *Handbook of Social Psychology*, Vol. 1, 5th edn. Hoboken, NJ: John Wiley and Sons. pp. 3–50.

Spence, K.W. (1956) *Behavior Theory and Conditioning.* New Haven, CT: Yale University Press.

Strube, M.J. (2005) 'What did Triplett really find? A contemporary analysis of the first experiment in social psychology', *American Journal of Psychology*, 118: 271–86.

Triplett, N. (1898) 'The dynamogenic factors in pacemaking and competition', *American Journal of Psychology*, 9: 507–33.

Triplett, N. (1900) 'The psychology of conjuring deceptions', *American Journal of Psychology*, 11: 439–510.

Triplett, N. (1901) 'The educability of perch', *American Journal of Psychology*, 12: 354–60.

Zajonc, R.B. (1965) 'Social facilitation', *Science*, 149: 269–74.

Zimbardo, P.G. (1969) 'The human choice: Individuation, reason, and order versus deindividuation, impulse, and chaos', *Nebraska Symposium on Motivation*, 17: 237–307.

2

Attitudes and Behaviour

Revisiting LaPiere's
hospitality study

Joanne R. Smith and Deborah J. Terry

BACKGROUND

How do you feel about eating healthily, exercising regularly or saving energy? Like most people, you probably feel quite positive about all these things. But do you eat five portions of fruit and vegetables every day, do you exercise regularly, and do you always switch appliances off completely rather than leaving them on standby? Like most people, if honest, you would probably have to admit that you don't always engage in all of these behaviours. In many ways, it seems that humans have difficulty in 'practising what they preach'.

The question of the relationship between what people say and what they do has been of interest to social psychologists from the discipline's early days at the start of the last century. Initially, researchers simply assumed that there would be a strong correspondence between attitudes and action. Indeed, one of the reasons that individuals are interested in knowing the attitudes of others is precisely because of this assumption: if you know how a person feels about an issue, then this should be a good basis for predicting (and perhaps understanding) how they are going to behave in relation to that issue. If a man likes cooking, then presumably he will gravitate towards the kitchen when given a chance; if a woman likes driving fast, then presumably, if given a choice, she will buy a car that isn't sluggish. However, when psychologists began to explore the attitude–behaviour relationship empirically, these assumptions were very quickly called into question, because it immediately became apparent that things were not this simple. Moreover, this realization is typically traced back to a single piece of research that produced a particularly dramatic disconfirmation of the attitude–behaviour link: Richard LaPiere's (1934) hospitality study.

In the early 1930s LaPiere was a young researcher at Stanford University where he had recently been awarded his PhD in sociology, after having earlier completed a degree in economics at the same institution. Yet while he spent his entire career in the same academic establishment, it was LaPiere's appetite for travel (which he developed while working as an aircraft engineer in the First

World War) that provided him with most of the experiences that informed his scientific imagination. When LaPiere embarked on the work for which he would become well known he was not interested in the question of whether attitudes predict actions. This was because, as he saw it, attitudes *were* actions. As he put it, 'a social attitude is a behaviour pattern [exhibited in response to] ... designated social situations' (1934: 230). In other words, he reasoned that one can only determine how an individual feels about a particular attitude object by observing the individual's response in relevant social situations. To establish how a man feels about cooking we have to observe how he responds when given an opportunity to cook; to ascertain how a woman feels about driving fast we need to see how she responds to situations in which she is able to speed.

In many ways this might seem obvious but, at the time of LaPiere's research, there was a growing tendency – which has persisted to the present day – for researchers to assess attitudes simply by asking people to respond to attitude items on questionnaires. One reason for this is that the task of actually observing behaviour is often logistically complicated, time-consuming and expensive. Rather, than having to observe a person cooking or driving, then, it is far easier to simply ask them how they feel about these things (e.g., 'Do you like cooking?').

Yet for LaPiere, this reliance on the questionnaire method (although 'easy, cheap, and mechanical' (1934: 230)) was problematic and failed to do justice to the true meaning of attitudes. In particular, he argued that the use of questionnaires to measure attitudes rests upon the – unproven – assumption that there is a straightforward relationship between the symbolic (or verbal) response and the non-symbolic (or behavioural) response. In his research, he therefore set out to test this assumption by examining the relationship between symbolic and non-symbolic behaviour.

As part of his postgraduate study, LaPiere (1928) had already conducted research that touched upon this issue in work that explored attitudes in France and England towards groups with different skin colour. In particular, while studying at the London School of Economics, he had travelled through Europe and, in the course of everyday conversations with the people he met, he later recounted that he would often ask them 'Would you let a good Negro live at your home?' In France he observed that the overwhelming majority of people (78%) responded in a non-prejudiced way (i.e., replying 'Yes'). In England, however, the reverse was true: 81% of people answered the question in a prejudiced way (i.e., 'No'). However, aware that these answers represented only a verbal response to a symbolic situation, LaPiere sought to corroborate his data by looking at the policies of hotels regarding the admission of non-White guests. His rationale for looking at hotel policies was that, for economic reasons, hotel proprietors might be motivated to reflect the broader attitudes of society at the time – in particular, wanting to ensure that their White clientele were not offended by the hotel's policy of admitting or rejecting non-White guests.

In line with this reasoning, an examination of hotel policies did indeed reveal that these were aligned with the patterns that emerged from LaPiere's conversations: thus 77% of French hotels had policies that were non-prejudiced while 80% of English hotels had policies that were prejudiced. However, as LaPiere noted, these policies were still essentially verbal reactions to a symbolic situation rather than a direct assessment of how people behave. In both France and England the hotels certainly had *policies* that were in line with public opinion, but was this true of their actual *practice*? This was an issue that LaPiere sought to resolve in the classic study that he now set out to conduct.

THE HOSPITALITY STUDY

The inspiration for LaPiere's classic study came from a trip around the United States that he happened to take with a young Chinese student and his wife, Helen. Prior to embarking on this trip, LaPiere was concerned about the response that the group would receive from hotels (given the widespread antipathy towards Chinese people at the time). However, on their travels the group experienced no problems. But two months later, it happened that LaPiere was passing through the same region and – to avoid a potentially embarrassing situation – he called one of the hotels that he had visited previously to ask whether the establishment would be willing to accommodate an important Chinese gentleman that he was travelling with at the time. To his surprise, the response was a resounding 'No'. The gaping disparity between the response received at the hotel's reception desk and the response given over the telephone piqued LaPiere's interest and motivated him to conduct a more rigorous study. In this, he wanted to establish whether this disparity between policy and practice was typical, and, if so, what its cause might be.

Method and results

Beginning in 1930 and over a period of two years, LaPiere travelled extensively across the US with a young Chinese couple. In his words, the couple were 'personable, charming, and quick to win the admiration and respect of those they had the opportunity to become intimate with' (1934: 231). Testament to LaPiere's commitment as a researcher (and the aforementioned enthusiasm for travel), during this period, in addition to the original hotel, the group visited no fewer than 250 further establishments: 66 hotels, auto-camps and tourist homes and 184 restaurants and cafés. These businesses covered the full spectrum of those within the hospitality industry: from the most basic to the most luxurious.

LaPiere did not inform the Chinese couple that they were part of his research project, 'fearing that their behaviour might become self-conscious and thus affect the response of others towards them' (1934: 232). Upon arrival at each location, he allowed the couple to negotiate the relevant service (e.g., accommodation or a meal) while he tried to remain in the background, busying himself with the luggage or with his car (which was easy to do as he had a lifelong interest in mechanics). In this way, on most occasions (220 out of 251 instances – 88%) the couple were accompanied by LaPiere and this allowed him to compile 'accurate and detailed records' of the 'overt response' to the presence of the Chinese couple (1934: 232).

Although very simple in design, LaPiere's study produced a startling finding. In 251 requests for service, the Chinese customers were refused service only once – at what LaPiere notes was a 'rather inferior auto-camp' (1934: 232). The group was never refused service in any restaurant or café and, indeed, was treated with 'more than ordinary consideration in 72 of them' (1934: 232). This positive response to the Chinese couple was very much at odds with large-scale attitude surveys conducted at the time that, in line with LaPiere's concerns prior to embarking on his previous trip, revealed widespread antipathy towards Chinese people. For example, Daniel Katz and Kenneth Braly's (1933) study of the racial stereotypes of different national groups indicated that many Princeton students at the time considered Chinese people to be sly and deceitful. This led LaPiere to conclude that:

> The 'attitude' of the American people, as reflected in the behaviour of those who are for pecuniary reasons presumably most sensitive to the antipathies of their white clientele, is anything but negative towards the Chinese. (1934: 233)

To investigate further this apparent disconnection between the 'attitudes' revealed in large-scale surveys and the 'attitudes' observed in his own research, LaPiere sent a questionnaire to each of the 250 establishments six months after it had been visited by the group. LaPiere allowed this time to elapse in order to try to reduce any effects associated with the respondents' earlier experience of the Chinese guests. He received responses from 81 restaurants and cafés and 47 hotels, auto-camps and tourist homes (a 51% response rate). As an additional control, he also obtained responses from 96 restaurants and cafés and 32 hotels, auto-camps and tourist homes that had not been visited. In one version of the questionnaire, the establishment was simply asked the question '*Will you accept members of the Chinese race as guests in your establishment?*' In a second version, the question about Chinese people was embedded in a larger survey that asked the same question about other racial, ethnic and national groups.

Regardless of the version of the questionnaire that respondents received, the results were essentially the same. Moreover, they were again very striking: 92% of the restaurants and 91% of the hotels that had been visited by the group, and 94% of the hotels and 81% of the restaurants that had not been visited, indicated that they would *not* accept members of the Chinese race in their establishment (see Table 2.1). As in his earlier one-off observation, there was thus considerable disparity between what people did and what they said they would do.

This lack of correspondence between people's verbal response to a potential situation and their actual behaviour when in that situation confirmed LaPiere's reservations about the use of survey items to assess attitudes. He argued that although attitude questionnaires may be useful for measuring reactions to symbolic or abstract targets (e.g., a person's feelings about god or freedom), this form of measurement did not allow researchers to assess how people would respond in real and concrete situations:

Only a verbal reaction to an entirely symbolic situation can be secured by the questionnaire. It may indicate what the responder would actually do when confronted with the situation symbolized in the question, but there is no assurance that it will. (1934: 236)

Table 2.1   The response of different hospitality establishments to a question asking whether they would accept Chinese guests (adapted from LaPiere, 1934)

Response	Establishments visited	Establishments not visited
No	118	186
Not sure	9	9
Yes	1	1
Total	128	128

Note: When Chinese guests actually visited particular establishments, only one of these did not accept them.

IMPACT OF THE HOSPITALITY STUDY

THE EMERGING QUESTION: ARE ATTITUDES AND ACTION RELATED?

Although LaPiere's goal was ostensibly to challenge the use of questionnaires to assess attitudes, his 1934 study was widely interpreted (rightly or wrongly) as showing that attitudes do not always predict behaviour. In line with this reading, following his study, more papers appeared suggesting that the relationship between attitudes and behaviour was only very weak (e.g., Kutner et al., 1952) and these in turn prompted intense theoretical debate about the nature of the attitude–behaviour link (e.g., Campbell, 1963; Deutscher, 1969).

More than 40 years after LaPiere's study, this debate came to a head with the publication of Alan Wicker's (1969) seminal review of the available empirical evidence on the relationship between attitudes and behaviour. Wicker reviewed 42 experimental studies and found that the average correlation between attitudes and behaviour was only very low ($r \approx .15$).[1] On this basis, he concluded that 'taken as a whole, these studies suggest that it is considerably more likely that attitudes will be unrelated or only slightly related to overt behaviours than that attitudes will be closely related to actions' (1969: 65).

At the same time, however, other researchers maintained that attitudes *did* predict behaviour and sought to understand the weak relations identified in the literature. Some researchers highlighted methodological issues related to the measurement of

---

[1] r is the statistical notation for a *correlation coefficient*. This indicates the nature and strength of the relationship between two variables, and can vary from +1 (indicating a perfect positive relationship), through 0 (no relationship at all) to −1 (a perfect negative relationship); rs whose absolute value (i.e., whose positive or negative difference from 0) is greater than .5 are typically considered strong; those around .3 are generally considered moderate; and those whose absolute value is less than .1 are usually thought of as weak.

attitudes and behaviour that we will discuss further below. However, others proposed more complex models to explain when attitudes would predict behaviour and when they would not. More specifically, researchers argued that there was no simple attitude–behaviour relationship and that in order to predict behaviour accurately it is necessary to take *other* variables into account. Furthermore, these researchers were also keen to propose *theories* that would *explain* why attitudes and action are sometimes related and sometimes unrelated.

The most dominant of these 'other variables' approaches are the *theory of reasoned action* (Fishbein and Ajzen, 1975) and the *theory of planned behaviour* (Ajzen, 1991). According to both these theories, the most immediate determinant of behaviour is a person's *intention* to engage in that behaviour. Intention, in turn, is determined by attitudes (i.e., the person's evaluation of the target behaviour), subjective norms (i.e., the person's perception that others would approve of the behaviour), and, in the theory of planned behaviour, perceived behavioural control (i.e., the person's perception that the behaviour is under his or her control). In this way, as Figure 2.1 indicates, attitudes, norms and perceived control are seen to have additive effects on intentions, with the strength of each component varying depending on the behaviour in question and the person who is performing it (in particular, the group or population that they belong to).

A substantial body of research has established that both of these theories provide reasonably good accounts of the attitude–behaviour relationship (in particular, see meta-analyses by Albarracin et al., 2001; Armitage and Conner, 2001; Hagger et al., 2002). Attitudes correlate well with intentions (the average correlation, r, ranges between .45 and .60). The same is true for correlations between subjective norms and intentions ($.34 < r < .42$), and between perceived behavioural control and intentions ($.35 < r < .46$). Indeed, overall, in combination, attitudes, subjective norms and perceived behavioural control turn out to be very good predictors of intentions ($.63 < r < .71$). Furthermore, Sheeran (2002) observes that intentions are themselves good predictors of behaviour (average $r = .53$). Together with a number of methodological refinements (such as the principle of compatibility discussed below),

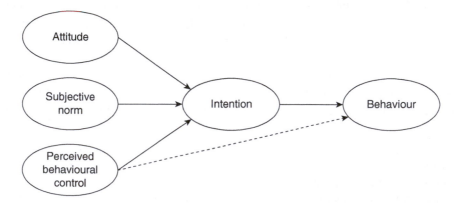

Figure 2.1 A schematic representation of the theory of planned behaviour (Ajzen, 1991)

the theoretical advance represented by the theories of reasoned action and planned behaviour suggests that it *is* possible to use attitudes to predict actions. Certainly, in light of such evidence, Wicker's (1969) conclusion that we should abandon the attitude concept altogether appears to be somewhat premature.

METHODOLOGICAL, CONCEPTUAL AND ETHICAL CRITICISMS

Despite the fact that the key finding of LaPiere's (1934) study has been replicated in a number of other domains, his results and conclusions have nevertheless been challenged on a number of methodological and theoretical grounds. First, there is the issue of the six-month interval between the two assessment points. Practically, we have no way of knowing whether the same individual responded to both the face-to-face request for service and the questionnaire request. This is a concern because it is likely that while LaPiere and the Chinese couple interacted with the desk clerk or waiter, the subsequent questionnaire was more likely to have been completed by the owner or manager of the establishment. If different people (with different roles) actually participated in the different phases of the study, then we would not necessarily expect a strong relationship between the symbolic (i.e., 'attitude') and non-symbolic responses (i.e., 'behaviour'). In addition, other research has shown that attitudes become more predictive of behaviour to the extent that they are measured at the same time rather than a long time apart (e.g., Schwartz, 1978). This is because attitudes can change over time, so that the person's attitude at the time behaviour is assessed may be quite different from the attitude they held previously or come to hold subsequently.

Other researchers have argued that the two measures of 'attitude' that LaPiere administered did not actually address the same attitude object. In particular, Ajzen and colleagues (1970) note that a different result might have been obtained if the verbal attitude measure more accurately reflected the behaviour of interest. That is, rather than asking 'Will you accept members of the Chinese race in your establishment?', LaPiere should perhaps have asked 'Will you accept a young, well-dressed, well-spoken, pleasant, self-confident, well-to-do Chinese couple accompanied by a mature, well-dressed, educated European gentleman as guests in your establishment?' (Ajzen et al., 1970: 270).

This suggestion speaks to the *principle of compatibility* (see Fishbein and Ajzen, 1975), which asserts that, in order to maximize the likelihood of their being correlated, attitudes and behaviour should be measured at the same level of specificity in terms of the target, action, context and time. For example, a person might have a positive attitude to exercise, but that doesn't necessarily mean that he or she will want to get up at 6 o'clock every morning in order to go to the gym.

To examine the compatibility issue, Davidson and Jaccard (1979) looked at the relationship between women's use of birth control pills (a behaviour of interest) and their attitudes (a) to birth control in general, (b) to birth control pills, (c) to using birth control pills, and (d) to using birth control pills in the next two years. Correlations between attitudes and behaviour were only weak for general attitudes to birth control ($r = .08$) but they were actually quite strong for the most specific attitude related to using birth control pills in the next two years ($r = .57$). Thus, as a measure of attitude becomes more compatible with the target behaviour in terms of the specifics of target, action, context and time, so the relationship between attitudes and behaviour becomes far stronger.

On a related note, critics have argued that what LaPiere (1934) assessed in his questionnaire was not in fact an attitude at all. Formally, an attitude can be defined as 'a psychological tendency that is expressed by evaluating a particular entity [the 'attitude object'] with some degree of favor or disfavor' (Eagly and Chaiken, 1993: 1). Yet, in these terms, LaPiere's study did not assess attitudes. Instead, it assessed *behavioural intentions*; that is, the degree to which a person intends to engage in a particular behaviour with respect to the attitude object (Ajzen et al., 1970; Dockery and Bedeian, 1989). Although we might expect behavioural intentions to be related to actual behaviour (as the theories of reasoned action and planned behaviour suggest), this relationship was likely to have been greatly attenuated by the violation of the principle of compatibility and the long period of time between the two measurements.

It is also important to consider the effect that the researcher and the particular Chinese couple may have had on the results. First, although LaPiere (1934) states that he made a conscious effort to control for any biasing effect of his presence by remaining in the background while the couple engaged with the staff at a particular establishment, as we noted above he was still actually present on most occasions. However, to be fair to LaPiere, he did record this as part of his data and he notes that the couple were served on each of the 31 occasions that he was absent. This suggests that LaPiere's presence was not crucial to the acceptance of the Chinese couple at the establishments visited.

Nevertheless, the group's acceptance may still have been an artifact of the particular Chinese couple involved in the research. As noted by LaPiere, the couple were personable and charming, well-dressed, spoke in unaccented English, and were 'skilful smilers' (1934: 232). Thus, the particular individuals who requested service in the establishments were potentially very different from the stereotypic representation that was likely to have been elicited in the questionnaire by the phrase 'members of the Chinese race'. It is possible that if the Chinese couple matched more closely the widespread stereotype of Chinese people at the time, then responses to the questionnaire and in the face-to-face interaction would have been more congruent.

The impact of situational constraints, such as norms, was also overlooked in LaPiere's (1934) analysis. Although LaPiere writes at length about the economic reasons that might be associated with accepting or not accepting members of stigmatized groups as guests, he does not consider the strong social and situational factors that are likely to have played an important role in the service workers' responses to their Chinese guests. People who hold negative attitudes towards particular groups may be reluctant to express these attitudes in their public behaviour because they also adhere to widely held norms of tolerance or politeness. In particular, because the participants in LaPiere's study were service workers, well-drilled in the importance of politeness and courtesy towards guests, norms of hospitality and courtesy may well have suppressed any discriminatory behaviour towards the Chinese couple in face-to-face interaction, even though discriminatory attitudes would readily be expressed in a private questionnaire.

From this discussion it is clear that a range of considerations (some subtle, some not-so-subtle) can have a bearing on the specific question of whether attitudes will be translated into behaviour. This is something that LaPiere himself was almost certainly well aware of. We can say this with some confidence because in his earlier graduate research (LaPiere, 1928) he had investigated attitudes towards Black people, yet he chose not to investigate attitudes towards this group in his later study. Why? As we have noted already, in part this was opportunistic since he and his wife happened to be travelling with a Chinese couple. At the same time, though, LaPiere was well aware of the fact that, at the time of his research, attitudes to Black people were extremely negative. More critically, the normative climate tended to encourage the public expression of such attitudes together with correspondingly discriminatory behavioural treatment (in particular, through the policy of segregation). Thus, if LaPiere had chosen to travel with a Black couple and then surveyed the establishments visited, it is likely that he would have found a very strong correspondence between the verbal and behavioural expressions of the attitude. And of course, had this been the case, then his study would not have emerged as one of the classic studies in social psychology.

One further point that needs to be made relates to the fact that, as we have remarked several times, LaPiere's (1934) work is usually interpreted as an examination of the attitude–behaviour relationship. Yet, interpreted in this way, it is clear that the study has a significant procedural problem. The reason for this is that LaPiere assessed behaviour *and then* attitudes, rather than assessing attitudes *and then* behaviour. Had LaPiere been interested in testing whether attitudes predict behaviour, then this would constitute a serious limitation to his work. However, it is important to remember that this was not his intention. Instead, as we explained earlier, his goal was to test the correspondence between verbal and behavioural expressions of attitudes. Thus, although the order of measurement poses problems for those who wish to interpret the hospitality study as evidence for the lack of a relationship between attitudes and behaviour, this methodological detail does not necessarily undermine LaPiere's original conclusions as to the lack of correspondence between verbal and behavioural responses.

Finally, although it may be unfair to judge classic studies on the basis of current norms, there are clearly some ethical issues associated with LaPiere's (1934) study. Specifically, there is the issue of informed consent. At no time were any of the participants in the study – either the Chinese couple or the service providers – aware that they were participating in the research. Moreover, while LaPiere informed his Chinese companions that they had been taking part in his research in 1934 when the findings were published, other participants were never debriefed as to the nature of the research or their involvement. Would they have objected, or refused to take part, had they known? Does this matter, since, in effect, they were simply doing their everyday jobs? However one imagines these questions being answered, the central message of LaPiere's research remains the same. Nonetheless, the fact that one can ask them makes it clear that even unobtrusive observational research has the potential to raise thorny ethical issues.

BEYOND THE HOSPITALITY STUDY

As we have seen, LaPiere's (1934) research raises a range of different types of question – methodological, conceptual and ethical. Indeed, this is one reason why it has aroused so much interest, and come to be seen as a classic study. It is also largely for this reason that the study continues to inspire debate and research among attitude researchers. Indeed, many of the questions that LaPiere raised about the nature of both attitudes and the attitude–behaviour relationship are as current today as they were three-quarters of a century ago.

WHAT IS AN ATTITUDE AND HOW SHOULD WE MEASURE IT?

In his work, LaPiere focused on the measurement of attitudes and the relationship between the conceptual definition of an attitude and the way in which attitudes were actually measured. At the time, he was concerned about the rise of paper-and-pencil techniques of attitude assessment and about the lack of correspondence between what he saw as the verbal and behavioural expressions of attitudes. As mentioned earlier, LaPiere believed that one could only truly assess attitudes by looking at individuals' behaviour because verbal and behavioural responses to an attitude object arise from a single 'acquired behavioural disposition' (Campbell, 1963: 97). In these terms, attitudes and behaviour are seen to be formally rather than causally related – that is, they are related because they are reflections of the same underlying state, not because one leads to the other. However, with a few notable exceptions (Kaiser et al., 2010), contemporary social psychologists tend to conceptualize attitudes as evaluative dispositions (e.g., Eagly and Chaiken, 1993), and this conceptualization has driven, and continues to drive, the way in which attitudes are measured.

One response to concerns that verbally expressed attitudes may not be an accurate representation of people's genuine feelings about a particular attitude object is to argue that the problem lies with the use of *explicit* attitudes (i.e., 'what people state out loud'). Accordingly, the recommended solution is to try to measure *implicit* attitudes (i.e., to establish 'what people feel inside'). Unlike explicit attitudes, such as those that individuals are aware of consciously and that are assessed by asking individuals to express their attitudes overtly in a questionnaire, implicit attitudes are assumed to be activated automatically in response to an attitude object and to guide behaviour unless overridden by controlled processes. In other words, implicit attitudes exist outside of conscious awareness or outside of conscious control.

Implicit attitudes are typically assessed through indirect measures, which are thought to capture attitudes that people may not be aware that they hold or attitudes that people might be unwilling to express due to social desirability concerns. Indirect measures such as the Implicit Association Test (IAT; Greenwald et al., 1998) and evaluative priming (Fazio et al., 1995) rely on response times to measure evaluative biases in relation to different attitude objects. These measures rest on the idea that exposure to a concept or stimulus (e.g., a picture of members of your own racial group) activates concepts in memory (e.g., a feeling that members of my group are generally positive), and then facilitates a positive response to related concepts (e.g., a positive word such as 'good') while simultaneously inhibiting responses to unrelated concepts (e.g., a negative word such as 'bad'). Individuals are seen to have a positive implicit attitude in favour of a given group when exposure to stimuli related to that group results in them responding faster to positive words than to negative words, and when exposure to stimuli related to other groups results in them responding faster to negative words than to positive words.

In recent years, implicit measures of attitudes have become very popular, particularly in the domains of prejudice and discrimination in which LaPiere was interested. This is because attitudes towards social groups are seen to be particularly susceptible to the influence of social desirability biases, due to widespread norms against the expression of negative attitudes (Crandall et al., 2002). However, implicit measures have also been employed in other attitude domains, such as consumer preferences, alcohol and drug use, and political preferences (Greenwald et al., 2009).

Moreover, the distinction between implicit and explicit attitudes raises interesting questions about the relationship between these constructs. Are implicit and explicit attitudes tapping distinct concepts such that people can hold opposing implicit and explicit attitudes towards the same attitude object (e.g., as suggested by Devine, 1989)? Or do implicit and explicit attitudes reflect a single underlying evaluation, such that the only difference between them is the extent to which they are affected by conscious processes (e.g., Fazio, 2001)?

Speaking to these questions, reviews of the relations between implicit and explicit attitudes have typically found only modest correlations (e.g., $r = .24$; Hoffman et al., 2005). However, there is considerable variability in the strength of this relationship (with some $rs > .40$ and others $< .10$) suggesting that additional factors, such as the desire to present the self positively and the strength of one's attitudes, are important (Nosek, 2005).

In reflecting on these issues, it is interesting to note that this contemporary debate about the distinction between, and relative validity of, implicit and explicit measures essentially revisits LaPiere's (1934) core concerns about the definition and measurement of attitudes. Yet despite increased interest in the role of implicit measures and the idea that such measures allow researchers to assess an individual's genuine or bona fide attitudes (because the expression of evaluations cannot be easily controlled or altered), it is important to note that even these measures are not direct observations of any evaluative disposition. Instead, we make inferences about an individual's attitudes from what we can observe, whether this is verbal expressions of like or dislike, physiological or cognitive reactions, or overt behaviour related to an attitude object. Moreover, all of these indicators are fallible. As Ajzen and Gilbert Cote point out:

> Verbal expressions of liking are subject to social desirability biases … , physiological reactions may reflect arousal or other reactions instead of evaluation … , and response latencies may be indicative not of personal attitudes but of cultural stereotypes. (2008: 289)

In addition, even overt actions can be misleading: just as people can use their verbal responses to deceive, so too can they deceive through their overt behaviour. Accordingly, in contrast to LaPiere's assertions, overt behaviour is not necessarily any more 'real' or 'authentic' than verbal responses.

ARE ATTITUDES RELATED TO BEHAVIOUR?

For all these reasons, the question of the nature of the relationship between attitudes and behaviours continues to be a central topic in social psychology. And while it is generally accepted that attitudes are related to behaviour, research also suggests that it is important to understand the circumstances that determine whether this link will be strong or weak. We have already considered some of the relevant factors here – such as the need for compatible measures and the importance of 'other variables'. In addition to those we have discussed, other research points to the importance of attitude accessibility (i.e., the extent to which an attitude is frequently invoked or expressed; Fazio, 1990) and social identity (i.e., the extent to which an attitude is associated with a salient group membership; Terry and Hogg, 1996). Nevertheless, in order to bring our discussion to a close, it is useful to reflect more broadly on the link between implicit attitudes and behaviour.

As noted above, there is now widespread use of tasks, such as the IAT, to measure implicit attitudes. However, just as Wicker (1969) did in his review of the literature on explicit attitudes, it is important to ask whether implicit attitudes actually predict behaviour and, if they do, do they predict it any better than explicit attitudes?

Both questions were recently addressed in a major review of existing studies conducted by Antony Greenwald and colleagues (2009). Surprisingly perhaps, this revealed that, in fact, the relationship between explicit attitudes and behaviour was generally stronger (mean $r = .36$) than the relationship between implicit attitudes and behaviour (mean $r = .27$) – although the strength of both relationships could best be described as moderate. However, speaking to the utility of implicit measures in the field of prejudice, this pattern was reversed for socially sensitive topics such as attitudes about different ethnic groups, such that here implicit attitudes were better predictors than explicit attitudes. Moreover, the predictive power of implicit and explicit attitudes was found to vary as a function of the type of behaviour. Implicitly assessed attitudes emerged as better predictors of behaviour that evades conscious control (e.g., non-verbal responses such as eye contact), while explicitly assessed attitudes were better predictors of deliberate behavioural responses (Fazio et al., 1995; cf. Greenwald et al., 2009).

CONCLUSION

Despite the fact that his work is now very widely known and debated, in his own lifetime LaPiere was disappointed by what he saw as its lack of impact. In particular, although he believed that his research demonstrated the dangers of relying on questionnaire methods when exploring attitudes, he reflected that his study

> did nothing to discourage the development of the paper-and-pencil test as the primary instrument of social investigation. Then and subsequently, the findings of that [the 1934] study were ignored by my peers and my questioning of methodological validity regarded as the views of a reactionary sociologist opposed to the application of truly scientific methods to the study of society. (LaPiere, 1969: 41)

But perhaps LaPiere should have been less critical – both of himself and of his colleagues. For while the nuances of his work are often overlooked and misunderstood, his efforts to highlight the dangers associated with equating different types of attitudinal and behavioural response are as relevant and as well-taken today as they were when he first made them. To be sure, the debate that surrounds these issues is now rather more complex than the one he initiated, but the basic terms of that debate are largely unchanged. In this sense, then, LaPiere can be seen not only to have opened up a major field of enquiry in social psychology but to have done so in a way that identified questions that proved to be of enduring importance. Not only can attitudes be considered 'the most distinctive and indispensable concept' in social psychology (Allport, 1935: 798), but also the need to study them in ways that are sensitive to the dynamics of social context remains paramount. As LaPiere urged us to understand, there is nothing about attitudes or behaviour – or their inter-relationship – that should ever be taken for granted.

FURTHER READING

LaPiere, R.T. (1928) 'Race prejudice: France and England', *Social Forces,* 7: 102–11.

LaPiere, R.T. (1934) 'Attitudes versus actions' *social Forces,* 13: 230–7.

It is well worth reading both the 1928 and 1934 papers by LaPiere for a vivid and engaging account of the methods and results of his research and the rationale for examining the relation between symbolic and non-symbolic behaviour.

Dockery, T.M. and Bedeian, A.G. (1989) '"Attitudes versus actions": LaPiere's (1934) classic study revisited', *Social Behaviour and Personality,* 17: 9–16.

Dockery and Bedeian revisit the 1934 study and provide a thorough account of both theoretical and methodological issues associated with this research.

Wicker, A.W. (1969) 'Attitudes versus actions: The relationship of verbal and overt behavioural responses to attitude objects', *Journal of Social Issues,* 25: 41–78.

Wicker's seminal paper in the study of attitude–behaviour relations provides a foundation for later examinations of this relationship such as the theories of reasoned action and planned behaviour.

Ajzen, I. (1991) 'The theory of planned behaviour', *Organizational Behaviour and Human Decision Processes,* 50: 179–211.

Fishbein, M. and Ajzen, I. (1975) *Belief, Attitude, Intention, and Behaviour: An Introduction to Theory and Research.* Reading, MA: Addison-Wesley.

Ajzen, I. and Gilbert Cote, N. (2008) 'Attitudes and the prediction of behaviour', in W.D. Crano and R. Prislin (eds), *Attitudes and Attitude Change.* London: Psychology Press. pp. 289–311.

For a more thorough discussion of the models of reasoned action and planned behaviour (which is worth considering given the dominance of these models in the attitude–behaviour field), the reader is directed to these publications.

REFERENCES

Ajzen, I. (1991) 'The theory of planned behaviour', *Organizational Behaviour and Human Decision Processes,* 50: 179–211.

Ajzen, I., Darroch, R.K., Fishbein, M. and Hornik, J.A. (1970) 'Looking backward revisited: A reply to Deutscher', *The American Sociologist,* 5: 267–73.

Ajzen, I. and Gilbert Cote, N. (2008) 'Attitudes and the prediction of behaviour', in W.D. Crano and R. Prislin (eds), *Attitudes and Attitude Change.* London: Psychology Press. pp. 289–311.

Albarracin, D., Johnson, B.T., Fishbein, M. and Muellerleile, P.A. (2001) 'Theories of reasoned action and planned behaviour as models of condom use: A meta-analysis', *Psychological Bulletin,* 127: 142–61.

Allport, G.W. (1935) 'Attitudes', in C. Murchison (ed.), *A Handbook of Social Psychology.* Worcester, MA: Clark University Press. pp. 798–844.

Armitage, C.J. and Conner, M. (2001) 'Efficacy of the theory of planned behaviour: A meta-analytic review', *British Journal of Social Psychology,* 40: 471–99.

Campbell, D.T. (1963) 'Social attitudes and other acquired behavioural dispositions', in S. Koch (ed.), *Psychology: A Study of a Science,* Vol. 6. New York: McGraw-Hill. pp. 94–172.

Crandall, C.S., Eshleman, A. and O'Brien, L.T. (2002) 'Social norms and the expression and suppression of prejudice: The struggle for internalization', *Journal of Personality and Social Psychology,* 82: 359–78.

Davidson, A.R. and Jaccard, J.J. (1979) 'Temporal instability as a moderator of the attitude–behaviour relationship', *Journal of Personality and Social Psychology,* 36: 715–24.

Deutscher, I. (1969) 'Looking backward: Case studies on the progress of methodology in sociological research', *The American Sociologist,* 4: 35–41.

Devine, P.G. (1989) 'Stereotypes and prejudice: Their automatic and controlled components', *Journal of Personality and Social Psychology,* 63: 754–65.

Dockery, T.M. and Bedeian, A.G. (1989) '"Attitudes versus actions": LaPiere's (1934) classic study revisited', *Social Behaviour and Personality,* 17: 9–16.

Eagly, A.H. and Chaiken, S. (1993) *The Psychology of Attitudes.* Belmont, CA: Thomson.

Fazio, R.H. (1990) 'Multiple processes by which attitudes guide behaviour: The MODE model as an integrative framework', in M.P. Zanna (ed.), *Advances in Experimental Social Psychology*, Vol. 23. San Diego, CA: Academic Press. pp. 75–109.

Fazio, R.H. (2001) 'On the automatic activation of associated evaluations: An overview', *Cognition and Emotion,* 15: 115–41.

Fazio, R.H., Jackson, J.R., Dunton, B.C. and Williams, C.J. (1995) 'Variability in automatic activation as an unobtrusive measure of racial attitudes: A bona fide pipeline', *Journal of Personality and Social Psychology,* 69: 1013–27.

Fishbein, M. and Ajzen, I. (1975) *Belief, Attitude, Intention, and Behaviour: An Introduction to Theory and Research.* Reading, MA: Addison-Wesley.

Greenwald, A.G., McGhee, D.E. and Schwartz, J.L.K. (1998) 'Measuring individual differences in implicit cognition: The implicit association test', *Journal of Personality and Social Psychology,* 74: 1464–80.

Greenwald, A.G., Poehlman, A.T., Uhlmann, E.L. and Banaji, M.R. (2009) 'Understanding and using the Implicit Association Test: III. Meta-analysis of predictive validity', *Journal of Personality and Social Psychology,* 97: 17–41.

Hagger, M.S., Chatzisarantis, N.L.D. and Biddle, S.J.H. (2002) 'A meta-analytic review of the theories of reasoned action and planned behaviour in physical activity: Predictive validity and the contribution of additional variables', *Journal of Sport and Exercise Psychology,* 24: 3–32.

Hofmann, W., Gawronski, B., Gschwendner, T., Le, H. and Schmitt, M. (2005) 'A meta-analysis on the correlation between the Implicit Association Test and explicit self-report measures', *Personality and Social Psychology Bulletin,* 31: 1369–85.

Kaiser, F.G., Byrka, K. and Hartig, T. (2010) 'Reviving Campbell's paradigm for attitude research', *Personality and Social Psychology Review,* 14: 351–67.

Katz, D. and Braly, K. (1933) 'Racial stereotypes of one hundred college students', *Journal of Abnormal and Social Psychology,* 28: 280–90.

Kutner, B., Wilkins, C. and Yarrow, P.R. (1952) 'Verbal attitudes and overt behaviour involving racial prejudice', *Journal of Abnormal and Social Psychology,* 47: 649–52.

LaPiere, R.T. (1928) 'Race prejudice: France and England', *Social Forces,* 7: 102–11.

LaPiere, R.T. (1934) 'Attitudes versus actions', *Social Forces,* 13: 230–7.

LaPiere, R.T. (1969) 'Comment on Irwin Deutscher's looking backward', *The American Sociologist,* 4: 41–2.

Nosek, B.A. (2005) 'Moderators of the relationship between implicit and explicit evaluation', *Journal of Experimental Psychology: General,* 134: 565–84.

Schwartz, S. (1978) 'Temporal stability as a moderator of the attitude–behaviour relationship', *Journal of Personality and Social Psychology,* 36: 715–24.

Sheeran, P. (2002) 'Intention–behaviour relations: A conceptual and empirical review', *European Review of Social Psychology,* 12: 1–36.

Terry, D.J. and Hogg, M.A. (1996) 'Group norms and the attitude–behaviour relationship: A role for group identification', *Personality and Social Psychology Bulletin,* 22: 776–93.

Wicker, A.W. (1969) 'Attitudes versus actions: The relationship of verbal and overt behavioural responses to attitude objects', *Journal of Social Issues,* 25: 41–78.

3

Cognitive Dissonance

Revisiting Festinger's End of the World study

Joel Cooper

BACKGROUND

On an autumn day in 1954, a well-known social psychologist read an article in his local newspaper. The psychologist had been a student of Kurt Lewin, often described as the seminal figure in the birth of modern social psychology. Like his mentor, this social psychologist believed that progress in the new science lay not only in testing theory in the laboratory but also in applying theory to phenomena in the real world.

At this time, Leon Festinger had already been responsible for two major theoretical contributions. In 1950 he had written a paper on the pressures for uniformity in groups (Festinger, 1950) and four years later turned his theoretical insight about group pressure into a focus on the individual, with his theory of social comparison processes (Festinger, 1954). Social comparison theory identified the strong need people have to evaluate their own opinions and abilities by comparing them with the opinions and abilities of others. However, he was now working on a new theory that would be transformative in the history of social psychology – what we would later know as the theory of *cognitive dissonance* (Festinger, 1957).

The new theory would move beyond social comparison to view the social world unabashedly from the perspective of the individual. According to Festinger, individuals represent the social world as a set of mental cognitions. Any behaviour, attitude or emotion was considered a cognition – that is, a mental representation within a person's mind. So, too, were the perceptions of the world around us. Our perceptions of other people, social groups and the physical world were all considered to be cognitive representations. Those representations existed in relationship to each other – sometimes fitting together consistently and sometimes inconsistently in people's minds. In his book-length monograph, Festinger (1957) would explain the arousal and reduction of dissonance with data and theory, and present a nuanced description of the events that create the discomfort of dissonance. However, the crux of the theoretical statement was elegant and straightforward: people abhor inconsistency among their cognitions and so mental representations that are inconsistent with each other create psychological discomfort akin to an unpleasant drive. Like other drive states, such as hunger, they need to be reduced. Moreover, the more important the cognitions to the individual, the greater the need to reduce any apparent inconsistency.

Imagine, then, Festinger's reaction when he read the following headline in a local newspaper:

PROPHECY FROM PLANET CLARION CALL TO CITY: FLEE THAT FLOOD.

IT'LL SWAMP US ON DEC. 21, OUTER SPACE TELLS SUBURBANITE

The two-column story described how a group of people in another state was preparing for the end of the world. It reported on a group of believers who had been receiving messages from beings on a distant planet called Clarion who had identified fault lines in the Earth's crust and warned the group that the Earth would soon be overwhelmed by a major cataclysm. Only those who truly believed the prophecy would be spared its devastation. As the headline suggested, the prediction was specific: the end of the Earth would come at midnight on 21 December 1955. The group of believers would be rescued by a space ship sent from Clarion that would whisk the believers to safety prior to the flood. The group was given the pseudonym of the Seekers by the researchers and they referred to its leader as Mrs Marion Keech.[1]

Could there be a more vivid example of cognitive inconsistency than the situation the Seekers would find themselves in on the morning of 22 December? A set of clear and definitive predictions had been made: the Earth was expected to come to an end at midnight on the previous night. A space ship was to have arrived at Mrs Keech's home to take the believers to safety. However, midnight would reveal that a space ship had not arrived and dawn would show that the cataclysmic flood had not occurred. The Sun would rise and the Earth would rotate as it always had.

In Festinger's view, the Seekers' mental representation of their prophecy and the disconfirmation they would witness on the morning of the 22nd would create a condition of cognitive dissonance. The inconsistency between the prediction and the observed event would create an unambiguous discrepancy. Festinger's fledgling theory of cognitive dissonance predicted that the members of the Seekers would experience this discrepancy as an unpleasant tension state and would need to find a way to reduce it.

How can people reduce their dissonance? Normally, when people are confronted with inconsistent cognitions, and suffer the unpleasant tension state of dissonance, they can change a cognition to reduce the discrepancy. If we believe that the distance between New York City and Paris is less than a thousand miles, and we are presented with information that the distance is 3,000 miles, it would

_____

[1]Mrs Keech (whose real name was Mrs Dorothy Martin) referred to herself as the 'Outer Space Subordinate', and before founding her group she had been an enthusiastic follower of L. Ron Hubbard's *Dianetics* movement – a forerunner to his later Church of Scientology.

not be surprising if we changed our belief in the distance between the two cities. But if we are committed to our belief – for example, if we had taken a public stance advocating the belief – then we try to hold onto it, even in the face of a contradictory cognition indicating the accurate distance.

When the Seekers expressed their belief in the celestial beings from the planet Clarion, they did so publicly. They suffered scorn from others. They sacrificed a great deal to be ready for the predicted cataclysm. Some sold their possessions, others emptied their bank accounts. There was strong commitment to the belief, making it very difficult to abandon. At the same time, the continued existence of Planet Earth on 22 December would be similarly undeniable. The inconsistent cognitions would be present and palpable on the morning of the 22nd.

In the face of these various circumstances, Festinger and his colleagues Henry Riecken and Stanley Schachter (1956) made a bold and controversial prediction. Their hypothesis was that the Seekers would not only persist in their belief but would actually become more ardent than they had been previously. They would hold tenaciously to their conviction that their prophecy had been correct all along; that the beings from Clarion had communicated with them correctly. Of course, they would not be able to maintain that the world had ended, but they could reaffirm their general belief pattern. Perhaps the date was wrong or perhaps there was another reason for the lack of destruction. But they would hold on to their belief system with greater tenacity than ever before.

The most obvious and notable change in the group's behaviour would be a sharp increase in their attempts to publicize their beliefs. In short, Festinger and his colleagues predicted that Mrs Keech and her followers would become evangelical proselytizers in their attempt to justify their belief system. 'If more and more people can be persuaded that the system of beliefs is correct, then clearly it must, after all, be correct' (Festinger et al., 1956: 28).

THE FIRST DISSONANCE STUDY: *WHEN PROPHECY FAILS*

Festinger and his colleagues leapt at the opportunity to study the effect of the disconfirmed prophecy. But time was short: there were only two months between the time the newspaper article appeared and the date of the anticipated cataclysm. So the investigators decided to study the Seekers through participant observation. And in order to do this, they decided to infiltrate the group, pretending to be newly converted members of the Seekers.

This was not easy. The investigators who called on Mrs Keech were treated politely but were rebuffed as potential group members. The Seekers had no interest in outsiders or in persuading others to become members. They were wary of the press and suspicious of strangers. Only after a senior member of the group suspected that the innocent strangers might have been sent by the celestial beings were the investigators finally allowed to join the group.

All of the messages about the destruction of Earth had come to Mrs Keech in the form of automatic writing séances. Automatic writing is a claim that another being has taken possession of an individual (a medium) and then uses the medium to communicate. The medium then writes a message that is believed to have come from another world. For the Seekers, Mrs Keech was the medium and the celestial beings from Clarion were the communicators. Automatic writing messages provided the group with specific instructions for the detailed preparations they must make in order to be saved from the cataclysm.

The group was told to expect a visitor from outer space to call upon them at midnight and escort them to a waiting spacecraft. The investigators were present as the group followed the carefully prepared script that would entitle them to enter the spacecraft. They went to great lengths for the preparation. One of the rules was to remove all metal from their persons. As midnight approached, zippers, bra straps and other objects were discarded. The space ship was to arrive precisely at midnight. The group was ready. The following sequence is an abridged version of the researchers' notes from that dramatic and traumatic night:

> *12:05 A.M. December 21.* No visitor. Someone in the group notices that another clock in the room shows only 11:55. The group agrees that it is not yet midnight.

> *12:10 A.M.* The second clock strikes midnight. Still no visitor. The group sits in stunned silence. The cataclysm itself is no more than hours away ... Midnight has passed and nothing has happened. There is no talking, no sound ... People sit stock still, their faces seemingly frozen and expressionless.

> *4:00 A.M.* The group has been searching for an explanation. None seems satisfactory. They comfort one another searching for a reason. Some, including Mrs Keech herself, begin to cry.

> *4:45 A.M.* Salvation! Mrs Keech is summoned to receive another message by automatic writing. When she returns she reads the message's momentous words to the group: 'For this day it is established that there is but one God of Earth and He is in thy midst and by his word have ye been saved. Not since the beginning of time has there been such a force for Good and light as now floods this room ...' (based on Festinger et al., 1956: 163–9)

The message was received with enormous enthusiasm. What did it mean? It meant that the cataclysm had been called off. Mrs Keech read, 'This little group, sitting all night long, had spread so much light that God had saved the world from destruction.' It meant that the disconfirmation of the specific prophecy had been explained. The belief system had been correct. A greater being – God of the Earth Himself – had tested this group of Seekers and found their goodness so overwhelming that he had decided to spare the world from destruction.

A second message arrived shortly thereafter. God had declared his message a Christmas message and ordered it to be released to the People of Earth. Mrs Keech and her group immediately phoned the newspapers: the Associated Press and every other news service they could think of. They took their message to their local newspaper even before it opened for business. As predicted by the investigators, proselytizing became the major avenue for reducing the dissonance caused by the prophecy's failure. The discrepant cognitions caused by the discordance of the prophecy from reality were changed into a more overarching message of how the small group of true believers had saved the world from destruction. This brilliant stratagem for dissonance reduction can be effective, but much more so if it receives social support. As Festinger and his fellow researchers had surmised, if everyone believed it was so, then it must have been so.

THE IMPACT OF *WHEN PROPHECY FAILS*

The development of cognitive dissonance in the social psychological literature has been characterized by rigorous and innovative experimental work in the laboratory. Looking back at the history of the discipline, there can be little doubt that the 1956 report by Festinger and his colleagues was one of the major works that propelled dissonance into an unparalleled position in social psychology. Dissonance was arguably the major intellectual force in the discipline throughout the 1960s and took on a variety of theoretical challenges in the decades to come. Almost all of the intellectual controversies were played out in experimental laboratories. There is therefore some irony in the fact that an *in vivo* participant observation study of a doomsday cult played such an important role in propelling the theory of cognitive dissonance to the centre stage of social psychology.

A further irony about Festinger et al.'s (1956) report is that its replicability is unclear. There is no doubt about the observations reported faithfully in *When Prophecy Fails.* However, our knowledge is compromised by not knowing about important parameters that may have facilitated the effect. Several years later, Jane Allyn Hardyck and Marcia Braden studied a group that they called the Church of the True Word, an evangelical church group associated with the Pentecostal movement. Four years prior to Hardyck and Braden's (1962) study, its leader, Mrs Shepperd, had received a prophecy that 'in fewer years than I have fingers on my right hand', there would be nuclear devastation. That was followed in the year of the study by a specific prophecy of the devastation. A group of 29 families – 135 people in all – built shelters to escape the devastation and stayed underground for 42 days.

They emerged from their shelters with their spirits high. The prophecy had not come true. Without the benefit of automatic writing to guide them, the group nonetheless reinterpreted the prophecy. Rather than the prophecy being about God's warning the world about nuclear destruction, the group reasoned that God was waking the world to the need for faith, love and brotherhood. Like Mrs Keech's group, they did not abandon their overall beliefs and did not come to feel that the prophecy was wrong. Like the Seekers, they changed the meaning of the prophecy to accommodate the reality. But they did not engage in the behaviour that had been the core prediction of Festinger et al.'s study: they did not proselytize.

Hardyck and Braden (1962) speculated that the conditions necessary for the seeking of social support might depend on factors not considered in the earlier work. Although both groups had specific predictions that were disconfirmed, the True Word group was considerably larger than the Seekers. Perhaps the size of the group mattered. With sufficient social support from *within* the group, there may be no need to seek additional converts. Hardyck and Braden (1962) also observed that the True Word group was respected by other members of the community as well as the larger Pentecostal sect in which it was embedded. The Seekers, on the other hand, were treated with derision from other members of the community. Parameters such as the magnitude of pre-existing social support or prior belief opposition may well determine whether disconfirmed prophecies lead to proselytizing or not.

THE SECOND DISSONANCE STUDY: THE PSYCHOLOGY OF INDUCED COMPLIANCE

With all due respect to Festinger et al.'s (1956) initial classic study, I think that a correct reading of the history of cognitive dissonance theory requires what boxing would call the one-two punch to understand the influence of *When Prophecy Fails*. For in truth, the study became an important part of the psychological literature only after Leon Festinger and J. Merrill Carlsmith (1959) subsequently published their controversial laboratory experiment on the consequences of induced compliance. Let's now consider the second part of the one-two punch in order to appreciate the impact of *When Prophecy Fails* and the development of cognitive dissonance.

BACKGROUND

Festinger and Carlsmith (1959) proposed a seemingly straightforward derivation from dissonance theory and set out to test it in the laboratory. As noted above, dissonance is said to arise from the perception that one's cognitions are inconsistent with each other. Imagine a woman who makes a statement that is at variance with her attitudes. For example, she may believe in a balanced governmental budget but make a contrary statement advocating high government spending. The statement and the attitude are inconsistent and the unpleasant drive state of dissonance should occur. Dissonance theory holds that the presence of dissonance will give rise to pressure to reduce it, such as changing one of the two cognitions to make them consistent with the other. The woman in this example cannot easily deny the fact that she took a position in favour of spending, so the cognition most easily changed is her attitude. In this way, dissonance causes her to become more in favour of deficit spending than before.

The crux of Festinger's second seminal experiment was to have a person make a statement that was at variance with his or her attitude, then measure the impact on the person's attitude. The inconsistency should produce attitude change consistent with the person's statement. Although there was no study in the psychology literature that had tested this prediction, it was consistent with what would have been predicted by several other balance theories that preceded dissonance theory. But what made dissonance unique among balance theories was the concept of dissonance as an *energy model*. And as a form of energy, it had a *magnitude*. In other words, there could be degrees of dissonance and degrees of pressure to change one's attitudes. Festinger and Carlsmith (1959) therefore set about studying that magnitude in a way that would excite the community of social psychologists.

They asked, what would be the consequence of providing an incentive for engaging in a behaviour that runs counter to one's attitude? Suppose a man were paid to make a statement contrary to his attitude. Would that lower the dissonance? Festinger and Carlsmith argued that it would, and the greater the incentive, the less the dissonance. Paying people a large sum of money to say something at variance with their attitude provides a clear reason for the attitude–discrepant behaviour and therefore reduces the magnitude of this aversive drive state. Put more directly, the larger the amount of money a person receives for making a statement contrary to his or her attitudes, the *less* their attitude should change.

This prediction was a direct challenge to the existing zeitgeist in psychology. The dominant approach to psychology, including social psychology, in the late 1950s was based on learning theory. This suggested that people learned as a direct function of reward. People changed their behaviour because they are reinforced or rewarded. The greater the incentive, the greater its influence on people's behaviour. Thus, according to learning theory, the larger the amount of money a person receives for making a statement contrary to his or her attitudes, the *more* their attitude should change. Festinger and Carlsmith (1959) challenged this proposition in a single stroke. They argued that, the smaller the incentive, the more people would be influenced by their own discrepant statements and that large incentives would eliminate the impact of behaviour on attitudes. This was a straightforward derivation from dissonance theory, but a challenge to the rule of reinforcement as a guiding principle of social psychology.

METHOD

Festinger and Carlsmith faced the dilemma of how to assess the dissonance predictions carefully and experimentally. In *When Prophecy Fails,* the testing situation had been chaotic and uncontrollable. Events happened in Mrs Keech's home in a fluid and evolving manner that the researchers could observe but not control. To address these problems, Festinger and Carlsmith would bring predictions of induced compliance into the laboratory where the variables could be tightly controlled and the prediction could be precise.

This was not a simple feat. Their goal was to find an attitude that participants agreed upon and then induce them to make a statement that was at variance with that attitude. They could then systematically vary the amount of incentive that the participants received for making their attitude–discrepant statement. And all of this needed to be done in a way that seemed real and involving to the participants.

The method that Festinger and Carlsmith (1959) created became the model for research for the next several decades. Its rigour and control were matched by its creativity. Indeed arguably, this study became as famous for its ingenious method-ology as it did for the findings it produced.

The first decision that the investigators made was to create a new attitude in the laboratory. They invented a task for students to perform and made sure that it would be perceived as truly dull and boring by anyone who performed it. That would constitute the attitude that participants would subsequently contradict by their verbal statements. To see how this worked, imagine that you were one of the student volunteers at Stanford University who participated in an experiment entitled 'Measures of Performance'. When you arrived, you would be seated in a waiting room for a few moments and then be called into the experimenter's office. In front of you is a large square board that contains 48 rectangular solid wooden pieces in monotonously even rows. The experimenter would give you your instruc-tions for the hour: you are to turn each peg ¼ turn with your right hand, then reverse the process by turning the pegs back again. When you finished this pro-cedure, you would be asked to do it again. And again. And again. That would be followed by an instruction to perform the task with the left hand. As the clock ticked off minute after tedious minute, the experimenter sat behind the partici-pant, fumbling with his stopwatch and a clipboard.

You finally come to the end of the peg-turning. The experimenter thanks you and tells you that you have been very helpful and that your participation is over. He also confesses something. He tells you that he has not been completely open with you about all that was going on in this experiment. The *real* purpose of the study, he explains, is to see how expectations affect performance on simple, manual tasks. He explains that half of the people who participate are actually in an experimental group. He double-checks with you. He asks if anyone had con-tacted you when you were sitting in the waiting room. You respond that there was no one else in the waiting room. The experimenter explains that you were in a control group. If you had been in the experimental group, his paid confederate would have met you in the waiting room and told you to expect that the study was really fun and exciting. He confesses that what he is really testing is whether people who expect the study to be fun perform differently from people – like you – who had no expectation.

You had no way to know this, but nothing the experimenter has told you so far was true. He does not care about how fast or how well you turned the pegs, and you were *not* in a control group. He has been setting the stage for the crucial next step in the experiment. After telling you about what his paid confederate would have done if you had been in the experimental group, it occurs to him that the next par-ticipant is scheduled to be in the experimental group and the paid confederate is late. After appearing momentarily befuddled, the experimenter has an enlightened stroke of ingenuity:

'Say, I have an idea,' he exclaims. 'I can hire you for the job'. Perhaps you feel honoured. You listen for the details. The experimenter continues: 'All you have to do is to go out into the waiting room where the next participant is waiting.' He checks the waiting room. 'Yes', he notes, 'the next person is already there. All you have to do is go out there and tell that guy that you were just in the "Measures of Performance" experiment and that it is one of the most fun experiences you've ever had as a psychology volunteer.' You consider the experimenter's offer while he adds that he can pay you for doing the job. He offers you either $1 for talking with the next person or $20, depending on the condition to which you had been randomly assigned. You agree.

You head to the waiting room where the next Stanford student is waiting patiently for the experiment. With the promise of pay in your pocket, you dive headlong into an extemporaneous speech, extolling the fun and interest of a procedure you privately believe was dull and boring. What you do not know is that you are not the experimenter's paid confederate. The 'next subject' in the waiting room is the real paid confederate. It is he who is working for the experimenters. He hears you out, thanks you for letting him know, and disappears behind the experimenter's office door, apparently to begin turning rectangular pegs.

With this elaborate procedure, Festinger and Carlsmith (1959) created all of the experimental conditions that they needed to test the hypotheses from dissonance theory. First, they created an attitude that was unanimously shared by all of their participants (that the Measures of Performance task was dull). They obtained the participants' agreement to make a statement that was in marked contrast to their real attitude, and they received either a high ($20) or low ($1) inducement to make the speech. Their prediction was that the behaviour (i.e., making the statement to the waiting participant that the task was fun) that was discrepant from the attitude (i.e., that the task was dull and boring) would create dissonance. The uncomfortable tension state of dissonance would lead to a change in attitude to bring it in line with the behaviour, but the amount of dissonance would be opposite to the size of the incentive: the higher the incentive for making the statement, the lower the dissonance. Festinger and Carlsmith predicted that participants would therefore express *more* positive attitudes towards the measures of performance task if they had been paid a trivial amount rather than a large amount for their statement.

How did they measure participants' attitudes? One more ruse was necessary. Prior to leaving, participants were asked to sign some papers at the department secretary's office. The secretary explained that the Psychology Department was conducting a survey about how students enjoyed the tasks they had performed in psychology experiments. The students were asked a series of questions about how interesting the tasks were and how much they enjoyed them. Only after they had done this did the participants finally find out what the study had really been about, as the experimenter now reappeared and explained all of the procedures and the hypotheses to them.

RESULTS

The results of the study, which are shown in Figure 3.1, confirmed the predictions. Control participants constituted a group of randomly assigned participants who merely performed the peg-turning task without being asked to make any counter-attitudinal statement. As expected, they expressed boredom with the task and had no interest in doing it again. However, also as predicted, making a statement that was discrepant from their attitude caused participants to change their attitudes to match their behaviour, but only when the incentive for doing so was very low. When participants made the very same statement but received a large financial reward for doing so, the statement produced no effect whatsoever on their attitudes. They held firm to their attitude that the peg turning was indeed a boring task. Apparently, and as predicted, dissonance was minimal when there was a large incentive to speak against one's attitude, but was maximal when the incentive was trivially small.

Figure 3.1 Attitudes towards a boring peg-turning task (from Festinger and Carlsmith, 1959)

Note: Responses made on a scale ranging from −5 to +5.

IMPACT OF THE COGNITIVE DISSONANCE STUDIES

Sometimes, the impact of research takes years to become fully appreciated by the community of scholars. However, the impact of Festinger and Carlsmith's (1959) study was immediate and enormous. In my view, it was the one-two punch of *When Prophecy Fails* and Festinger and Carlsmith's induced compliance study that made it happen. Readers inside and outside of the social psychology community were aware of the prophecy study. People's responses to a prophecy as bold and as wrong as the Seekers' attracts attention. The fact that Festinger and his colleagues (1956) not only reported it but used a theory to predict the outcome was duly noted. However, the study was not experimental, it did not control any of its variables, and (as later research showed) the relationship of proselytizing to dissonance reduction could certainly be debated.

In their subsequent study, Festinger and Carlsmith (1959) not only showed support for dissonance theory in a tightly controlled experiment, but also they did so with experimental panache (a feature that would characterize dissonance research for a generation). Moreover, they took direct aim at the leading theoretical notion in all of psychology – the idea that reinforcement produces change.

Additional fascinating findings were added to the experimental literature from the perspective of dissonance theory. Aronson and Mills (1959) systematically varied how onerous an initiation process was in order to join a group. They predicted and found that people liked the group better the more they suffered to join it. In later research, Aronson and Carlsmith (1962) showed that the effects of threats and punishments offered to children for *refraining* from behaving in a desired activity were also governed by the same dissonance rules. When children were warned not to play with an attractive toy and did not play with this toy, they showed more permanent attitude change by devaluing the attractive toy if they received a lower rather than higher threat. The higher the threat, the less effective was the threat on their attitudes. These studies focused on hedonic rewards and reinforcements to make dissonance theory predictions that seemed to defy common wisdom and the reinforcement notions that underlay them.

Dissonance had no shortage of critics. But the hallmark of a good theory is that it provokes both criticism and support. It provokes honest experimentation to find the flaws (e.g., Chapanis and Chapanis, 1964; Rosenberg, 1965) and subsequent experimentation to restore the findings and broaden the perspective (e.g., Linder et al., 1967). The conclusion from a decade of research following the seminal studies presented here is that dissonance theory was substantially correct, that it made some interesting and non-obvious predictions, but there were some persistent limiting conditions on the phenomenon that the theory could not accommodate. Ultimately, the theory had to change.

BEYOND THE TWO CLASSIC DISSONANCE STUDIES

The research on dissonance theory in the decades following the two seminal studies produced a number of important conclusions, some consistent with the theory and some less so. In the original work, Festinger (1957) had surmised that the key motivational factor that caused inconsistency to lead to attitude change was an aversive drive-like state that he labelled dissonance. At the time, he had no evidence for this assumption but it was the key factor that drove the predictions of the two classic studies discussed above, as well as many others. We now know that his guess was correct. We know this because (a) we can measure physiological changes (e.g., in skin conductance (SCR) and brain activity (EEG)) and the psychological discomfort that follow from advocating a position contrary to one's attitudes (Croyle and Cooper, 1983; Elliot and Devine, 1994; Harmon-Jones, 1999; Losch and Cacioppo, 1990); (b) we can increase dissonance by having participants ingest an arousing drug and decrease it with a sedative (Cooper et al., 1978); and (c) we can eliminate attitude change following attitude–discrepant behaviour by having people misattribute their arousal to something other than their discrepant behaviour. For example, if people believed they were aroused from the side effects of a pill they had ingested rather than their discrepant behaviour, then attitude change did not occur (Zanna and Cooper, 1974).

On the other hand, research has also shown that the impact of counterattitudinal behaviour on attitudes is not ubiquitous. It occurs only under certain specifiable conditions. For example, Darwyn Linder and colleagues (1967) showed that Festinger and Carlsmith's (1959) induced compliance results only occur if people believe they had the choice to agree to make their counterattitudinal speech. In addition, Cooper and Worchel (1970) showed that making a counterattitudinal statement did not produce dissonance unless it led to some consequential event. In this study, we repeated Festinger and Carlsmith's (1959) classic experiment but we systematically varied whether the confederate (i.e., the 'waiting participant') was or was not convinced by the real participant's assertion that the task was interesting. We found that attitude change occurred only when the confederate was convinced. Under these conditions, the negative impact of duping a fellow student to believe something untrue led to attitude change. When he was not convinced, people seemed to use a 'no harm, no foul' principle. Although the statement about the task was still inconsistent with their attitudes, the fact that the statement failed to have any impact on others eliminated the participants' dissonance.

Why should dissonance only occur under certain conditions? The original theory was silent about the impact of such variables as choice and consequences. The persistent set of limiting conditions suggested a need for a fresh perspective on the theory and that is what Russell Fazio and I provided in 1984. In our *New Look* model of dissonance (Cooper and Fazio, 1984), we argued that dissonance was *not* brought about by cognitive discrepancies *per se*. Rather, we argued that dissonance is a state of uncomfortable arousal that occurs when a person accepts responsibility for bringing about an unwanted consequence. Behaviour that is inconsistent with attitudes typically arouses dissonance because people typically feel that they have acted freely and because inconsistent behaviour typically produces an unwanted event. However, we argued that dissonance is caused by the consequences of discrepant behaviour and not the inconsistency as such (Scher and Cooper, 1989).

Other scholars took note of the limiting conditions of dissonance and suggested alternative views of the impact of attitude–discrepant behaviour (e.g., Beauvois and Joule, 1999; Harmon-Jones, 1999). Elliot Aronson (1992) argued for the key motivating role of the self, suggesting that dissonance occurs primarily when one's self-esteem has been threatened by inconsistent cognitions. Claude Steele (1988) concurred with the importance of the self but viewed attitude-inconsistent behaviour as a damage to self that could be repaired by reaffirming one's global self-system.

Borrowing from these insights, Stone and Cooper (2001) modified the earlier New Look model and adopted a *self-standards* model. They realized that the New Look had been silent about how a person decides whether an action has brought about an aversive consequence. What makes the outcome of an act unwanted, unwelcome, or unpleasant? They extended dissonance theory again, this time to argue that people need to assess the consequences of their behaviour against a standard of judgment. Sometimes, that standard of judgment is unique to the individual's self concept, violating a personal code that he or she would rather not violate. Sometimes, that standard is normative, violating a code of conduct that society has established for behaviour. Adopting concepts from social cognition, the self-standard model lays out the conditions under which different standards are made accessible and therefore play a role in the dissonance process.

CONCLUSION

Commenting on dissonance theory at its thirtieth anniversary in 1987, Festinger noted that he was personally pleased that dissonance theory was undergoing change. All theories need to change, he said. If they remain static, they are probably not good theories at all. From the moment that Festinger and his colleagues opened their newspaper to read about the doomsday cult, the die was cast for the creation of a foundational theory in the social psychology literature. The empirical and theoretical battles that tested dissonance against other theories strengthened the theory and revealed its limits. From those active battles, new versions of dissonance were formed. Festinger would smile at the current state of dissonance theory. It has evolved and, in so doing, has become stronger. Festinger's prophecy has not failed at all.

FURTHER READING

Festinger, L., Riecken, H.W. and Schachter, S. (1956) *When Prophecy Fails.* Minneapolis: University of Minnesota Press.

This book presents a preliminary statement of cognitive dissonance theory in the context of the real world group who prepared for the Earth to be destroyed. The setting is dramatic and the methodological issues are presented in an honest and fascinating way.

Festinger, L. and Carlsmith, J.M. (1959) 'Cognitive consequences of forced compliance', *Journal of Abnormal and Social Psychology*, 58: 203–10.

Festinger and Carlsmith's classic experiment is a must-read derivation of cognitive dissonance theory known for its iconoclast predictions and its clever methodology.

Zanna, M.P. and Cooper, J. (1974) 'Dissonance and the pill: An attribution approach to studying the arousal properties of dissonance', *Journal of Personality and Social Psychology,* 29: 703–9.

Zanna and Cooper's experiment provided a new methodological approach to assessing one of the key assumptions of cognitive dissonance, namely that dissonance produces arousal and that it is the arousal that motivates change.

Cooper, J. and Fazio, R.H. (1984) 'A new look at dissonance theory', in L. Berkowitz (ed.), *Advances in Experimental Social Psychology*, Vol. 17. Orlando, FL: Academic Press. pp. 229–64.

As dissonance research began to accumulate, the theory needed to adapt to the new findings. Cooper and Fazio's paper presented the first comprehensive change to the theory.

Stone, J. and Cooper, J. (2001) 'A self-standards model of cognitive dissonance', *Journal of Experimental Social Psychology,* 37: 228–43.

The modern face of dissonance is probably best represented by Stone and Cooper's self-standards model.

Cooper, J. (2007) *Cognitive Dissonance: Fifty Years of a Classic Theory*. London: Sage.

This book is an integration of a half-century of research dedicated to the theory that began when Festinger and his colleagues infiltrated and studied the Seekers doomsday cult more than 50 years ago.

REFERENCES

Aronson, E. (1992) 'The return of the repressed: Dissonance theory makes a comeback', *Psychological Inquiry,* 3: 303–11.

Aronson, E. and Carlsmith, J.M. (1962) 'The effect of the severity of threat on the devaluation of forbidden behavior', *Journal of Abnormal and Social Psychology,* 66: 584–8.

Aronson, E. and Mills, J. (1959) 'The effect of severity of initiation on liking for a group', *Journal of Abnormal and Social Psychology,* 59: 177–81.

Beauvois, J. and Joule, R.V. (1999) 'A radical point of view on dissonance theory', in E. Harmon-Jones and J. Mills (eds), *Cognitive Dissonance: Progress on a Pivotal Theory in Social Psychology.* Washington, DC: American Psychological Association. pp. 43–70.

Chapanis, N.P. and Chapanis, A. (1964) 'Cognitive dissonance', *Psychological Bulletin,* 61: 1–22.

Cooper, J. (2007) *Cognitive Dissonance: Fifty Years of a Classic Theory*. London: Sage.

Cooper, J. and Fazio, R.H. (1984) 'A new look at dissonance theory', in L. Berkowitz (ed.), *Advances in Experimental Social Psychology*, Vol. 17. Orlando, FL: Academic Press. pp. 229–64.

Cooper, J. and Worchel, S. (1970) 'The role of undesired consequences in the arousal of cognitive dissonance', *Journal of Personality and Social Psychology,* 16: 312–20.

Cooper, J., Zanna, M.P. and Taves, P.A. (1978) 'Arousal as a necessary condition for attitude change following induced compliance', *Journal of Personality and Social Psychology,* 36: 1101–6.

Croyle, R. and Cooper, J. (1983) 'Dissonance arousal: Physiological evidence', *Journal of Personality and Social Psychology,* 45: 782–91.

Festinger, L. (1950) 'Informal social communication', *Psychological Review*, 57 : 271–82.

Festinger, L. (1954) 'A theory of social comparison processes', *Human Relations*, 1: 117–40.

Festinger, L. (1957) *A Theory of Cognitive Dissonance.* Stanford: Stanford University Press.

Festinger, L. and Carlsmith, J.M. (1959) 'Cognitive consequences of forced compliance', *Journal of Abnormal and Social Psychology,* 58: 203–10.

Festinger, L., Riecken, H.W. and Schachter, S. (1956) *When Prophecy Fails.* Minneapolis: University of Minnesota Press.

Hardyck, J.A. and Braden, M. (1962) 'Prophecy fails again: A report of a failure to replicate', *Journal of Abnormal and Social Psychology*, 65: 136–41.

Harmon-Jones, E. (1999) 'Toward an understanding of the motivation underlying dissonance effects: Is the production of aversive consequences necessary?', in E. Harmon-Jones and J. Mills (eds), *Cognitive Dissonance: Progress on a Pivotal Theory in Social Psychology*. Washington, DC: American Psychological Association. pp. 71–103.

Linder, D.E., Cooper, J. and Jones, E.E. (1967) 'Decision freedom as a determinant of the role of incentive magnitude in attitude change', *Journal of Personality and Social Psychology,* 6: 245–54.

Losch, M.E. and Cacioppo, J.T. (1990) 'Cognitive dissonance may enhance sympathetic tonus, but attitudes are changed to reduce negative affect rather than arousal', *Journal of Experimental Social Psychology,* 26: 289–304.

Rosenberg, M.J. (1965) 'When dissonance fails: On eliminating evaluation apprehension from attitude measurement', *Journal of Personality and Social Psychology*, 1: 28–42.

Scher, S.J. and Cooper, J. (1989) 'Motivational basis of dissonance: The singular role of behavioral consequences', *Journal of Personality and Social Psychology*, 56: 899–906.

Steele, C.M. (1988) 'The psychology of self-affirmation: Sustaining the integrity of the self', in L. Berkowitz (ed.), *Advances in Experimental Social Psychology*, Vol. 21. San Diego, CA: Academic Press. pp. 261–302.

Stone, J. and Cooper, J. (2001) 'A self-standards model of cognitive dissonance', *Journal of Experimental Social Psychology,* 37: 228–43.

Zanna, M.P. and Cooper, J. (1974) 'Dissonance and the pill: An attribution approach to studying the arousal properties of dissonance', *Journal of Personality and Social Psychology,* 29: 703–9.

4

Norm Formation

Revisiting Sherif's autokinetic illusion study

Dominic Abrams and John M. Levine

It's not a matter of what is true that counts but a matter of what is perceived to be true.

Henry Kissinger

BACKGROUND

What is Truth? This is the ultimate question behind Muzafer Sherif's research on norm formation and the reason that his research using the autokinetic illusion is as relevant today as it was when he first published it in 1935. In the simplest terms, Sherif sought to understand how people come to see particular views of the world as correct and to demonstrate and analyse the critical role that *other people* play in this process.

Philosophers, poets and scientists have struggled with the problems of truth and reality for centuries, ultimately driven by the conviction that the world will be a better place the more our understanding of it approaches 'reality'. However, alongside a strictly empiricist scientific view of what is reality, there are at least two alternative visions. One, which vexed Sherif, is founded in the idea that religious faith can transcend science as a guide to reality. The other, which Sherif persuasively advocated, is that reality, and thus truth as we are able to understand it, is fundamentally a construction. Moreover, he argued that reality is not simply a psychological construction – in that we need our brains and senses to perceive it – but rather it is a *social* psychological one in that we need a social framework to give our perceptions meaning.[1]

---

[1]Sherif's blend of Gestalt theory – what would later be known as social constructionism – is by no means a singular or coherent school of thought. Outside psychology, the origins of his ideas can be traced back to structural theories in sociology, particularly those of Durkheim (1915), but also to research in cultural anthropology. The ideas also link and track forward to the Chicago School of sociology, symbolic interactionism, ethnomethodology and even postmodernist and discursive orientations.

Whereas later research by Solomon Asch (1951; see Chapter 5) and Stanley Milgram (1964; see Chapter 7) was concerned with why or when social rules, roles and norms are followed or resisted, Sherif raised some fundamental prior questions. These included what is a norm, what is the social psychological function of a norm, and how do norms develop and hold their potency?

Sherif's masterstroke was to demonstrate his insights using a phenomenon that had hitherto been regarded as a minor problem of visual perception, namely the autokinetic illusion. We will briefly describe the specific questions that Sherif chose to examine, before we describe the paradigm in more detail and consider how he linked this line of studies to the wider questions with which he was concerned. For Sherif, these studies illustrated the mechanisms through which social structure, culture, and society become embedded in consciousness and thereby shape people's perception and understanding of the world. The underlying rationale and description of the research is provided in his enormously influential 1936 book, *The Psychology of Social Norms.* Here he explained why he adopted the autokinetic effect and why he used his research to establish a metatheoretical critique of individualism and reductionism in social psychology. He was at pains to point out that there is no separation between society and the individual – that neither is more fundamental than the other. Stridently rejecting the reductionist theorizing of Floyd Allport (1924), he was able to show that even the perception of physical reality can have a social basis.

THE AUTOKINETIC ILLUSION (AKI) STUDIES

The autokinetic effect is an illusion whereby a pinpoint of light in an otherwise darkened surrounding appears to move spontaneously. This phenomenon is well known to astronomers, who first noticed it while observing stars on dark nights. Psychologists have also long been interested in the psychophysiological basis for the effect (Adams, 1912), which is attributable to various properties of the visual perception system (Levy, 1972). When a person is shown a pinpoint of light in a dark room repeatedly, the light appears to move erratically each time, particularly if the observer does not know his or her distance from the light. Indeed, if seated in a chair that does not have a back on it, the observer may even feel unsure of his or her spatial bearing. Sherif identified this illusion as an ideal vehicle for studying how people make sense of a stimulus in the absence of any frame of reference.

Sherif used the AKI to investigate several questions. First, how would people make sense of a stimulus that was completely ambiguous? Would they make random or chaotic judgments, hoping to be accurate on at least some occasions, or would some systematic approach to judgment emerge? Second, if two individuals were asked to judge the same stimulus, would their differing perceptions of this illusion result in even more randomness and anarchy or would they somehow produce a coordinated system for judgment? Third, supposing such a system were established, would it have a life beyond the presence of the particular individuals concerned? Would the system persist in a group even after the people who initially developed it departed? And would people continue to use the system of judgment even after they left the situation?

METHOD AND RESULTS

Sherif's experiments were conducted in a dark room in the Columbia University psychological laboratory. By today's standards these experiments were quite basic (see Sherif, 1935, for technical details). The individual experiment involved 19 male participants, and the group experiments – in fact just two conditions – involved 40 male participants, all university students.

The pinpoint of light was shown to participants for two seconds on each trial, using a relatively simple apparatus that consisted of a screen, a metal light box (which showed the pinpoint of light) with a shutter (controlled by the experimenter) and a timer. The participants sat 18 feet away at a table with a telegraph key in front of them and were given the following instructions:

> When the room is completely dark, I shall give you the signal READY, and then show you a point of light. After a short time the light will start to move. As soon as you see it move, press the key. A few seconds later the light will disappear. Then tell me the distance it moved. Try to make your estimates as accurate as possible.

After the light had been shown for two seconds from the point at which the participant indicated they had seen it start to move, the shutter was closed and the participants called out their estimates in inches or fractions of inches. The experimenter recorded the responses on a note pad (in the dark), turning one page for each trial. This procedure was followed for 100 judgments.

In the individual experiment, participants returned to the laboratory on two consecutive days and repeated the exercise. It was found that each person established his own median[2] and range of values during the course of the first session and also maintained that median with decreasing variation around the median on the two subsequent sessions. Sherif thus argued:

> When individuals perceive movements which lack any other standard of comparison, *they subjectively establish a range of extent and a point (a standard or norm) within that range which is peculiar to the individual* ... the norm serves as a reference point with which each successive experienced movement is compared and judged. (1936: 96, emphasis in original)

The important point here is that, when left to their own devices, individuals generated their own frame of reference for judgment. Put another way, if no norm exists in an uncertain and ambiguous situation, then individuals generate one such that their judgments do have a reference or anchor point. Indeed, Sherif did not regard

---

[2]The median is the middle point in a distribution that separates the upper 50% of the distribution from the lower 50% of the distribution.

a norm as a single point on a scale or a single judgment, but rather saw it as a modal[3] or median point *together* with its frame of reference. When left to their own devices, different individuals generated different norms, and, having established them, used them again on subsequent occasions. In this regard, he commented:

> We purposely chose a stimulus situation in which the external factors are unstable enough, within limits, to allow the internal factors to furnish the dominating role in establishing the main characteristics of organization. This enables us to say that any consistent product in the experience of the individual members of the group, differing from their experience as isolated individuals, is a function of their interaction in the group. (1936: 98)

This is the essential point Sherif wished to make – namely that the group process could not be reduced to an aggregate of individual processes, and indeed that the group process could continue to influence individuals even when they were no longer in the group.

To test this latter idea, the group experiments involved two phases, with counterbalanced ordering. Participants either completed the first session as individuals and then three subsequent sessions as members of two- or three-person groups, or they completed the first three sessions as members of groups and the final session as individuals. The group sessions required a signal system so that participants could indicate to the experimenter who was responding (Sherif allowed participants to respond in any sequence they chose).

As indicated in Figure 4.1, the results (which were presented separately for each group) were highly consistent. When starting as individuals (as shown in the

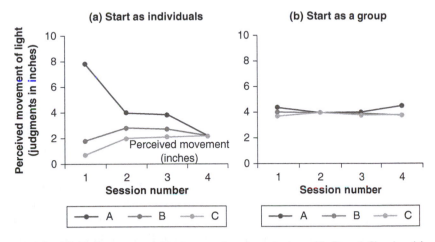

Figure 4.1 Typical patterns of judgment for three judges (A, B and C) who (a) start as individuals (in Session 1) and then come together as a group (in Sessions 2, 3 and 4) or (b) start as a group (in Sessions 1, 2 and 3) and then make judgments as individuals (in Session 4). Data from Sherif, 1936: 102–3

---

[3]The mode is the most frequent or popular value in a distribution.

left-hand graph), estimates of the light's movement that were quite different in the first session converged quickly in the second session (when judgments were made as a group) and then maintained their convergence in subsequent sessions. When starting as a group (the right-hand graph), convergence happened rapidly within the first session and remained constant in the next two (group) sessions, and then persisted when participants made judgments alone in the final session.

THEORETICAL SIGNIFICANCE

Sherif's interpretation of these findings was that 'there is a factual psychological basis in the contentions of social psychologists and sociologists who maintain that new and supra-individual qualities arise in the group situations' (1936: 105). He noted that in his studies each group established its own range and median and that when this norm changed, it affected the group as a whole. Moreover, these norms were 'social products', which, once established, continued to have meaning and influence beyond the conditions of their inception. In other words, groups seemed to have a binding power that locked individuals into their judgments. Sherif further dismissed the idea that one member may be leading and the others following, arguing that this did not happen in the experiments and that, in any case, a leader who ignored the rest of the group once its norm was settled would cease to be followed.

Sherif was also highly sensitive to the generalizability of his results and was keen to make the point that the patterns of findings he had unearthed were relevant to a broad range of social contexts in which groups form norms – arguing that the experimental paradigm he had created possessed important characteristics that were representative of a range of group situations outside the laboratory. In particular, he argued that when old norms no longer fit the situation (for example, when authority is no longer legitimate), the plastic and unstable situation that follows promotes the development and standardization of new norms. In times of political upheaval, as well as in times of famine or disaster, these norms are often manifested in slogans, which define the new reality in terms of a new frame of reference. Sherif also noted the cunning way in which would-be political leaders may first 'prepare an unstructured field', or create the appearance of uncertainty and free choice, in order to give their slogans more impact.

Sherif's ambit was very wide. He considered his definition of norms to include things that today psychologists parcel into numerous smaller packets such as values, morals, attitudes and affect. For Sherif, all of these constructs can be subsumed under the heading of norms. They all have a focal or figural point and all involve a frame of reference. However, they differ in their period of gestation, development and reach. He regarded values as the most enduring frame of reference through which specific attitudes and behaviours are manifested. He illustrated how categorization is a vital basis for discrimination based on values. He highlighted Jean Piaget's (1932) work on the moral judgment of the child, arguing that the developmental shift from heteronomous (rule-based) to autonomous (principle-based) morality is a demonstration of the 'progressive interiorization of values in the case of an especially important type of social norms' (Sherif, 1936: 135), namely those surrounding fairness and equality.

Sherif had a further concern with political propaganda and value change. He regarded values as essentially sociological, as the established social frameworks within which attitudes are formed and expressed. However, he was keenly aware that even values could change under sufficiently unstable and ambiguous conditions. He wondered how it is possible for a political regime to persuade its people to engage in acts of war or become infused with hatred of another group (an issue that he would later reprise in his famous Boys' Camp studies, see Chapter 9).

To explore this issue, Sherif (1937) conducted a further variant of the AKI study, this time using a confederate who was primed to respond within a specific range while making judgments alongside a naïve participant. A different range and median was used for each of seven different participants to establish that it was possible to produce convergence to different norms. Sherif demonstrated both that individuals did converge to the norm of the confederate within the session and that participants stuck closely to that norm in a subsequent session when tested alone (even though some later claimed that they had actually tried to resist that confederate's norm). Echoing much future work on persuasion and indirect minority influence (e.g., see Chapter 6), Sherif (1936) observed that even though people may feel hesitant about fully accepting a friend's opinion when it is first aired, they often later fall back upon that opinion, using it as a reference point or anchor.

Sherif attacked the idea that his experiments lacked generalizability by drawing on anthropological evidence that even people's most basic needs and activities are bound by social frames of reference and rules. He specifically targeted Floyd Allport (1924) as 'grossly lacking perspective' and as promoting a 'picture of men shaped in competitive individualistic bourgeois society' (Sherif, 1936: 144). Sherif discussed different cultural practices in areas such as kinship and parental care, and he also illustrated how dietary restrictions may be based on beliefs about the influence of particular animals or trees on the mother; how property can be defined as other than a personal possession (Rivers, 1924); and how, in contrast to US culture, Samoan culture views cooperation rather than competition as normative (Mead, 1928). He also noted how sexual rules and rituals differ in different cultures (Malinowski, 1927). His essential point was that even the most basic human needs are met within a socially agreed frame of reference, or set of norms. In other words, such needs are socially regulated.

Sherif then explored in more detail the idea of 'interiorization' of norms, arguing that this is really the process of socialization. He drew, somewhat loosely, on Sigmund Freud's theorizing about the ego and superego (Freud, 1927) to argue that these represent the interiorization of values – the subjective acceptance of the frame of reference provided by those values. He distinguished this idea from the Durkheimian view that society stands as a distinct entity that imposes its reality on people, arguing instead that values and norms are realized through everyday interaction and socialization within social groups.

Sherif went on to address various implications of his theorizing. For one, he disputed that he was propagating a group, or institutional, fallacy that individuals cognitively represent the entire social structure within which they exist. Rather, he argued,

> the social in the individual is not an exact replica in miniature of the whole structure-and-value system of his society. The social in him cannot extend beyond the social stimulus situations that he faces and incorporates in himself in the course of his development. (1936: 187)

On the basis of his AKI findings, Sherif also argued that the social psychologist must be aware of the individual's location in a social structure even if the individual is not aware of it him- or herself. The analogy is that the experimenter may be aware that different individuals set up their own norms in the AKI experiment, but until they are exposed to others' judgments, those individuals are not aware of the different norms. Nor are groups of individuals necessarily aware that other groups establish different norms.

A second key issue is the extent to which norms are passed from one generation to another. Sherif argued that new norms are continually developed in response to changing circumstances, but some older norms continue. Where these conflict with existing needs and conditions, they are termed 'survivals'. Such survivals often serve the interests of powerful dominating groups (e.g., morally questionable religious practices, oppression of particular social groups). Moreover, in an intriguing and perhaps over-optimistic analysis of social change, Sherif argued that the ensuing friction does not bring about anarchy but rather 'the formation of a new superstructure of norms' (1936: 202).

FOLLOW-UP STUDIES

It was not until after the end of the Second World War that Sherif's work on the autokinetic effect was systematically followed up. An important question was how enduring the norms would prove to be following participation in the AKI paradigm. Bovard (1948) showed, with just nine participants, that norms induced by a confederate remained stable after 28 days. Hoffman and colleagues (1953) established that it was possible, and more efficient, to establish a norm using a light source that actually moved, and moreover that a longer exposure time (7 seconds) was likely to produce a stronger effect. Using this training technique with 46 males from military training units, Rohrer and colleagues (1954) trained participants by moving the light source either 2 inches or 8 inches. An hour later, in the immediate group phase, the light point was kept static, allowing estimates to be based entirely on illusory movement. Each group consisted of one individual trained at 2 inches and one individual trained at 8 inches, who made judgments on 50 exposures. A year later, participants were tested individually for a further 50 exposures. As might be expected, the participants trained at 2 inches and 8 inches (who averaged 3.08 and 8.74 inches, respectively, in their estimates in the training phase) converged so that their estimates averaged 6.29 inches and 6.41 inches, respectively, in the immediate group phase. More strikingly, these new group-based norms persisted so that a year later the individual mean estimates of individuals who had initially been trained at 2 inches and 8 inches were 5.50 and 5.09 inches, respectively. The correlations between estimates in the group phase and the individual phase a year later were also very high ($r = .92$ for the participants trained at 2 inches and $r = .60$ for those trained at 8 inches). These results highlight the point that the average established by each group was not merely a matter of short-term conformity but was accepted as a valid norm that, in the absence of any contrary evidence, persisted beyond the first experimental setting and was fully reinstated when the participants found themselves in the same setting a year later.

Meanwhile, researchers pursued other methods of examining norm formation with ambiguous stimuli, addressing such questions as whether it mattered how far away the individual's initial judgments were from those of the group. For example, Goldberg (1954) examined group conformity in white males' ratings of the intelligence of African American males from photographs. Goldberg concluded that group influence was established quickly and that conformity was a constant proportion of the initial distance between the individual and the group. Thus, individuals who were initially more distant from the group norm showed a larger shift towards it in absolute terms but not in proportionate terms, which was equal regardless of initial distance. An implication of the finding that proportionate influence was constant is that, even in apparently consensual groups, influence may be arising, albeit almost imperceptibly, drawing members closer and closer to the norm.

Other research focused on personality variables that might account for people's desire to converge to a norm. Vidulich and Kaiman (1961) examined whether individuals who were very high or very low in dogmatism (or closed mindedness) would converge more or less to a high-status (professor) or low-status (student) confederate's judgments. They found that the closed (dogmatic) participants conformed more to the high-status confederate whereas the open (non-dogmatic) participants showed the opposite response pattern.

In another variation, Kelman (1950) examined how success, failure, or ambiguous outcomes on a task would affect the extent to which participants conformed to a confederate who gave consistently higher estimates than the participant's own individual norm. Findings showed that a group that failed converged more, while a group that succeeded converged less (relative to the ambiguous feedback group), presumably because the successful group had its prior independence reinforced. Later, Sampson and Insko (1964) confirmed a prediction from balance theory that if participants found the source of influence to be unlikeable, they would converge less than if they found the source to be likeable.

BEYOND THE AUTOKINETIC ILLUSION STUDIES I

A*LTERNATIVE INTERPRETATIONS AND FINDINGS*

The first serious challenge to Sherif's interpretation of norm formation came from C. Norman Alexander and colleagues (1970) who proposed an alternative explanation for the AKI findings. They argued that 'tendencies toward structuring reside in the expectations that individuals bring to the events in a situation, expectations that are shaped in part by the nature of the situation itself' (1970: 108). More specifically, they argued that Sherif's initial findings did not reflect the ambiguity of the stimulus but rather were attributable to the fact that participants believed that the experimenter was moving the light and so there was an objectively correct answer regarding its movement. It was therefore reasonable that they should expect agreement around a correct estimate (i.e., a norm). It follows that if this expectation is removed – so people do not expect there to be any structure or stability to a stimulus situation – then they should not impose a norm on it.

To test this hypothesis, Alexander and colleagues conducted an experiment in which participants were simply told that the light was in fact stationary and that any movements were illusory. Specifically, participants were told that:

> You should not be surprised... [Alone:... if the direction and distance the light appears to move changes each time you look at it. / Together:... if you see the light moving a different direction and for a different distance than anyone else.] In fact, you should not be surprised if the direction and distance the light appears to move changes each time you look at it. (1970: 113)

Thus, it was argued, when the participants (10 individuals and 5 pairs of individuals) responded to 60 trials they should not be surprised by variable patterns of movement and should have no expectation that they would agree with others. Unlike the findings from Sherif's studies, participants reported that, across trials, both the direction and distance of the light appeared to change. Moreover, in both the alone and together conditions, there was no evidence of convergence to a norm or reduction in variance over trials.

In a second experiment, standard instructions (like those Sherif used) were given but a confederate either converged with or diverged from the participant in blocks of 15 trials that were run alternately with the participant's trials. When the confederate converged, the ten participants showed the normal Sherif-type of convergence. However, when the confederate diverged they did not follow the confederate. Why? Alexander and colleagues concluded that this was because 'situational expectations and role definitions rather than inherent psychological tendencies to regard inconsequential chaos as uncomfortable' (1970: 120) explained perceptual convergence in the AKI paradigm.

However, in 1976, Nicholas Pollis and colleagues provided an effective rebuttal of this alternative interpretation. They pointed out that Alexander and colleagues'

(1970) variation of the paradigm actually induced expectations of divergence, or at least non-convergence, and hence did provide a kind of predictability. That is, the situation was not one that induced uncertainty. This is because participants did not expect that there should be consistent agreement. To test this possibility, Pollis and colleagues added a third condition to the design of Alexander and colleagues' study, in which participants were given no expectation other than the knowledge that the AKI was an illusion. The results were quite clear. Participants who made judgments in pairs showed greater convergence and less variability over trials than did those who judged alone. Moreover, in all three conditions, participants showed convergence over the course of the trials. Thus, the findings not only failed to replicate those of Alexander and colleagues but also strongly reinforced Sherif's original interpretation that norms form and participants converge when the situation is perceived to be unstructured.

The power of the group as an aid to development of norms was also demonstrated by Pollis and Montgomery (1966), who asked participants to establish norms either together or alone, and either in natural (pre-existing) groups or in groups of strangers. The investigators then retested participants and found that when participants later judged the AKI, the group norm was sustained more when it had been formed by participants together in the natural group than in all other conditions.

Sherif also continued to conduct AKI studies. In particular, Sherif and Harvey (1952) focused on the ego functions of norm formation. They argued that 'the effect of extreme stress, uncertainty, lack of stable anchorages may be to increase suggestibility in the sense of increasing the likelihood of accepting a standard for behaviour from a source other than the individual's own' (1952: 276). In this way it was suggested that an unstructured and uncertain stimulus situation would induce anxiety and result in wider ranges of judgments around the norm, such that while there would be more inter-individual variability in judgments, there also would be greater convergence to a group norm.

To test this idea, participants gave 50 judgments alone and then a few days later responded in pairs. There were three conditions. In the simple condition, participants had a chance to view the experimental room, which was smaller than in the other conditions, thereby providing more anchorages and reference points for perception. The experimenter was also friendly and encouraging. In the intermediate condition, the study was conducted in a very large (81 x 54 ft) room, but participants never saw the apparatus or room in the light. In the difficult condition, the larger room was used again but this time participants had to find their seats using a complex arrangement of stairs and ropes. In addition, the experimenter made no attempt to establish rapport with the participants. In other words, this last condition was highly disorientating. The results largely confirmed Sherif and Harvey's predictions, with greater convergence in the intermediate and difficult conditions than in the simple condition.

In a test of the robustness of norms created in the AKI paradigm, Robert Jacobs and Donald Campbell (1961) conducted a large-scale study (with 175 participants and various group sizes) in which after every 30 trials one member of the group left and was replaced by a new member. Moreover, in each group one, two or three confederates initially imposed a 'cultural norm', or anchor. These confederates anchored naïve subjects to a norm of 15.5 inches, which was much larger than the typical norm for solitary judgments (which averaged 3.8 inches). Jacobs and Campbell found that 'significant remnants of the culture persisted for four or five generations beyond the last confederate' (1961: 657), although gradually it decayed such that the final norm reverted to the 'natural' level. Of course, this study can be interpreted as showing either that the initial norm was strong (because it continued for several generations) or weak (because it eventually disappeared). Like the Asch (1951) conformity studies (see Chapter 5), Jacobs and Campbell's study thus illustrates both the power of social influence and individuals' ability to resist such influence.

Mark MacNeil and Sherif (1976) responded to Jacobs and Campbell's study by arguing that a norm involves more than its central tendency. It also includes its latitude – or range – of acceptable precepts or behaviours. Given that the typical latitude, or range, for the norm in the AKI paradigm is around 7 inches (with a central tendency of 4 inches), the cultural norm provided by Jacobs and Campbell was arguably implausible in regard to both its central tendency and latitude. MacNeil and Sherif argued that new norms should persist longer if they are not clearly arbitrary in relation to the 'natural' norm.

To examine this possibility, these researchers conducted a study using the replacement member procedure developed by Jacobs and Campbell. Groups consisted only of naïve participants or of three confederates who were replaced by naïve participants in successive generations, so that the groups were composed of only naïve participants by the fourth generation. In the 'moderately arbitrary' condition, the confederates centred on a mode of 12 inches with a range of 9–15 inches. In the 'most arbitrary' condition, they centred on a mode of 18 inches with a range of 15–21 inches. Consistent with MacNeil and Sherif's predictions, convergence to the arbitrary norm both was greater and persisted for many more trials in the moderately arbitrary than in the most arbitrary condition.

IMPACT OF THE AUTOKINETIC ILLUSION STUDIES

S herif's work had a huge impact. In numerous ways the autokinetic illusion studies provided the cornerstone for much of the subsequent work on social influence in groups. Sherif's methodology was explicitly intended to lay bare the essential processes that contribute to informational group influence (Deutsch and Gerard, 1955). The use of ambiguous stimuli as the starting point for studying group processes became increasingly common. It is no accident that Henri Tajfel's (e.g., 1978) groundbreaking work on intergroup discrimination (see Chapter 10) started by stripping down Sherif and Sherif's (1953) studies on intergroup conflict (see Chapter 9) to a situation in which the basis of categorization and group membership was arbitrary and minimal, leaving participants with no real idea of the authentic basis for group identity. Similarly, Serge Moscovici's (1976, 1980) work on minority influence owes much to the use of an unstable stimulus situation (e.g., in which participants had to judge the colour of an afterimage; see Chapter 6).

A second key contribution of Sherif's work was to establish that it is viable and meaningful to study group processes in terms of distinctive group products and with a distinctive level of analysis that does not reduce everything to individual psychology. Sherif's original advocacy of a non-reductionist social psychology was sidelined for many years as ego psychology, on the one hand, and approaches spanning behaviourism and social cognition (and now social neuroscience), on the other hand, focused on more micro levels of analysis. Yet Sherif's arguments and perspective – in particular his critique of reductionism – spurred the development of the 'European' perspective in social psychology, led by both Tajfel (1979) and Moscovici (1961, 1981), which asserted that the larger social structure must be considered in order to make sense of individual behaviour. What, perhaps, was missing from Sherif's ideas was recognition that an adequate analysis of social norms must consider more than just values and frames of reference, but also broader themes such as social structure and ideology. Relevant ideas are incorporated in approaches such as social representations theory (Deaux and Philogene, 2001; Jovchelovitch, 2007) and system justification theory (Jost and Hunyadi, 2005).

Sherif (1966) was unhappy that much of the work following up his AKI studies focused on the moderating role of personality or other individual differences. It was not that he felt these were unimportant, but rather that he felt they were not relevant to the key themes in his work on norm formation that permeated his later work in other areas. These included 'frame of reference, the problem of what constitutes a social situation, problems of level of organization and interdisciplinary approach, gradations of stimulus structure, anchorage (reference point), cultural products, social norm (in the generic sense), social perception, and ego involvements' (1966: xv). For example, his work on conflict and cooperation showed how intergroup interdependence generated new norms (e.g., Sherif and Sherif, 1953), and norms and frame of reference were also central to his work on reference groups in adolescence (Sherif and Sherif, 1964) and attitudes and attitude change (Sherif and Hovland, 1961). Putting these various elements together, Sherif summarized his perspective as follows:

> A social attitude (say on religion, politics or war) cannot be adequately presented as a single point, as in most attitude measures. The individual's stand on social issues, toward people and groups, is not a point, but a categorization of those he accepts and those he rejects …[;] the relative sizes of a person's latitudes of acceptance, rejection and noncommitment were proposed as operational indicators of the degree of the individual's involvement. (1966: xx)

BEYOND THE AUTOKINETIC ILLUSION STUDIES II

NEW APPROACHES TO NORM FORMATION

Sherif's ideas have contributed both directly and indirectly to modern research on 'shared reality'. Hardin and Higgins (1996) argued that social verification plays a key role in people's confidence in their judgments across an array of domains, and therefore 'efforts to establish shared reality should dominate social interaction' (1996: 38). John Levine and E. Tory Higgins (2001) argued that this is as true for groups as it is for individuals (see also Echterhoff et al., 2009). Indeed, shared reality is central to numerous group phenomena, including trans-active memory (Moreland et al., 1996), group beliefs (Bar-Tal, 1990), and shared mental models (DeChurch and Mesmer-Magnus, 2010). Critically (and drawing from Sherif), Levine and Higgins (2001) pointed out that shared reality has a temporal aspect whereby, over the course of becoming a member of a group, people come to accept and embrace its shared reality. Moreover, the process of imparting that reality to new members may itself consolidate the shared reality among old-timers (see Levine et al., 1996). Also, drawing on Sherif's wider point that norms include a frame of reference that affects judgment and behaviour, Levine and colleagues (2000) showed how a shared reality, operationalized as either a promotion-focused task orientation or a prevention-focused task orientation, could affect the riskiness of the strategy used in a multi-trial recognition memory task. The key point underlined by this research is that groups establish a shared reality not just regarding the correct answer to a problem but also regarding the best means for arriving at such an answer.

Social identity and self-categorization theory have also focused on the nature of the social frame of reference. In particular, it has been argued that self-categorization provides psychological boundaries for influence, such that people are more likely to share a social reality with people who are members of their own category (the ingroup) than with members of another category (the outgroup). For example, John Turner (1985) developed a theory of 'referent informational influence' (see also Abrams and Hogg, 1990; Turner, 1991), arguing that 'uncertainty is a social product of disagreement between people categorized as identical to self. The perception of others as an appropriate reference group for social comparison creates the shared expectations of agreement necessary for the arousal of uncertainty and mutual influence' (1985: 93).

This idea was tested by Dominic Abrams and colleagues (1990) in an important extension of the Sherif AKI studies. They proposed that the expectation of agreement should be influenced by social categorization, in line with referent informational influence theory. In their study, on each exposure, three naïve participants judged the movement of a light and then heard the judgments of three confederates. The confederates were each instructed to yoke their estimates to those of a specified naïve participant by estimating 5cm higher for the first 3 trials and then remaining within +/− 2cm of the third estimate for the remaining 22 trials.

In the control condition, participants were given seat numbers and were instructed to call out their numbers before giving their estimates (in cm) for the movement of the light. To test the role of categorization, Abrams and his colleagues (1990) added two further conditions. In the categorization condition, naïve and confederate participants were given different category labels (H and J), ostensibly as part of a randomization procedure. When participants made their estimates, they were asked to say their category label. In the group identity condition, this categorization was further reinforced by first having participants in the two groups play a game, apparently to ensure that there were no initial differences between them. When making estimates, they had to say which group they were in.

Recall that the initial difference between the confederates' norm and the naïve participants' norm was 5cm. Sherif would predict that the naïve participants should converge towards the higher estimates made by the confederates in all three conditions. In contrast, referent informational influence theory would predict no convergence to the confederates in the categorization and group identity conditions, and limited convergence to the confederates in the control condition, because of the implicit categorization arising from the fact that the naïve and confederate participants had an answering sequence that correlated with their seat numbers (i.e., the three naïve participants were in seat numbers 1 to 3 and so responded before the three confederates). Results confirmed these predictions. The experiment therefore showed that when categorization was salient, two distinct norms could emerge in parallel within the same, otherwise-unstructured stimulus environment. Far from weakening Sherif's conclusions, these findings strengthen his argument that people seek structure – a frame of reference – when they form new norms. When a categorization is meaningfully correlated with differences in judgments, people will use that categorization to establish distinct norms, or, to put it another way, different shared realities.

Subsequent studies using stimulus situations other than the AKI have shown similar effects. For example, considering the role of anonymity and depersonalization in norm formation, Tom Postmes and colleagues have argued that group norms emerge based on within-group accommodation to a prototype that emerges from ingroup communications. Their social identity model of deindividuation effects (SIDE) holds that this process is facilitated by computer-mediated communications because of their anonymity and their potential to make common ingroup categorizations salient while reducing the salience of individual identity. For example, Postmes and colleagues (1998) showed that when groups were primed with prosocial or efficiency interaction goals, they converged on this norm more when members were anonymous than when they were identifiable. Moreover, Postmes and colleagues (2000) showed that computer-mediated groups spontaneously generated both a social identity and distinctive communication norms linked to that identity. Finally, consistent with the idea that people want to share the reality of particular social groups and not others, evidence shows that they are likely to overestimate ingroup (but not outgroup) consensus around their own behaviour or opinion (Robbins and Krueger, 2005) and that even children anticipate that ingroups and outgroups will hold different opinions (Abrams, 2011; Piaget and Weil, 1951).

CONCLUSION

Sherif's work on norm formation and persistence is a truly classic contribution not only to the field of social psychology but to the behavioural sciences as a whole. By raising fundamental questions about the nature and function of social norms and developing a clever experimental paradigm for testing his ideas, Sherif revolutionized thinking about how social influence operates. For example, his research using the autokinetic illusion provided a major impetus for conceptual and empirical work on the important phenomenon of shared reality. And his metatheoretical critique of individualism and reductionism in social psychology helped lay the intellectual groundwork for what is arguably the most influential current theoretical perspective on intergroup and intragroup processes, namely the social identity approach. Indeed, contrary to the ambiguity and uncertainty harnessed so ingeniously in his autokinetic experiments, there is little uncertainty that, some 75 years after they were published, Sherif's ideas continue to be a solid reference point and generative force in our discipline.

FURTHER READING

Sherif, M. (1936) *The Psychology of Social Norms*. New York: Harper and Row.

This book, while quite short, is by any standards a classic. It is highly readable, vibrant and fascinating, as well as hugely impressive in its breadth.

Abrams, D. and Hogg, M.A. (1990) 'Social identity, self-categorization and social influence', *European Review of Social Psychology*, 1: 195–228.

Abrams and Hogg provide a useful summary that links traditional social influence research to the social identity approach.

Turner, J.C. (1991) *Social Influence*. Milton Keynes: Open University Press.

A more extended treatment of the social identity approach is provided by Turner.

Postmes, T., Spears, R. and Lea, M. (2000) 'The formation of group norms in computer-mediated communication', *Human Communication Research,* 26: 341–71.

This paper provides a more specific example of how the social identity approach can be applied, showing how norms emerge even when groups have no face-to-face interaction but rather communicate via computers. This research illustrates how different groups or communities can create their own customs and rules for communication.

Levine, J.M. and Higgins, E.T. (2001) 'Shared reality and social influence in groups and organization', in F. Butera and G. Mugny (eds), *Social Influence in Social Reality: Promoting Individual and Social Change*. Seattle: Hogrefe and Huber. pp. 33–52.

Levine and Higgins review work illustrating the critical role that shared reality plays in group affairs. They discuss how group members seek shared reality before interaction, achieve shared reality during interaction, and are influenced by shared reality following interaction.

Jost, J.T. and Hunyadi, O. (2005) 'Antecedents and consequences of system-justifying ideologies', *Current Directions in Psychological Science,* 14: 260–5.

Jost and Hunyadi explain their theory of system justification which deals with the way social groups develop normative beliefs such that they accept a social structure that affects them unfairly.

Moscovici, S. (1981) 'On social representations', in J.P. Forgas (ed.), *Social Cognition: Perspectives on Everyday Understanding.* London: Academic Press. pp. 181–209.

Moscovici elaborates his theory of social representations, a much wider concept than norms, which elaborates the assumption that people construct or connect to a socially shared system of interpretation and meaning.

REFERENCES

Abrams, D. (2011) 'Wherein lies children's intergroup bias? Egocentrism, social understanding and social projection', *Child Development*, 82(5): 1579–93.

Abrams, D. and Hogg, M.A. (1990) 'Social identity, self-categorization and social influence', *European Review of Social Psychology,* 1: 195–228.

Abrams, D., Wetherell, M.S., Cochrane, S., Hogg, M.A. and Turner, J.C. (1990) 'Knowing what to think by knowing who you are: Self-categorisation and the nature of norm formation, conformity, and group polarisation', *British Journal of Social Psychology,* 29: 97–119.

Adams, H.F. (1912) 'Autokinetic sensations', *Psychological Monographs,* 59: 32–44.

Alexander, C.N. Jr., Zucker, L.G. and Brody, C.L. (1970) 'Experimental expectations and autokinetic experiences: Consistency theories and judgmental convergence', *Sociometry,* 33: 108–22.

Allport, F.H. (1924) 'The group fallacy in relation to social science', *Journal of Abnormal and Social Psychology,* 19: 60–73.

Asch, S.E. (1951) 'Effects of group pressure upon the modification and distortion of judgments', in H. Guetzkow (ed.), *Groups, Leadership, and Men.* Pittsburgh, PA: Carnegie Press. pp. 177–90.

Bar-Tal, D. (1990) *Group Beliefs: A Conception for Analyzing Group Structure, Processes and Behavior.* New York: Springer Verlag.

Bovard, E.W. Jr. (1948) 'Social norms and the individual', *Journal of Abnormal and Social Psychology,* 43: 62–9.

Deaux, K. and Philogene, G. (eds) (2001) *Representations of the Social.* Oxford: Blackwell.

DeChurch, L.A. and Mesmer-Magnus, J.R. (2010) 'The cognitive underpinnings of effective teamwork: A meta-analysis', *Journal of Applied Psychology,* 95: 32–53.

Deutsch, M. and Gerard, H. (1955) 'A study of normative and informational social influences upon individual judgment', *Journal of Abnormal and Social Psychology,* 51: 629–36.

Durkheim, E. (1915) *The Elementary Forms of the Religious Life.* London: Allen and Unwin.

Echterhoff, G., Higgins, E.T. and Levine, J.M. (2009) 'Shared reality: Experiencing commonality with others' inner states about the world', *Perspectives on Psychological Science,* 4: 496–521.

Freud, S. (1927) *The Ego and the Id.* London: L and V Woolf.

Goldberg, S.C. (1954) 'Three situational determinants of conformity to social norms', *Journal of Abnormal Psychology,* 49: 325–9.

Hardin, C.D. and Higgins, E.T. (1996) 'Shared reality: How social verification makes the subjective objective', in R.M. Sorrentino and E.T. Higgins (eds), *Handbook of Motivation and* Cognition, Vol. 3. New York: Guilford. pp. 28–84.

Hoffman, E.L., Swander, D.V., Baron, S.H. and Rohrer, J.H. (1953) 'Generalization and exposure time as related to autokinetic movement', *Journal of Experimental Psychology,* 46: 171–7.

Jacobs, R.C. and Campbell, D.T. (1961) 'The perpetuation of an arbitrary tradition through several generations of a laboratory microculture', *Journal of Abnormal and Social Psychology,* 62: 649–58.

Jost, J.T. and Hunyadi, O. (2005) 'Antecedents and consequences of system-justifying ideologies', *Current Directions in Psychological Science,* 14: 260–5.

Jovchelovitch, S. (2007) *Knowledge in Context: Representations, Community and Culture.* London: Routledge.

Kelman, H.C. (1950) 'Effects of success and failure on "suggestibility" in the autokinetic situation', *Journal of Abnormal and Social Psychology,* 46: 267–85.

Levine, J.M., Bogart, L.M. and Zdaniuk, B. (1996) 'Impact of anticipated group membership on cognition', in R.M. Sorrentino and E.T. Higgins (eds), *Handbook of Motivation and Cognition,* Vol. 3. New York: Guilford. pp. 531–69.

Levine, J.M. and Higgins, E.T. (2001) 'Shared reality and social influence in groups and organization', in F. Butera and G. Mugny (eds), *Social Influence in Social Reality: Promoting Individual and Social Change.* Seattle: Hogrefe and Huber. pp. 33–52.

Levine, J.M., Higgins, E.T. and Choi, H.S. (2000) 'Development of strategic norms in groups', *Organizational Behavior and Human Decision Processes,* 82: 88–101.

Levy, J. (1972) 'Autokinetic illusion: A systematic review of theories, measures and independent variables', *Psychological Bulletin,* 78: 457–74.

MacNeil, M.K. and Sherif, M. (1976) 'Norm change over subject generations as a function of arbitrariness of prescribed norms', *Journal of Personality and Social Psychology,* 34: 762–73.

Malinowski, B. (1927) *Sex and Repression in Savage Society.* New York: Harcourt, Brace & Company.

Mead, M. (1928) *Coming of Age in Samoa: A Psychological Study of Primitive Youth for Western Civilization.* New York: William Morrow & Co.

Milgram, S. (1964) 'Group pressure and action against a person', *Journal of Abnormal and Social Psychology,* 69: 137–43.

Moreland, R.L., Argote, L. and Krishnan, R. (1996) 'Socially shared cognition at work: Transactive memory and group performance', in J.L. Nye and A.M. Brower (eds), *What's Social about Social Cognition?* Thousand Oaks, CA: Sage. pp. 57–84.

Moscovici, S. (1961) *La Psychanalyse, son Image et son Public.* Paris: Presses Universitaires de France.

Moscovici, S. (1976) *Social Influence and Social Change.* London: Academic Press.

Moscovici, S. (1980) 'Towards a theory of conversion behavior', in L. Berkowitz (ed.), *Advances in Experimental Social Psychology*, Vol. 13. London: Academic Press. pp. 209–39.

Moscovici, S. (1981) 'On social representations', in J.P. Forgas (ed.), *Social Cognition: Perspectives on Everyday Understanding.* London: Academic Press. pp. 181–209.

Piaget, J. (1932) *The Moral Judgment of the Child.* London: Kegan Paul.

Piaget, J. and Weil, A.M. (1951) 'The development in children of the idea of the homeland and of relations to other countries', *International Social Science Journal,* 3: 561–78.

Pollis, N.P. and Montgomery, R.L. (1966) 'Conformity and resistance to compliance', *Journal of Psychology,* 63: 35–41.

Pollis, N.P., Montgomery, R.L. and Smith, T.G. (1976) 'Autokinetic paradigms: A reply to Alexander, Zucker and Brody', *Sociometry,* 38: 358–73.

Postmes, T., Spears, R. and Lea, M. (1998) 'Breaching or building social boundaries? SIDE-effects of computer-mediated communication', *Communication Research,* 25: 689–715.

Postmes, T., Spears, R. and Lea, M. (2000) 'The formation of group norms in computer-mediated communication', *Human Communication Research,* 26: 341-71.

Rivers, W.H.R. (1924) *The History of Melanesian Society.* Cambridge: Cambridge University Press.

Robbins, J.M. and Krueger, J.I. (2005) 'Social projection to ingroups and outgroups: A review and meta-analysis', *Personality and Social Psychology Review,* 9: 32–47.

Rohrer, J.H., Baron, S.H., Hoffman, E.L. and Swander, D.V. (1954) 'The stability of autokinetic judgments', *Journal of Abnormal and Social Psychology,* 49: 595–7.

Sampson, E.E. and Insko, C.A. (1964) 'Cognitive consistency and performance in the autokinetic situation', *Journal of Abnormal and Social Psychology*, 68: 184–92.

Sherif, M. (1935) 'A study of some social factors in perception', *Archives of Psychology,* 27(187): 23–46.

Sherif, M. (1936) *The Psychology of Social Norms.* New York: Harper and Row.

Sherif, M. (1937) 'An experimental approach to the study of attitudes', *Sociometry,* 1: 90–8.

Sherif, M. (1966) *Introduction to the Torchbook Edition of the Psychology of Social Norms.* New York: Harper and Row.

Sherif, M. and Harvey, O.J. (1952) 'A study in ego functioning: Elimination of stable anchorages in individual and group situations', *Sociometry,* 15: 272–305.

Sherif, M. and Hovland, C.I. (1961) *Social Judgment: Assimilation and Contrast Effects in Communication and Attitude Change.* Oxford: Yale University Press.

Sherif, M. and Sherif, C.W. (1953) *Groups in Harmony and Tension.* New York: Harper and Row.

Sherif, M. and Sherif, C.W. (1964) *Reference Groups: Exploration into Conformity and Deviation of Adolescents*. New York: Harper and Row.

Tajfel, H. (ed.) (1978) *Differentiation Between Social Groups: Studies in the Social Psychology of Intergroup Relations*. London: Academic Press.

Tajfel, H. (1979) 'Individuals and groups in social psychology', *British Journal of Social Psychology*, 18: 183–90.

Turner, J.C. (1985) 'Social categorisation and the self-concept: A social cognitive theory of group behaviour', in E.J. Lawler (ed.), *Advances in Group Processes*, Vol. 2. Greenwich, CT: JAI Press. pp. 77–121.

Turner, J.C. (1991) *Social Influence*. Milton Keynes: Open University Press.

Vidulich, R.N. and Kaiman, I.P. (1961) 'The effects of information source status and dogmatism upon conformity behavior', *Journal of Abnormal and Social Psychology*, 63: 639–42.

5

Conformity

Revisiting Asch's line-judgment studies

Jolanda Jetten and Matthew J. Hornsey

'2 + 2 = 5'

George Orwell, *Nineteen Eighty-Four*

BACKGROUND

Obviously, 2+2 does not equal 5. However, as Orwell suggests, if you find yourself in a world where people believe this to be true, you might start to doubt your judgment. Perhaps you even start to think that this must be true; 'They are right and so I must be wrong.'

For some decades now social psychologists have had a key interest in the factors that lead us to go along with others' views rather than stand strong and resist the pressure to conform. Of particular importance in advancing our knowledge about conformity and resistance were the line-judgment studies by Solomon Asch (1951, 1955). Asch asked why we sometimes abandon our firmly held convictions and bring our attitudes and judgments in line with those of other people, even if we know that they are wrong and we are right. That is, why do we at times yield to conformity pressures and seem to uncritically adopt the majority point of view?

As Asch (1955) writes, his interest in conformity started when he read about classic research by, among others, the psychologist Edward L. Thorndike. In these studies, people are asked to give their opinion on a topic and after doing so they are confronted with an authority figure or group of peers saying the opposite. What typically happens in these studies is that when people are asked again for their opinion, they shift their views and attitudes towards those expressed by the peers or authority. Like many others, Asch was puzzled by this finding. Why would people change their mind when the authority or majority did not even present any arguments to support their views? Why would the sheer number of opponents or the fact that an authority provides another attitude lead to conformity?

THE LINE-JUDGMENT STUDIES

To address such questions, Asch devised an experimental paradigm that was modelled closely on the experimental set-up in these suggestion studies. However, there was one important difference: in his experiments he created a situation in which various features of the task and the social context made it extremely difficult to resist conformity pressure despite it being very clear that conforming would mean giving an incorrect response.

Perhaps the best way to explain the experiment is to invite you to imagine that you were a participant in one of these studies. After arriving at the laboratory, you find yourself in the company of between seven and nine other participants and you are told that you are all taking part in a psychological study of visual judgment. The experimenter informs you that you will be comparing the length of various lines. You are shown two large white cards (see Figure 5.1). One has a reference line and on the other card you see three comparison lines (labeled A, B and C). Your task is to say out loud which of the three comparison lines is similar in length to the reference line. One of the three lines is clearly the same length as the reference line and the other two are obviously shorter or longer. You think this will be easy.

Participants are seated and they are presented with several trials where they have to call out their answers in the order in which they are seated. You are seated in a position where almost all the other participants have to call out their response before you. The study starts quite uneventfully; everyone agrees which comparison line is similar in length to the reference line. This is getting boring. But then, suddenly, on the third trial, the first participant calls out what is obviously the wrong answer. For example, given lines like those in Figure 5.1, they say 'A' rather than 'B'. They must have made a mistake and you reassure yourself that they cannot be correct by looking again closely at the lines. But then, the second and third persons give the same answer as the first person. Number four and five also call

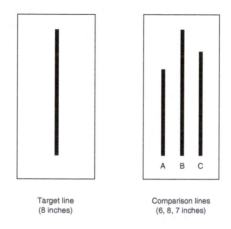

Target line   Comparison lines
(8 inches)   (6, 8, 7 inches)

Figure 5.1   The stimuli in Asch's standard line-judgment studies. The participant's (seemingly very easy) task is to say which of the comparison lines (A, B or C) matches the target line on the left out a letter associated with a line that appears to be clearly much longer (or shorter) than the reference line. Are they all blind? Then it is your turn. What do you answer? Should you just go along with their response (even though, privately, you are pretty sure they are wrong), or should you stick to your own judgment even though you are the only one giving this answer?

Unbeknownst to you, the other participants are not actually real participants at all, but are assistants of the experimenter ('confederates') who have been instructed to call out wrong answers on 12 critical trials. The study was not about visual perception, but an investigation into conformity. The results show that it is fairly difficult to withstand conforming in such contexts, even though it is clear that the majority is wrong. There are a number of ways in which the key findings have been reported and, for now, we focus on the way the results are typically reported in the majority of social psychology textbooks. The responses on the critical trials (where the majority clearly gave the wrong response) are presented in Figure 5.2. One popular way of summarizing these findings is to say that 76% of participants conformed at least once to an incorrect answer given by the majority.

To put this number in perspective, Asch also examined conformity under conditions where no confederates were involved and when everyone was a naïve participant who called out the line that they felt best matched the length of the reference line. Under such conditions, hardly anyone gave the wrong response – the task was indeed incredibly easy. On this basis, Asch remarked that 'whereas in ordinary circumstances, individuals matching the lines will make mistakes less than 1 percent of the time, under group pressure, the minority subjects swung to acceptance of the misleading majority's wrong judgments in 36.8 percent of the selections' (Asch, 1955: 32–3).

Regardless of whether participants conformed or not, it is clear that the experience of being in the minority, and of being confronted with a majority who appeared to be seeing something very different to what the participants were seeing with their own eyes, was unsettling. It must have been a troubling experience to be a participant in this study. Indeed, film footage from the study

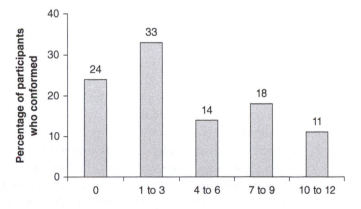

Figure 5.2 Percentage of participants that conformed to the majority on the 12 critical trials in Asch's standard line-judgment study (adapted from Asch, 1955)

shows participants squinting and looking at the lines from different angles, in a vain attempt to discover what the majority is seeing and they are not (see Figure 5.3). Asch (1952) himself provides detailed accounts of the changes in non-verbal behaviour that an onlooker would witness when observing the naïve participant over the course of the experiment:

> After the first one or two disagreements he would note certain changes in the manner and posture of this person. He would see a look of perplexity and bewilderment come over this subject's face at the contradicting judgments of the entire group. Often he becomes more active; he fidgets in his seat and changes the position of his head to look at the lines from different angles. He may turn around and whisper to his neighbor seriously or smile sheepishly. He may suddenly stand up to look more closely at the card. At other times he may become especially quiet and immobile. (1952: 454)

Figure 5.3 The naïve participant (sixth person from the left) is confused but also more alert when other respondents unanimously call out the wrong response (from Asch, 1955: 31)

FOLLOW-UP STUDIES

From the moment its findings were first published, Asch's study attracted considerable attention. And having obtained such intriguing results, Asch and others set about conducting a series of further studies to examine in greater detail the context and features of the task that led to more or less conformity. As they are typically understood in textbooks, the studies themselves are seen as evidence of what is termed *normative influence*. This analysis suggests that the fear of standing out as different motivates people to compromise their motivation to be accurate and to conform to an obviously incorrect majority.

As it turns out, any fears participants might have had about expressing their deviant opinion were well-founded. In one variant of the line-judgment study, Asch inverted the typical paradigm. This time there was just one confederate who was instructed to call out the wrong answer and the confederate was surrounded by several true participants. Here the (unfortunate) confederate was openly and loudly ridiculed. As a further demonstration of the power of normative influence, Morton Deutsch and Harold Gerard (1955) created a situation in which participants could witness the (incorrect) responses of the majority but were allowed to record their own responses privately (thus eliminating fear of ridicule and, by extension, the power of normative influence). In this variant, the level of conformity plummeted (see also Abrams et al., 1990; Insko et al., 1983). Interestingly, however, conformity was not reduced to zero. For some participants, the power of the situation was enough to convince them that the majority answer was the correct answer after all. In other words, the study provides evidence not only of normative influence (i.e., 'going along' with others) but also of *informational influence* (i.e., being convinced by others).

Other follow-ups focused on other conditions that affect conformity levels. Perhaps unsurprisingly, resistance was enhanced when the majority gave answers that were more blatantly incorrect (Asch, 1955). Asch (1955) was also interested in whether the sheer size of the majority, or the unanimity of its members, enhanced conformity. Here a first series of studies showed that the size of the majority only mattered up to a point: when confronted with just one other confederate giving the wrong responses, participants answered independently and gave the correct response on nearly all trials (all but 3%). When there were two confederates giving wrong answers, conformity to their incorrect judgments increased to 14%. Conformity increased still further to 32% when confronted with a majority of three confederates, but did not increase substantially after that. Indeed, if there were 15 confederates, the rate of conformity was very slightly lower (31%; see Asch, 1955).

Asch also examined to what extent conformity would be affected by the extent to which the majority was unanimous. Results of these studies were even more striking. When there was one other individual who failed to conform to the incorrect majority response (either a confederate or another naïve participant), conformity dropped dramatically. Interestingly too, the other dissenter was perceived especially warmly and positively by participants. From their perspective, it must have been reassuring to be in the company of at least one other person who perceived the lines in the same way. Other studies examined conformity when the dissenter disagreed not only with the majority but also with the participant (i.e., still giving an obviously wrong answer, but a different one to the majority). Here conformity to the majority giving the wrong answer was relatively low (occurring on only 9% of critical trials). This led Asch to conclude that what undermined conformity was not the direction of dissent (i.e., whether the dissenter was right or wrong), but the fact that dissent had occurred at all.

The studies have also inspired research which aims to establish who is most likely to conform. Do children conform more than adults? Do women conform more than men? Are there differences across countries in levels of conformity? One of Asch's early studies examined conformity among children. He compared the responses of a cohort of younger children (7 to 10 years old) to those of older children (over 10 years old), and found that those who were younger conformed more than those who were older. This pattern has since been replicated in more recent studies. For example, in a study that used a slightly different paradigm to Asch, Michael Walker and Maria Andrade (1996) found that the younger partici-pants were, the more they conformed: conformity levels were 42% among 6- to 8-year-olds, 38% for 9- to 11-year-olds, and 9% for those 12 to 14 years old, but there was no conformity at all among those aged between 15 and 17.

Looking at national differences in conformity in the Asch paradigm, Rod Bond and Peter Smith (1996) conducted a statistical analysis in which they compared conformity levels across countries that promote individualism (e.g., the US) and countries that have a more collectivist orientation (e.g., Hong Kong). Their analysis of 133 Asch line-judgment studies showed that conformity was higher in collectiv-ist countries than in individualist countries, presumably because conformity is more valued in the former than the latter. Their study also revealed a robust effect whereby women were more likely to conform than men. Interestingly too, the researchers found that levels of conformity had dropped significantly over the decades, with conformity levels being relatively low in more recent studies. Indeed, two replication attempts (LaLancette and Standing, 1990; Perrin and Spencer, 1981) using the line-judgment paradigm uncovered only one incident of conformity between them. This is not to say that normative-influence principles no longer apply, but it does suggest that the people are more prepared to use their minority voice than they were in the 1950s.

IMPACT OF THE LINE-JUDGMENT STUDIES

Asch's programme of studies is iconic within social psychology. The studies do not have the same theatricality as some other studies in the same tradition (in particular, Stanley Milgram's shock experiments and Philip Zimbardo's Stanford Prison Experiment; see Chapters 7 and 8) and so have had limited impact with in popular culture.[1] Nevertheless, as a result of Asch's elegant, programmatic approach, the studies have proved foundational to those interested in the study of conformity. It is hard to imagine an introductory textbook that would not make reference to them or a student of psychology who would not have been exposed to the findings and ideas that Asch explored so masterfully.

It is not hard to understand why the Asch study results attracted so much atten-tion. In particular, this is because the results seemed to speak powerfully to instances where people appear to be going along with the majority in a sheep-like fashion. For example, conformity of the form observed in Asch's studies has been

---

[1] Asch's studies may have been the inspiration, however, for the pop culture phenomenon of the 'No soap, radio' pranks that emerged in New York in the mid-1950s. In these pranks, a joke-teller and a confederate laugh uproariously at a joke that ends with the nonsense line 'No soap, radio'. The goal was to get the victim to laugh even though the joke makes no sense.

argued to underlie behaviours as diverse as going along with Nazi propaganda, succumbing to eating disorders such as bulimia (where people are not able to resist the majority pressure for thinness; Crandall, 1988), and engaging in football hooliganism and other types of crowd violence (Le Bon, 1895). As Gustave Le Bon had argued half a century earlier, Asch's studies appear to show that, in a group or crowd, the individual is unable to resist peer pressure and becomes a slave to the will of the collective. In Le Bon's words: 'An individual in a crowd is a grain of sand amid other grains of sand, which the wind stirs up at will' (1895: 13). In this view, conformity is seen as an irrational influence that leads people to conform in a mindless way. In this vein, Serge Moscovici later commented: 'The Asch studies are one of the most dramatic illustrations of conformity, of blindly going along with the group, even when the individual realizes that by doing so he turns his back on reality and truth' (1985: 349). Conformity is thus typically associated with the dark side of humanity: it reveals people's inability to resist even when they know the majority is wrong – to the extent that they are not even able to resist the pressure to agree with something as silly as an assertion that $2 + 2 = 5$.

BEYOND THE ASCH STUDIES

ALTERNATIVE INTERPRETATIONS AND FINDINGS

But is it really the case that conformity is a reflection of weakness and cowardice? Is it really sheep-like to take seriously what other people say even when they are clearly wrong? Put differently, can we see conformity in the Asch line-judgment experiments as normal, or perhaps even as a sensible thing to do? And is it the case that those who conformed were mindlessly and blindly following the majority? To answer these questions, we need to look more closely at the specifics of these studies and reflect on what it must have been like to be a participant in them.

In this regard, it is particularly revealing to read what participants said when asked after the study to elaborate on what it was that dictated their responses. Indeed, these data are every bit as informative as details of the levels of conformity to the incorrect majority responses. In line with the reasoning that conformity resulted from normative influence, many of those who conformed spontaneously mentioned that they went along with the group because – even though they did not think the majority was right – they did not want to appear foolish or to be the odd one out. However, there were also other reasons why people conformed. Some mentioned they did not want to 'spoil the study results' (Asch, 1955: 33) and believed they were acting in everyone's interest by not rocking the boat and going along with the majority. Still others believed that the first person to call out the wrong response must have had a visual impairment. When Confederates 2 and 3 also called out the wrong response, they simply concluded that these participants were conforming, possibly because they did not want to make the first person look like a fool. Interestingly, these participants thus interpreted the context as one where everyone was conforming to the wrong response of the first person. For all these participants, though, their privately held beliefs regarding the right response differed from their public responses: they trusted their own eyes, but as a result of the situational context, decided it was better to comply with the majority. Others, though, not only complied with the majority, but also appeared to change their privately held belief as to what the correct response was (thereby displaying so-called *conversion*). For example, they believed that they themselves were victims of optical illusions, and that the majority was actually right – simply because it was inconceivable that so many people could be wrong. They convinced themselves that 'I must be wrong and they must be right'.

Significantly too, although Asch himself also considered in detail the responses of those who resisted majority pressure, those responses are less often summarized in social psychological textbooks. So what exactly did those who resisted say? Asch reports two classes of individuals: those who were confident of their own judgment and appeared to respond without much consideration of the majority, and those who believed that the majority may be correct, but could not stop themselves calling out what they saw. For example, Asch (1952) describes the debrief interview with Participant 1 who resisted conformity on all critical trials. When the experimenter asks after the study, 'Who do you suppose was right?' this participant responds: 'There was absolutely no doubt in my mind, I still think I am right.' When asked: 'Do you think everyone else is wrong?', this participant said: 'Well, if I didn't I wouldn't have given these answers. Right now I have all the confidence in my judgment. I still don't understand how this difference could have come about' (1952: 466). In other words, those who resisted appeared to be more concerned about being correct and about being true to their own perceptions. This did not mean that they were not deeply disturbed by the experience. For example, Asch (1952: 466) notes that the participant described above, who resisted conformity on all critical trials, walked over to the experimenter at the end of the discussion and asked, 'Is there anything wrong with me?' After being given a full debrief, this participant felt a deep sense of relief and he walked out of the room saying: 'This is unlike any experience I have had in my life – I will never forget it as long as I live' (1952: 467).

These accounts provide a number of important insights. In particular, looking at the way that participants explained their responses, it becomes clear that people were actively trying to make sense of the situation by developing different theories as to why the majority was giving these obviously wrong responses. Some of these theories justified conforming (e.g., 'They must all be too polite to disagree with that poor first person who clearly has a visual impairment'), and others justified non-conformity (e.g., 'In this confusing context, the best I can do is just trust my own eye-sight'). It thus appears that accounts suggesting that people were blindly and passively following the majority are failing to do justice to what the experience must have been like. Participants did not sit back and simply let the majority overwhelm them. Rather, they were critically engaged and tried actively to make sense of the situation in order to develop a theory that would allow them to resolve the highly dissonant experience of contradiction between what they were seeing and how the majority was responding (for a related discussion of the strength of such dissonance, see Chapter 3).

To understand the nature of those theories that participants developed, it is instructive to look more closely at the specifics of the studies. Two aspects of the experimental context in particular are important: (a) the content of the task, and (b) the opposition by the majority. In relation to the first aspect, the task is one where (a) the participant knows that only one response is right and it appears clear which response is correct; (b) whether the right or wrong response is given does not appear consequential and does not necessarily reflect personal values; and (c) participants are isolated when giving responses and an immediate response is required, making it impossible to establish why the majority is giving the wrong response. Let us discuss these characteristics in turn and consider how they may have affected responses.

By making one response obviously right, and two other responses obviously wrong (see Figure 5.1), a context was created whereby, due to the clarity of the judgment, there was very little need to gather information from others about what the right response would be (a situation very different from that which prevailed in Muzafer Sherif's earlier autokinetic studies; see Chapter 4). But in everyday life, conformity is rarely an all-or-nothing judgment of this form. Instead, it involves subjective judgments where we can accept some influence from others, but also partially reject it. For example, I might conform to the majority of my friends that a movie we saw together was awful, but might still disagree when discussing whether the special effects were convincing or not. In addition, dissent in this case does not create discomfort, because it is easy to accept that one has a different perspective on reality to others. In this regard, it has been pointed out that it is the very obviousness of the answer in the Asch paradigm that led to such high conformity levels (Ross et al., 1976). Participants were almost certainly unprepared for the sheer and utter bizarreness of the situation that they were confronted with. This meant that many participants were probably so overwhelmed by the context, and so poorly equipped to deal with it, that it was easiest for them just to go along with the majority.

As Asch himself mentioned, the simplicity of the set-up also contributed to conformity in another way: 'The individual had nothing to "gain" by acting one way or another; usual considerations of interest were excluded' (1952: 469). This is precisely what one participant mentioned when discussing his responses afterwards. He said: 'If it had been a political question, I don't think I'd have agreed if I had a different feeling ... I probably wanted my own ideas, but it was easiest to string along' (Asch, 1952: 471). In line with this point, many have argued (and shown) that conformity levels would be much lower if responses were associated with important outcomes or outcomes that were personally meaningful (Crutchfield, 1955; Hornsey et al., 2003; Jahoda, 1959).

Turning to the nature of the majority, there are a number of interesting observations that can help us understand why it is perhaps not so surprising that participants went along with a majority that was so clearly wrong. Asch himself

(1952) certainly did not think that the majority was a force that could be easily ignored. He emphasizes that, once we find ourselves in the midst of a group, we are not indifferent to it and individuals are concerned about what others around them think. He says:

> The individual comes to experience a world that he shares with others. He perceives that the surroundings include him, as well as others, and that he is in the same relation to the surroundings as others. He notes that he, as well as others, is converging upon the same object and responding to its identical properties. Joint action and mutual understanding require this relation of intelligibility and structural simplicity. In these terms, the 'pull' toward the group becomes understandable. (1952: 484)

In other words, giving in to majority pressure is not an act of indifference or mindlessness. Quite the opposite: it shows that individuals are *mindful* of the views of others around them. It shows that they are interested in maintaining harmony within the group and willing to go along with what others think is right. This is important because it is precisely through the acceptance of social influence from others that groups are able to function effectively and maintain cohesion. This analysis is consistent with theorizing within the social identity tradition whereby conformity, and social influence more generally, are seen as originating

> in the need of people to reach agreement with others perceived to be interchangeable in respect of relevant attributes (psychological ingroup members in the given situation) in order to validate their responses as correct, appropriate and desirable. (Hogg and Turner, 1987: 150)

Thus, when surrounded by members of the same group who undergo the same experience as oneself, those others become valid sources of information that tell us how to interpret the world (Turner, 1991). In this view, rather than an irrational force that makes people blurt out responses that are obviously wrong, conformity in the Asch line-judgment experiments appears to be an entirely appropriate response. Asch puts it even more strongly when he says: 'The group is part of the given conditions. Not to take it into account, not to allow oneself to be in any way affected by it, would be willful' (1952: 484).

THE NEGLECTED IMPORTANCE OF RESISTANCE

A survey of popular social psychology texts suggests that Asch's line-judgment studies are particularly remembered for what they tell us about conformity, not what they tell us about resistance. Especially telling is the fact that they are routinely referred to as 'Asch's conformity studies'. However, closer inspection suggests that the studies generated just as much resistance as conformity. In that sense, it is revealing how results are presented. Often it is stated that 76% conformed on at least one trial and that about a third conformed on average on critical trials by going along with the majority. What is rarely highlighted is the other side of the coin: 'about one-quarter of the subjects were completely independent and never agreed with the erroneous judgment of the majority' (Asch, 1955: 33) or that only about 11% of participants conformed on almost all trials (see Figure 5.2). It thus seems that for every one time a participant conformed, he or she dissented twice. Given this, it seems reasonable to ask why we see the studies as studies of conformity. Why are they not reported as studies providing insight into dissent – as evidence of participants standing strong and going against the majority despite enormous pressure?

This is not a minor point. For resistance is not simply the absence of conformity. Rather, it is a process that is quite different from conformity and guided by different considerations. Yet the idea that individuals are able to resist a majority that is clearly wrong has generally been of little interest to those who typically comment on Asch's work. One possible reason for this is that social psychology in general appears more interested in what makes people conform than in what makes them dissent and show defiance in the face of group pressure (see Jetten and Hornsey, 2011, 2014). As Marie Jahoda remarks:

> Not only is there widespread consensus among many diagnosticians of the climate of our times that this is an age of conformity; the relevant psychological literature is almost unanimous in its emphasis on conditions accounting for conformity. Actually, there is, of course, ample evidence for the existence of independence not only in common-sense observations but also in every single experiment which rejects the null-hypothesis of independence ... There is a tacit implication in many of these experiments that those insubordinate subjects who are outside the hypothesis-confirming majority are a nuisance. (1959: 99; see also Moscovici, 1976)

Not much has changed in the 60 years since Jahoda made her observation. This is unfortunate for a number of reasons – not least because it appears that by focusing on conformity at the expense of resistance we have come to paint a picture of group life that is incomplete and, at times, plain wrong. Indeed, as Asch showed, resistance is just as common in group life as is conformity (Haslam and Reicher, 2007; Reicher and Haslam, 2006; see Chapters 7 and 8). Moving beyond Asch's studies, this point is also clear when we look around us and tally both acts of conformity and resistance in daily life. Both occur and dissent is just as much part of daily life as conformity.

What is more, we often like and identify with people who are able to withstand conformity pressures and rebel – in particular when they do not go along with a majority that is obviously wrong or misguided. Consider for example the now classic film and play *Twelve Angry Men,* which tells the story of a jury that has to decide whether a defendant is guilty or not. Even though they have not carefully examined the evidence, 11 of the jurors quickly agree that the defendant is guilty. One of the jurors, however, resists going along with this majority and forces the group to carefully check the evidence. By dissenting with the majority despite considerable pressure, as the story unfolds, it is clear that the majority is wrong and that the dissenter was right in standing firm in his claim that the evidence for a guilty verdict cannot be sustained. As viewers, we identify with the dissenter. He is the hero of the story, and, interestingly, the majority is portrayed as consisting of weak people who are guided by prejudice and an inability to be true to themselves.

There is another reason why it is unfortunate that there has not been more attention paid to the evidence of resistance in the Asch line-judgment studies. This is that, up to the present day, by focusing on the minority who conformed on some trials, we have neglected to explain – or even try to explain – why a majority of participants resisted conforming on a majority of trials. When we focus on conformity instead of dissent, we also focus on understanding uniformity instead of difference, and on passive responding rather than active behaviour by group members. As a result, theorizing about dissent and the willingness to stand out is quite underdeveloped and this has led to a failure to understand the way in which groups (and society more broadly) *change* (see Turner, 2006). Indeed, social change often has its roots in one individual (or a group of people) questioning whether the majority's view of reality is really correct and standing firm in their belief that it is not.

Yet when one reads (or re-reads) Asch's original reports of his studies it is clear that he was certainly not only interested in conformity. In fact, it is apparent that he warned against portraying people as conforming beings. Thus, he observes:

> Current thinking has stressed the power of social conditions to induce psychological changes arbitrarily. It has taken slavish submission to group forces as the general fact and has neglected or implicitly denied the capacity for men for independence, for rising under certain conditions above group passion and prejudice. (Asch, 1952: 451)

Asch's own deliberations provide a much more nuanced view of how he was trying to explore these countervailing processes in his research, and of what he felt were the implications of his work. Thus, it is true that, on the one hand, he expresses alarm about the willingness of participants to go along with a majority that is clearly wrong. As he puts it:

> That we have found the tendency to conformity so strong that reasonably intelligent and well-meaning young people are willing to call white black is a matter of concern. It raises questions about our ways of education and about the values that guide our conduct. (1955: 34)

Yet, on the other hand, he finishes the article by reflecting:

> Yet anyone inclined to draw too pessimistic conclusions from this report would do to remind [her/]himself that the capacities for independence are not to be underestimated. [S]he may also draw some consolation from a further observation: those who participated in this challenging experiment agreed nearly without exception that independence was preferable to conformity. (1955: 34)

Indeed, Asch was just as much convinced of the vitality and realness of independence as he was of the power of conformity. Even if we find that people conform, he says:

> We should be skeptical, however, of the supposition that the power of social pressure necessarily implies uncritical submission to it: Independence and the capacity to rise above group passion are also open to human beings. (1955: 32)

Nevertheless, it seems that only one-half of Asch's message has survived and that the other part has been largely forgotten. His message and purpose has thus been transformed over the years: so that rather than trying to understand the interplay between independence and conformity, consumers of his work have focused solely on people's inclination to conform.

CONCLUSION

So what should one conclude from the Asch line-judgment studies? Of course, the studies tell us about conformity and the confusion one experiences when confronted with a majority that is clearly wrong. But perhaps more important is the question of what this finding tells us about human behaviour more generally. Rather than arguing that the findings show us how easily people succumb to peer pressure, we would suggest that the studies inform us instead, first, that it is important for people to be validated by others and, second, that in many contexts other people are the most useful and important source of such validation. Both conformity and resistance can be a path towards actively achieving a greater understanding of the world around us and both are therefore equally rational (see Spears, 2010). Again, we can refer to Asch in order to illustrate this point. In the following passage he quotes from the reflections of the astronomer Tycho Brahe upon discovering a new star in 1572:

> When according to my habit, I was contemplating the stars in a clear sky, I noticed that a new and unusual star, surpassing the other stars in brilliancy, was shining almost directly above my head; and since I had, almost from boyhood, known all the stars of the heavens perfectly (there is no great difficulty in attaining that knowledge), it was quite evident to me that there had never before been any star in that place in the sky, even the smallest, to say nothing of a star so conspicuously bright as this. I was so astonished at this sight that I was not ashamed to doubt the trustworthiness of my own eyes. But when I observed that others, too, on having the place pointed out to them, could see that there was really a star there, I had no further doubts. (quoted in Asch, 1952: 493)

Because we can only know reality by agreeing with others about that reality, is it really that surprising that at times we do not believe our own eyes until others have told us that what we see is true? And, if they seem to be seeing something different – not seeing the star in Tycho Brahe's case – would that not lead us to conclude, over time at least, that 'they must be right and I must be wrong'? As Asch remarks, Tycho Brahe's story tells us that he was profoundly concerned with validating and corroborating what he saw. Indeed, 'had he remained the only one who continued to see the star, he would have been an unhappy man indeed' (1952: 494). Put simply, then, we *need* other people to tell us that what we are seeing is right, in order for us to understand that it *is* right. For this reason, to stop listening to others (and to stop conforming) would be the *ir*rational thing to do.

FURTHER READING

Asch, S.E. (1952) *Social Psychology*. Englewood Cliffs, NJ: Prentice-Hall.

Asch, S.E. (1955) 'Opinions and social pressure', *Scientific American*, 193: 31–5.

To get a better feeling for the line-judgment studies, you may want to read Asch's classic reports. The 1952 textbook provides detailed and rich accounts of what participants said after taking part and illustrates well what it must have been like to be a participant in the study. The 1955 paper reflects on what to conclude from the findings and provides considerable food for thought. Both texts show quite clearly that Asch was interested in both conformity and dissent.

Turner, J.C. (1991) *Social Influence*. Milton Keynes: Open University Press.

If you are interested in social influence processes more broadly and in questions about why people conform, then you need to read Turner's comprehensive overview of the literature.

Moscovici, S. (1976) *Social Influence and Social Change*. New York: Academic Press.

This book by Moscovici has become a classic in the field and reveals Moscovici's frustration with social psychologists' one-sided interest in conformity.

Spears, R. (2010) 'Group rationale, collective sense: Beyond intergroup bias', *British Journal of Social Psychology*, 49: 1–20.

A similar sentiment to Moscovici was voiced more recently by Spears when he ponders why it is that social psychologists insist on seeing the group as a source of bias and irrationality.

Jetten, J. and Hornsey, M.J. (2014) 'Deviance and dissent in groups', *Annual Review of Psychology, 65*: 461–85.

As a counterpoint to the received view, Jetten and Hornsey's *Annual Review of Psychology* article reviews research showing that when it comes to creativity, learning, organizational functioning and so on, dissent, difference, deviance and defiance are just as much a part of group life as conformity and just as essential for good group functioning.

REFERENCES

Abrams, D., Wetherell, M.S., Cochrane, S., Hogg, M.A. and Turner, J.C. (1990) 'Knowing what to think by knowing who you are: Self-categorization and the nature of norm formation, conformity, and group polarization', *British Journal of Social Psychology,* 29: 97–119.

Asch, S.E. (1951) 'Effects of group pressure upon the modification and distortion of judgment', in H. Guetzkow (ed.), *Groups, Leadership and Men.* Pittsburgh, PA: Carnegie Press. pp. 177–90.

Asch, S.E. (1952) *Social Psychology*. Englewood Cliffs, NJ: Prentice-Hall.

Asch, S.E. (1955) 'Opinions and social pressure', *Scientific American,* 193: 31–5.

Bond, R. and Smith, P. (1996) 'Culture and conformity: A meta-analysis of studies using Asch's (1952b, 1956) line judgment task', *Psychological Bulletin*, 119: 111–37.

Crandall, C.S. (1988) 'Social contagion of binge eating', *Journal of Personality and Social Psychology,* 55: 588–98.

Crutchfield, R. (1955) 'Conformity and character', *American Psychologist,* 10: 191–8.

Deutsch, M. and Gerard, H. (1955) 'A study of normative and informational social influences upon individual judgment', *Journal of Abnormal and Social Psychology,* 51: 629–36.

Haslam, S.A. and Reicher, S.D. (2007) 'Beyond the banality of evil: Three dynamics of an interactionist social psychology of tyranny', *Personality and Social Psychology Bulletin,* 33: 615–22.

Hogg, M.A. and Turner, J.C. (1987) 'Social identity and conformity: A theory of referent informational influence', in W. Doise and S. Moscovici (eds), *Current Issues in European Social Psychology*, Vol. 2. Cambridge, UK: Cambridge University Press. pp. 139–82.

Hornsey, M.J., Majkut, L., Terry, D.J. and McKimmie, B.M. (2003) 'On being loud and proud: Non-conformity and counter-conformity to group norms', *British Journal of Social Psychology,* 42, 319–35.

Insko, C.A., Drenan, S., Solomon, M.R., Smith, R. and Wade, T.J. (1983) 'Conformity as a function of the consistency of positive self-evaluation with being liked and being right', *Journal of Experimental Social Psychology,* 19: 341–58.

Jahoda, M. (1959) 'Conformity and independence', *Human Relations,* 12: 99–120.

Jetten, J. and Hornsey, M.J. (eds) (2011) *Rebels in Groups: Dissent, Deviance, Difference and Defiance*. Wiley-Blackwell.

Jetten, J. and Hornsey, M.J. (2014) 'Deviance and dissent in groups', *Annual Review of Psychology, 65*: 46–85.

LaLancette, M.-F. and Standing, L. (1990) 'Asch fails again', *Social Behavior and Personality,* 18: 7–12.

Le Bon, G. (1895) *La Psychologie des foules* (*The Crowd: A Study of the Popular Mind*, 1982, Atlanta: Cherokee Publishing Company).

Moscovici, S. (1976) *Social Influence and Social Change*. New York: Academic Press.

Moscovici, S. (1985) 'Social influence and conformity', in G. Lindzey and E. Aronson (eds), *Handbook of Social Psychology*, Vol. 2. New York: Random House. pp. 347–412.

Perrin, S. and Spencer, C. (1981) 'Independence or conformity in the Asch experiment as a reflection of cultural and situational factors', *British Journal of Social Psychology,* 20: 205–9.

Reicher, S.D. and Haslam, S.A. (2006) 'Rethinking the psychology of tyranny: The BBC Prison Study', *British Journal of Social Psychology*, 45: 1–40.

Ross, L., Bierbrauer, G. and Hoffman, S. (1976) 'The role of attribution processes in conformity and dissent: Revisiting the Asch situation', *American Psychologist,* 31: 148–57.

Spears, R. (2010) 'Group rationale, collective sense: Beyond intergroup bias', *British Journal of Social Psychology*, 49: 1–20.

Turner, J.C. (1991) *Social Influence*. Milton Keynes: Open University Press.

Turner, J.C. (2006) 'Tyranny, freedom and social structure: Escaping our theoretical prisons', *British Journal of Social Psychology*, 45: 41–6.

Walker, M.B. and Andrade, M.G. (1996) 'Conformity in the Asch task as a function of age', *Journal of Social Psychology*, 136: 367–72.

6

Minority Influence

Revisiting Moscovici's blue-green
afterimage studies

Robin Martin and Miles Hewstone

BACKGROUND

Does a majority always overcome a minority, such that people bend their will to the power of the majority, or is it possible for a minority to change the view of the majority? Looking at research on social influence, one might think that the pressures towards conformity mean that the views of the majority will inevitably prevail. Indeed, Asch's classic conformity studies (see Chapter 5) showed that people will publicly agree with the objectively incorrect judgments of a majority on an unambiguous task involving the judgment of line lengths. Moreover, subsequent studies showed that people will conform to the majority for a number of reasons including the desire to be accepted by the majority and therefore not appear to be different (reflecting *social approval*; 'I want to be in the majority group'), and also because people assume that the majority is more likely to be accurate and correct in its judgments than a minority (reflecting *social consensus*: 'Many pairs of eyes must be better than just a few').

Up until the late 1960s, research in social psychology was dominated by a focus on the conditions under which a majority can cause individuals to conform to its position – a phenomenon that the French social psychologist Serge Moscovici referred to as a *conformity bias*. However, from the late 1960s, and due especially to Moscovici's own work, researchers began to ask a different question – can a numerical minority influence the attitudes of the majority? As Moscovici noted in his (1976) book *Social Influence and Social Change* it seems likely that the answer must be 'Yes' for the simple reason that if people only conformed to the majority, then new ideas would never emerge, innovations would never occur, and society would never change. However, history is replete with individuals (e.g., Galileo, Freud), as well as minority groups (e.g., the Suffragettes, the anti-slavery movement), who have advocated views that challenged mainstream attitudes. Furthermore, over time, the views of these minorities clearly changed the ways that the majority thought and acted.

In thinking about social influence more broadly, Moscovici argued that, in focusing so much on majority influence, the conformity bias had led researchers to view social influence as a one-way street, where the minority always falls into line with the majority. However, as the few examples mentioned above clearly demonstrate, it is possible for a minority to change the attitudes and behaviour of the majority. Indeed, in a powerful critique, Moscovici suggested that Asch's studies on majority influence were, in fact, studies of minority influence. That is, when thinking about the wider population outside the laboratory (who would presumably see the lines in the same way as the naïve participant), Asch's studies demonstrate that a small but consistent minority (Asch's confederates) can alter the judgments of a member of the majority.

To test his ideas about minority influence, Moscovici and his colleagues developed a paradigm where participants made judgments about the colour of a slide (Moscovici et al., 1969). In these 'blue-green' experiments, groups of up to six naïve participants sat in front of a screen and viewed a series of blue slides that varied in their light intensity. After each slide, each participant was asked, in turn, to name aloud the colour of that slide. When all the participants had named the colour of the slide, the next slide was presented. Under these conditions, virtually everybody called the slides 'blue', showing that they were perceived as being unambiguously blue. However, in some experimental conditions, a numerical minority within the group (two of the six group members) were confederates of the experimenter and gave pre-agreed responses. In this case they replied 'green' to the slides – a response that was clearly different from that of the naïve participants. Also, as in the Asch studies, the confederates gave their colour judgments aloud before the naïve participants gave theirs. The key finding of the study was that having a minority consistently calling the blue slides 'green' in this way resulted in an increase in the number of times that the naïve answers also called these slides 'green'. Specifically, while less than 1% of participants (actually 0.25%) called them green in a control condition where participants were not exposed to the views of any confederates, now 8.42% did. Contrary to the idea that people always conform to a majority (as might be expected based on the earlier Asch studies), the studies thus show that a numerical minority is able to change the judgments of a majority.

But how can we explain minority influence? Although the blue-green studies demonstrated that minority influence was possible, these studies did not provide any insights into *how* and *why* minority influence occurs. Clearly, the social approval and social consensus accounts that are used to explain majority influence are not very useful in this respect, because joining the minority puts people in a deviant group and at risk of losing social approval. Accordingly, Moscovici suggested that minorities need to exert influence in different ways. Specifically, he suggested that they need to be consistent, confident, and committed in their judgments and, in this way, they encourage members of the majority to question their own views. This then opens up the possibility for influence to occur.

To try to integrate and explain both majority and minority influence, Moscovici developed *conversion theory* (Moscovici, 1980; for reviews see Martin and

Hewstone, 2008; Martin et al., 2008). As represented schematically in Figure 6.1, the cornerstone of conversion theory is that both majorities and minorities can cause influence, but, to some extent, do so via different processes. According to conversion theory, majorities and minorities lead people to focus their attention on different aspects of the situation, which then produces attitude change at different levels of influence. As noted above, when faced with a majority, people want to be part of the majority group to gain social approval and because they assume that it is correct. They therefore go along with the majority position without considering the content of its arguments in detail. This leads to public compliance but without private change. However, when faced with a minority, people want to avoid being seen as part of a deviant group but, at the same time, they are intrigued by the minority's views and want to understand why it holds a different view from the majority. This leads to a detailed consideration of the content of the minority position, to evaluate its arguments, resulting in public rejection but private acceptance and change. It is the different predictions made for majority and minority influence across different levels of influence (public versus private) that form the core theoretical novelty of conversion theory. Majorities are expected to lead to more public than private change, while minorities do the opposite.

At the end-point of this process, research in majority and minority influence makes a distinction between the *manifest* (public) and *latent* (private) levels of influence. The main difference between the manifest and latent levels is the degree to which the participants are consciously aware of the change in their responses. At the manifest level, people are aware that their responses have changed. At the latent level, however, this change may be outside conscious awareness. Going beyond the manifest or public level of influence that had been the focus of previous research (e.g., Asch's line-judgment studies), this analysis therefore leads to the prediction that minority influence is likely to be greater at the latent or private level and, furthermore, that this change will be unconscious to the individual. This leads to the intriguing possibility that people may change their attitudes or behaviour after exposure to a minority position but be unaware that such change has occurred.

This chapter focuses on one set of studies, referred to as the 'afterimage studies', which were the first to examine majority and minority influence beyond

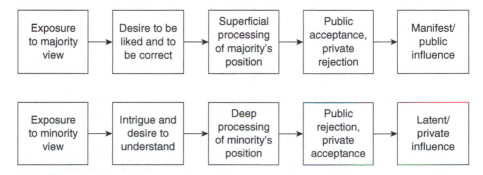

Figure 6.1 A schematic representation of conversion theory

the manifest or public level, at a more latent and unconscious level of influence. This is important because we cannot assume that what people say publicly is what they truly believe. In the case of the Asch studies many people publicly agreed with the majority but when responses were taken in private, and therefore were unknown to majority group members, rates of conformity fell dramatically. Moreover, when asked by Asch to explain their responses in his studies, many participants stated that they knew that the majority was wrong but went along with it out of a fear of appearing different or deviant. In their afterimage studies Moscovici and Personnaz (1980) had the novel idea of setting out to show that, in contrast to a majority, a numerical minority could change the way people see the world (in this case colours) even though they would be unaware of this change. Through the use of a clever methodological technique, the afterimage studies were able to examine people's perceptions of colours beyond what they publicly said but at a more latent and unconscious level.

THE BLUE-GREEN AFTERIMAGE STUDIES

The original blue-green studies described above showed that a consistent minority can change the public judgments given by naïve participants. But these studies were unable to examine the impact of the minority on a more latent/private level of influence. This is because only one type of response was measured, namely the slide colour (manifest influence), and no measure of latent influence was taken. Critically, then, such studies cannot tell us whether participants' private judgments were also affected by the minority.

METHOD

To address this methodological issue, the afterimage paradigm was developed by Moscovici and his colleague Bernard Personnaz (1980). This relied upon a well-known perceptual effect: the perception of complementary chromatic afterimages. When a person stares at a coloured stimulus and then looks at a white background, he or she will briefly perceive a different colour to that of the original stimulus (termed the 'afterimage'). Since afterimages result from the physiological properties of the eyes' rod and cone cells, there is a predictable relationship between the colour of the stimulus and that of the afterimage (Brindley, 1962). You can easily experience this perceptual phenomenon by staring at a blue colour for about 30 seconds and then quickly changing your gaze onto a white sheet of paper. You will notice that a colour will appear briefly on the page, but that it soon decays. The colour that appears on the white page is the afterimage of the initial colour you stare at. For example, if you stare at a blue object, then the afterimage colour should be yellowish.

Applying this principle of afterimage perception to the afterimage studies, if a confederate who calls the blue slide 'green' exerts no influence on other group members, then one would expect participants to perceive afterimages towards the complementary colour of blue (i.e., yellow), no matter what they had said the slide colour was in public. However, if the confederate does actually succeed in changing participants' perception then those participants should perceive an afterimage towards the complementary colour of green (i.e., red/purple). Moscovici and Personnaz (1980) argue that, although the afterimage responses are directly related to slide perception, they are recorded using different responses than those used for the public responses (because the latent responses involve judgments based on colours not mentioned in the public phases of the study). And since participants are presumably unaware of the afterimage effect, then these responses can be considered to represent the latent level of influence. Through this ingenious method it was possible to obtain both manifest (slide colour) and latent (afterimage colour) measures of influence in such a way that participants were not aware of the link between the two.

The afterimage paradigm involved just two participants who were shown a series of blue slides. The slides were projected onto a screen and for each slide the participants were required to make two responses: (a) identifying the colour of the slide (either blue or green) and (b) judging the colour of the slide afterimage. The afterimage judgment was obtained by participants viewing a white screen, after looking at the blue slide, on which an afterimage briefly developed. Afterimage responses were recorded on a nine-point scale (1 = yellow, 2 = yellow/orange, 3 = orange, 4 = orange/red, 5 = red, 6 = red/pink, 7 = pink, 8 = pink/purple, 9 = purple). In fact, the same slide, which was unambiguously blue, was used throughout the experiment.

The experiment had four phases, with each phase consisting of a number of trials or presentations of a slide. As we describe the methodology, you may like to reflect on how you might feel if you were a participant in this study. Having agreed to take part in a study on colour perception you are asked to sit next to someone whom you think is also a naïve participant in the experiment (the participant is actually a confederate of the experimenter, and in his original studies Moscovici used female participants and a female confederate).[1] Together with the other participant you sit facing the screen and are told that a series of slides will be shown on the screen, and that you will be asked to indicate the colour of the slide and the afterimage. The procedure for forming the afterimage and the nature of the response format is explained to you.

The first phase (Pre-influence) then commences and consists of five trials in which the slide and afterimage judgments are recorded in private on a response form. Before Phase 2 (Influence) commences, you are informed of the responses of previous participants in the experiment. In the majority condition, you are told that 81.2% of previous participants saw the slide as green and that 18.2% saw it as blue (the percentages were reversed in the minority condition). This feedback is in fact fictitious, but it serves to associate a 'green' response with either a numerical majority or a minority position.

---

[1]Interestingly, Moscovici argued that he preferred to use women as confederates and participants in his blue-green studies 'because of their greater involvement in evaluating the colour of an object' (Moscovici et al., 1969: 368).

Phase 2 commences and consists of 15 trials in which you and the other participant are asked to say aloud only the judgment of the slide colour (no after-images are formed at this point). In the experimental conditions (majority or minority) the participant next to you, who always gives their response aloud first, responds 'green' to every slide – clearly at odds with the fact that the slide is unambiguously blue. What would be your reaction to your co-participant calling the obviously blue slides 'green'? Disbelief? Confusion? Suspicion? And would your reaction be different if you believed that a green response was shared by a numerical majority or minority of previous participants?

Phase 3 (Post-influence I: Confederate present) consists of another 15 trials in which you are asked to give both the slide and afterimage judgments with responses recorded in private (only five trials were used in Experiment 2). Before commencing the final phase, the confederate informs the experimenter that she has to leave because of an important appointment. This is planned, in order to leave you alone to respond to the final set of slides, because it is thought you might be more likely to agree with the confederate when she is not present. Therefore, Phase 4 (Post-influence II: Confederate absent) consists of you completing a further five trials alone so that your responses for both slide and afterimage are made in private. At the end of the study, you are fully debriefed about the procedure and the role of the confederate in the experiment.

In reflecting on how you might have felt if you were a participant in one of these studies it is useful to highlight a number of points. First, the study is presented to the participants as one concerning color perception and not majority or minority influence. Therefore, participants were not expecting to be influenced by anyone. Also at no time did the experimenter or confederate try to convince the naïve participant to change their responses. Second, the naïve participant did not know that the confederate was giving predetermined responses to the slides. The confederates were highly trained and acted like normal participants. Third, when the study started no communication was allowed between the participants so it was not possible to question the confederate's responses. Fourth, the confederate only gave the 'green' answers aloud in the second phase of the study and so there was no attempt to influence the naïve participant in the other phases. It might be tempting to think that the naïve participant was not fooled by this procedure but, as with the Asch study, the combination of the experimental procedures and well-trained confederates leads to a highly realistic situation. The first author of this chapter, who has conducted several studies with this paradigm, can attest that very few people question the authenticity of the confederate (and if they do, they are eliminated from the study).

RESULTS

Now let us turn to the results of the two experiments described by Moscovici and Personnaz (1980). The first experiment consisted of three conditions: majority source, minority source, and control. The control condition was the same as the source conditions except that it involved two naïve participants and no response feedback was given. The results for the perceived colour of the slide (manifest response) showed that in the first phase (Pre-influence) all the participants reported the slide as being blue, confirming the unambiguous nature of the stimulus. In the second phase (Influence), the number of 'green' responses rose slightly to 5%, but there was not a reliable difference between the experimental conditions. In fact, these results do not support Moscovici's (1980) conversion theory, which predicts that a majority leads to compliance to its position, such that there should be a greater number of 'green' responses in the majority condition than in the minority and control conditions.

For the afterimage scores, which represent the latent response, the pattern of means was consistent with conversion theory. As predicted, and as can be seen in Figure 6.2, there was a significant shift in afterimage judgments towards the complementary colour of green in the minority condition between Pre-influence and both Post-influence phases. In other words, the participants reported the colour of the afterimage as being nearer the complementary colour of green when they believed that such a response was shared by a minority of people. In addition, there were no reliable shifts in the perceived afterimage in either the majority or the control conditions. The latter findings are important, as they show that the changes in the afterimages were only observed when the confederate's response was believed to represent a numerical minority position and not when it represented a numerical majority position – even though the confederate gave the same response in each condition.

Figure 6.2 Afterimage scores as a function of condition and phase (based on Moscovici and Personnaz, 1980, Experiment 1)

Note: Scores on nine-point scale with higher scores indicating a judgment closer to the complement of green (red-purple). Moscovici and Personnaz (1980) report mean standardized scores; these raw means were obtained from Moscovici (1980).

These findings were replicated in a second experiment. Once again, there was a significant change in afterimage judgments towards the complement of green for those in the minority condition, but not for those in the majority condition.

To summarize, these afterimage studies suggest that a numerical minority was able to produce a genuine change in perception, as shown by changes in afterimage scores. However, a numerical majority was not able to produce the same perceptual change. In this way, the results for the latent measure (afterimage colour) seem to provide support for the claim that a minority can produce change on a latent/unconscious level. The studies thus not only provided additional evidence for the idea that minorities can influence the majority (thereby extending Moscovici et al.'s 1969 initial blue-green studies), but also provided the first evidence to support the idea that majorities and minorities exerted influence through different processes that lead to different outcomes.

IMPACT OF THE BLUE-GREEN AFTERIMAGE STUDIES

The original Moscovici and Personnaz (1980) paper has had a massive impact in the study of group consensus and minority influence and is one of the most cited articles in this area. There appear to be four main reasons why the studies have had such impact.

First, the results are counterintuitive, and they challenge many assumptions concerning social influence and provide a stark counterpoint to the conformity bias that characterized much early research and theorizing about social influence. Moreover, the claim that numerical minorities can change perception, if true, would appear to have major implications for understanding not only social influence processes, but also the physiological processes involved in colour perception. Indeed, the authors of one leading text on group processes describe the results of the afterimage studies as 'Astounding! Astonishing! Implausible?' (Baron et al., 1992: 81). As this quotation suggests, the studies have had a mixed reaction amongst social psychologists, as evident in an anonymous review of one of our own research papers (Martin, 1998) that questioned aspects of the original Moscovici and Personnaz (1980) study thus: 'As an unconvinced sceptic, I welcome new research which drives new stakes into the heart of an old vampire ... that refuses to die.'

Second, the methodology that these studies developed was ingenious, and the afterimage studies have been a catalyst for other researchers to examine conversion effects. The afterimage studies also encouraged researchers to develop other new paradigms in order to examine the impact of minorities beyond the public/manifest level to a 'deeper' or latent level of influence that is beyond conscious knowledge (e.g., Alvaro and Crano, 1997). It additionally led to a much better understanding of how to develop manifest and latent measures of influence (see Martin and Hewstone, 2001).

Third, as noted by Brewer and Crano (1994), the results of replications of the Moscovici and Personnaz (1980) study 'are as interesting as they are controversial' (1994: 395), in part because they have proved inconsistent. Subsequent research has sometimes, but not always, found afterimage shifts that are similar to those observed in the Moscovici and Personnaz (1980) experiments, but not exclusively for a minority source (as described below).

Fourth, the paper reporting these results was published in the same year as Moscovici's (1980) conversion theory and – although the afterimage studies are not the only evidence that supports this – their findings are in many ways the most emblematic of what has become a highly influential analysis of social influence (Martin et al., 2008).

BEYOND THE BLUE-GREEN AFTERIMAGE STUDIES

ALTERNATIVE INTERPRETATIONS

A number of alternative interpretations have been put forward for the results of the afterimage studies that revolve around factors (other than source status) that can lead to increased attention to the slides and therefore changes in afterimage judgments. This section considers three interpretations that seek to explain why participants might pay greater attention to the slides – these focus on (a) unexpected responses from confederates, (b) participant suspicion and (c) repeated slide exposure.

UNEXPECTED RESPONSES

In a direct replication of the afterimage studies, Machteld Doms and Eddy Van Avermaet (1980) found afterimage shifts towards the complementary colour of green for *both* a majority and minority. These researchers also included a 'no information' condition in which the confederate called the slides 'green' but no feedback (percentage) information was given (i.e., the confederate's responses were not linked to a majority or minority position). Interestingly, there was no shift in afterimages across the phases in the no-information condition. Since afterimage shifts only occurred when the deviant response (calling slides 'green') was associated with a source position, this led Doms and Van Avermaet to suggest that the shifts might be part of a general tendency to pay closer attention to stimuli when a response is unexpected or unusual. They claim that this did not happen in the no-information condition because the confederate's response was not supported by anyone else and therefore might have been seen as biased and invalid. However, while there may be a general tendency to increase attention following an unexpected response, this cannot explain why Moscovici and Personnaz (1980) did not find afterimage shifts in the majority condition, in which participants also received the unexpected response.

Participant suspicion

In a partial replication of Moscovici and Personnaz (1980), Richard Sorrentino and colleagues (1980) examined only minority influence. After their study they asked participants to rate how suspicious they were of the experimental procedure. Interestingly, they found afterimage shifts towards the complementary colour of green only for those participants who were highly suspicious of the experiment (see also Martin, 1998). In their explanation, these researchers suggest that highly suspicious participants may stare more intensely at the stimulus than unsuspicious participants do, and that the shift in afterimages may be due to this greater attention to the stimulus. The researchers also report separate data from an informal study on the impact of slide intensity on afterimages, to suggest a link between intensity of attention to the slide and afterimage shifts. However, Sorrentino and colleagues (1980) only took judgments of how suspicious participants were after the study, and it is not known whether participant suspicion led to changes in afterimage judgments or whether participants' perceptions of changes in afterimage judgments led to increased suspicion.

Repeated slide exposure

In our own work, we have drawn attention to the fact that all the afterimage studies analyse changes in the overall afterimage response between each phase of the experiment but do not examine changes *within* each phase (Martin, 1998; see also Martin, 1995). Across five afterimage experiments, Martin (1998) found a significant within-phase shift in afterimage judgments in all the phases (see also Laurens and Moscovici, 2005), an effect that was more pronounced for participants who reported being suspicious of the study. This effect indicated that participants' afterimage judgments shifted towards the complementary colour of green (i.e., red) over progressive trials within each phase of the experiment (see also Laurens and Moscovici, 2005).

Why the within-phase effect occurs is not fully known, but Martin (1998) has suggested that it may be due to a perceptual phenomenon that arises from repeated exposure to the same stimulus in the context of afterimage methodology. Specifically, a basic study consists of different phases that require changing levels of brightness – starting by viewing the slides and then moving to less bright situations when the participants receive instructions for the next phase. It is possible that between phases the participants' eyes adapt to the less bright environment so that when they first look at the bright slide they subsequently perceive fainter (and lighter) afterimages that, in the case of a blue stimulus, would lead to afterimages closer to the complement of blue (yellow). Over time, as the eyes adapt, participants begin to perceive darker afterimages that, in this case, would be towards the complementary colour of green (red-purple). Thus, the effects of changing light conditions and repeated slide exposure can give the illusion of afterimage shifts towards the complementary colour of green without any influence having occurred at all.

These three explanations are distinct, but not mutually exclusive. Indeed, they could all be at work in these studies. Together, they raise many concerns about the original Moscovici and Personnaz (1980) results and demonstrate that afterimage shifts can occur as a consequence of a number of methodological factors that are unrelated to whether the source of influence is a majority or minority. Importantly, though, obtaining afterimage shifts towards the complementary colour of green by various manipulations does not, alone, disprove the claim that numerical minorities can also bring about change on a latent and unconscious level.

METHODOLOGICAL ISSUES

The foregoing discussion alerts us to a number of methodological issues associated with the afterimage studies. Before we consider some of these, we should highlight the point that Moscovici and Personnaz were themselves aware of these. Thus, in the first set of studies that used this paradigm they remarked that 'the phenomenon we describe is more suggestive than it is firmly established' (1980: 274).

LACK OF EFFECT ON MANIFEST RESPONSES

A criticism of the afterimage studies is that virtually no evidence has been found for influence at the manifest or public level – that is, in participants' perception of the colour of the slides. Most studies report that on only very few occasions do participants agree with the confederate that the slide is green. However, it should be noted that the paradigm was primarily designed to examine latent/private influence, and there is robust support from other research that majorities have a greater impact on the manifest/public level (Martin and Hewstone, 2008).

SOURCE MANIPULATION

In the afterimage studies, source status (majority vs. minority) is manipulated by false feedback from previous participants' responses. Given that the confederate's responses are likely to be seen as extremely unusual (calling blue slides 'green'), it would seem to be extremely difficult to convince participants in the majority condition that over 80% of people also see the slides as green. Indeed, this might be the reason why those in the majority condition did not show reliable levels of conformity at the manifest level (slide judgment). In this regard it should be noted that Moscovici and Personnaz's (1980) experiments do not include a source manipulation check to establish how many participants agreed with the intended manipulation of the size of the source, nor were participants asked how credible this information was.

MEASUREMENT ISSUES

Sorrentino and his colleagues (1980) have criticized the afterimage judgment scale employed by Moscovici and Personnaz (1980) in terms of the labels it employed (see also Laurens, 2001). In their variant, they instead asked participants to select a coloured chip that best matched the colour they saw. No evidence of conversion due to minority influence was found with this method. Another attempt to try to improve the measurement of perceived slide and afterimage colour has been the use of a spectrometer, which is able to measure the wavelength of light (Personnaz, 1981). However, one procedural difficulty with this technique is that it requires participants to move their gaze from the slide to the white screen (to form an after-image) and then to the spectrometer to make a judgment for a perceptual phenomenon that forms very rapidly and decays quickly. Nevertheless, Personnaz's spectrometer study is one of the few studies to have replicated the original after-image effects with a different measure of the latent response.

MANIFEST–LATENT RESPONSE CRITERIA

In order to test the relative impact of majorities and minorities on manifest and latent responses, it is important to overcome the problem of response generaliza-tion or inhibition across the two types of responses. Martin and Hewstone (2001) identified three important criteria that need to be satisfied in order to establish manifest and latent responses:

1. There needs to be a link between the manifest and latent response dimension, such that change on the manifest response results in a corresponding change in the latent response (*manifest–latent correspondence*). No afterimage study has reported the relationship between the slide (manifest) and afterimage (latent) scores, presumably because of the lack of influence on slide judgments.

2. The relationship between the manifest and latent response should be consistent and insensitive to situational factors (*manifest–latent consistency*). As discussed earlier, afterimage perception varies as a function of repeated exposure, with scores moving towards the complementary colour of green over successive trials (within each phase). These problems make it difficult to disentangle changes in afterimage scores due to the independent variables (in this case source status) from those arising from situational or procedural factors.

3. Participants should not be aware of the link between the manifest and latent responses, and ideally they should use different response codes (*manifest–latent perceived independence*). Even if participants were unaware of the afterimage effect before the study began (which should be measured at Pre-influence), they would surely become aware of the link between slide and afterimage during the study. Given the short time between slide presentation and afterimage perception it is clear that the former causes the latter (in fact, as the projector is switched off there is nothing else that could cause the afterimage).

Having established these three criteria, it is interesting to note that Moscovici and Personnaz's original afterimage studies, and subsequent replications, have failed to meet all three. Indeed, the studies' methodological shortcomings can be seen to lie at the heart of much of the controversy that this line of research has fuelled – to the extent that they have overshadowed the original theoretical contribution they sought to develop.

CONCLUSION

I n a major review of the afterimage studies that we conducted some time ago we stated that they 'continue to amaze and puzzle researchers' (Martin and Hewstone, 2001: 17). Not least this is because, to the best of our knowledge, no subsequent research has fully replicated the pattern of results of the original studies. Furthermore, a number of reasonably convincing alternative explanations have been put forward to explain their (and other) findings. On balance, then, there is little to support the view that the afterimage studies demonstrate that a numerical minority is able to cause a perceptual change on a latent level. It should be noted, however, that while the studies are often cited as some of the best evidence in favour of conversion theory, they are certainly not the only source of empirical support, and overall the theory is well supported by other avenues of research (for a review, see Martin et al., 2008).

Nonetheless, we believe that the afterimage studies represent an iconic series of studies that have shaped the development of the research area in two important aspects. First, they were pioneering studies that examined minority influence at a latent and unconscious level and, in doing so, they encouraged the development of new paradigms to explore these effects. Second, because they were developed to test conversion theory, they have encouraged researchers to pay greater attention to the underlying psychological processes involved in majority and minority influence – and this focus remains at the very core of research into this topic (see Martin and Hewstone, 2008).

The studies are thus a powerful reminder of the fact that science does not always progress in a linear fashion, with the discovery of one truth leading straightforwardly on to the next. For progress to occur, it is not always essential that paradigms are perfect, that data are neat and tidy, or even that initial results prove reliable. Instead, then, science progresses through powerful ideas that create an appetite for new paradigms and data that challenge existing preconceptions and serve a valuable heuristic function in making us rethink our assumptions (Hewstone and Martin, 2010). Moscovici and Personnaz's (1980) studies did just that, making social influence researchers think harder about what they were pro-posing, and what they expected to see, even if they themselves did not always agree. In this respect, the legacy of Moscovici's work is perhaps the most powerful testimony to the reality of minority influence and to its potential to have latent and enduring influence.

FURTHER READING

Moscovici, S. (1980) 'Towards a theory of conversion behavior', in L. Berkowitz (ed.), *Advances in Experimental Social Psychology*, Vol. 13. London: Academic Press. pp. 209–39.

Here Moscovici outlines the basics of conversion theory and the different processes involved in both majority and minority influence, and presents supporting evidence, including the afterimage studies.

Moscovici, S. and Personnaz, B. (1980) 'Studies in social influence: V. Minority influence and conversion behavior in a perceptual task', *Journal of Experimental Social Psychology*, 16: 270–82.

Moscovici and Personnaz review in detail the two studies described in this chapter. It is also interesting to look at this paper in relation to the two replications published in the same volume of the *Journal of Experimental Psychology* (Doms and Van Avermaet, 1980; Sorrentino et al., 1980) and to read the 'note added in proof' by Moscovici and Personnaz (1980: 282) in which they attempt to explain the difference in results between their experiments and those of these other researchers.

Martin, R. (1998) 'Majority and minority influence using the afterimage paradigm: A series of attempted replications', *Journal of Experimental Social Psychology*, 34: 1–26.

Martin offers the most comprehensive testing of the afterimage paradigm across five experiments, and presents evidence that afterimage judgments change within phases.

Personnaz, M. and Personnaz, B. (1994) 'Perception and conversion', in S. Moscovici, A. Mucchi-Faina and A. Maass (eds), *Minority Influence*. Chicago: Nelson-Hall. pp. 165–83.

This paper discusses many studies, several of which are unpublished, to claim that afterimage shifts can occur via a number of mechanisms associated with minority influence.

Martin, R. and Hewstone, M. (2001) 'After-thoughts on after-images: A review of the literature using the afterimage paradigm in majority and minority influence', in C. De Dreu and N. De Vries (eds), *Group Innovation: Fundamental and Applied Perspectives*. Oxford: Blackwell. pp. 15–39.

Martin and Hewstone (2001) are more critical of the paradigm, but their review notes that the afterimage studies have played a central role in shaping research in this area.

REFERENCES

Alvaro, E.M. and Crano, W.D. (1997) 'Indirect minority influence: Evidence for leniency in source evaluation and counter-argumentation', *Journal of Personality and Social Psychology*, 72: 949–65.

Baron, R.S., Kerr, N. and Miller, N. (1992) *Group Process, Group Decision, Group Action*. Buckingham: Open University Press.

Brewer, M.B. and Crano, W. (1994) *Social Psychology*. St Paul, MN: West Publishing.

Brindley, S.G. (1962) 'Two new properties of foveal afterimages and a photochemical hypothesis to explain them', *Journal of Physiology*, 164: 168–79.

Doms, M. and Van Avermaet, E. (1980) 'Majority influence, minority influence and conversion behavior: A replication', *Journal of Experimental Social Psychology*, 16: 283–92.

Hewstone, M. and Martin, R. (2010) 'Minority influence: From groups to attitudes and back again', in R. Martin and M. Hewstone (eds), *Minority Influence*. Hove, E. Sussex: Psychology Press (Taylor & Francis). pp. 365–94.

Laurens, S. (2001) 'Logique cachée du paradigme bleu/vert', *Bulletin de Psychologie*, 54: 383–8.

Laurens, S. and Moscovici, S. (2005) 'The confederate's and others' self-conversion: A neglected phenomenon', *Journal of Social Psychology*, 145: 191–207.

Martin, R. (1995) 'Majority and minority influence using the afterimage paradigm: A replication with an unambiguous blue slide', *European Journal of Social Psychology*, 25: 373–81.

Martin, R. (1998) 'Majority and minority influence using the afterimage paradigm: A series of attempted replications', *Journal of Experimental Social Psychology*, 34: 1–26.

Martin, R. and Hewstone, M. (2001) 'After-thoughts on after-images: A review of the literature using the afterimage paradigm in majority and minority influence', in C. De Dreu and N. De Vries (eds), *Group Innovation: Fundamental and Applied Perspectives*. Oxford: Blackwell. pp. 15–39.

Martin, R. and Hewstone, M. (2008) 'Majority versus minority influence, message processing and attitude change: The Source-Context-Elaboration Model', in M. Zanna (ed.), *Advances in Experimental Social Psychology*, 40: 237–326.

Martin, R., Hewstone, M., Martin, P.Y. and Gardikiotis, A. (2008) 'Persuasion from majority and minority groups', in W. Crano and R. Prislin (eds), *Attitudes and Attitude Change*. New York: Psychology Press. pp. 361–84.

Moscovici, S. (1976) *Social Influence and Social Change*. London: Academic Press.

Moscovici, S. (1980) 'Towards a theory of conversion behavior', in L. Berkowitz (ed.), *Advances in Experimental Social Psychology*, Vol. 13. London: Academic Press. pp. 209–39.

Moscovici, S., Lage, E. and Naffrechoux, M. (1969) 'Influence of a consistent minority on the response of a majority in a color perception task', *Sociometry*, 32: 365–80.

Moscovici, S. and Personnaz, B. (1980) 'Studies in social influence: V. Minority influence and conversion behavior in a perceptual task', *Journal of Experimental Social Psychology*, 16: 270–82.

Personnaz, B. (1981) 'Study in social influence using the spectrometer method: Dynamics of the phenomena of conversion and covertness in perceptual responses', *European Journal of Social Psychology*, 11: 431–8.

Sorrentino, R.M., King, G. and Leo, G. (1980) 'The influence of the minority on perception: A note on a possible alternative explanation', *Journal of Experimental Social Psychology*, 16: 293–301.

7

Obedience

Revisiting Milgram's shock experiments

**Stephen Reicher and
S. Alexander Haslam**

BACKGROUND

In 1961 our understanding of the human capacity for evil was utterly transformed by two events. One took place in the Jerusalem District Court, the other in a Psychology Laboratory at Yale University. Although very different, over time, researchers' understandings of these two events were fused into a unified model of evil that dominated popular and scientific thinking for half a century.

Hannah Arendt on Adolf Eichmann

First, in early April, Adolf Eichmann walked into a courtroom in Jerusalem. Eichmann had been Head of the Reich Main Security Office Sub-Department IV-B4 during the Second World War. This was the department that dealt with Jewish Affairs and 'evacuation'. In other words, Eichmann was the person who arranged the deportation of Jews to the Nazi death camps. He was the chief bureaucrat of the Holocaust (see Cesarani, 2005, for a detailed biography).

After the war, Eichmann fled to Argentina where he lived under the name of Ricardo Klement. But in 1959 the Israeli intelligence agency, Mossad, learned of his whereabouts. On 11 May 1960 he was kidnapped and smuggled to Israel in the uniform of an El Al flight attendant. After an intensive interrogation, Eichmann was indicted on 15 charges, notably crimes against humanity, crimes against the Jewish people, and war crimes. On 11 April 1961, the date the trial began, he was seen in public for the first time.

For those sitting and waiting in the courtroom, Eichmann's appearance was a shock. They had expected to see a strutting, arrogant Nazi officer. For surely someone who had committed such monstrous acts would be a monster himself – someone quite extraordinary and clearly different from ordinary decent folk. But what they saw instead was a rather non-descript character. Eichmann was slightly hunched, balding, insignificant. He sat in his bulletproof booth fastidiously taking notes. He looked to all the world like an unexceptional bureaucrat.

One of those sitting in the audience on that day was Hannah Arendt, a famous German-Jewish historian and philosopher who had previously written several important texts on totalitarianism. But these were to be eclipsed by the reports she wrote of the trial for *The New Yorker* – later to be published in book form as *Eichmann in Jerusalem* (Arendt, 1963/1991). More specifically, her impact was concentrated into a three-word phrase that she employed in the sub-title of the book, but only once in the book itself, to encapsulate the lesson that she learned from Eichmann at his trial: 'the lesson of the word-and-thought-defying *banality of evil*' (1963/1994: 252, emphasis added).

What Arendt meant by the 'banality of evil' was not that the acts of Nazis like Eichmann were banal, but rather that the perpetrators *themselves* were – and that they were acting on the basis of banal motives. Eichmann and his ilk, she suggested, were moved less by great hatreds than by the petty desire to do a task well and to please their superiors. Indeed, they concentrated so much on these tasks that they forgot about their consequences. As Arendt put it, Eichmann 'had no motives at all. He merely, to put the matter colloquially, never realized what he was doing' (1963/1994: 287).

This idea – that ordinary people can commit extraordinary acts of evil through sheer thoughtlessness and inattention – was profoundly shocking and deeply controversial. But it gained credibility through support from an altogether different form of evidence.

STANLEY MILGRAM ON OBEDIENCE

The Eichmann trial closed on 14 August 1961. Exactly a week before, on 7 August, Stanley Milgram began his famous obedience experiments at Yale University. Milgram was born in 1933, the year Hitler came to power, to Jewish parents of East European origins (see Blass, 2004, for a rich and detailed biography). The Holocaust loomed large throughout his youth, and during the war the family followed events in Europe closely. In a speech at his Bar-Mitzvah (the traditional Jewish coming-of-age ceremony) in 1946, the young Stanley declared: 'As I come of age and find happiness in joining the ranks of Israel, the knowledge of the tragic suffering of my fellow Jews throughout war-torn Europe makes this also a solemn event and an occasion to reflect upon the heritage of my people – which now becomes mine' (cited in Blass, 2004: 8).

This heritage and the questions it raised were evident in Milgram's academic work. He started his research career by looking at the phenomenon of conformity. He was particularly interested in whether different nations – Germans in particular – differed in their degree of conformity. But he was dissatisfied with the traditional way that such research was conducted. It tended to address fairly trivial instances of conformity. Most notably, Solomon Asch (1956) had conducted studies to see if people would change their judgments of physical stimuli (such as the length of lines) in order to fit in with the views of a majority (see Chapter 5). As Milgram himself put it:

I was dissatisfied that the test of conformity was judgment about *lines*. I wondered whether groups could pressure a person into performing an act whose human import was readily apparent, perhaps behaving aggressively toward another person. (cited in Blass, 2004: 62)

But then, Milgram asked, what might happen even if there was no group but only instructions from an experimenter: 'Just how far would a person go under the experimenter's orders?' As Milgram later remarked, 'It was an incandescent moment' (Blass, 2004: 62). The reason for this was that it was at this point that he conceived of the design for his studies of obedience to authority.

As described in more detail below, the basic set-up for these studies involved a learning experiment in which the participant found himself in the role of a 'teacher' who had to administer ever-increasing levels of electric shock to a 'learner' each time the learner gave a wrong answer. In fact, the learner was a confederate who had been carefully trained to play the role, and the impressive shock machine that appeared to deliver shocks of increasing magnitude was also bogus – but the teacher (the only true participant in the study) did not know this. For him (and all participants in the early study were male) the situation was very real indeed.

Milgram initially intended to examine national differences in the level of shock that people would be prepared to inflict. He would start out in America, but then examine the phenomenon in other countries. The United States would form a baseline. After all, who could seriously expect ordinary Americans to inflict great harm on someone simply because an experimenter told them to? Indeed, to confirm this point, Milgram asked 110 respondents – groups of psychiatrists, college students and middle-class adults – to predict what they would do under these circumstances. You may want to ask yourself the same question. How far would you go? Would you be prepared to administer a 'strong shock' of 135 volts? What about an 'intense shock' of 225 volts? Or would you go as far as 'danger severe shock' at 375 volts?

Among Milgram's respondents, most said that they would break off before the shock level became particularly painful or harmful. As Milgram noted in his 1974 book *Obedience to Authority* (his classic account of the studies), not a single person said they would go up to the maximum level of 450 volts.

Yet when Milgram conducted pilot studies with Yale University students this was not what happened. Most of the participants in what became known as the baseline condition proved willing to obey the experimenter all the way to the bitter end. Indeed, in the very first pilot study that he ran, *all* the students went up to 450 volts. As Stanley's wife Alexandra recalls, at first Milgram simply dismissed this as something to do with 'Yalies' (A. Milgram, 2000). However, when the study was repeated with ordinary Americans a sizeable proportion of them also proved willing to administer shocks right up to the 450-volt level. Milgram sat up and took note. For he realized he had discovered the 'phenomenon of great consequence' of which he had always dreamed (Blass, 2004: 62). And now he proceeded to 'worry it to death' – that is, to investigate the precise circumstances that would (and would not) produce such obedience. He never did get round to looking at national differences in obedience. It was enough that he had demonstrated in the laboratory what Arendt claimed to have observed in the courtroom: that ordinary people can inflict extraordinary harm on their fellow human beings. What is more, like Arendt (by whom he was heavily influenced), he concluded that this comes about because people pay more attention to the task of carrying out instructions than to the actual consequences of that task. In other words, they are concerned only to follow – not to ask where they are being led.

THE JOINT IMPACT OF ARENDT AND MILGRAM

Both Arendt's historical study and Milgram's psychological studies have had tremendous impact on their own. For example, in 2011 *The Guardian* newspaper in Britain included *Eichmann in Jerusalem* in their 100 greatest non-fiction books of all time. And according to Muzafer Sherif (whose own classic studies are discussed in Chapters 4 and 9), 'Milgram's obedience experiment is the single greatest contribution to human knowledge ever made by the field of social psychology, perhaps psychology in general' (cited in Takooshian, 2000: 10). The studies were extensively covered in the *New York Times*, they have been featured in television documentaries in several countries, and they have even been made into a television play with William Shatner – Captain Kirk from the original *Star Trek* – as the Milgram-like lead. In 2015 they were also the basis for the film *Experimenter* (with Peter Sarsgaard in the role of Milgram and Winona Ryder as his wife), which was premiered to critical acclaim at the Sundance Film Festival.

But although each of these contributions has been influential on their own, it is the combination of Arendt and Milgram's ideas that has been most powerful. Arendt's history of Eichmann and the Holocaust provides social relevance for Milgram's studies. Milgram's studies provide scientific credibility for Arendt's specific claims. The two strands weave together to make what has often appeared to be an uncontestable model of the psychology of human atrocities. This suggests that all of us are capable of becoming perpetrators of evil because this results more from inattention than from intention. As Peter Novick puts it in his analysis of *The Holocaust in American Life*:

> From the sixties on, a kind of synergy developed between the symbol of Arendt's Eichmann and the symbol of Milgram's subjects, invoked in discussing everything from the Vietnam War to the tobacco industry, and, of course, reflecting back on discussions of the Holocaust. (2000: 137)

THE OBEDIENCE STUDIES

Milgram's obedience studies are great drama as well as great science (Reicher and Haslam, 2011a). Anyone who watches Milgram's famous film of the studies – itself entitled *Obedience* – will be gripped as they see participants agonizing over what to do, remonstrating and arguing with the experimenter, torn between their obligations to him and their awareness of what they are doing to the learner. This is not accidental. For as well as being a brilliant psychologist, Milgram was an accomplished artist. He wrote children's stories, he composed musicals, and he was a keen film-maker (Millard, 2011, 2014). Moreover, Milgram very carefully calibrated the obedience studies through a series of pilots in order to create just the right amount of dramatic tension. For instance, he carefully selected confederates who would act as the 'experimenter' and the 'learner' in the studies so that the former was stern and intellectual, the latter 'mild and submissive [and] not at all academic' – indeed 'perfect as a victim' (cited in Russell, 2011: 159). This combination, he believed, would make it more likely that people would be willing to inflict shocks.

At the same time, Milgram did not want to make obedience too straightforward. In the pilot study that we mentioned above, participants inflicted shocks without ever seeing the 'learner' or ever getting any form of feedback from them — simply pressing the switches on the shock generator without seeing or hearing the consequences. In this study, almost every participant went 'blithely' up to the maximum shock level (Milgram, 1965a). But the lack of any force countervailing *against* the pressure to deliver shocks removed any tension in the studies and made them uninteresting to Milgram.

Equally, Milgram was deeply concerned with the *look* of the studies. In particular, he designed the shock generator very carefully. It was very important that it looked imposing and professional. An early version with only 12 switches, and a 30-volt gap between each, was replaced with the model containing 30 switches and 15-volt gap between them. The idea was that this would make it easier for people to progress through the sequence. Tellingly, the labels associated with the different shock levels were also modified. Originally, the 450-volt switch was labelled 'Lethal'. But this was felt to be too stark and too off-putting, so it was later replaced by the ominous, but more ambiguous 'XXX' (Russell, 2011).

After all these careful modifications, Milgram had a credible and compelling paradigm. But it is important to recognize that this was the outcome of a long and careful process of balancing the forces that make it easier to obey the experimenter with those that make it easier to heed the learner. The dramatic brilliance of the studies lies precisely in the fact that both elements were addressed and neither was allowed to dominate the other.

Figure 7.1 Diagram of the control panel on the shock generator (from Milgram, 1974: 28)

METHOD AND RESULTS

In addition to all the pilot studies, 18 different studies are listed in *Obedience to Authority* (Milgram, 1974), but there were also a number of other variants that he did not report there, and which have come to light more recently as researchers have gained access to the rich Milgram archive in the Sterling Library at Yale which contains, amongst other things, audio recordings of the experiment, Milgram's notebooks, and the post-experimental responses of participants (e.g., see Rochat and Blass, 2014). The different variants of the paradigm vary in a number of ways, including how many experimenters there were, whether the participant was alone or delivered shocks in the company of others, whether the learner was shocked against his will or actually demanded to be shocked. We will return to some of the variants later. However, it is probably clearest to start by outlining the best known or 'new baseline' condition (Milgram, 1974, Study 5). Then we can consider some of the most significant variants.

THE 'BASELINE' CONDITION

Participants for all studies were recruited through an advertisement in the local paper. It read: 'We will pay five hundred New Haven men to help us complete a scientific study of memory and learning.' Of those who volunteered 40% were blue-collar workers, 40% were white-collar workers, and 20% were professionals. They were invited to come to the elegant Interaction Laboratory of Yale University (although in some subsequent conditions, the study took part in shabby offices in the nearby industrial city of Bridgeport). When they arrived, two other people were present. One was the 'experimenter', who was dressed in a grey technician's coat. The other was supposedly another volunteer (although actually he was a confederate). The experimenter explained that the study was concerned with the effect of punishment – electric shocks – on learning. Accordingly, one of the participants would serve as a 'teacher' and the other as a 'learner'. A draw was then made to decide who would take which role – but this was rigged to ensure that the volunteer was always the teacher and the confederate was always the learner. Next, the teacher and learner were taken to another room and the learner was strapped into a chair and electrodes were attached to his body. The experimenter declared that 'although the shocks can be extremely painful, they cause no permanent tissue damage' (Milgram, 1974: 19).

The learning task involved word pairs. First, the teacher read out a series of such pairs (e.g., blue–box). Then, in the 'testing phase' he read a target word from one of the pairs (in this example, blue) along with four other words (e.g., sky, ink, box, lamp). The learner then had to say which of these four words was originally paired with the target (in this instance, box). If the learner gave a wrong answer, the teacher had to deliver an electric shock by depressing one of the switches on the shock generator, moving one level higher with every error. There were 30 switches, increasing 15 volts at a time up to a maximum of 450 volts. If participants continued all the way to the maximum level, they were instructed to continue at this level of shock for subsequent errors. After two more trials, the experiment was terminated.

This basic structure is just the start. Both the learner and the experimenter had carefully devised scripts to follow during the experiment. In the baseline condition, as the learner was being strapped into the electric chair, he mentioned that he had a slight heart condition. Then, during the task itself, he made specific responses at different shock levels. Despite the learner being in another room, these responses could be heard clearly by the teacher. They start at 75 volts with an expression of pain. At 150 volts the learner first demands to leave the study. He exclaims 'Get me out of here, please! My heart's starting to bother me. I refuse to go on. Let me out.' He intensifies his protestations over time and refers to his heart condition again at 195 and 330 volts. At 300 volts the learner screams 'I absolutely refuse to answer any more!' and repeats three times 'Get me out of here.' After 330 volts he stops responding or making any sound (for full details see Milgram, 1974: 56–7).

The script for the experimenter had to be somewhat more flexible since his urgings depended on the way that the teacher responded to his task. If the teacher hesitated and showed concern about going on, the experimenter responded using a predetermined set of prods. These were as follows:

> Prod 1: Please continue [or Please go on].
>
> Prod 2: The experiment requires that you continue.
>
> Prod 3: It is absolutely essential that you continue.
>
> Prod 4: You have no other choice, you *must* go on.

These were given in an escalating series, so that a higher-level prod was only given after a lower-level one had failed to persuade the teacher to continue. In addition, there were two special prods in response to specific objections by the teacher. If he asked about physical danger to the learner, the experimenter replied: 'Although the shocks may be painful, there is no permanent tissue damage, so please go on.' If the teacher objected that the learner did not want to continue, the experimenter replied: 'Whether the learner likes it or not, you must go on until he has learned all the word pairs correctly. So please go on.'

When the sessions were finished, Milgram devised an extensive post-experimental procedure that involved telling participants that the shocks were not real and that the learner had not been harmed in any way. They then had a friendly meeting with the learner who told them that they were a good person. If they had defied the experimenter they were told that this was the right thing to do. If they had not, they were told that this was perfectly normal. Later they received a full written report about the studies and also a follow-up questionnaire that assessed their thoughts and feelings about participating in the studies.

In this baseline condition 26 out of 40 participants (65%) went all the way to the maximum level and never defied the experimenter – this was despite the screams, the demands to be released, the invocations of heart disease and,

Figure 7.2 A participant in one of Milgram's obedience experiments (from the film *Obedience*)

Source: Yale University archive

ultimately, the learner's ominous silence. Of those 14 who did refuse to go on, the largest number (six) did so at the 150-volt level. No more than two people broke off at any other single level.

MAIN VARIANTS

Perhaps the best-known set of variants addresses the physical proximity of the learner to the experimenter. In the first of these (the 'remote' experiment), the learner is in a separate room and his voice cannot be heard by the teacher. The only feedback comes at 300 volts when there is banging on the wall. In the second (voice-feedback) study, the set-up is almost identical to the 'baseline' variant except that there is no mention of a heart condition at any point. The third variant (proximity) is like the second, except that it involves the teacher and learner being in the same room so there is visual as well as auditory feedback. Finally, in the fourth (touch proximity), the teacher has to press the learner's hand onto a metal shock plate. The number (out of 40 participants) and percentage of people who obey to the end in these studies is respectively 26 (65%), 25 (62.5%), 16 (40%) and 12 (30%). Again, apart from the remote condition (where the first point that people break off – as well as the point where most people break off – is at 300 volts when banging on the wall is heard), more people break off at 150 volts than at any other point.

Another set of variants deals with the various roles involved in the study. Thus, in one study, it is the learner who demands that the shocks are delivered. At 150 volts the experimenter calls a halt to the study but the learner indicates a willingness to continue. No-one heeds the learner. At the 150-volt mark, all 20 participants in this condition stop, and none (0%) continue to the end. In another study, the person demanding that shocks be delivered is not a scientist in a lab coat, but just an ordinary man, ostensibly a volunteer for the study, just like the participant. In this situation only 4 out of 20 people (20%) obey to the end. In yet another study, there are two scientist experimenters who argue with each other as to whether shocks should be delivered. Here again, not one of the 20 participants (0%) is fully obedient and 18 of them stop at the 150-volt mark. In a fourth study, not only is the person making demands an ordinary man, but also the learner who receives shocks is the scientist. Once more, not one of the 20 participants (0%) is fully obedient and all of them stop at the 150-volt mark. In a fifth and final study of this series, both the person demanding the shocks and the person receiving the shocks is a lab-coated scientist. This time, obedience rises to the same level as the baseline condition (13 out of 20 participants go to 450 volts, 65%) and six of the seven participants who break off do so at 150 volts.

There are also two variants dealing with what Milgram terms 'group effects'. In the first of these, there are three teachers – two are actors and one is the real participant. At 150 volts one of the actors refuses to continue. At 210 volts the second does likewise. Here only 4 of the 40 (10%) participants continue obeying the experimenter to the end. Of those who don't, the largest number break off, along with the second dissenting actor, at 210 volts. In the other variant, there are two experimenters (one an actor, the other the real participant). The actor actually administers the shocks; the participant only assists. This time, 37 of the 40 participants (92.5%) are prepared to administer the full set of shocks.

Finally, of the many other variants, three are notable. When women are used instead of men, there is no difference in obedience levels. Out of 40 participants, 26 are fully obedient (65%). When the study was conducted in Bridgeport, full obedience was displayed by 19 out of 40 participants (47.5%). When the learner made the experimenter agree, prior to the shocks starting, that the study would be ended when the learner demanded it, obedience fell further to 16 out of 40 participants (40%). It is worth commenting, once again, that in all these conditions more people dropped out at 150 volts than any other level.

To summarize, then, three points are worth noting (for further discussion see Reicher, Haslam and Smith, 2012). First, the levels of obedience in these studies vary massively from over 90% to 0%. Milgram's studies thus demonstrate *dis*obedience as well as obedience. The critical questions, thus, have to do with *when* people obey as much as *why* people obey. Second, participants do not obey just anyone: their obedience seems to be contingent upon a legitimate authority providing clear guidance. Third, people are highly responsive to other voices in the study. They are most likely to break off the first time the learner demands to quit (150 volts in most studies, 300 volts in the remote condition; Packer, 2008). Equally, in the first 'group variant', they are most likely to stop when there is a consensus amongst others to do so (at 210 volts).

The Milgram paradigm, then, is one in which the participant is assailed on all sides by different voices demanding different things. The participants seem to be attentive to all these voices and their dilemma is which to prioritize over the others.

EXPLAINING THE FINDINGS

In his early papers on the 'Obedience to Authority' studies (which, as we have just seen, might better be termed the 'Obedience and Disobedience to Authority' studies) and in the notes that he took while he was conducting the studies, Milgram places considerable emphasis on the tension that arises in the studies as participants are torn between 'the competing demands of two persons: the experimenter and the victim' (Milgram, 1963: 378), and he considers a wealth of factors that pull them towards the one or the other. Thus, for instance, the importance and prestige of the research (ostensibly to advance knowledge about learning and memory) is a factor that pulls participants towards the experimenter (and hence obedience reduces when the research is associated with a commercial enterprise rather than Yale University). The status and prestige of the researcher (as a legitimate scientist) is equally important in this regard (and hence obedience reduces and even disappears when the researcher is just an ordinary person).

But obedience does not just rely on who the experimenter is, but on the *relationship* between the participant and the experimenter. Thus, Milgram uses the notion of 'incipient group formation' as an important element in explaining the effects of proximity on obedience (Milgram, 1965: 64). In the remote and voice-feedback variants, experimenter and teacher are alone together in the same room and this helps them bond. But in the proximity and touch proximity conditions, the teacher and learner no longer have a wall between them. They don't face the experimenter alone. 'They have an ally who is close at hand and eager to collaborate in a revolt against the experimenter' (Milgram, 1965a: 64). In another paper, Milgram (1965b) makes a similar point about the relationship between the real participant and his fellow actor-teachers in the first group condition: 'there is identification with the disobedient confederates and the possibility of falling back on them for social support when defying the experimenter' (1965b: 133). In other words, the way that the physical environment impacts on the configuration of social relationships in the studies plays an important part in determining which voice the participant will heed and which he will ignore. As Milgram observed in his notebook:

> The subjects have come to the laboratory to form a relationship with the experimenter, a specifically submissive relationship in the interest of advancing science. They have not come to form a relationship with the subject, and it is this lack of relationship in the one direction and the real relationship in the other that produces the results.... Only a genuine relationship between the Victim and the Subject, based on identification, or marriage, etc. could reverse the results. (Milgram, Box 46, Yale archive; cited in Haslam, Reicher, Millard and MacDonald, 2015: 60)

Attention to such factors dominated Milgram's early accounts of his findings, and they are still referred to in his 1974 book. However, over time, they became overshadowed by an alternative explanation, which he outlines in the Introduction to *Obedience to Authority*:

> After witnessing hundreds of ordinary people submit to the authority in our own experiments, I must conclude that Arendt's conception of the banality of evil comes closer to the truth than one might dare imagine. The ordinary person who shocked the victim did so out of a sense of obligation – a conception of his duties as a subject – and not from any peculiarly aggressive tendencies. (1974: 6)

Milgram refers to this state of immersion in one's role as the 'agentic state', and the shift from acting in terms of one's own purposes to acting as an agent for someone else's is termed the 'agentic shift' (1974: 132–4).

Even Milgram's most ardent admirers are highly sceptical about the 'agentic state' explanation (e.g., Blass, 2004). If nothing else, this is because there is no evidence that the different levels of obedience witnessed across the study variants relate to differences in the extent to which participants enter into this state (Mantell and Panzarella, 1976). This is unsurprising, given two aspects of the explanation. The first is that the agentic state is conceptualized mechanically as an all-or-nothing affair: one is either completely in or completely out of it. Such a stark view does not allow for different degrees of involvement and hence of obedience. Indeed, it is this aspect of the account that drew some of the fiercest criticism. Thus, John Darley wrote that:

> The first time I read this, I was startled and appalled by ... the odd and pseudoscientific/pseudophysiological concept of the agentic state, by the notion of the 'trigger' that switches an individual between normal and agentic functioning, and by the dichotomous and all-or-nothing character of being in one state or another. And I continue to be. (1992: 207)

However, the second aspect of the agentic state explanation is, perhaps, even more problematic. This concerns the way in which it conceptualizes one of the several relationships in the study – that between participant and experimenter. For here it loses sight of the fact that a key feature of the studies concerns the way in which participants are torn between different relationships and different obligations. It therefore fails to address the ways in which the balance of relationships varies between the different studies or to answer the key question of why participants heed one of the voices that is appealing to them rather than the others. In short, the agentic state explanation reduces a multi-vocal reality to a uni-vocal account. This not only makes the account unconvincing, but also obscures the many other rich insights that Milgram provided in the course of his research.

Although it is now nearly a quarter of a century old, Ross (1988) thus provides the best summary of the prevailing view when he states that we really have no firm understanding of why people behaved as they did in the studies (see also Miller, 2016; Reicher, Haslam and Miller, 2014). Milgram undoubtedly supplied us with a compelling phenomenon, but we still await a satisfactory explanation. What is clear, however, is that any account must be inadequate if it suggests that there is something inherent in the human psyche which compels us to obey. A convincing explanation must be one that is rich enough to explain the complex patterning of obedience and disobedience that Milgram discovered in the process of worrying the phenomenon to death.

BEYOND THE OBEDIENCE STUDIES

There have been two major obstacles that have prevented progress in understanding the underpinnings of obedience and disobedience. The first is ethical, the second is conceptual.

OVERCOMING ETHICAL OBSTACLES

Milgram's studies are nearly as famous for the ethical storm that they provoked as for their demonstration that ordinary men can commit acts of extraordinary harm. From the moment the studies were first reported, many observers noted that participants who had obeyed the experimenter would be deeply disturbed when confronted with what they had done – notwithstanding Milgram's attempts to reassure them that they had done nothing wrong. For his critics (of whom there have been many; for recent discussion see Brannigan, Nicholson and Cherry, 2015), Milgram had himself committed acts of inhumanity in the guise of studying inhumanity. In an influential commentary that appeared in *American Psychologist*, Diana Baumrind (1964) accused Milgram of failing to treat his participants with the respect they deserved and of undermining their self-esteem and dignity. Shortly after the research was first publicized in the *New York Times* of 26 October 1963, an editorial in the *St. Louis Post-Dispatch* described Milgram's work as 'open-eyed torture' (cited in Blass, 2004: 121). Bruno Bettelheim, a famous psychoanalyst who himself had written about behaviour in the concentration camps and who had positively reviewed Arendt's *Eichmann in Jerusalem* in the *New Republic* (15 June 1963), went even further. He declared the studies to be 'vile' and 'in line with the human experiments of the Nazis' (cited in Blass, 2004: 123). Milgram even became the subject of attacks by fictional characters. In Dannie Abse's play *The Dogs of Pavlov*, the protagonist Kurt calls the obedience studies 'bullshit', 'fraudulent' and 'a cheat' (see Milgram, 1974: 198).

Milgram (1964) responded to such criticism by claiming that 'no-one who took part in the obedience study suffered damage, and most subjects found the experience to be instructive and enriching' (Blass, 2004: 124). He backed up his claims with evidence taken from post-experimental questionnaires. These showed that, of the 656 people who participated in the studies, 83.7% were 'glad' or 'very glad' to have participated, 15.1% were neutral, and 1.3% were 'sorry' or 'very sorry' to have taken part. In terms of distress, more than half the participants said that they had suffered some level of discomfort during the studies; roughly a third said they had been bothered since; and 7% said that they had been bothered quite a bit. So while the figures bear out Milgram's contention that once the nature of the studies had been explained to participants 'most' 'responded positively' and felt 'it was an hour well-spent' (Milgram, 1974: 198), it is an over-statement to say that 'no-one' suffered any damage.

But even if we accept that very few participants were harmed by their experience, this does not mean that the studies are ethically unproblematic. Indeed, it is clear from examination of post-experimental responses in the Yale archive that one key reason why participants were not distressed – and in fact were rather happy – is that Milgram encouraged them to think that they had not done anything wrong (in being prepared to harm the learner) but instead had actually done something virtuous (in being prepared to stick to their difficult task in order to advance scientific understanding). Faced with this evidence, one might reasonably ask whether it is ethically acceptable for participants to be led to feel happy about having been prepared to administer ostensibly lethal punishments to a total stranger in the interests of science (Haslam et al., 2014).

Whatever one's position on these issues, what is not in doubt is that ethical considerations have rendered the obedience studies, in their original form, impossible to replicate to this day. However, researchers have developed a number of strategies in order to surmount this considerable obstacle. One is to use alternative and less harmful behaviours in order to investigate obedience. These include giving negative feedback to job applicants in order to make them more nervous (Meeus and Raaijmakers, 1986, 1995), crushing bugs (Martens et al., 2007), performing an on-line analogue task which involves applying negative labels to increasingly positive groups (Haslam, Reicher and Birney, 2014), or simply persisting at a long and tedious task (Navarick, 2009). These are all ingenious solutions, but the problem is that they lack the one thing that gave Milgram's studies their impact – the fact that the behaviour he was investigating in his laboratory (doing serious physical harm to others) was akin to the phenomena that concerned him outside the laboratory.

A second strategy has been to revisit and re-analyse Milgram's own studies for new insights. Thus, for instance, Steven Gilbert (1981) shows the importance of the gradual increase in shock intensity which deprives participants of a qualitative breakpoint that would allow them to justify breaking off and becoming disobedient. Dominic Packer (2008), by contrast, highlights how the reactions of the learner can provide such a justification. This relates to the fact (noted above) that the point at which most people break off is 150 volts, where the learner first asks to be released from the study. Likewise, Nick Haslam and colleagues conduct statistical analysis to identify the various features of Milgram's paradigm that induced participants to continue all the way to 450 volts when they did (Haslam, Loughnan and Perry, 2014). They conclude that eight factors were important: the experimenter's directiveness, legitimacy, and consistency; group pressure to disobey; the indirectness, proximity, and intimacy of the relation between teacher and learner; and the distance between the teacher and the experimenter. These studies are valuable, but there is only so far one can go with the existing data since one is limited to the constructs that Milgram considered important (and hence examined). As a result, researchers cannot examine the importance of alternative constructs that might help us understand the findings.

A third strategy, then, has been to study historical examples of obedience and disobedience from a psychological perspective. A notable example of this is François Rochat and Andre Modigliani's (1995) analysis of resistance to the official oppression of minorities by the villagers of Le Chambon in Southern France during the Second World War (see also Rochat and Modigliani, 2000). The researchers use this to examine the conditions that made Le Chambon such a shining example – and such an exception to what happened elsewhere. We shall return to these conditions presently. For now, it is worth noting that Rochat and Modigliani's work is not only an important contribution to the obedience literature, but also an excellent example of how psychologists can use historical case studies to formulate questions, address hypotheses, and validate theories (see Chapter 11). This should not be seen as opposed to, but rather as complementing, experimental studies that can systematically disentangle the relevance and contribution of different factors.

Recently, though, three new approaches to the experimental study of obedience have been developed that allow us to address real harm-doing without harming participants in the process. The first employs virtual reality simulations of the Milgram paradigm. In these it has been shown that behaviour in these simulations corresponds closely to that which is observed in the original paradigm (Slater et al., 2006). The second involves using a technique called Immersive Digital Realism to train actors to play the role of normal participants in the Milgram paradigm (Haslam, Reicher and Millard, 2015). Like regular participants, these actors are not told about the paradigm in advance, and it transpires that their behaviour – in particular, their responses to different prods and different experimental variants – closely mirrors that of Milgram's own participants. The third is based on the observation that what people do at 150 volts is a very accurate predictor of whether they will obey up to 450 volts. So why not stop the studies at the 150-volt mark where one can see if people will obey without getting them to actually do something harmful? This was the strategy adopted by Jerry Burger (2009a) in his replication of the Milgram paradigm. Following an extensive debate on Burger's studies in *American Psychologist*, the general consensus seems to be that, after half a century, we are in a position to re-open meaningful research on obedience. To quote Alan Elms, who assisted Milgram in his original studies, 'Burger and other social psychologists should be able to come up with many additional situational variables that have remained untouched during the Dark Age of obedience research proscription' (2009: 35).

FROM REPLICATION TO EXPLANATION

Let us turn, now, from how people have sought to study obedience since Milgram, to what they have had to say. Here we immediately encounter a second obstacle to progress in understanding the phenomena. For the question that dominates much of the subsequent research is whether or not people will still obey to the extent that they did in the original studies (e.g., Blass, 1999; Burger, 2009b; Meeus and Raaijmakers, 1986; Twenge, 2009). The problem with this question is that it tends to focus on the (high) level of obedience in one of the experimental variants (generally the 'baseline' study) rather than addressing the huge differences in obedience across studies. Once one addresses these differences, the question no longer makes sense. There is no set level of obedience to be explained. Instead, as we have already noted, the key question is what explains the *variability* in obedience. The issue – as we have previously suggested – becomes not *whether* but *why* people obey and disobey. The priority is to explain obedience, not just describe it.

But it is important not to overstate the case: there may be a *tendency* to focus on whether people are obedient, but equally there have been important insights into when and why people obey. First of all, several authors point to the need to consider the importance of disobedience as well as obedience (Bocchario and Zimbardo, 2010; Dimow, 2004; Jetten and Mols, 2014; Passini and Morselli, 2009; Rochat and Modigliani, 1995). Second, a number of analyses point to features of the various relationships in the obedience paradigm that might help explain whether people obey or disobey authority. Wim Meeus and Quinten Raaijmakers (1995), for instance, argue that obedience does not result from an inability to resist scientific authority but rather from a cultural tendency to identify with the social system, combined with a tendency not to identify with our fellow citizens but to see them in terms of specific role positions – an analysis which suggests that in the Milgram studies participants relate to the learner in terms of the different roles that the two of them occupy rather than in terms of their common citizenship.

However, it is perhaps Rochat and Modigliani (1995) who provide the richest analysis of the way in which the quality of social relationships influences the way people position themselves in relation to a destructive authority and its victims. They note that the villagers of Chambon were descendants of the persecuted Protestant minority in France (the Huguenots) and this meant that they likened the collaborationist Vichy Government to their own persecutors, and saw commonality between themselves and those who were persecuted. What is more, they show that the villagers had a strong norm of resisting violence to the extent that even those who disapproved of the help given to minorities kept silent. Their analysis concludes that once the persecutors became 'them' and the persecuted became 'us', the choice of whom to side with – of whether to obey or defy authority – became easy.

IDENTIFICATION AND INFLUENCE

We began this chapter by describing the hunched and balding figure of Adolf Eichmann and noted how, through the eyes of Hannah Arendt, his appearance gave rise to the notion of the banality of evil. We then saw how Arendt's analysis fused with the figure of Milgram's obedient participants to provide a compelling new analysis of human evil. Yet over the ensuing pages we have questioned this analysis by reconsidering Milgram's own explanation of his findings. This led us to conclude that people do not helplessly slip into a state where they can do nothing else but obey authority. Instead, to understand obedience, it is clear that we need to address the different relationships that people form with authorities, with victims, and indeed with their peers. But where does that leave us with Arendt? Whatever the psychological evidence might say, is there not sound historical evidence to support the view that harm is perpetrated through inattention?

Not really. In fact, over time, Arendt's analysis has been more thoroughly questioned than Milgram's. Vetlesen (2005), for instance, argues that Eichmann deliberately put on an act to convince the judges and jury that he was no monster. Vetlesen acerbically comments that 'in suggesting that he [Eichmann] was "merely thoughtless", [Arendt] in fact adopts the very self-presentation he cultivated' (2005: 5). Had she stayed on at the trial for more than just the first few days, and listened to evidence from his victims, she would have discovered a very different Eichmann. This is the Eichmann described in David Cesarani's biography (2004), which presents evidence that Eichmann was a committed Nazi and anti-Semite who perfected new ways of deporting Jews from their homes (see also Stangneth, 2014). In 1944 he went to Hungary to send the Jewish populations to the death camps. Far from simply obeying orders, he argued with his superior, Himmler, who wanted to do a deal with the allies by trading Jewish lives for war materials. Eichmann fervently believed in the extermination of all Jewish people. He was not inattentive to what he was doing; he celebrated what he was doing. And after the war, he expressed satisfaction with the murders he had organized, regretting only that he hadn't been even more successful. What Cesarani says of Eichmann, Lozowick (2002) says of 'Hitler's bureaucrats' in general. These were people who were 'true believers', who worked hard and showed considerable ingenuity in killing people. They identified fully with Hitler and the Nazi system. For them, Jews were simply the enemy.

Daniel Goldhagen (1996) underlines this last point with graphic intensity. He refers to an infamous picture of a Nazi officer leading a small girl to a pit where she would be shot and killed. He makes the obvious point that the officer was fully aware of what he was about to do, and he asks what prevented him from showing the compassion and protection that would normally be accorded to a young child. Goldhagen's answer hinges on the point that the officer presumably did not see a young child but a Jew, 'a young one, but a Jew nonetheless' (1996: 217). Here, then, one is reminded of Rochat and Modigliani's (1995) analysis, but in reverse: active identification with authority as 'us', combined with fervent disidentification with the Jewish victim as 'them', made the choice to oppress straightforward.

In sum, the historical evidence, like the psychological evidence, is at odds with the 'inattentiveness' hypothesis (Haslam and Reicher, 2007; Overy, 2014). Instead, evidence from both sources points to an alternative approach. We harm others to the extent that we listen to the appeals of malicious authorities above those of its victims. At the same time, there is now converging evidence that this has something to do with the extent to which we identify with one over the other (Haslam et al., 2014, 2015; Reicher and Haslam, 2011a; Reicher et al., 2012). In our present state of knowledge, as we are just emerging from what Elms, quoted above, called 'the Dark Age of obedience research proscription', this is more a working hypothesis than a firm conclusion. However, like any good hypothesis, the aim is less to mark where we have got to than to signpost where we should be going.

There are three areas in particular that need to be addressed in the future – although in each case they also represent a return to suggestions made by Milgram before his theory of the 'agentic state' took centre stage.

First, we need to investigate the way in which different situational arrangements affect group formation and identification between the participant and the different parties within the obedience paradigm (Reicher and Haslam, 2011a, 2011b). Can we show, for instance, by directly measuring identification, that the different proximity conditions affect obedience by influencing the extent to which they lead to identification with the experimenter over the learner (or vice versa)? Moreover, can we show that such an explanation can make sense of variation in obedience across studies (Haslam et al., 2015; Reicher et al., 2012)? Finally, can we show that further socially relevant variations will affect obedience via relative identification? Most obviously, what happens when the learner (or the experimenter) is a member of an outgroup, a despised outgroup, or a feared enemy outgroup as Jewish people were perceived in Nazi Germany?

Second, we need to understand what sort of appeals make people side with the experimenter rather than with the learner, as well as the impact that participants' own discourse has on their ability to disengage from these parties. Milgram (1965b) himself notes that one of reasons why participants may continue to obey is that they lack the rhetorical resources to challenge the legitimacy of the experimenter's requests and hence to relinquish their obligations to him (see also Hollander and Maynard, 2016; Rochat and Modigliani, 1995). It follows that a focus on the negotiation of identities and obligations is of both theoretical and practical importance. For one way to mitigate against 'crimes of obedience' may involve training people to contest demands from authorities that they feel violate shared norms of propriety.

Third and last, there is one specific aspect of the language used in the obedience studies that is particularly important and particularly ironic in light of the way that the studies are popularly represented. When people are asked to sum up the studies in a single sentence, they generally say something like 'People blindly obey orders' (Reicher and Haslam, 2011a). However, if you look closely at the exhortations, prods and prompts used by the experimenter in the studies, it is clear that some are simple requests (e.g., prod 1: 'Please go on'), some are justifications on the basis of scientific value (e.g., prod 2: 'The experiment requires that you continue'), but only one is a direct order (prod 4: 'You have no other choice, you must go on'). Moreover, all the evidence points to the fact that, when this order is given, people react badly. In his 1974 book Milgram gives just one illustration of this. When the participant – a Professor of Old Testament liturgy – is given this fourth prod, he responds 'If this were Russia, maybe, but not in America. *(The experiment is terminated.)*' (Milgram, 1974: 48). In their replication study Burger and colleagues found that every time the experimenter gave this final prod, participants refused to continue (Burger, Girgis and Manning, 2011), and in controlled studies of our own we observe that prod 4 is singularly ineffective in securing compliance (Haslam et al., 2014, 2015).

This is powerful evidence against the notion that participants in Milgram's studies are simply following orders. It suggests instead that people are seeking out justifications for acting one way rather than another, from people they trust and identify with. Indeed, the problem with orders is precisely that they are generally given by people who we don't identify with and who can't otherwise justify what they ask us to do (see Haslam et al., 2011). Indeed, as the British historian Ian Kershaw (1993) has noted, one thing that made the Nazi state so efficient was precisely the fact that its leaders did not have to issue orders to their followers. Instead, those followers did what they did because they thought it was the right thing to do. The same would seem to be true of the obedient participants in Milgram's studies (see Haslam et al., 2014). This point, however, remains to be confirmed by further research in the process of establishing the impact of various forms of invitations, requests and orders to harm others.

CONCLUSION

So, at the end of this long journey, where precisely have we got to? First and foremost, it is clear that Milgram provided us with evidence of probably the most compelling phenomenon ever uncovered by a social psychologist. Indeed, although it was first reported half a century ago, it is so important and (sadly) still so relevant that there can be no more pressing area for social psychologists to study.

Yet despite this, the phenomenon that Milgram so carefully described still lacks a compelling explanation. Nevertheless, recent methodological innovations, alongside forensic historical analysis, provide us with methods that are allowing us to recommence investigation. Moreover, we also have some clear pointers about how to proceed. There are exciting prospects ahead.

FURTHER READING

Milgram, S. (1974) *Obedience to Authority: An Experimental View*. New York, NY: Harper & Row.

As the classic account of Milgram's studies, this provides a rich description of most of the studies. More controversially, it introduces the 'agentic state' explanation of the findings. The book concludes with two very informative appendices, one on ethical issues in the research and the other on individual differences in obedience.

Blass, T. (2004) *The Man who Shocked the World: The Life and Legacy of Stanley Milgram*. New York: Basic Books.

For a wider perspective on Milgram, the man, and his work, Blass's authoritative biography is a highly enjoyable and informative read.

Russell, N.J.C. (2011) 'Milgram's obedience to authority experiments: Origins and early evolution', *British Journal of Social Psychology*, 50: 140–62.

A fascinating account of the background to the obedience studies is also provided in this recent paper by Nestar Russell.

Finally, for a range of resources, visit the website www.stanleymilgram.com.

REFERENCES

Arendt, H. (1963/1994) *Eichmann in Jerusalem: A Report on the Banality of Evil*. New York: Penguin.

Asch, S. (1956) 'Studies of independence and conformity: A minority of one against a unanimous majority', *Psychological Monographs: General and Applied*, 70: 1–70.

Baumrind, D. (1964) 'Some thoughts on ethics of research: After reading Milgram's "Behavioral study of obedience"', *American Psychologist*, 19: 421–3.

Blass, T. (1999) 'The Milgram paradigm after 35 years: Some things we now know about obedience to authority', *Journal of Applied Social Psychology*, 29: 955–78.

Blass, T. (2004) *The Man who Shocked the World: The Life and Legacy of Stanley Milgram*. New York: Basic Books.

Bocchiaro, P. and Zimbardo, P.G. (2010) 'Defying unjust authority: An exploratory study', *Current Psychology*, 29: 155–70.

Brannigan, A., Nicholson, I. and Cherry, F. (2015) 'Unplugging the Milgram machine', *Theory and Psychology* (Special Issue), 25: 551–696.

Burger, J. (2009a) 'In their own words: Explaining obedience through an examination of participants' comments'. Paper presented at the Meeting of the Society of Experimental Social Psychology, Portland, ME, 15–17 October.

Burger, J. (2009b) 'Replicating Milgram: Would people still obey today?', *American Psychologist*, 64: 1–11.

Burger, J.M., Girgis, Z.M., and Manning, C.C. (2011) 'In their own words: Explaining obedience to authority through an examination of participants' comments', *Social Psychological and Personality Science*, 2: 460–6.

Cesarani, D. (2004) *Eichmann: His Life and Crimes*. London: Heinemann.

Cesarani, D. (2005) *After Eichmann: Collective Memory and the Holocaust since 1960*. London: Routledge.

Darley, J. (1992) 'Social organization for the production of evil', *Psychological Inquiry*, 3: 199–218.

Dimow, J. (2004) 'Resisting authority: A personal account of the Milgram obedience experiments', *Jewish Currents*, January.

Elms, A.C. (2009) 'Obedience lite', *American Psychologist*, 64: 32–6.

Gilbert, S.J. (1981) 'Another look at the Milgram obedience studies: The role of a graduated series of shocks', *Personality and Social Psychology Bulletin*, 7: 690–5.

Goldhagen, D. (1996) *Hitler's Willing Executioners: Ordinary Germans and the Holocaust*. London: Little, Brown.

Haslam, N., Loughnan, S. and Perry, G. (2014) 'Meta-Milgram: An empirical synthesis of the obedience experiments', *PLoS ONE*, 9(4): e93927.

Haslam, S.A. and Reicher, S.D. (2007) 'Beyond the banality of evil: Three dynamics of an interactionist social psychology of tyranny', *Personality and Social Psychology Bulletin*, 33: 615–22.

Haslam, S.A., Reicher, S.D. and Birney, M. (2014) 'Nothing by mere authority: Evidence that in an experimental analogue of the Milgram paradigm participants are motivated not by orders but by appeals to science', *Journal of Social Issues*, 70: 473–88.

Haslam, S.A., Reicher, S.D. and Millard, K. (2015) 'Shock treatment: Using immersive digital realism to restage and re-examine Milgram's 'Obedience to Authority' research. *PLoS ONE*, 10(3): e109015.

Haslam, S.A., Reicher, S.D. Millard, K. and McDonald, R. (2015) '"Happy to have been of service": The Yale archive as a window into the engaged followership of participants in Milgram's "obedience" experiments', *British Journal of Social Psychology*, 54: 55–83.

Haslam, S.A., Reicher, S.D. and Platow, M.J. (2011) *The New Psychology of Leadership: Identity, Influence and Power*. New York: Psychology Press.

Hollander, M.M. and Maynard, D.W. (2016) 'Do Unto Others…? Methodological advance and self-versus other-attentive resistance in Milgram's "Obedience" experiments', *Social Psychology Quarterly*, 79(4): 355–75.

Jetten, J. and Mols, F. (2014) '50:50 hindsight: Appreciating anew the contributions of Milgram's obedience experiments', *Journal of Social Issues,* 70: 587–602.

Kershaw, I. (1993) 'Working towards the Führer', *Contemporary European History*, 2: 103–8.

Lozowick, Y. (2002) *Hitler's Bureaucrats: The Nazi Security Police and the Banality of Evil* (trans., H. Watzman). London: Continuum.

Mantell, D.M. and Panzarella, R. (1976) 'Obedience and responsibility', *British Journal of Social and Clinical Psychology*, 15: 239–45.

Martens, A., Kosloff, S., Greenberg, J., Landau, M.J. and Schmader, T. (2007) 'Killing begets killing: Evidence from a bug-killing paradigm that initial killing fuels subsequent killing', *Personality and Social Psychology Bulletin,* 33: 1251–64.

Meeus, W.H.J. and Raaijmakers, Q.A. (1986) 'Administrative obedience: Carrying out orders to use psychological-administrative violence', *European Journal of Social Psychology,* 16: 311–24.

Meeus, W.H.J. and Raaijmakers, Q.A. (1995) 'Obedience in modern society: The Utrecht studies', *Journal of Social Issues,* 51: 155–75.

Milgram, A. (2000) 'My personal view of Stanley Milgram', in T. Blass (ed.), *Obedience to Authority: Current Perspectives on the Milgram Paradigm*. Mahwah, NJ: Erlbaum. pp. 1–7.

Milgram, S. (1963) 'Behavioral study of obedience', *Journal of Abnormal and Social Psychology*, 67: 371–8.

Milgram, S. (1964) 'Issues in the study of obedience: A reply to Baumrind', *American Psychologist,* 19: 848–52.

Milgram, S. (1965a) 'Liberating effects of group pressure', *Journal of Personality and Social Psychology*, 1: 127–34.

Milgram, S. (1965b) 'Some conditions of obedience and disobedience to authority', *Human Relations*, 18: 57–76.

Milgram, S. (1974) *Obedience to Authority: An Experimental View*. New York, NY: Harper & Row.

Millard, K. (2011) 'The window in the laboratory: Stanley Milgram as filmmaker', *The Psychologist*, 24(9): 658–61.

Millard, K. (2014) 'Revisioning obedience: Exploring the role of Milgram's skills as a film-maker in bringing his shocking narrative to life', *Journal of Social Issues*, 70: 439–55.

Miller, A.G. (2016) 'Why are the Milgram experiments still so famous — and controversial?', in A.G. Miller (ed.), *The Social Psychology of Good and Evil*. New York: Guilford. pp. 185–223.

Navarick, D.J. (2009) 'Reviving the Milgram obedience paradigm in the era of informed consent', *The Psychological Record,* 59: 155–70.

Novick, P. (2000) *The Holocaust in American Life*. Boston, MA and New York, NY: Houghton Mifflin.

Overy, R. (2014) 'Ordinary men, extraordinary circumstances: Historians, social psychology, and the Holocaust', *Journal of Social Issues*, 70: 515–30.

Packer, D.J. (2008) 'Identifying systematic disobedience in Milgram's obedience experiments: A meta-analytic review', *Perspectives on Psychological Science*, 3: 301–4.

Passini, S. and Morselli, D. (2009) 'Authority relationships between obedience and disobedience', *New Ideas in Psychology,* 27: 96–106.

Perry, G. (2011) *Behind the Shock Machine: The Untold Story of the Notorious Milgram Psychology Experiments.* Melbourne: Scribe Publications.

Reicher, S. and Haslam, S.A. (2011a) 'After shock? Towards a social identity explanation of the Milgram "obedience" studies', *British Journal of Social Psychology*, 50: 163–9.

Reicher, S.D. and Haslam, S.A. (2011b) 'Culture of shock: Milgram's obedience studies fifty years on', *Scientific American Mind*, 22(6): 30–5.

Reicher, S.D., Haslam, S.A. and Miller, A.G. (2014) 'What makes a person a perpetrator? The intellectual, moral, and methodological arguments for revisiting Milgram's research on the influence of authority', *Journal of Social Issues,* 70: 393–408.

Reicher, S.D., Haslam, S.A. and Smith, J.R. (2012) 'Working towards the experimenter: Reconceptualizing obedience within the Milgram paradigm as identification-based followership', *Perspectives on Psychological Science*, 7: 315–24.

Rochat, F. and Blass T. (2014) 'Milgram's unpublished obedience variation and its historical relevance', *Journal of Social Issues*, 70: 456–72.

Rochat, F. and Modigliani, A. (1995) 'The ordinary quality of resistance: From Milgram's laboratory to the village of Le Chambon', *Journal of Social Issues*, 51: 195–210.

Rochat, F. and Modigliani, A. (2000) 'Captain Paul Grueninger: The Chief of Police who saved Jewish refugees by refusing to do his duty', in T. Blass (ed.), *Obedience to Authority: Current Perspectives on the Milgram Paradigm*. Mahwah, NJ: Lawrence Erlbaum. pp. 91–110.

Ross, L.D. (1988) 'Situationist perspectives on the obedience experiments', *Contemporary Psychology*, 33: 101–4.

Russell, N.J.C. (2011) 'Milgram's Obedience to Authority experiments: Origins and early evolution', *British Journal of Social Psychology*, 50: 140–62.

Slater, M., Antley, A., Davison, A., Swapp, D., Guger, C., Barker, C., et al. (2006) 'A virtual reprise of the Stanley Milgram obedience experiments', *PLoS ONE*, 1: e39.

Stangneth, B. (2014) *Eichmann before Jerusalem: The Unexamined Life of a Mass Murderer*. New York: Random House.

Takooshian, H. (2000) 'How Stanley Milgram taught about obedience and social influence', in T. Blass (ed.), *Obedience to Authority: Current Perspectives on the Milgram Paradigm*. Mahwah, NJ: Erlbaum. pp. 9–24.

Twenge, J.M. (2009) 'Change over time in obedience: The jury's still out, but it might be decreasing', *American Psychologist*, 64: 28–31.

Vetlesen, A.J. (2005) *Evil and Human Agency*. Cambridge: Cambridge University Press.

8

Tyranny

Revisiting Zimbardo's Stanford Prison Experiment

**S. Alexander Haslam and
Stephen Reicher**

BACKGROUND

On 21 August 1971, George Jackson – a 30-year-old left-wing radical – was shot dead by correctional officers in California's San Quentin State Prison. Jackson was a Black Panther who had been jailed for murdering a correctional officer, John V. Mills, in retaliation for Mills having shot three black inmates from his guard tower in Soledad Prison in Monterey County, California. The circumstances of Jackson's death are controversial, but three weeks later they were the catalyst for a five-day riot involving around 1,000 inmates at New York State's Attica Correctional Facility. In this, a further 33 inmates and 10 guards died.

Accounts from prisoners at Attica suggest that their uprising was a response to the appalling conditions that they were forced to endure inside the prison. On top of physical privation, these included regular taunting from guards, frequent beatings and alleged torture. Furthermore, according to *Time* magazine, after the riot, 'Nothing was done to prevent reprisals. Inmates were made to run naked through gauntlets of enraged guards, who had "anesthetized their humanity"' (1972: 22).

These episodes of spiralling violence shocked Americans and made international news. This is unsurprising, since, at the time, the Attica uprising was the bloodiest confrontation on American soil since the Civil War. Amongst other things, it motivated a series of enquiries into the US prison system and led people to ask questions about the psychology of those who were involved – especially the psychology of those correctional officers whose job it was to represent authority and the rule of law. What had led them to go so far beyond the bounds of civility and decency? What had led them to betray the morals and values they were meant to be upholding and descend into brutal, thuggish tyranny?

Important as they were at the time, some 33 years later, Americans and the rest of the world would ask these very same questions with even greater force. This time they were responding to graphic evidence of American soldiers subjecting Iraqi detainees to appalling abuse inside Abu Ghraib Prison, 20 miles west of Baghdad. In a lurid documentary shown on *60 Minutes II* and in photographs that made news around the world, images showed soldiers smiling proudly as they subjected detainees to a series of degrading humiliations. Hooded and naked, prisoners were pictured piled on top of each other on the floor, standing in stress positions on boxes with wires attached to their hands, or being threatened by menacing dogs. How was it possible that 'the fine young men and women sent overseas on the glorious mission of bringing democracy and freedom to Iraq' could contemplate, let alone perpetrate, such acts (Zimbardo, 2007: 324)? How could any reasonable human being do such things?

In both 1971 and 2004, the search for answers to these pressing questions led journalists, politicians, academics, lawyers and the general public inexorably towards one psychologist and one classic social psychological study – Philip Zimbardo and the Stanford Prison Experiment (SPE).

Zimbardo was a full professor at Stanford who had completed his PhD at Yale in 1959, nine years after graduating from James Monroe High School in the Bronx in the same class as Stanley Milgram. Like Milgram (see Chapter 7), Zimbardo was interested in exploring the ways in which social influences can contribute to extreme behaviours. However, where Milgram had been concerned to investigate the behaviour of individuals in tightly controlled experimental settings, Zimbardo wanted to explore the free-flowing dynamics that emerge when groups interact within a prison environment.

Of course, like many criminologists before him, Zimbardo might have explored these questions by conducting research inside one of the many hundreds of penal establishments spread across the United States. Clearly, though, if he had found evidence of brutality akin to that in San Quentin or Attica, it would have been hard to know to what extent this was a reflection of the prison system itself. In particular, he would not have been able to rule out the possibility that extreme behaviour was a product of the personalities and characters of those who worked and who were incarcerated there. Accordingly, Zimbardo took two bold initiatives. First, he used funds he had received from the Office of Naval Research to build his own prison in the basement of the Stanford Psychology Department (see Figure 8.1). Second, he recruited 24 male college students to serve as prisoners and guards.

Figure 8.1   The Psychology Department in Jordan Hall at Stanford University where the SPE was brought to a close on 20 August 1971 (left) and San Quentin State Prison (right) where George Jackson was killed the following day. Permission: Penni Gladstone Photography.

THE STANFORD PRISON EXPERIMENT

A s fate would have it, the day before George Jackson died in San Quentin, Zimbardo's own prison study was being brought to a close just 52 miles away. The experiment had been scheduled to last for two weeks but it had been brought to an end after just six days. As Zimbardo reported to Congressional Hearings two months later, the reason for this premature termination was that the mock prison he had created had become a living hell:

> At the end of only six days we had to close down our mock prison because what we saw was frightening ... In less than a week, the experience of imprisonment undid (temporarily) a lifetime of learning; human values were suspended, self-concepts were challenged, and the ugliest, most base, pathological side of human nature surfaced. We were horrified because we saw some boys ('guards') treat other boys as if they were despicable animals, taking pleasure in cruelty, while other boys ('prisoners') became servile, dehumanized robots. (Zimbardo, 1971: 154)

Indeed, the level of abuse in the 'prison' was so intense that five of the participants who had been assigned to be prisoners had needed to be released early because they were showing disturbing signs of psychopathology. Again, then, as with the abuses witnessed in real prisons, the critical question was, how had this come about?

Prior to this point, it had been common for psychologists to answer such questions by arguing that brutality and oppression are a straightforward reflection of the pathological dispositions of those who become agents of tyranny. This *dispositional hypothesis* argues that pathological systems are produced by people who are themselves in some sense pathological. For example, researchers had argued that people who are sympathetic to tyrannical regimes have an authoritarian personality type that makes them deferential to strong leaders and disdainful of weak groups. However, the participants in the SPE were 'normal healthy male college students' (Haney et al., 1973: 5) and they had been randomly assigned to their roles as guards or prisoners. Accordingly, the extreme behaviour witnessed in the study could not be explained simply as a manifestation of participants' deviant personality.

As an alternative to this dispositional account, Zimbardo argued passionately for a *situational hypothesis* – suggesting that people's behaviour is primarily determined by the social context in which they find themselves. As he put it to the Congressional Hearings:

> Individual behavior is largely under the control of social forces and environmental contingencies rather than 'personality traits', 'character', 'will power', or other empirically unvalidated constructs. Many people, perhaps the majority, can be made to do almost anything when put in psychologically compelling situations – regardless of their morals, ethics, values, attitudes, beliefs, or personal convictions ... The mere act of assigning labels to people, such as 'prisoners' and 'guards' and putting them in

situations where these labels acquire validity and meaning, is sufficient to elicit pathological behavior ... The prison system ... is guaranteed to generate severe enough pathological reactions in both guards and prisoners as to debase their humanity. (Zimbardo, 1971: 155)

For Zimbardo, then, the SPE provided an opportunity to 'untangle the dispositional versus situational knot' and, in the process, it generated dramatic and compelling evidence of the tendency for 'negative situational forces to overwhelm positive dispositional tendencies' (Zimbardo, 2004: 39, 40).

METHOD

Zimbardo's confidence in making these claims is underpinned by four features of the SPE's methodology (Zimbardo, 2004: 38–9). As already noted, the first of these is that the *participants* had normal personalities and no prior history of psychopathology. The study started by placing an advert in a newspaper inviting college students to take part in a 'psychological study of prison life'. Seventy-five people responded to this advert and Zimbardo's student assistants, Craig Haney and Curtis Banks, interviewed them in order to select the 24 who were most 'mature, emotionally stable, normal, intelligent' (Zimbardo, 1971: 153). As Zimbardo reported to the Congressional Hearings, they appeared – like the boys in Sherif's earlier camp studies (see Chapter 9) – to represent 'the cream of the crop of this generation' (1971: 153).

This assessment was confirmed, among other things, by the measurement of participants' authoritarianism. This revealed that, on average, participants scored in the normal range. Moreover, at the start of the study there was no difference in the average level of the prisoners' and guards' authoritarianism. This was to be expected in light of the study's second important feature – the *random assignment* of participants to guard and prisoner groups. Thus, in contrast to a real prison, the participants had not exercised any form of choice prior to finding themselves in a particular group (indeed, when asked, most had said they wanted to be prisoners). Instead, the experimenters had assigned them to groups by tossing a coin so that, for each participant, there was an equal probability that he would be a guard or a prisoner.

A third important feature of the study was that Zimbardo attempted to create 'an experimental setting that came as close to a functional simulation of the psychology of imprisonment as possible' (Zimbardo, 2004: 39). In the first instance he sought to ensure this by placing himself in the role of Prison Superintendent, and another student assistant, David Jaffe, in the administrative role of Prison Warden.[1]

---

[1] Jaffe had been selected for the role of warden because, as part of a class assignment for Zimbardo, he and some fellow students had previously created a prison in his college dormitory over the course of a weekend. His results – which anticipated those of the SPE – motivated Zimbardo to design a more extensive and controlled replication.

He also solicited the help of Carlo Prescott – an ex-convict who had previously spent 17 years in San Quentin – to construct a *prison-like environment* that captured relevant features of a prison of the time. Central to this were details that reinforced the low status of the prisoners and the high status of the guards. The study thus started with the prisoners being 'arrested' at their home by members of the Palo Alto police force, then fingerprinted and taken into a detention cell. After this they were blindfolded and taken to the 'prison', where they were stripped naked, sprayed with what was said to be a delousing agent, and then placed in one of three very small (6 × 9 ft) 'cells' that they would share with two other prisoners. They were forced to wear chains on one ankle, smocks without underwear, rubber sandals and a cap made from nylon stocking. To preserve the reality of the prison, whenever the prisoners left the main prison area, they also wore bags over their heads so that they could not see the outside world. In contrast, the guards wore khaki shirts and trousers, carried a whistle and a night stick (baton), and wore reflective sunglasses. And whereas the prisoners were kept in the prison around the clock, the guards were assigned to work in one of three eight-hour shifts and could go home when not on duty.

The fourth significant feature of the SPE was that the roles to which the participants were assigned were *novel*. The participants had signed up to take part in a 'psychological study of prison life' and knew that they would get $15 a day 'for 1–2 weeks'. Their contract guaranteed minimal rights (e.g., 'adequate diet, clothing, medical care'), but also indicated that some of their basic civil rights (e.g., to privacy) might be suspended, 'excluding physical abuse' (Haney et al., 1973: 7). Beyond this, though, they did not know what to expect. In particular, this meant that:

> Participants had no prior training in how to play the randomly assigned roles. Each subject's prior societal learning of the meaning of prisons and the behavioral scripts associated with the oppositional roles of prisoner and guard [were] the sole source of guidance. (Zimbardo, 2004: 39)

Rather than being given formal training, the guards were therefore simply informed that it was their task to 'maintain the reasonable degree of order within the prison necessary for its effective functioning' (Haney et al., 1973: 7). To this end, the day before the study started, the guards and prison warden worked together to devise a set of 17 rules by which the prison would be run. Although, ominously, Rule 17 stated that 'failure to obey any of the above rules may result in punishment', the guards were not instructed to run the system in a way that involved abusing the prisoners. Instead, this was something that they would work out for themselves.

RESULTS

As already noted, the ultimate outcome of the SPE is well known and easy to relate: the guards' brutality towards the prisoners led Zimbardo to call the study to a premature close on the morning of the sixth day. However, the process of arriving at this point was convoluted and harder to describe formally. One reason for this is that the study was never written up in detail in a peer-reviewed psychology journal and hence no single 'authorized' publication provides a definitive account of events. Instead, key accounts of the study's findings are provided in different outlets produced for different audiences, in different forms, and at different points in time.

Nevertheless, from these various sources it is clear that the SPE went through at least three distinct phases before its termination. The first phase was one of *settling in* and involved the participants adjusting to the situation in which they found themselves. At this point neither prisoners nor guards were 'completely into their roles' and both groups displayed 'considerable hesitation and some awkwardness' (Zimbardo, 2007: 54). For example, during roll calls, the prisoners did not take their subordinate position especially seriously and the guards were not sure how to assert their authority. Guards, in particular, expressed diverse feelings about their role: some felt guilty and uneasy; some thought they were being too polite to prisoners and that they needed to exert more discipline. Those guards on the night shift appeared to be most comfortable with their role, led by Guard Hellman, an individual who came to earn the nickname 'John Wayne'. He enjoyed getting the prisoners to recite their prisoner number during roll call and gave them press-ups when they made mistakes. And when one of the prisoners showed dissent, the guards on the night shift ordered him into 'the Hole' – a small (2 × 7 ft) windowless closet that the experimenters had set aside to be used for solitary confinement. However, this – together with a number of other small incidents – started to annoy the prisoners and 'combine[d] to give [them] a new collective identity as something more than a collection of individuals trying to survive on their own' (Zimbardo, 2007: 51).

The emergent sense of shared grievance among the prisoners led the study into a second phase: *rebellion*. Angered and frustrated by the treatment that the guards were starting to mete out, some of the prisoners started to formulate plans for rebellion. They began by displaying signs of insubordination – complaining about their conditions, swearing at the guards, and refusing to follow their orders. This culminated in the occupants of two cells removing their caps and prison numbers and barricading themselves in their cell. As one cried out in a rallying call to his fellow prisoners, 'the time has come for violent revolution!' (Zimbardo, 2007: 61).

The overall effect of the rebellion was to embolden and empower the prisoners, but it also galvanized the guards in counterreaction and ushered in the study's long third phase: *tyranny*. The guards started by calling for reinforcements and together they decided to meet force with force. They broke into the barricaded cells, stripped the prisoners naked and forced the rebellion's ringleader into solitary confinement. As well as starting to harass and intimidate the prisoners more vigorously, guards also now worked to undermine solidarity among the prisoners through a strategy of 'divide and rule'. This involved singling out prisoners in the cell who had not participated in the revolt for special privileges and reorganizing the cells so that those prisoners who had rebelled were mixed in with those who had not been involved.

Zimbardo's role in instigating or condoning these actions is unclear. Nevertheless it is apparent that he was far from a detached observer. For example, in his role as superintendent, he recruited one rebel (Prisoner #8612) to act as a 'snitch' – offering him preferential treatment for informing on his fellow prisoners. To top this off, Prisoner #8612 came away from his meeting with Zimbardo with the belief that it was no longer possible to leave the prison, and he returned to his fellow prisoners screaming '*You can't get out of here!*' As Zimbardo recounts, this had a 'transformational impact on the prisoners' (2007: 71). For with the prisoners' collective will now crushed, and that of guards consolidated, the scene was set for the guards to progressively dominate, oppress, and brutalize the prisoners.

Importantly, not all of the guards went down this path. Zimbardo observes that 'about a third became tyrannical in their arbitrary use of power ... [becoming] quite inventive in their techniques of breaking the prisoners and making them feel worthless' (1971: 154). Of the remaining guards, some strove to be 'tough but fair' while others endeavoured to be 'good guards', being friendly to the prisoners and doing them small favours. However, it is for the behaviour of the most abusive guards – epitomized by 'John Wayne' – that the study is best known. Over the course of the next four days they subjected the prisoners to increasingly degrading persecution. Roll calls lasted several hours and non-compliant prisoners (in particular, a new prisoner who went on hunger strike in protest at his conditions) were singled out for taunting and humiliation. Others were forced to do push-ups with a guard's foot on their back, or to do menial repetitive tasks including washing out toilet bowls with their bare hands, or to play homoerotic games of leapfrog.

The experimenters also got 'caught up' in these dynamics. Thus, when on Day 3 of the study a rumour spread that the prisoners were planning an escape, Zimbardo introduced a new prisoner as an informer to find out about, and help foil, the plot. When this strategy appeared to be failing, he formulated a second plan in which the guards were instructed 'to chain the prisoners' legs together, put bags over their heads' and move them to another room in the building (Zimbardo, 2007: 97). The experimenters also went to great lengths to convince visitors (in particular, the prisoners' relatives) that the prison system was harmless, at the same time that they ran mock parole boards which belittled and verbally abused the prisoners. As the study moved towards its conclusion, then, it was not just the guards and prisoners who succumbed to the power of their role, but also the experimenters. Indeed, not only does Zimbardo cite this realization ('the horror of realizing that *I* could easily have traded places with the most brutal guard'; 1971: 113) as one of his main reasons for ending the study, but he also sees it as one of the SPE's most important messages:

> I began to talk, walk, and act like a rigid institutional authority figure more concerned about the security of 'my prison' than the needs of the young men entrusted to my care as a psychological researcher. In a sense, I consider the extent to which I was transformed to be the most profound measure of the power of the situation. (Zimbardo, 2004: 40)

IMPACT OF THE STANFORD PRISON EXPERIMENT

CHALLENGING DISPOSITIONALISM

As a vehicle for advancing Zimbardo's situationist thesis, the SPE has proved enormously influential. This is partly because, as well as speaking to core issues in social psychology, the SPE also generated heated ethical debate (e.g., Savin, 1973; Zimbardo, 1973). Indeed, this ultimately prompted the American Psychological Association to tighten guidelines for participation in psychological research in order to ensure that the abuses witnessed at Stanford would never be repeated.

Testimony to the study's impact, the original article by Haney and colleagues has been cited over 1,300 times; the SPE website receives an average of more than 3,000 visitors a day; and the study has inspired several feature films (notably *Das Experiment* in 2001, *The Experiment* in 2010 and *The Stanford Prison Experiment* in 2015). In line with Zimbardo's rationale, the great strength of the study is that it shows that extreme behaviour – in this case a willingness to participate in acts of extreme brutality that help to perpetuate a system of tyranny – cannot be understood simply with recourse to the personalities of those involved. In large part this is because, as Zimbardo argues, the SPE provides stark and vivid evidence of the capacity for people's characters to be *transformed* by the context in which they find themselves.

This point has been taken on board by a great many commentators as they struggle to explain the willingness of seemingly civilized people to engage in acts of brutality and barbarism. The historian Christopher Browning (1992) thus draws parallels between the behaviour of guards in the SPE and the activities of Reserve Police Battalion (RPB) 101, a mobile Nazi killing unit that roamed German-occupied Poland and murdered at least 38,000 Jews between July 1942 and November 1943. Browning shows that the members of this unit were not fanatics or even particularly pro-Nazi, and were not forced to do what they did. As the title of his book puts it, for Browning they were just 'ordinary men' who, like Zimbardo's guards, succumbed to a system that 'alone was a *sufficient* condition to produce aberrant, anti-social behavior' (1992: 168, original emphasis).

More recently, though, there has been a massive resurgence of interest in the SPE as analysts have attempted to come to terms with the horrific images that emerged from Abu Ghraib in early 2003. Indeed, the parallels between the two prisons are striking, and Zimbardo himself recalls the 'shock of recognition' when he watched the *60 Minutes II* programme in which the abuses of Iraqi detainees were revealed: 'these images made me relive the worst scenes of the Stanford Prison Experiment. There were the bags over prisoners' heads; the nakedness; the sexually humiliating games' (2004: 328).

Initial responses by military and political leaders attempted to dismiss these abuses as isolated incidents, and as the perverted actions of a few 'rogue soldiers'. However, Zimbardo questioned this account and went so far as to present himself as an expert witness for the defence at the trial of Ivan 'Chip' Frederick, a staff sergeant accused of torturing detainees at Abu Ghraib. On the basis of evidence from the SPE, Zimbardo challenged the idea that Frederick did what he did simply because he was a 'bad apple'. Instead, like the guards in the SPE, Zimbardo describes him as a 'chip off the best block' who was unwittingly perverted by the 'bad barrel' in which he found himself (2004: 344).

BEYOND THE STANFORD PRISON EXPERIMENT

CHALLENGING SITUATIONISM AND ADVANCING INTERACTIONISM

In presenting the above analysis, Zimbardo won himself many supporters, most notably among those who saw the dispositional 'bad apple' narrative as an attempt by US authorities to distance themselves from events at Abu Ghraib, and to deny all responsibility for them. Nevertheless, he also attracted criticism. For example, in a letter to *The Observer* (the official magazine of the Association for Psychological Science) Vladimir Konečni observed that:

> Even someone fully convinced of the sufficient applicability of the empirical results marshalled by Zimbardo ... is presumably forced by the existence of guards who did not 'misbehave' to admit that a pure situational explanation cannot be at issue but rather one involving the interaction of situational factors with those of personality, attitudes and expectations. (2007: 9)

Later that year, this same *interactionist* argument was articulated in another letter to *The Observer* in which a group of 49 psychologists protested that 'Zimbardo has misrepresented the scientific evidence in an attempt to offer a purely situational account of the antisocial acts perpetrated at Abu Ghraib' (Donnellan et al., 2007). 'The scientific consensus', they continued, 'is that people vary in their propensity for antisocial behaviour and that environments transact with personalities.' It is notable too that Zimbardo's evidence at Frederick's trial was met with similar scepticism by the Army prosecutor, Christopher Graveline:

> Impossible to resist the situational forces?... Clearly the situation a person faces plays a significant role in his actions, but to say that bad action becomes inevitable negates the responsibility, free will, conscience and character of the person. (Graveline and Clemens, 2010: 179)

QUESTIONING THE SPE: WHAT WAS 'NATURAL', 'NOVEL' AND 'NORMAL'?

Beyond their intellectual difficulties with Zimbardo's situationist position, another reason why commentators and researchers resile from the suggestion that there was 'a certain inevitability' to the abuse shown by guards at Abu Ghraib is that they have reflected closely on the procedural features of the SPE which are used to support this conclusion. Scrutiny of this form was first provided by Ali Banuazizi and Siamak Movahedi (1975) in a probing *American Psychologist* article that exposed several grounds on which Zimbardo's claims could be questioned.

First, the claim that guard aggression was 'emitted simply as a "natural" consequence of being in the uniform of a "guard" and asserting the power inherent in that role' (Haney et al., 1973: 12) seems inconsistent with the content of Zimbardo's briefing of his guards before the start of the SPE. In this he instructed them:

> You can create in the prisoners feelings of boredom, a sense of fear to some degree, you can create a notion of arbitrariness that their life is totally controlled by us, by the system, you, me – that they'll have no privacy at all. ... There'll be constant surveillance. Nothing they do will go unobserved. They'll have no freedom of action, they can do nothing, or say nothing that we don't permit. We're going to take away their individuality in various ways. In general what all this leads to is a sense of powerlessness. (Zimbardo, 1989)

As Philip Banyard observes: 'it is not, as Zimbardo suggests, the guards who wrote their own scripts on the blank canvas of the SPE, but Zimbardo who creates the script of terror' (2007: 494). Moreover, the idea that the experimenter's guidance is critical to the production of particular outcomes is also supported by a seldom-cited study that Sid Lovibond and his colleagues conducted at the University of New South Wales in the late 1970s (Lovibond et al., 1979). This incorporated three conditions in which guards were instructed to run a prison along very different lines. Challenging any suggestion that guard brutality is either natural or inevitable, the researchers found that if guards were encouraged to engage in 'participatory' practices (e.g., respecting prisoners as individuals and including them in decision-making processes) then the resultant regime was both moderate and benign (which is one reason why the study has not attracted much attention).

Second, while Zimbardo claims that it was the guards who dreamed up the various abuses that were meted out to prisoners in the SPE, it would appear that in this they were simply making use of props and procedures that had been provided by the experimenters (e.g., chains, bags over the head, forced nudity). In some cases the guards were also clearly instructed to use these tools. But even where they were not, the fact that Zimbardo and Jaffe – in their roles as Prison Superintendent and Warden – did not intervene to stop any prisoner abuse presumably communicated to participants some sense that what they were doing was 'appropriate'. In this way the guards' behaviour can be understood as their response to a range of cues and demands that were embedded in the SPE's design (see Banuazizi and Movahedi, 1975). Indeed, this concern was expressed rather more forcibly by Zimbardo's chief advisor, Carlo Prescott, in a letter that he wrote to *The Stanford Daily* in 2005:

> My opinion, based on my observations, was that Zimbardo began with a preformed
> blockbuster conclusion and designed an experiment to 'prove' that conclusion ... How
> can Zimbardo ... express horror at the behavior of the 'guards' when they were
> merely doing what Zimbardo and others, myself included, encouraged them to do or
> frankly established as ground rules? (2005: 8)

More recently, a third objection to the SPE has focused on Zimbardo's claim that
participants in the study were simply normal college students. This point arises
from research by Thomas Carnahan and Sam MacFarland (2007) at Western
Kentucky University that sought to assess whether there is anything unusual
about the type of person who volunteers to participate in such a study. To answer
this question, these researchers placed two adverts in a local newspaper. One
contained exactly the same wording as the original advert for the SPE, indicating
that 'college students [were] needed for a psychological study of prison life'; the
other was worded identically but simply omitted the phrase 'of prison life'. When
Carnahan and MacFarland subsequently compared the personality profile of the
two sets of volunteers, they found that they were very different. Specifically, those
who responded to the invitation to take part in 'a study of prison life' (rather than
just 'a study') tended to be more authoritarian, more Machiavellian, more narcis-
sistic and more socially dominant. They were also less empathic and less altruistic.

Carnahan and MacFarland acknowledge the difficulty of making inferences
about the students who volunteered for the SPE on the basis of these findings. Not
least, this is because they cannot explain differences in the behaviour of prisoners
and guards, and the results are inconsistent with evidence that participants in the
SPE had normal levels of authoritarianism (Haney and Zimbardo, 2009).
Nevertheless, Carnahan and MacFarland's findings raise the possibility that those
who would volunteer for a study like the SPE may not be quite so 'normal' as is
generally suggested and that here, as in prisons more generally, certain types of
people may be more likely to select themselves into particular situations than others.
Again, this suggestion fits both (a) with Zimbardo's own evidence that only one-
third of his guards engaged in extreme forms of tyrannical behaviour (a figure
which, as it happens, corresponds to the proportion of abusive members of RPB
101; Browning, 1992), and (b) with the idea that abuse is the product of an *interaction* between the individual and his or her environment rather than simply a
product of one or other of these elements in isolation.

Extending the SPE:
The role of social identity and leadership

These various challenges to Zimbardo's situationist account are in many ways
crystallized by another prison study that we conducted 30 years after the SPE –
The BBC Prison Study (BPS) (Reicher and Haslam, 2006; see also Haslam and
Reicher, 2005, 2009). This revisited issues raised by the SPE using the same basic
paradigm as Zimbardo's study – seeking to examine the behaviour of 15 men who
had been randomly assigned to roles as guards or prisoners within a specially
constructed prison-like environment over a period of up to two weeks.

Importantly, the BPS differed from the SPE in two key respects. First, unlike Zimbardo, we did not assume any role within the prison, so that we could study group dynamics without directly managing them. Second, the study involved a number of manipulations that had been devised on the basis of *social identity theory* (SIT). This theory was developed at the University of Bristol in the 1970s by Henri Tajfel and John Turner and, among other things, it suggests that people do not automatically take on roles associated with group membership, but do so only when they have come to *identify* with the group in question (Tajfel and Turner, 1979; see Chapters 9 and 10). This suggests that the roles will only be accepted when they are seen as an expression of a person's sense of self (i.e., the social identity of 'us'). Moreover, the theory suggests that when members of a low-status group (e.g., prisoners) come to develop a sense of shared social identity this can be a basis for them to collectively *resist* oppression rather than just succumb to it (see Haslam and Reicher, 2012a).

The analysis provided by SIT can be used to reinterpret a number of key events in the SPE. In the first instance, it suggests that guards only came to identify with their role, and to define that role in brutal terms, because a tyrannical social identity was actively promoted by Zimbardo in his guard briefing ('We're going to take away their individuality ...'). Similarly, it suggests that prisoners only became passive because (and after) their social identity had been systematically broken down by the actions of the guards and the experimenters. Rather than guard aggression and prisoner submission being 'natural' expressions of role, SIT therefore provides a basis for seeing these outcomes as specific responses to the *particular* structures that Zimbardo's leadership created in the SPE.

This conclusion is lent further support by several key findings from the BPS (Reicher and Haslam, 2006). First, the study provided no evidence of guards succumbing blindly to their role. Instead, in the absence of leadership from the experimenters, the guards disagreed among themselves about how to interpret their role and, as a result, they never developed a shared sense of identity. This meant not just that they were unable to run the prison along tyrannical lines, but that they had difficulty running it at all. Second, among the prisoners there was also no evidence that they were overwhelmed by the context in which they found themselves such that they succumbed uncritically to the demands of their role. Indeed, on the contrary (and as predicted by SIT), as their sense of shared identity increased they displayed increasing resistance to the guards. This culminated on Day 6 of the study when a group of prisoners mounted a revolt that brought the guards' regime to an end and which ushered in a new 'Commune' in which prisoners and guards came together to run the prison along collaborative rather than conflictual lines.

For a number of reasons, however, on Day 7 of the study the Commune itself began to run into difficulty. Significantly too, now tyranny *did* begin to rear its head. Specifically, a group composed of former prisoners and former guards proposed a coup in which the guard–prisoner divide would be reinstated and they would be the 'new guards'. They requested black berets and black sunglasses as symbols of this new authoritarian system, and talked about ways of using force to ensure that prisoners 'toed the line'. As at Stanford, this new regime never came to pass because we brought the study to an early close on Day 8.

Yet while the outcome of the BPS is superficially similar to that of the SPE, the path that led to this outcome suggests a very different analysis of tyranny from that proposed by Zimbardo. In the first instance, this is because when participants in the BPS became committed to tyranny they were not acting in terms of roles assigned by the experimenters, but instead had *rejected* those roles and adopted new ones. When they sought to advance the goals of a tyrannical group this was therefore an *active choice* that reflected high levels of identification with the group and its mission. Related to this point, it was also the case that there was *variation* in participants' enthusiasm for this tyrannical solution, and that those who were most enthusiastic were the participants who had been most authoritarian at the study's outset. In line with data from the SPE and RPB 101, individual differences do therefore appear to be implicated in the development of tyranny. Significantly, though, it is apparent that in the BPS individuals did not exert a stable level of influence on events – in part because their personal psychology was transformed and *given meaning* by emergent group dynamics. Among other things, this meant that authoritarian participants were only in a position to express and advance their authoritarian ambitions once they had been galvanized by a sense of shared identity that had both steeled them and drawn more moderate individuals to their cause.

All this suggests that tyranny arises neither from disposition nor situation alone, nor even from a mechanical interaction between these elements. Instead it arises from a *dynamic interactionism* in which individuals who are inclined towards tyranny (in part as a result of prior group experience) come to exert influence over others (and therefore over events) only when they come to represent a shared social identity and are able to exercise *leadership* on that basis (Haslam and Reicher, 2007, 2012b). It was these processes that allowed particular leaders to come close to tyranny in the BPS, and it was these same processes that allowed Zimbardo and some of his guards to create tyranny in the SPE. And while the SPE leaves us with unanswered questions about what would motivate a leader to promote tyranny in the way that Zimbardo did in his guard briefing, a strength of the BPS is that it gives us some insight into the social and historical dynamics that take groups and their leaders down this path.

CONCLUSION

The Stanford Prison Experiment is rightly recognized as a classic study in social psychology. Fundamentally, this is because it provides powerful testimony of the capacity for people who have reasonable claims to be considered normal, decent and civilized to perpetrate acts that are abnormal, indecent and uncivilized. In the falsificationist tradition that points to the power of a single case to demand a major rethinking of established wisdom, it remains a trump card that can be played to counter arguments that tyranny is perpetrated only by those who have strong inclinations towards tyranny, or that barbarianism is the preserve only of barbarians. This dispositionalist argument was used to explain brutality in the 1970s, it remains popular today, and it is likely to have continued appeal for the foreseeable future. For this reason the core message of the SPE is unlikely to lose either its appeal or its relevance in the years ahead.

Yet while the SPE provides a strong basis for questioning dispositionalism, it is also the case that in the 45 years since it was conducted researchers have issued major challenges to Zimbardo's staunch situationism. First, close analysis points to ways in which the tyranny observed in the SPE can be explained with reference to methodological features that Zimbardo has tended to overlook or downplay. Second, studies that have revisited the paradigm of the SPE have generated data which suggest that dispositions play a role in drawing people into particular contexts and also in orienting them towards particular group activities once there. Third, a wealth of evidence suggests that in seeking to explain tyranny (both in experiments and in the world at large) we need to move beyond the question of whether it is a product of people's dispositions *or* the situation in which they find themselves, to understand instead how these elements combine. Indeed, even here the evidence takes us beyond the simple suggestion that tyranny is just a question of whether particular people find themselves in particular places. For it appears that the interaction of person and context which leads to tyranny (and also to resistance) is *dynamic* such that, on the one hand, group contexts transform individuals but, on the other, individuals transform contexts, primarily through their capacity to represent, lead and mobilize groups.

The great strength of the SPE is that it throws out a bold invitation to consider these various issues in depth and thereby to advance our understanding of a range of important social processes – not just those that give rise to tyranny, but also those that fuel resistance. Yet in many ways, this has also been the study's great weakness. For not only did the ethical concerns that the study aroused serve to deter researchers from replicating Zimbardo's methods, but so too the stature of the SPE has often deterred those who approach the study from looking beyond the simplistic narrative that Zimbardo provides. When they do, it becomes apparent not just that there is much more to see, but also that there is a lot more that needs explaining.

FURTHER READING

Haney, C., Banks, C. and Zimbardo, P. (1973) 'A study of prisoners and guards in a simulated prison', *Naval Research Reviews*, September: 1–17. Washington, DC: Office of Naval Research.

This article provides a succinct account of the SPE.

Zimbardo, P. (2007) *The Lucifer Effect: How Good People Turn Evil*. London: Random House.

The world had to wait another 34 years for the extensive account that Zimbardo provided in this 551-page volume. This became an international best-seller and a platform for worldwide publicity largely because it couples an extensive and highly readable account of the SPE with an analysis of atrocities at Abu Ghraib – drawing on Zimbardo's role as an expert witness at the trial of Ivan Frederick.

Graveline, C. and Clemens, M. (2010) *The Secrets Of Abu Ghraib Revealed: American Soldiers on Trial.* Dulles, VA: Potomac Books.

Graveline and Clemens were Army prosecutors at the same trial. Their 2010 book provides a disturbing account of goings-on in the prison and on this basis they raise questions about the validity of Zimbardo's analysis.

Banuazizi, A. and Movahedi, S. (1975) 'Interpersonal dynamics in a simulated prison: A methodological analysis', *American Psychologist*, 30: 152–60.

Carnahan, T. and McFarland, S. (2007) 'Revisiting the Stanford Prison Experiment: Could participant self-selection have led to the cruelty?', *Personality and Social Psychology Bulletin*, 33: 603–14.

These two papers provide evidence that suggests that demand characteristics and selection biases may have played a role in the SPE's findings.

Reicher, S.D. and Haslam, S.A. (2006) 'Rethinking the psychology of tyranny: The BBC Prison Experiment', *British Journal of Social Psychology*, 45: 1–40.

This article challenges Zimbardo's study on a range of other grounds, in the course of presenting a detailed account of findings from the 2002 BBC Prison Study.

REFERENCES

Banuazizi, A. and Movahedi, S. (1975) 'Interpersonal dynamics in a simulated prison: A methodological analysis', *American Psychologist*, 30: 152–60.

Banyard, P. (2007) 'Tyranny and the tyrant', *The Psychologist*, 20: 494–5.

Browning, C. (1992) *Ordinary Men: Reserve Police Battalion 101 and the Final Solution in Poland.* London: Penguin Books.

Carnahan, T. and McFarland, S. (2007) 'Revisiting the Stanford Prison Experiment: Could participant self-selection have led to the cruelty?', *Personality and Social Psychology Bulletin*, 33: 603–14.

Donnellan, M.B., Fraley, R.C. and Krueger, R.F. (2007) 'Not so situational', *APS Observer*, 20(6): 5.

Graveline, C. and Clemens, M. (2010) *The Secrets Of Abu Ghraib Revealed: American Soldiers on Trial.* Dulles, VA: Potomac Books.

Haney, C., Banks, C. and Zimbardo, P. (1973) 'A study of prisoners and guards in a simulated prison', *Naval Research Reviews*, September: 1–17. Washington, DC: Office of Naval Research.

Haney, C. and Zimbardo, P.G. (2009) 'Persistent dispositionalism in interactionist clothing: Fundamental attribution error in explaining prison abuse', *Personality and Social Psychology Bulletin,* 35: 807–14.

Haslam, S.A. and Reicher, S.D. (2005) 'The psychology of tyranny', *Scientific American Mind*, 16(3): 44–51.

Haslam, S.A. and Reicher, S.D. (2007) 'Beyond the banality of evil: Three dynamics of an interactionist social psychology of tyranny', *Personality and Social Psychology Bulletin*, 33: 615–22.

Haslam, S.A. and Reicher, S.D. (2009) *The BBC Prison Study website*. Available at: www.bbcprisonstudy.org.

Haslam, S.A. and Reicher, S.D. (2012a) 'When prisoners take over the prison: A social psychology of resistance', *Personality and Social Psychology Review*, 16: 152–79.

Haslam, S.A. and Reicher, S.D. (2012b) 'Contesting the "nature" of conformity: What Milgram and Zimbardo's studies really show', *PLoS Biology, 10*(11): e1001426.

Konečni, V.J. (2007) 'Bad apples and bad barrels: Bad metaphors and blind spots regarding evil?', *APS Observer*, 20(5): 9–10.

Lovibond, S.H., Mithiran, X. and Adams, W.G. (1979) 'The effects of three experimental prison environments on the behaviour of non-convict volunteer subjects', *Australian Psychologist*, 14: 273–87.

Prescott, C. (2005) 'The lie of the Stanford Prison Experiment', *The Stanford Daily*, 28 April: 8. Available at: www.stanforddaily.com/2005/04/28/the-lie-of-the-standford-prison-experiment/.

Reicher, S.D. and Haslam, S.A. (2006) 'Rethinking the psychology of tyranny: The BBC Prison Study', *British Journal of Social Psychology*, 45: 1–40.

Savin, H.B. (1973) 'Professors and psychological researchers: Conflicting values in conflicting roles', *Cognition*, 2: 147–9.

Tajfel, H. and Turner, J.C. (1979) 'An integrative theory of intergroup conflict', in W.G. Austin and S. Worchel (eds), *The Social Psychology of Intergroup Relations*. Monterey, CA: Brooks/Cole. pp. 33–48.

Time (1972) 'A year ago at Attica', 100(13), 25 Sept: 22.

Zimbardo, P.G. (1971) 'The psychological power and pathology of imprisonment', *Hearings before Subcommittee No.3 of the Committee on the Judiciary House of Representatives Ninety-Second Congress, First sessions on corrections – Part II, Prisons, prison reform, and prisoners' rights: California* (Serial No. 15, 25 October). Washington, DC: US Government Printing Office.

Zimbardo, P.G. (1973) 'On the ethics of intervention in human psychological research: With special reference to the Stanford Prison Experiment', *Cognition*, 2: 243–56.

Zimbardo, P. (1989) *Quiet Rage* (video). Stanford, CA: Stanford University.

Zimbardo, P.G. (2004) 'A situationist perspective on the psychology of evil: Understanding how good people are transformed into perpetrators', in A. Miller (ed.), *The Social Psychology of Good and Evil*. New York: Guilford. pp. 21–50.

Zimbardo, P. (2007) *The Lucifer Effect: How Good People Turn Evil*. London: Random House.

9

Intergroup Relations and Conflict

Revisiting Sherif's Boys' Camp studies

Michael J. Platow and John A. Hunter

BACKGROUND

From 1949 to 1954, the Turkish-born social psychologist Muzafer Sherif and his colleagues conducted three field experiments with schoolboys who were attending summer camps in various locations in the United States. The studies came to be known collectively as 'the Boys' Camp studies', and they are probably the most famous and influential field studies in the discipline of social psychology.

The timing of the studies – falling squarely between the end of the Second World War and the onset of the Cold War – places the Boys' Camp studies well within that body of psychological work seeking answers to the intergroup atrocities of Nazi Germany. These atrocities, together with Sherif's own experiences – witnessing the rise of Fascism, imprisonment in Turkey for his criticism of Nazism, and narrowly escaping being killed by Greek soldiers – loomed large in Sherif's thinking. Moreover, the historical period in which the Boys' Camp studies were conducted was a time of increasing decolonization and the development of nationalist senti-ments among colonized peoples. These, too, represented dynamic intergroup relations that shaped Sherif's thinking. Finally too, the fact that the third study was conducted on the eve of the Civil Rights era in the United States (where Sherif lived and worked) meant that race relations were emerging as a focal point for politics and social action.

All these developments were a concern to Sherif, but when he sought to under-stand them as a social psychologist, he found himself confronted with models that sought to explain intergroup relations in terms of biological processes, individual processes (e.g., personality and individual frustration), or purely *intra*group pro-cesses. But taking his lead from other notable scientists (e.g., Albert Einstein), Sherif understood the necessity of developing theoretical concepts that addressed pro-cesses at the same level as the research questions that were being asked (e.g., Sherif, 1951). Thus, to understand intergroup phenomena (i.e., the ways that groups behave towards each other) he believed that it was critical to take an intergroup approach. To be sure, being a *psychologist*, he saw the individual's 'perception of the social world', coupled with the individual's 'learning about it' and appraisals and evaluations of it, as a key focus of his analysis (Sherif and Sherif, 1969: 8). But, in Sherif's thinking (and that of his colleague and wife, Carolyn), the individual should not be conceived in isolation from the rest of the world, but as interdependent with it, so that the individual 'is not merely the recipient of sociocultural influences ... [but] is an active participant in the reaction of social influences' (Sherif and Sherif, 1969: 9). He believed that 'interpersonal relations occur within larger organized contexts, so that it is very difficult to consider other individuals as discrete social stimuli' (1969: 15). Individual behaviour, while made possible only through individual minds, *cannot* be understood through analysis of those individual minds individually and removed from the social context. Humans, he asserted, do not live alone, but have 'identifications and commitments in religion, politics, ideology and so on' (1969: xiii), creating social organization which, in turn, 'recasts man' (1969: 19).

It is this reciprocal interplay between individuals and their context that lies at the heart of Sherif's theoretical thinking. For him, the progress and pattern of intergroup behaviour represented *normal* social-psychological functioning, and is neither 'irrational' (Sherif and Sherif, 1969: 269), nor a 'problem of *deviate behaviour*' (Sherif et al., 1961: 198).

In practice, however, it can sometimes appear as if Sherif took a very one-sided approach to intergroup relations. As we describe below, he and his colleagues did all they could in their Boys' Camp studies to show that biological and personality constructs could not account for their findings. As a consequence, these studies ultimately bear testament to the strength of the social context, and this is possibly the most significant legacy of his work. To achieve that, he worked hard to demonstrate the power of the social context in shaping both intragroup and intergroup attitudes and behaviours. But his goal was never to discard completely other potential factors because:

> Theories of intergroup relations which posit single factors (such as the kind of leadership, national character, individual frustrations) as sovereign determinants of intergroup conflict or harmony have, at best, explained only selectively chosen cases. (Sherif et al., 1961: 199)

In the end, then, Sherif knowingly adopted a model of intergroup relations based upon small-group interactions (Sherif, 1951). At the same time, however, by moving out of the laboratory and choosing to conduct intensive field experiments, Sherif was ultimately able to test hypotheses and make inferences that extended well beyond the scope of nearly all social-psychological experimentation prior to, and since, his groundbreaking work. Indeed, the Harvard-based psychologist Roger Brown described the third, most famous, of the three Boys' Camp studies (the Robbers Cave study, named after the park in Oklahoma where it was conducted) as 'the most successful field experiment ever conducted on intergroup conflict'. And it was this quotation that the *New York Times* reproduced in its obituary for Sherif after his death from a heart attack in October 1988.

THE BOYS' CAMP STUDIES

OBJECTIVES AND DESIGN

The key goal of the Boys' Camp studies was to examine experimentally how intergroup attitudes and behaviours – such as prejudice and discrimination – are affected by the nature of intergroup relations. Like all researchers, the first challenge that Sherif and colleagues faced was the translation of their broad conceptual notions of groups and intergroup relations into specific experimental practices. Sherif began the empirical work by attempting to define precisely the 'minimal essential properties of groups' (Sherif et al., 1955: 371). Note that the very claim that groups have 'properties' reveals Sherif's belief that groups had a material reality. Of course, he recognized the importance of group members' psychological internalization of, for example, group norms, and the importance of group members' 'identity and self conception[s]' as they related to their groups (Sherif et al., 1961: 8). But a group, in Sherif's work, is more than a psychological representation; it is

> a social unit which consists of a number of individuals who, at a given time, stand in more or less definite interdependent status and role relationships to one another and which explicitly or implicitly possess a set of values or norms regulating the behavior of members at least in matters of consequence to the group. (Sherif et al., 1955: 372)

However, Sherif and his colleagues also needed to clarify one more concept: intergroup relations. For them, intergroup relations were conceptualized as 'functional relationships between two or more groups ... and their respective members' (Sherif and Sherif, 1969: 223). Embedded here, again, is the basic premise that these relations entail actual, material interactions. Moreover, these relationships occur *both* between individual group members *and* between the groups as entities. To study such relations, then, Sherif needed to employ a method that involved actual interactions: first, between people *within* at least two separate groups, and then *between* these groups.

To achieve these goals within the Boys' Camp studies, Sherif and his colleagues devised a strategy that involved three experimental phases, each of which lasted approximately one week – (1) *ingroup formation*, (2) *intergroup conflict* and (3) *reduction of intergroup conflict*. As can be seen from Table 9.1, each study incorporated slightly different variants of these phases, and Experiment 2 did not involve the third phase. In each study, the participants were boys who were naïve to the experimental hypotheses and, in fact, to the fact that they were taking part in an experiment at all. Instead, they believed they were attending a normal summer camp (although their parents, of course, did know about the researchers' purpose).

PARTICIPANTS

In selecting participants, Sherif and his colleagues actively worked to ensure 'homogeneity of subjects as to sociocultural and personal backgrounds' (Sherif et al., 1961: 59). All were white (i.e., of European descent) boys around 12 years of age,

Table 9.1 Outline of the three phases of the three Boys' Camp studies (based on Sherif and Sherif, 1969)

	Experiment		
Year conducted	1949	1953	1954
Example reference	Sherif, 1951	Sherif et al., 1955	Sherif et al., 1961
The groups	'Bull Dogs' and 'Red Devils'	'Panthers' and 'Pythons'	'Eagles' and 'Rattlers'
Location of study	Connecticut	'Upstate' New York	Robbers Cave, Oklahoma
Phase 1: Ingroup formation			
Spontaneous interpersonal choices	X	X	
Arbitrary division into two matched sets according to specified criteria	X	X	X
Phase 2: Intergroup conflict			
Win–lose competition	X	X	X
Planned frustration of ingroups	X	X	
Phase 3: Reduction of conflict			
Common enemy, individual activities, adult intervention	X		
Contact without interdependence	X		X
Provision of superordinate goals			X

of Protestant backgrounds, and of normal physical and psychological development. School records were reviewed, interviews were conducted with parents, and psychological tests (e.g., of intelligence and personality) were administered. The goal was to obtain a sample of participants who, as far as possible, were *least likely* to have some psychological, familial or sociocultural (e.g., experience of discrimination) attribute that might contaminate the study's findings. In short, these boys were thoroughly normal. And this meant that if they ultimately came to behave viciously towards each other, this could not be attributed to any inherent deficiencies in their character or background.

METHOD AND RESULTS

PHASE 1: INGROUP FORMATION

The first phase in all three studies was one of ingroup formation *prior to* any subsequent intergroup interactions. In the first two days of Experiments 1 and 2, all boys were given the opportunity to develop spontaneous, interpersonal friendships.

After this period, however, the experimenters systematically assigned the boys to two distinct categories. These cut across any friendships they had initially formed, so that friends were now separated. This allowed the researchers to observe the emergence of group processes in the absence of any pre-existing ties. Experiment 3 brought two sets of boys to the research camp sites and kept them apart for all of Phase 1.

For the rest of Phase 1, Sherif and his colleagues created conditions that would ultimately transform these categories into social groups. The boys engaged in a series of activities that required interdependent interactions and shared goals. Maintaining the cover story of the summer camp, these activities included things like a treasure hunt (with a collective reward), and the collective building of dams and lean-tos (Sherif et al., 1955). Sometimes the boys simply went hiking, swimming and canoeing. The experimenters tried to limit competition within these forming groups, and competitive games (e.g., baseball) were held at bay until Phase 2 when explicit intergroup competition was introduced.

As Phase 1 progressed, the essential properties of groups that Sherif had previously identified emerged. The boys differentiated themselves into the roles of leaders and followers, and norms of behaviour emerged. For example, the boys took on different roles when camping and preparing food (see Figure 9.1). Some boys adopted leadership roles, with this leadership ultimately being recognized by both the other boys and the experimenters themselves. In addition, very strong norms developed that guided behaviour within each group, including norms promoting toughness and discouraging the expression of homesickness (Sherif et al., 1961). Boys who transgressed these norms were punished in various ways: for example, by being given the 'silent treatment' or by having to remove stones from a swimming hole (Sherif and Sherif, 1969).

Figure 9.1 Boys collaborate in camping and food preparation activities (from Sherif et al., 1961)

PHASE 2: INTERGROUP CONFLICT

After having established two distinct groups, Sherif next wanted to study the emergence of negative intergroup attitudes and behaviours. Would groups that had behaved fairly in the *intra*group phase of the research carry this form of behaviour into the intergroup phase? Or are intergroup attitudes and behaviours – like prejudice and discrimination – shaped by specific, material intergroup relations? And, if so, what is the nature of these relations?

To begin, recall that in the 1954 study, the boys did not initially know of the existence of the other group. This is an extremely important point. Although Sherif believed that functional, material intergroup relations were the cause of negative (and, ultimately, positive) intergroup attitudes and behaviours, he and his colleagues observed that negative attitudes were expressed *even before* actual intergroup contact. For example, upon discovering that there was another group nearby, one boy exclaimed, 'They better not be in our swimming hole' (Sherif et al., 1961: 94), and another referred to them as 'nigger campers' (1961: 95). Thus, even prior to competition, the boys already perceived a type of negative interdependence such that 'What is ours is not theirs'. And, associated with this, they also expressed highly prejudicial attitudes.

When the two groups were finally brought together, Sherif did so with the specific goal of examining the role of *intergroup competition for limited and valued resources*. He predicted that intergroup competition of this nature would lead to intergroup hostilities, negative intergroup stereotypes and enhanced *within*-group solidarity. To test this hypothesis, the boys competed over a series of days in a tournament composed of a series of typical summer-camp activities: baseball, tug-of-war, tent-pitching competitions, and song and skit competitions. Across all of these competitions, the original groups that developed during Phase 1 were maintained. Moreover, the experimenters intentionally chose subjectively evaluated competitions (e.g., song and skit) to allow the judges (i.e., the experimenters themselves) to control overall patterns of success and failure. Importantly, the competitions became strongly ego-involving for the boys, so much so that Sherif (1951: 416, italics in original) observed that '*group efforts and goals* became intensely *personal* ones for the individual members'.

Sherif's predictions were substantiated. As the competition progressed, increasingly negative intergroup attitudes were expressed. This hostility started with the groups disparaging each other and trading insults (e.g., 'You're not Eagles, you're pigeons', Sherif et al., 1961: 102; see Figure 9.2). Over time though, these confrontational words escalated into confrontational acts. Thus, after one loss, a boy from the losing group vowed to fight anyone from the winning group the next time the two met. On another occasion, when the losing group discovered the winning group's flag, their insults spiralled into actual burning of the flag. And during one lunch, hostility became so strong that, after shouting at each other across the room, the boys began throwing cups and knives at the other group and then went on to raid each others' cabins.

Figure 9.2 Expressions of negative intergroup attitudes resulting from intergroup competition in the Robbers Cave study (from Sherif et al., 1961)

Sherif and his colleagues, however, were interested in more than these spontaneous expressions of intergroup prejudice and hostility. They also wanted a systematic measure of the boys' intergroup attitudes. To this end, they asked boys from each group to rate the other boys from their own and the other group on a series of positive traits ('brave', 'tough', 'friendly') and negative traits ('sneaky', 'smart alecs', 'stinkers'). As Table 9.2 shows, negative intergroup attitudes were expressed not only in the comments that were made in the heat of competition, but also in ratings made upon colder reflection.

Finally, *inter*group competition also led to changes in *intra*group relations. As we have already mentioned, in Phase 1, specific role structures had developed within each group, with some boys assuming leadership roles and others occupying follower roles. However, after the broader social context changed in Phase 2, so too did this lead to changes in these role structures. For example, one boy who had been a relatively low-status bully in the group formation phase rose to the status of leader during the intergroup phase (Sherif and Sherif, 1969). Likewise, a Phase 1 leader fell from power during the Phase 2 when he expressed reluctance in the outgroup competition. In this way, Sherif's research showed that successful leadership is not about possessing a particular set of leadership characteristics (e.g., in the way that personality theories of leadership propose). Instead, the qualities required of a leader varied dramatically as a function of changes in social context.

Table 9.2 Ratings of ingroup and outgroup favourability at the end of Phase 2 in the Robbers Cave study (adapted from Sherif et al., 1961)

	Group being rated	
	Rattlers	Eagles
Group providing ratings		
Rattlers	4.86	2.76
Eagles	2.08	4.70

Note: Boys systematically rated the outgroup more negatively than their ingroup

PHASE 3: REDUCTION OF INTERGROUP CONFLICT

In the 1949 field experiment, a de-escalation in intergroup enmity was observed when the two groups combined to compete against an outside baseball team. In light of this, the researchers recognized that intergroup collaboration against a third party ('a common enemy') might be a way to promote intergroup harmony among the *original* two enemies.

Over the next few years, Sherif and his colleagues considered a number of ways of exploring this hypothesis. It was not, however, until the 1954 Robbers Cave study that they examined conflict reduction systematically. First, the researchers wanted to know whether intergroup contact, *in the absence of intergroup competition*, would lead to a reduction in intergroup hostility. Seven specific episodes of contact (involving eating, watching movies and setting off fireworks) were initiated over two days. Yet despite the repeated and positive nature of the contact tasks, this approach was ineffective. Indeed, rather than reducing hostility, contact between the two groups merely afforded new opportunities 'for overt acts of hostility and further exchanges of unflattering invectives' (Sherif et al., 1961: 209).

Next, a new hypothesis was tested: that negative intergroup attitudes and behaviours would be reduced, if not eliminated, under conditions in which the two groups were required to *cooperate* for the attainment of a mutually valued, *super-ordinate* goal. Importantly for Sherif, attainment of this goal could not be 'achieved by the efforts of one group alone' (Sherif et al., 1961: 52).

To test this hypothesis, several clever situations were engineered in which the two groups of boys had to work together in order to achieve goals that could not be achieved by either group alone. Specifically, the boys had to cooperate in order to (a) repair the camp's water supply, (b) pool enough money to watch a movie, (c) pull the food truck up a hill, and (d) set up camp. The implementation of these cooperative tasks over the next four to five days saw a gradual reduction in name calling, the use of derogatory terms, hostile expressions and the avoidance of out-group members. And again these findings were confirmed in intergroup ratings. Even more telling, however, the boys cheered when they found they could all take the same bus home, performed skits and songs for each other on the last night at the camp, and the winners of the last bean-toss game used their prize money to buy drinks for the losers.

THE IMPACT OF THE BOYS' CAMP STUDIES

As we have already noted, Sherif's Boys' Camp studies constitute one of the most influential social-psychological programmes of research on group and intergroup relations ever conducted. In them, Sherif and his colleagues were able to create psychologically meaningful groups (e.g., with a history, norms and internal status relations) and to demonstrate systematically the profound impact that variations in relationships both within and between the groups had on psychology and behaviour. In so doing, they were 'able to recreate many phenomena ... usually associated with long-term complex social and historical developments' (Tajfel, 1978: 435). Beyond this core intellectual contribution, however, there are also

Table 9.3 Three social-psychological lessons and corollaries from Sherif and his colleagues' Boys' Camp studies

Lesson 1	Groups have a material reality that includes interdependencies and role and status relationships
Corollary to Lesson 1	Interdependencies, and role and status relationships within groups, will vary dynamically with the nature of intragroup and intergroup relations
Lesson 2	Groups have a psychological validity, with group members identifying with the group and adopting the group's goals as their own personal goals
Lesson 3	Intergroup impressions (e.g., stereotypes), attitudes (e.g., prejudice) and behaviours (e.g., discrimination, hostility) are psychologically meaningful outcomes of the nature of intergroup relations
Corollary 1 to Lesson 3	Intergroup competition for limited resources causes negative intergroup impressions, attitudes and behaviour
Corollary 2 to Lesson 3	Sustained cooperation between groups necessary to achieve compelling superordinate goals will have a cumulative effect in reducing intergroup hostility
Corollary 3 to Lesson 3	Intergroup contact alone is not sufficient to reduce intergroup hostility

three more specific conclusions that can be drawn from the Boys' Camp studies. These are summarized in Table 9.3.

First, the studies demonstrate that *groups have a material reality* that includes interdependencies, and role and status relationships, but that these vary dynamically as a function of the nature of intragroup and intergroup relations. To some audiences, this might seem to be an obvious point. Yet one of Sherif's key successes in the Boys' Camp studies was to counter claims that groups in fact do *not* exist (at least as scientific entities), and that the only material reality lies at the level of the individual (e.g., Allport, 1924). Indeed, the Boys' Camp studies demonstrated unequivocally the presence and importance of social-psychological variables that exist *only* at the conceptual level of the group. It is conceptually impoverished, and empirically wrong, for example, to seek to understand the effectiveness of a leader without reference to the group that he or she leads (see also Haslam et al., 2011).

Second, the Boys' Camp studies demonstrated that *groups have substantive psychological meaning and significance for their members*. As Sherif noted, the boys in his studies identified strongly with their groups. These groups were psychologically real, engaging and self-defining. This meant that the successes of their groups were the boys' own successes, and the failures were their own failures. Moreover, even before material intergroup relations occurred, boys from one group expressed negative intergroup attitudes, and physical objects and locations became imbued with group-based meaning: it was not *the* swimming hole, but *our* swimming hole. These findings were destined to have a substantial impact on later thinking about the social psychology of groups and intergroup relations (e.g., see Chapter 10). Prior to the publication of the Boys' Camp studies, psychologists had typically explained stereotypes, prejudice and discrimination in terms either of some form of biological factor, *individual* psychological (decontextualized) characteristic, or *intra*group property (see Sherif and Sherif, 1969, for a review). Moreover, this pursuit continued even after the publication of these studies (e.g., Hamilton and Gifford, 1976; Sibley and Duckitt, 2008; see Chapter 14). However, the boys in these studies had been specifically selected to rule out alternative explanations of the findings based upon supposed psychological deficits.

Third, the studies also showed that *intergroup impressions, attitudes and behaviours* are both (a) *consequences of intergroup relations* (as opposed to causes) and also (b) *psychologically meaningful for group members*. Specifically, in the studies, intergroup impressions (i.e., *stereotypes*) were shown to vary meaningfully in both content and valence so as to reflect changes in the competitive and cooperative relationships between the two groups. Making this observation, however, neither condones nor excuses the holding and expression of negative stereotypes of groups in society at large. Rather, it provides a clear path to follow in pursuing broader social change: to reduce negative stereotypes and foster positive intergroup attitudes, one needs to change the real relationships between real groups from which they arise. In this respect, seeking to promote intergroup harmony simply by bringing members of the two groups together to see that 'they're all just normal, decent people' can be seen as dangerously naïve. Recall Sherif's failed attempts at promoting intergroup harmony by bringing together the boys from the two groups for mutually enjoyable, *but non-cooperative*, activities. These showed that intergroup contact alone is not sufficient to reduce intergroup hostility.

CRITICISMS OF THE BOYS' CAMP STUDIES

One common criticism of Sherif's work – levelled by both biographers and critical social psychologists (e.g., Brannigan, 2006; Grandberg and Sarup, 1992) – is that, for him and his colleagues, hypothesis testing typically came rather late in the research process. That is, following immersion in a given problem the researchers would develop insights about the nature of the problem, which they would then seek to confirm empirically. As a result, Sherif and his colleagues have been criticized for seeking to devise experiments that would *verify* (rather than test) their hypotheses (e.g., see Sherif, 1948: 357). For epistemological reasons, this type of approach will tend to have high external validity, but it is not well suited to the discovery of new insights (Cherry, 1995). Nevertheless, as we have noted, the Boys' Camp studies did, in fact, serve to counter much of the received wisdom at the time – and they still have this function today.

The Boys' Camp studies are often lauded for their innovative and methodological rigour (e.g., Billig, 1976; Fine, 2004; Pettigrew, 1992). The incorporation of mixed methods to study the developing and cumulative effects of real-time intergroup relations are, without doubt, outstanding. However, the implementation of the studies was not unproblematic. For example, the 1953 study was terminated when the boys discovered that they were being manipulated by the camp authorities – and for this reason the study is largely forgotten. Likewise, in the Robbers Cave study, two of the larger boys from the Eagle group became homesick and had to be sent home. This had at least two important consequences. First, the Rattler group, thought by the boys to be tougher, became the numerical majority group. Second, the experimenters felt that they needed to rig the eventual outcome of the tournament because other homesick Eagles were in 'some danger of disorganization ... in case of their defeat' (Sherif et al., 1961: 100). As Sherif and his colleagues (e.g., 1961: 128) acknowledge, these various intrusions by the experimenters may well have affected intergroup relations and the study's findings – yet they are not included in the overall theoretical analysis that Sherif provides.

Michael Billig (1976) has also pointed out that each of the field experiments actually contained *three* groups: two group of boys *and* one group of experimenters. In this manner, the main message of the study may not be how competition and cooperation affect intergroup attitudes and behaviours, but rather how one powerful group (i.e., the experimenters) can manipulate two less powerful groups (e.g., the Rattlers and the Eagles). Indeed, seeing the photographs of one group of boys raiding the cabin of the other group has always struck us as rather curious. How were the boys to interpret their supposed camp counsellors photographing their raid? We suspect that they took the photographing (and the fact that no punishment ensued) as a sign that their activities were condoned.

In relation to theory, several authors (e.g., Brewer and Brown, 1998; Turner, 1975) have also stressed that Sherif and his colleagues failed to distinguish between competition based on real, material competition and more symbolic competition (e.g., based on values, prestige, social status). However, these two broad types of competition can be seen to have quite different consequences for diverse forms of intragroup and intergroup behaviour (see e.g., Stephan and Stephan, 2000; Tajfel and Turner, 1979). Moreover, recent research that has examined both kinds of competition has revealed that each makes a *unique* contribution to our understanding of intergroup discrimination (Aberson and Gaffney, 2008).

The evidence from the Boys' Camp studies clearly shows that competition leads to increased intergroup discrimination, and that cooperation towards superordinate goals leads to a reduction in intergroup discrimination. Nevertheless, Sherif and his colleagues report much anecdotal evidence to suggest (a) that the boys showed ingroup favouring attitudes *before* the formal introduction of competition (see Sherif, 1966: 80; Sherif and Sherif, 1969: 239); and (b) that, although cooperation towards superordinate goals reduced ingroup favouritism, it did not eradicate it completely. This means that other social-psychological processes are clearly at play, ones that Sherif and his colleagues failed to address directly.

With regard to social-psychological processes, one of the major strengths of Sherif's research – its location in the field (as opposed to laboratory) – is also one of its biggest weaknesses. Because there were so many variables interacting in the field experiments (e.g., mutual frustration, ingroup bullying, intergroup attribution, the anticipation of competition, the consequences of winning or losing), it remains almost impossible to discern specifically what it was about any given situation that led to the observed effects (Dion, 1979; Rabbie, 1982; Platow and Hunter, 2001).

Finally, there are potential ethical criticisms with this programme of research. As a result of the experimental manipulations, the boys displayed high levels of intergroup hostility in which outgroup members – together with 'poor' ingroup members – were both verbally and physically assaulted. Some were called 'yellow', some were threatened with physical violence, while others were actually attacked. There were also examples of ostracism and ridicule (see Sherif, 1967: 92; Sherif et al., 1961: 93). To be sure, such things would be part-and-parcel of many boys' experiences at summer camp, but that does not make them any less harmful, and one might question the role that the experimenters played in encouraging them. And although these experiences could be seen as less noxious than those associated with subsequent studies (see Chapters 7 and 8), one needs also to remember that the participants here were children not adults.

BEYOND THE BOYS' CAMP STUDIES

E ach of the critiques above is valid. However, it is important to recognize that the Boys' Camp studies are not the end-point in the study of groups and intergroup relations, but rather the *foundation* for the 50 years of social-psychological research since. In the first instance, the findings of the Boys' Camp studies have been replicated in other field and experimental settings, cultures and diverse social categories (e.g., Brown, 2010; Platow and Hunter, 2001; Sherif and Sherif, 1969). Indeed, many of the critiques have themselves served as the basis for subsequent research, with the result that social psychologists now have more knowledge about the way in which many of the studies' uncontrolled variables do, in fact, impact upon intergroup relations.

But while the critiques remain valid, so too are the lessons learned. Indeed, since Sherif developed his theoretical analysis, researchers have gone on to clarify its ability to explain such things as rapid changes in the onset and dissipation of intergroup discrimination, and the process by which ingroup love evolves into outgroup hate (Brewer, 1999; Brown et al., 1986; Struch and Schwartz, 1989).

SOCIAL IDENTITY

The theoretical perspectives that are most directly indebted to Sherif and his colleagues are those that have, like him, eschewed an individualistic approach to intergroup relations: in particular, *social identity theory* (Tajfel and Turner, 1979) and *self-categorization theory* (Turner et al., 1987; collectively referred to as the *social identity approach*; see Haslam, 2004). Building upon Sherif's insights, this approach recognizes and emphasizes the importance of the broader social context – including specific relations between groups – in shaping group life. It also extends upon Sherif's observations regarding the importance of group identification as a basis for group behaviour – in particular stereotyping and prejudice (e.g., Oakes et al., 1994; Tajfel, 1978; Turner, 1982; see Chapter 10).

At the same time, it is true that there are fundamental differences between Sherif's analysis and the social identity approach. For example, Sherif focused on the analysis of 'structural properties of group interaction and formation, group products ... and the reciprocal functional relationships between groups and individual members' (Sherif and Cantril, 1947: 282). Analyses of these relationships, however, are less important in social identity analyses of intergroup behaviour – in part, as a result of Henri Tajfel's own minimal group studies which established that group-based behaviour could emerge in the absence of *intra*group interdependence, structure and roles (see Chapter 10). Interestingly, this behaviour took the form of ingroup favouritism *in the absence of intergroup competition*, which, as we have seen, was actually observed in the Robbers Cave study. In this sense, social identity theorizing (and associated empirical work) served to tease out the profound significance of Sherif's research in ways that his own theorizing did not. Accordingly, as John Turner observes, 'Tajfel and Turner were in agreement with Sherif and felt that he would have been a social identity theorist – they were certainly, in principle, Sherifians' (Turner and Reynolds, 2010: 16).

COMMON INGROUP IDENTITY

Related to such developments, Sherif's work also provided a platform for the *common ingroup identity approach* to prejudice reduction advanced by Samuel Gaertner and John Dovidio (e.g., Gaertner et al., 1993, 2000; see Chapter 13). In this approach, cognitive re-categorization of 'us' and 'them' into 'all of us' is argued to be the basis for reducing prejudice. This, indeed, was precisely the process that Sherif believed occurred in the context of intergroup cooperation for a superordinate goal in Phase 3 of his studies (e.g., see Sherif, 1951: 421).

Again, however, there are definite differences between Sherif's analysis and the common ingroup identity model. For example, a variety of factors are assumed to lead to this cognitive re-categorization rather than just successful cooperation for a superordinate goal. The common ingroup identity model also recognizes that cognitive re-categorization processes may be different for members of minority and majority groups (e.g., Dovidio et al., 2007), a factor not considered by Sherif and his colleagues.

LEADERSHIP

Sherif's Boys' Camp studies have also informed recent analyses of *leadership* (e.g., Platow et al., 2003; see also Haslam et al., 2011). In particular, the changes to leaders' status observed in Phase 2 of the Boys' Camp studies show that neither even-handedness nor attempts to control others through power guarantee leadership success in all situations. Instead, leadership is contingent upon leaders advancing ingroup interests that vary with context. Moreover, in this respect too, Sherif also anticipated the argument of self-categorization theorists that 'leadership is not a quality of leaders alone but rather of the *relationship* between leaders and followers' (Haslam et al., 2011). All this is not to say that self-categorization analyses of leadership have not developed our understandings beyond the Boys' Camp studies. They have. But, once again, these developments were ones for which Sherif laid important groundwork, in outlining essential concepts and in clarifying the importance of group-level social-psychological processes.

CONCLUSION

A simple conclusion from the Boys' Camp studies, and one that tends to be the focus of most discussion of them, is that intergroup competition leads to prejudice, and that intergroup cooperation reduces it. Insightful as this may be, the legacy of Sherif's studies is much wider and deeper than this – for they provide a very broad platform on which to build an understanding of the social psychology of groups and intergroup relations. And while it is true that the studies are not without fault, their shortcomings in no sense destroy either the lessons or the intellectual contributions that Sherif, his colleagues and the many other researchers who followed in his footsteps drew from them. Indeed, in this regard, it is hard to overestimate the continued impact that the studies have had on contemporary theoretical approaches to the study of intergroup relations, particularly the social identity approach. Certainly, it is undeniable that had the Boys' Camp studies not been conducted, our understanding of the social-psychological underpinnings of stereotyping, prejudice, and discrimination would be seriously impoverished.

Over half a century ago Muzafer Sherif and his colleagues set out to provide social-psychological answers to some of the most pressing questions of their day. Unfortunately, and despite the legacy of Sherif's work, the questions and social problems that inspired the Boys' Camp studies remain just as pressing. We can only speculate as to why their lessons have not been taken up more vigorously in the pursuit of social change. Some reasons lie in the critiques we outlined above. Yet we also suspect that problems have arisen because in focusing on the findings of his research, researchers and commentators have failed to attend to Sherif's deeper intellectual contributions – leading them to persist in trying to explain intergroup antagonism through analyses of individual differences or cognitive error.

And here too, one further reason for the failure to make practical progress is that researchers often fail to come to grips with the material realities that give rise to such antagonism. This was a problem that both Muzafer and Carolyn Sherif (1969: 284) recognized when they observed:

> If two groups are irrevocably committed to conflicting objectives, there is little point in discussing conditions that are conducive to reducing the conflict. They will continue to cast blame for the state of things on each other. ... In short, there are very real conflicts of vital interest that preclude the emergence of superordinate goals.

Thus, the process of bringing together groups that are entrenched in conflict, with the goal of promoting cooperation for a superordinate goal, is challenging in itself, and requires not just sound psychological understanding but also strong *political* will.

But this should not deter us. For as Muzafer and Carolyn observed, 'in modern world torn by strife, it is becoming more and more urgent that social scientists of all descriptions analyse conditions and trends that effectively foster [the] peaceable and productive pursuit of life' (1969: 284). Certainly, the scale of this task did not deter Sherif – a man who, as his colleague O.J. Harvey observed, 'in the domain of ideas and social issues' had 'a passion that carried him into areas and expanses of thought that few have equalled' (1989: 1326).

FURTHER READING

There are many published reviews, critiques and interpretations of Sherif's Boys' Camp studies. Interested readers will find some of these in our references below. However, we fear that reading (only) reviews misses the elegance, the insight, and both the depth and breadth of Sherif's work. For this reason, five of the six further readings that we recommend are by Sherif and his colleagues themselves. Without reading Sherif directly, many of his more important contributions will be lost in attempts to simplify his story.

Sherif, M., Harvey, O.J., White, B.J., Hood, W.R. and Sherif, C.W. (1961) *Intergroup Conflict and Cooperation: The Robbers Cave Experiment*. Norman, OK: Institute of Group Relations, University of Oklahoma.

A detailed book outlining the Robbers Cave Experiment.

Sherif, M. (1951) 'A preliminary experimental study of inter-group relations', in J.H. Rohrer and M. Sherif (eds), *Social Psychology at the Crossroads*. New York: Harper & Row. pp. 388–424.

Sherif, M., White, B.J. and Harvey, O.J. (1955) 'Status in experimentally produced groups', *American Journal of Sociology*, 60: 370–9.

These articles present portions of the other two Boys' Camp studies.

Sherif, M. (1956) 'Experiments in group conflict', *Scientific American*, 195: 54–8.

This short paper presents a succinct and accessible overview of all three studies.

Sherif, M. and Sherif, C.W. (1969) *Social Psychology*. New York: Harper & Row.

This is a classic social-psychology textbook, one that is matched by no other since; by reading this book, readers will gain further understanding of the Boys' Camp studies, but will be able to appreciate Sherif's intense scholarship.

Oakes, P.J., Haslam, S.A. and Turner, J.C. (1994) *Stereotyping and Social Reality*. Oxford: Blackwell.

Finally, this book presents a self- categorization analysis of stereotyping. In some ways, it only loosely references Sherif and his colleagues; however, the intellectual debt owed to Sherif is substantial, and most clearly articulated in Chapter 8 of the book.

REFERENCES

Aberson, C.L. and Gaffney, A.M. (2008) 'An integrated threat model of explicit and implicit attitudes', *European Journal of Social Psychology*, 39: 808–30.

Allport, F.H. (1924) 'The group fallacy in relation to social science', *Journal of Abnormal Psychology and Social Psychology*, 19: 60–73.

Billig, M. (1976) *Social Psychology and Intergroup Relations*. London: Academic Press.

Brannigan, A. (2006) *Introduction to the Aldine Translation Edition of M. Sherif: Social Interaction: Processes and Products*. Piscataway, NJ: Transaction Publishers.

Brewer, M.B. (1999) 'The psychology of prejudice: Ingroup love or outgroup hate?', *Journal of Social Issues*, 55: 429–44.

Brewer, M.B. and Brown, R.J. (1998) 'Intergroup relations', in D.T. Gilbert, S.T. Fiske and G. Lindzey (eds), *The Handbook of Social Psychology*, 4th edn. New York: McGraw-Hill. pp. 554–94.

Brown, R.J. (2010) *Prejudice: Its Social Psychology*, 2nd edn. Malden, MA: Wiley.

Brown, R.J., Condor, S., Mathews, A., Wade, G. and Williams, J.A. (1986) 'Explaining intergroup differentiation in an industrial organization', *Journal of Occupational Psychology*, 59: 273–86.

Cherry, F. (1995) *The 'Stubborn Particulars' of Social Psychology: Essays on the Research Process*. London: Routledge.

Dion, K.L. (1979) 'Intergroup conflict and intragroup cohesiveness', in S. Worchel and W.G. Austin (eds), *The Social Psychology of Intergroup Relations*. Monterey, CA: Brooks/Cole. pp. 33–47.

Dovidio, J.F., Gaertner, S.L. and Saguy, T. (2007) 'Another view of "we": Majority and minority group perspectives on a common ingroup identity', *European Review of Social Psychology*, 18: 296–330.

Fine, G.A. (2004) 'Forgotten classic: The Robbers Cave experiment', *Sociological Forum*, 19: 663–6.

Gaertner, S.L., Dovidio, J.F., Anastasio, P.A., Bachman, B.A. and Rust, M.C. (1993) 'The common ingroup identity model: Recategorisation and the reduction of intergroup bias', *European Review of Social Psychology*, 4: 1–26.

Gaertner, S.L., Dovidio, J.F., Banker, B.S., Houlette, M., Johnson, K.M. and McGlynn, E.A. (2000) 'Reducing intergroup conflict: From superordinate goals to decategorization, recategorization, and mutual differentiation', *Group Dynamics: Theory, Research and Practice*, 4: 98–114.

Grandberg, D. and Sarup, G. (1992) 'Muzafer Sherif: Portrait of a passionate intellectual', in D. Grandberg and G. Sarup (eds), *Social Judgment and Intergroup Relations: Essays in Honor of Muzafer Sherif*. New York. Springer-Verlag. pp. 3–54.

Hamilton, D.L. and Gifford, R.K. (1976) 'Illusory correlation in interpersonal perception: A cognitive basis of stereotypic judgments', *Journal of Experimental Social Psychology*, 12: 392–407.

Harvey, O.J. (1989) 'Obituary: Muzafer Sherif (1906–1988)', *American Psychologist*, 44: 1325–6.

Haslam, S.A. (2004) *Psychology in Organizations: The Social Identity Approach*, 2nd edn. London: Sage.

Haslam, S.A., Reicher, S.D. and Platow, M.J. (2011) *The New Psychology of Leadership: Identity, Influence and Power*. New York: Psychology Press.

New York Times (1988) 'Obituary: Muzafer Sherif, 82, psychologist who studied hostility of groups', 27 October. Retrieved from: http://www.nytimes.com/1988/10/27/obituaries/muzafer-sherif-82-psychologist-who-studied-hostility-of-groups.html.

Oakes, P.J., Haslam, S.A. and Turner, J.C. (1994) *Stereotyping and Social Reality*. Oxford: Blackwell.

Pettigrew, T.F. (1992) 'The importance of cumulative effects: A neglected emphasis of Sherif's work', in D. Grandberg and G. Sarup (eds), *Social Judgement and Intergroup Relations: Essays in Honour of Muzafer Sherif*. New York. Springer-Verlag. pp. 89–104.

Platow, M.J., Haslam, S.A., Foddy, M. and Grace, D.M. (2003) 'Leadership as the outcome of self-categorization processes', in D. van Knippenberg and M.A. Hogg (eds), *Identity, Leadership and Power*. London: Sage. pp. 34–47.

Platow, M.J. and Hunter, J.A. (2001) 'Realistic intergroup conflict: Prejudice, power, and protest', in M. Augoustinos and K.J. Reynolds (eds), *Understanding the Psychology of Prejudice and Racism*. London: Sage. pp. 195–212.

Rabbie, J.M. (1982) 'The effects of intergroup competition on intragroup and intergroup relationships', in V.J. Derlega and J. Grzelak (eds), *Cooperation and Helping Behaviour: Theories and Research*. New York: Academic Press. pp. 123–49.

Sherif, M. (1948) *An Outline of Social Psychology*. New York: Harper.

Sherif, M. (1951) 'A preliminary experimental study of inter-group relations', in J.H. Rohrer and M. Sherif (eds), *Social Psychology at the Crossroads*. New York: Harper & Row. pp. 388–424.

Sherif, M. (1966) *In Common Predicament: Social Psychology of Intergroup Conflict and Cooperation*. Boston: Houghton-Mifflin.

Sherif, M. (1967) *Group Conflict and Co-operation: Their Social Psychology*. London: Routledge and Kegan-Paul.

Sherif, M. and Cantril, H. (1947) *The Psychology of Ego-involvements*. New York: Wiley.

Sherif, M. and Sherif, C.W. (1969) *Social Psychology*. New York: Harper & Row.

Sherif, M., Harvey, O.J., White, B.J., Hood, W.R. and Sherif, C.W. (1961) *Intergroup Conflict and Cooperation: The Robbers Cave Experiment*. Norman, OK: Institute of Group Relations, University of Oklahoma.

Sherif, M., White, B.J. and Harvey, O.J. (1955) 'Status in experimentally produced groups', *American Journal of Sociology*, 60: 370–9.

Sibley, C.G. and Duckitt, J. (2008) 'Personality and prejudice: A meta-analysis and theoretical review', *Personality and Social Psychology Review*, 12: 248–79.

Stephan, W. and Stephan, C.W. (2000) 'An integrated threat theory of prejudice', in S. Oskamp (ed.), *Reducing Prejudice and Discrimination*. Mahwah, NJ: Erlbaum. pp. 23–46.

Struch, N. and Schwartz, S.H. (1989) 'Intergroup aggression: Its predictors and distinctness from in-group bias', *Journal of Personality and Social Psychology*, 56: 364–73.

Tajfel, H. (ed.) (1978) *Differentiation Between Social Groups: Studies in the Social Psychology of Intergroup Relations*. London: Academic Press.

Tajfel, H. and Turner, J.C. (1979) 'An integrative theory of intergroup conflict', in W.G. Austin and S. Worchel (eds), *The Social Psychology of Intergroup Relations*. Monterey, CA: Brooks/Cole. pp. 33–48.

Turner, J.C. (1975) 'Social comparison and social identity: Some prospects for intergroup behaviour', *European Journal of Social Psychology*, 5: 1–34.

Turner, J.C. (1982) 'Toward a cognitive redefinition of the social group', in H. Tajfel (ed.), *Social Identity and Intergroup Behavior*. Cambridge, UK: Cambridge University Press. pp. 15–40.

Turner, J.C., Hogg, M.A., Oakes, P.J., Reicher, S. and Wetherell, M.S. (1987) *Rediscovering the Social Group: A Self-categorization Theory*. Oxford: Basil Blackwell.

Turner, J.C. and Reynolds, K.J. (2010) 'The story of social identity', in T. Postmes and N. Branscombe (eds), *Rediscovering Social Identity: Core Sources*. Hove: Psychology Press.

10 | Discrimination

Revisiting Tajfel's minimal
group studies

Russell Spears and Sabine Otten

BACKGROUND

It is fitting that this chapter follows one on Sherif's famous Boys' Camp studies. For, after these studies, research on another set of boys was to become equally famous. The studies in question were led by the British social psychologist, Henri Tajfel, a Polish-born Jew whose first-hand experience of Nazism had fuelled a lifelong interest in issues of prejudice, conflict and intergroup relations. Extending the earlier work of Sherif, his *minimal group studies* were designed to reduce the group or category to its most minimal elements and then establish at what point conflict and discrimination between groups would rear their heads. As it turned out, the intergroup discrimination arising from the highly recognizable phenomenon of gangs of boys fighting over territory and resources also arose when all obvious features that might produce such conflict (e.g., a history of antagonism, a scarcity of resources) were stripped away. Indeed, by this means the studies provided striking evidence that boys (and later adults) would discriminate in favour of their own group in the absence of any visible signs of the groups themselves – a phenomenon typically referred to as *minimal ingroup bias*.

In this chapter we first outline the minimal group paradigm and the phenomenon of minimal ingroup bias together with the motivations that inspired them – as presented in Tajfel's original classic studies (Tajfel et al., 1971). We then examine early attempts to explain the study's findings, which spawned (after a false start) the development of a major new theory of social behaviour: *social identity theory*. This symbiotic relationship between data and theory contributed to the impact of the original studies, which has been enormous. As we will see, in part, this reflects the controversy surrounding the results of Tajfel's studies. The phenomenon these reveal is not in dispute but the studies have evoked a range of explanations, and many that have involved a critique of the social identity account. As a result, finding the best explanation for minimal ingroup bias has proved a bit like solving an Agatha Christie 'whodunit', with many twists and turns along the way.

One interesting question we might have about the minimal group studies is how one would even look for something that researchers had hitherto assumed was not there. To pursue the Agatha Christie metaphor, this was a murder mystery without a body. Evidence for the realistic basis of conflict between groups had already been established in Sherif's classic Boys' Camp studies. As discussed in Chapter 9, these showed that tensions arise between groups when they have to compete for scarce resources. But, as set out in the influential 1971 paper in which Tajfel and his colleagues presented the findings of the first minimal group studies, two related themes seemed to motivate Tajfel's quest to go beyond Sherif's ideas. First, he emphasized the importance of the social context in which behaviour was embedded and acquired meaning. Thus, he observed:

> A network of intergroup categorizations is omnipresent in the social environment; it enters into our socialization and education all the way from 'teams' and 'team spirit' in the primary and secondary education through teenage groups of all kinds to social, national, racial, ethnic or age groups. (Tajfel et al., 1971: 153)

A second impetus was Tajfel's earlier work on the cognitive aspects of prejudice (1969) in which he attributed an important sense-making role to social categorization. The above quote thus continues:

> The articulation of an individual's social world in terms of its categorization in groups becomes a guide for his [or her] conduct in situations to which some criterion of intergroup division can be meaningfully applied. (Meaningful need not be 'rational'.) An undifferentiated environment makes very little sense and provides no guidelines for action … . Whenever … some form of intergroup categorization can be used it will give order and coherence to the social situation. This is an aspect of intergroup conduct that is … present in all intergroup situations. The present experiments are designed to show that it can on its own determine differential group behaviour. (Tajfel et al., 1971: 153)

We reproduce these ideas in some detail because, as we shall see, the second motif in particular (i.e., the idea that intergroup distinctions can give meaning to social situations) turns out to be remarkably prophetic. And although these ideas do not provide a wholly satisfactory answer to the question of exactly why Tajfel was motivated to probe further into the minimal conditions for intergroup conflict, we should, nevertheless, be grateful that he did. For the impact of the ensuing research proved to be anything but minimal.

THE MINIMAL GROUP STUDIES

MINIMAL GROUP BIAS:
A PHENOMENON IN SEARCH OF AN EXPLANATION

So what are the minimal conditions for conflict to emerge between groups? Tajfel and colleagues outlined six factors that they sought to investigate, and whose influence they sought to rule out (1971: 153–4). They did this by conducting studies that had the following features:

1. No face-to-face interaction (within or between groups).

2. Complete anonymity.

3. No link between the criteria for categorization into groups and the nature of the responses requested from participants.

4. Respondents should not derive any (utilitarian) value from their responses (to rule out self-interest).

5. A strategy designed to differentiate between groups should be in competition with rational/utilitarian principles of obtaining the maximum benefit for all. In particular, benefit to the participant's own group (the *ingroup*) should be contrasted with a strategy in which the ingroup gains more than the other group (the *outgroup*).

6. Responses should be made as important and real as possible (i.e., involve concrete rewards rather than some form of evaluation).

METHOD

THE SOCIAL CATEGORIZATION PROCEDURE

Social categorization was established in two different ways for the two studies (Experiments 1 and 2) that have become the classic procedures in the field. The key point, though, is that these both involved assigning the participants to groups on a completely arbitrary basis.

In Experiment 1 the schoolboys were categorized by means of a dot estimation procedure: they were asked to estimate the number of dots projected on a screen, presented for a fraction of a second. On the basis of 40 of these trials the boys were told that they were either in a group of under-estimators (i.e., a group who under-estimated the number of dots) or a group of over-estimators. In fact, though, they were assigned at random to these categories.

In Experiment 2 the now-famous preference for the paintings of Klee vs. Kandinsky was used. Here participants indicated their aesthetic preferences for a series of 12 paintings (six by each painter) designated as A or B for each paired choice (although in fact some pairs contained two by the same painter!). Once again, actual assignment to categories was random.

After being assigned to groups in this way, participants were told that they would engage in a task that involved giving real money rewards (and penalties in Experiment 1) to other people. They would not know these people and it was stressed that they could never reward or penalize themselves. They were then placed in cubicles to complete this task alone.

THE 'TAJFEL' MATRICES

In the next phase, participants completed reward matrices (one matrix per page) designed to examine how they would choose to reward members of the two

```
Matrix 1

IG no. 42:  23  22  21  20  /19\ 18  17  16  15  14  13  12  11
OG no. 31:  5   7   9   11  \13/ 15  17  19  21  23  25  27  29

Matrix 2

IG no. 42:  7   8   9   10  /11\ 12  13  14  15  16  17  18  19
OG no. 31:  1   3   5   7   \9/  11  13  15  17  19  21  23  25
```

Figure 10.1   Examples of differential Tajfel matrices (adapted from Tajfel et al., 1971)

Note: Participants were required to choose one response option per matrix, which involved circling one vertical pair of numbers. In the examples here, the choices both involve giving more points to the ingroup (IG) member than the outgroup (OG) member – a strategy of maximum difference (MD).

groups (their ingroup and the outgroup).[1] The matrices were designed to measure the pull of particular reward strategies when set in opposition to others (see Bourhis et al., 1994, for an excellent overview of the matrices and the scoring method). Examples of two matrices taken from Experiment 2 are presented in Figure 10.1.

Although in the original studies some matrices involved rewarding two ingroup members and two outgroup members, the theoretically most interesting cases are those involving 'differential' matrices that (as in these examples) involve assigning points to an ingroup versus an outgroup member.

In line with the pre-conditions, the designated group members never included the self, ostensibly ruling out self-interest. Calculating the pull scores to establish strategies involves looking at responses on more than one matrix, but the different possible strategies can be illustrated by considering response options in the two example matrices presented in Figure 10.1. Here, responses to the left of Matrix 1 would represent a combination of two strategies: maximum ingroup profit (MIP), which involves giving the most possible points to the ingroup, and maximum difference in favour of the ingroup (MD), which involves ensuring that the ingroup member gets more points than the outgroup member. On the other hand, a response to the right-hand end of Matrix 1 would involve a strategy of maximum joint profit (MJP) in which the gains for both the ingroup and the outgroup member are maximized. Turning to Matrix 2, a response to the left-hand end would reveal a preference for MD but at the expense of MIP and MJP, which converge for preferences more to the right. In both examples, responses towards the middle of the scales suggest a strategy of fairness (F). Because it is useful to have a clear grasp of these different strategies, they are summarized in Table 10.1.

---

[1] These matrices were actually designed by Claude Flament who was officially second author on the paper. However, thanks to the wisdom of a copy editor who thought it more convenient to group authors by university affiliation, he is listed fourth in the paper itself.

Table 10.1 Different reward strategies examined using the Tajfel matrices

| Strategy | Abbreviation | Choice that best represents strategy in example matrices | | Explanation |
		Matrix 1	Matrix 2	
Fairness/	F	17	13	Most similarity in IG and OG
Parity		17	13	points
Maximum	MD	23	7	Biggest positive difference between
Difference		5	1	IG and OG points in favour of the IG
Maximum	MJP	11	19	Most combined points for IG
Joint Profit		29	25	and OG
Maximum	MIP	23	19	Most points for IG
Ingroup Profit		5	25	

RESULTS

The results from Experiment 1 showed that when allocations involved two ingroup or two outgroup members, participants displayed an overwhelming preference for a strategy of fairness. However, when it came to differential matrices that involved rewarding an ingroup versus an outgroup member, they were now more discriminatory in favour of the ingroup (although the modal response was still for fairness). In other words, these matrices produced evidence of significant *ingroup bias*. Moreover, participants' support for this strategy did not change when the categorization procedure was given a value connotation that might justify discrimination (i.e., if the ingroup was denoted as *more* or *less* accurate than the outgroup).

Experiment 2 was designed to distinguish further between the different reward strategies participants were using. Specifically, it contrasted MJP with MIP and/or MD (where MIP and MD coincided this can be called *ingroup favouritism*, whereas when MD is contrasted with MIP and MJP this reflects a maximum difference strategy). The clear result was that MD exerted a significant pull when opposed to the other strategies. Although MIP was always combined with either MJP or MD (as can be seen from Matrix 1; a problem that has persisted) it also exerted a stronger pull than MJP, but less than MD. In short, the differentiation matrices provide consistent evidence of ingroup favouritism and maximum difference strategies (and these findings were replicated in an additional pilot study). In other words, the boys in these studies seemed to want to favour their ingroup – at the expense of the outgroup – even though the group in question had very little meaning beyond the minimal context that Tajfel had created.

INTERPRETING THE MINIMAL GROUP STUDIES:
THE EMERGENCE OF SOCIAL IDENTITY THEORY

INITIAL INTERPRETATION:
NORMS, DEMANDS AND EXPECTATIONS

Although there was also strong evidence for a fairness strategy in Tajfel and colleagues' first experiment, this is often forgotten in secondary reporting of the results of this (and subsequent) minimal group studies. However, consistent support for the MD strategy (in contrast to MJP and MIP) also provides evidence of discrimination. Initially, Tajfel and his colleagues interpreted this as supporting a generic social norm to discriminate.

Note that Tajfel and colleagues referred to MD as a differentiation strategy (albeit one involving discrimination), but many subsequent accounts interpreted this as an example of outgroup *derogation* (because it harms the outgroup at the expense of benefiting the ingroup). Indeed, secondary accounts have been prone to jump to the conclusion that minimal ingroup bias (and specifically MD) means that discrimination and even outgroup derogation are an inevitable consequence of the mere social categorization of people into groups. This is clearly an over-interpretation (and over-generalization). One of the problems that has dogged the paradigm and in particular the matrices is that, in the MD strategy, positive differentiation and derogation are confounded, and this problem has never adequately been addressed (and is rarely if ever discussed).

In reflecting further on their findings, Tajfel and his co-workers (1971) considered three alternative interpretations: (a) demand characteristics (the idea that participants were responding to cues that conveyed the experimenter's hypothesis), (b) expectations of reciprocity, and (c) anticipation of future interaction. Demand characteristics are important to consider in such an artificial situation, and were addressed in subsequent research. For example, Lindsay St Claire and John Turner (1982) found that if people were asked to role-play being members of the groups (rather than being categorized themselves) and then complete the matrices accordingly they did not show the same degree of ingroup bias (MD and MIP) but tended to predict fairness. Moreover, this seems to also argue against a normative explanation. The sheer number of times that the minimal ingroup bias effect has been replicated also suggests that the phenomenon is real and more than simply an effect of demand characteristics (given the equally plausible demands for fairness).

In the case of expectations of reciprocity, Tajfel and colleagues admitted that they had no data that spoke to this issue and hence this explanation could not easily be ruled out. As we shall see, despite the attempts to eliminate this form of self-interest, it has never really gone away. Yet while the anticipation of further interaction could also have been an issue (in that the boys would return to the same school), Tajfel proposed that the most rational strategy – given that they did not know who was in 'their' group – was to opt for an MJP strategy. However, as we have seen, this strategy held little appeal.

THE SOCIAL IDENTITY EXPLANATION:
THE MINIMAL GROUP FINDINGS INSPIRE A THEORY

Despite being initially favoured by Tajfel, the generic norm explanation quickly fell from favour. One concern was the potential circularity of a normative account: if there is a competitive norm (e.g., among participants from western countries), where does it come from and what explains that? Moreover the strong(er) preference for fairness that was apparent from the very first study could also support an equally plausible explanation in terms of a fairness norm (see also St Claire and Turner, 1982). The challenge, then, is to explain which norm operates when, and because a normative account cannot do this, it was pushed back into the long grass. Having said this, dismissing normative processes may have been premature. For example, Margaret Wetherell (1979) subsequently used normative arguments to explain evidence that Maori children showed less ingroup favouritism than more westernized Pakeha New Zealanders.

Nevertheless, almost as soon as the 1971 paper was published, Tajfel's story started to shift (Tajfel, 1972; see Diehl, 1990). In particular, in the process of dismissing additional interpretations, a new explanation in terms of *social identity* started to emerge (Tajfel, 1974; Turner, 1975). Turner (1975) talked of 'social competition' between the minimal groups and contrasted this with Sherif's (1967) notion of 'realistic' competition: a social identity explanation of differentiation in minimal groups had started to crystallize.

The central idea of the new explanation was that social categorization into groups, and membership in one of these groups, provides a basis for anchoring the self in the ingroup. At this point, Tajfel famously defined social identity as 'that part of the self-concept corresponding to our group membership' (1978: 63). To become an identity, however, clearly implies some *identification*. Tajfel's definition of social identity therefore continues 'together with the value and emotional significance attached to that group membership' (1978: 63).

A further element was a *social comparison* process: understanding the meaning of our group involves a comparison with other relevant groups of which we are not members (facilitated by the social categorization process). To see the ingroup as 'us' implies a contrast with 'them'. Here Tajfel and Turner also posited a motivational process whereby groups strive for 'positive group distinctiveness', which entails them positively differentiating their ingroup from the relevant comparison outgroup, on valued dimensions, and thereby gaining a positive social identity. This was the key process now used to explain positive differentiation and especially the MD strategy in the minimal group paradigm. Moreover, this process now became a central element in social identity theory more generally, which was elaborated to explain processes of social change in status hierarchies (Tajfel and Turner, 1979).

What was perhaps not clear from this explanation for the minimal ingroup bias was whether this motivated process of differentiation starts from the investment in a social identity, or whether it is used to *create* or consolidate a (distinctive) sense of identity. We will return to this issue towards the end of this chapter, but it is useful to refer back to Tajfel's own reference to the quest to create meaning and coherence that is tied up with the social categorization (and later the identification) process (see above). That idea became rather sidelined by the generic norm explanation. In the new social identity explanation it is probably true to say that this same idea (focusing on creating meaning and coherence) also became sidelined by the focus on the quest to create a *positive* social identity. As a result, positive differentiation became more bound up with enhancing the ingroup and raising self-esteem (i.e., through self-enhancement) than with creating (group) distinctiveness *per se*. This became known as the 'self-esteem hypothesis', and it soon came to dominate the social identity agenda as an explanation for the findings of the minimal group studies.

THE SELF-ESTEEM HYPOTHESIS

The focus on self-esteem can be traced back to the original social identity researchers – Henri Tajfel and John Turner – and their proposition that individuals strive to achieve or maintain a positive social identity (Tajfel and Turner, 1979). Oakes and Turner (1980) were the first to explicitly test this idea. They showed that the opportunity to discriminate on the Tajfel matrices did indeed raise participants' scores on a measure of self-esteem. It is worth noting, though, that subsequent reviews have criticized the use of measures of personal global self-esteem in these and other studies (see Hewstone et al., 2002; Long and Spears, 1997; Rubin and Hewstone, 1998) since this seems to go against the more group-level spirit of social identity theory.

Moreover, although much research (with both minimal and real groups) was concerned to address the self-esteem hypothesis, the results proved rather mixed (Rubin and Hewstone, 1998). However, research that conceptualizes esteem as a state rather than trait variable (i.e., something that is context-specific rather than fixed), at the group level, and also as specific to the domain of ingroup bias, has generated more support. For example, a study led by Jackie Hunter and colleagues found evidence for enhanced collective esteem in a domain important to the ingroup after ingroup favouritism in a minimal group setting (Hunter et al., 1996). Literature reviews also suggest reasonable support for the self-esteem hypothesis when such criteria are met (see Hewstone et al., 2002; Rubin and Hewstone, 1998, for reviews). Nevertheless, most of this evidence has emerged from research on naturally occurring groups rather than minimal groups. Consequently it is not clear whether enhancing group identity and esteem is the only or even most important mechanism that drives minimal ingroup bias (specifically the MD strategy) in the minimal group studies.

IMPACT OF THE MINIMAL GROUP STUDIES

The influence of the minimal group studies is difficult to overestimate. Conservative estimates indicate that the original 1971 article has been cited over 1500 times on Web of Science (Tajfel's most cited research article by some distance), and the minimal group studies are rarely excluded from treatments of prejudice, discrimination and intergroup relations in social psychology and intro-ductory psychology textbooks. Whether the studies are accurately presented is another matter: as we have noted, a particular problem is that they are often used to warrant the conclusion that discrimination is pervasive and inevitable.

The influence of the minimal group studies (and social identity theory more generally) on other theories within social psychology is also very considerable (although again the question of whether the portrayal is always accurate is pertinent). For example, within social dominance theory, evidence for ingroup favouritism is used to argue that intergroup discrimination is a generic feature of many intergroup relations (Sidanius and Pratto, 1999). Likewise, evidence of ingroup favouritism is used within system justification theory (Jost and Banaji, 1994) to suggest that groups (especially those with high-status) often seek to justify their position through displays of bias towards others.

Perhaps just as influential has been the impact of the minimal group findings outside of social psychology in anthropology, evolutionary psychology, and behavioural economics. In particular, as we will see below, the minimal group paradigm and its findings have been used to argue for humans' evolutionary tendency to favour ingroups and distrust outgroups (Dunbar et al., 2005). This takes us well beyond Tajfel's original grounding of the minimal ingroup studies (and evidence of bias) in an appreciation of norms, social meaning, and a quest for positive group distinctiveness. Nevertheless, it shows that the paradigm (and the findings it generated) has been so influential as to live a life of its own, well beyond its original scope.

BEYOND THE MINIMAL GROUP STUDIES

THE ROLE OF SIMILARITY

One early idea that was proposed as an alternative interpretation of minimal ingroup bias was that, rather than categorization driving discrimination, this was simply caused by participants' perception that other ingroup members were simi-lar to themselves. This meshed with belief-congruence theory (Rokeach, 1969) and similarity-attraction principles, which suggest that we are prone to dislike others (and by extension other groups) who have different views and values to our own. Could ingroup favouritism therefore be explained by the assumed similarity with those in the ingroup (and dissimilarity with those in the outgroup)? This explanation does not necessarily invalidate the effect of social categorization (as Tajfel's own work had shown, categorization can indeed lead people to accentuate similarities within categories and differences between them). However, it does point to a different mechanism.

Further experiments by Michael Billig and Tajfel (1973) in which similarity and social categorization were manipulated independently seemed to rule out this idea. These showed that social categorization produces stronger ingroup bias than simi-larity. Furthermore, a study by Michael Diehl (1989) that also manipulated similarity at the group level actually found greater discrimination towards a *similar* outgroup. This contradicts belief-congruence principles and supports the idea that outgroup similarity might actually threaten group distinctiveness and motivate greater positive differentiation (Tajfel, 1982; see below).

THE ROLE OF INTERDEPENDENCE AND RECIPROCITY

Despite the original attempts to put the question of self-interest to sleep, it keeps returning rather like a restless zombie. Indeed, ruling out the role of self-interest in the minimal group studies has proven no easier than ruling it out in instances of altruism (a debate that continues to rage in psychology more generally). Recall that, in the minimal group paradigm, participants always allocate rewards to another ingroup or outgroup member but never to themselves. Formally, then, there is no opportunity for self-interest. However, researchers have argued that there may be an *expectation* that ingroup members will favour their own group, and so it makes sense (and is rational) to favour other members of the ingroup. In other words, there are assumptions of interdependence or *reciprocity* within the ingroup that could explain ingroup favouritism.

Jaap Rabbie and his colleagues were early proponents of this view (e.g., Rabbie et al., 1989) and proposed a 'Behavioural Interaction Model' to formalize this interdependence and reciprocity argument. To test this, they devised an experiment with different conditions that made it explicit whether participants would receive reward allocations from (i.e., be dependent on) the ingroup (ID), the outgroup (OD) or both (IOD). In this research participants tended to favour the ingroup when dependent on its members for rewards, but to favour the outgroup when dependent on its members. This seems to confirm the power of interdependence and reciprocity. However, participants still tended to favour the ingroup in the more balanced IOD condition and, in a critique of this research, Richard Bourhis and colleagues (1997) point out that parity or fairness would be a more valid prediction in this case if only reciprocity was at work.

A series of further studies have also manipulated explicit dependence on the ingroup and/or outgroup for rewards in the MGP. For example, as well as manipulating explicit categorization, Lowell Gaertner and Chet Insko (2000) also manipulated whether a dependence structure was present or absent (i.e., participants were the only ones allocating rewards or others allocated them too). The prediction here was that the sole ability to allocate (i.e., where there is no dependence) should eliminate dependence on others, and thereby eliminate ingroup favouritism. This prediction held, but only for men: their responses were no more discriminatory than non-categorized men. However, women participants showed ingroup favouritism irrespective of the dependence structure – present or absent.

In a second study, Gaertner and Insko (2000) asked participants to allocate rewards but varied whether the other allocator was an ingroup member or an outgroup member, and whether participants would personally receive rewards or not. Participants favoured their ingroup over the outgroup, but only when they were dependent on an ingroup member for their own outcomes. Another study by Wolfgang Stroebe and colleagues (2005) orthogonally manipulated participants' dependence on the ingroup (yes, no) and the outgroup (yes, no) for rewards. As in Gaertner and Insko's study, this showed that ingroup-favouring strategies were clearly strongest when there was dependence on the ingroup rather than the outgroup.

These studies that manipulate group dependence more explicitly point to a relatively consistent pattern that provides evidence of what has been termed 'bounded (generalized) reciprocity' (see also Yamagishi and Kiyonari, 2000). In other words, people tend to respond to the dependency structure and then recip-rocate with favouritism toward those on whom they are dependent, but this effect is considerably stronger for dependence on the ingroup (hence 'bounded'). This idea is also supported by recurring evidence that people do indeed tend to expect the ingroup to reward fellow ingroup members more (Gaertner and Insko, 2000; Jetten et al., 1996; Stroebe et al., 2005).

Some important questions remain, however. Most obviously, what is special about *ingroup* reciprocity? It is perhaps no surprise that people expect reci-procity from the ingroup, but if reciprocity is the critical thing, why does it appear to be less effective when it is explicitly forthcoming from a minimal outgroup? To answer this question, researchers have tended to fall back on evolutionary arguments, proposing that from an evolutionary perspective there may be good reasons to trust the ingroup and to distrust or even fear the out-group (Gaertner and Insko, 2000; Yamagishi et al., 1999). Gaertner and Insko also use evolutionary arguments to develop a *post hoc* explanation of the gender asymmetry in their first study – suggesting that, unlike men, women tend to favour the ingroup, irrespective of group dependence. However, a problem here is that standard evolutionary arguments might lead one to expect men to be generally more competitive than women (e.g., Sidanius et al., 1994; Yuki and Yokota, 2009). And while it is difficult to rule out these evolutionary arguments, it is just as difficult to prove them.

Clearly, though, bounded reciprocity could be an important factor that helps to explain ingroup bias in the MGP. However, an objection to the suggestion that this provides a complete explanation is that it seems to be better suited to explaining ingroup favouritism (i.e., MIP) than the maximum differentiation strategy (MD). If bounded reciprocity is concerned with self-interest why do group members sacri-fice self-interest as they do in MD? In this regard, Marilyn Brewer (1999) has claimed that social identity theory (and the findings of the minimal group studies) are better able to explain 'ingroup love' than 'outgroup hate'.[2] Nevertheless, this criticism would seem to apply even more to the bounded reciprocity argument: after all, this is more about reciprocating within the ingroup than harming the outgroup. In sum, then, self-interest may help explain why participants strive to

_____

[2] Despite the MD effect, most minimal group studies show stronger evidence for rewarding the ingroup rather than derogating the outgroup (see Mummendey and Otten, 1998).

maximize ingroup profit, but it struggles to explain why they sacrifice ingroup profit in order to deprive an outgroup of benefits.[3] In this, it appears to tell part of the story, but is not the whole story.

THE ROLE OF THE INDIVIDUAL SELF:
PROJECTION AND SELF-ANCHORING

As Tajfel noted when he embarked on this line of research, and as we will consider in more detail in the final section, the idea that social categorization helps give meaning to social situations would seem to play a central role in the minimal group studies. However, while there is little doubt that social categories can provide meaning to complex social situations in this way, some researchers have raised the question whether *minimal* social categories can serve this function. By definition, minimal groups are not grounded in previous experiences, nor in already existing and easily accessible stereotypes. So how can minimal groups provide their new members with meaning?

Twenty-five years after Tajfel and colleagues' seminal 1971 paper, Mara Cadinu and Myron Rothbart thus stated: 'Overall, in-group favoritism in the minimal group paradigm is a well-established phenomenon, but the exact reasons for this favoritism remain unclear' (1996: 661). While also starting from the same premise that group members strive to give meaning to the categories they belong to, Cadinu and Rothbart (1996) proposed an explanation that stressed the role of the individual self in this process. More specifically, they proposed two processes that may account for intergroup bias in the MGP. On the one hand, because social categorization implies that the self and the ingroup share certain characteristics, people will be prone to *project* (aspects of) the typically positive representation of the individual self onto the ingroup (self-anchoring), thereby forming a positive ingroup representation. In other words, they will entertain thoughts of the form 'I am good; I am in this group; therefore this group must be good'. At the same time, Cadinu and Rothbart suggest that people will also apply an 'oppositeness heuristic', assuming that ingroup and outgroup do indeed differ ('My group is good; the other group is different; therefore that group must be less good').

Cadinu and Rothbart (1996) provided evidence for this self-anchoring explanation by showing that manipulating the accessibility of the individual self prior to judgments about minimal groups affected ingroup but not outgroup ratings – making judgments of the ingroup more similar to those of the self. Moreover, Sabine Otten and Dirk Wentura (2001) showed that the degree of overlap between self and ingroup ratings predicted the degree to which members of minimal groups showed evaluative intergroup bias. There was no evidence, however, that similarity or dissimilarity in the mental representations of self and

---

[3]This is not to deny that evolutionary arguments can also be imagined for MD (e.g., a strategy of intergroup competition along realistic conflict lines might motivate use of MD, but this remains speculative given the absence of realistic conflict in the MGP).

outgroup was a relevant predictor of intergroup bias in a minimal group setting (see also Robbins and Krueger, 2005, for a similar conclusion).

Typically, self-anchoring research has focused on ingroup favouritism at the level of trait ratings. As a result, Cadinu and Rothbart (1996: 675) only speculated about the role of self-anchoring in intergroup allocation strategies: 'According to the self-anchoring process, if ingroup members are assumed to be similar to the self, allocation strategies toward ingroup members should be similar to allocation strategies toward the self.'

In sum, the findings on self-anchoring in minimal groups suggest that positive representations of the ingroup result from the projection of positive self character-istics onto this group, and that the positive differentiation from the outgroup is a by-product of this differentiation. In this way, an *inter*group phenomenon, namely the positive differentiation of minimal ingroups from outgroups, can be traced back to an *intra*group phenomenon, namely the link between self and ingroup. At the same time, the self-anchoring approach is consistent with the idea that differ-entiation between minimal groups is at least partly motivated by striving for meaning. While the classical interpretation focuses on 'us–them' distinctions as a tool to structure social reality, the self-anchoring approach focuses on the self as a tool that gives meaning to the novel ingroup and thereby suggests that the indi-vidual self may play a bigger role in minimal group settings than initially assumed. Again, though, the approach cannot convincingly explain why group members sac-rifice maximum ingroup profit for the sake of maximum differentiation between ingroup and outgroup. Thus, as with self-interest models, self-anchoring princi-ples seem to provide a partial rather than a complete explanation of Tajfel and colleagues' original findings.

COMING FULL CIRCLE: THE ROLE OF GROUP DISTINCTIVENESS

As we suggested earlier, tests of the social identity explanation of minimal ingroup bias became somewhat side-tracked by the self-esteem hypothesis. One conse-quence of this was that researchers neglected the role of group distinctiveness that was central to Tajfel's original explanation. In short, gaining positivity was empha-sized at the expense of gaining distinctiveness. Moreover, the very question of what is distinctive about the ingroup (in contrast to the outgroup) has not been discussed. To address this, in some of our own research we have therefore distin-guished 'reactive distinctiveness' motivated by an established outgroup that is explicitly similar to the ingroup, from a 'creative distinctiveness' process relevant to unknown or minimal groups (Spears et al., 2002, 2009).

Two studies by Daan Scheepers and colleagues (2002) provided some initial evidence for the importance of group distinctiveness for minimal intergroup bias. This research created groups following quasi-minimal categorization procedures, and compared strategies of ingroup bias for groups given a group competition goal (relevant to realistic conflict principles; Sherif, 1967) with groups without such a goal (i.e., effectively minimal groups). For example, in one experiment, participants were given an opportunity to differentiate between group products at Time 1 (or were not) and then given a group goal manipulation relating to intergroup competition (or not). Our rationale was that the absence of a prior opportunity to differentiate between the groups would motivate the groups to *create* group distinctiveness and a meaningful group identity, especially in the condition where there was no subsequent group goal (the most minimal condition). At the same time, participants who *did* have the opportunity to differentiate between groups at Time 1 (creating a group identity), and who had the group goal of future competition, were also expected to discriminate, as predicted by realistic conflict principles. The results of our studies confirmed predictions. That is, ingroup bias was highest in conditions where either both factors were absent (consistent with creative distinctiveness) or both were present (realistic conflict).

Building on these results, a further study used the classic Klee/Kandinsky minimal-group-paradigm procedure to assign participants to groups, but for some participants also added a 'meaningful' condition in which extra information was given about the minimal basis for categorization. We predicted that attaching this meaning to group identity would eliminate the need to create a distinctive group identity, and thus reduce or eliminate ingroup bias. This was what we found: participants showed more ingroup bias (on matrices and evaluative ratings) when groups were minimal rather than meaningful. This supports the idea that discrimination in the minimal group paradigm is a way of achieving group distinctiveness that gives meaning to the participants' assigned group identity. Moreover, the studies also provided evidence that social identification increased in the minimal conditions – a pattern which again supports the idea that positive differentiation serves to create groups that are meaningful for participants.

In sum, there is now evidence that one factor that contributes to responses in the minimal group paradigm is the opportunity this provides for creating coherence and meaning through the *creation* of positive group distinctiveness (Spears et al., 2009). This idea was apparent both in the thinking that Tajfel brought to his original 1971 article, and in the logic of social identity theory (e.g. Tajfel, 1978; Tajfel and Turner, 1979). There is some irony in the fact that it took 30 years for the idea to be tested, but also some relief to discover that Tajfel's initial hunches proved to be well-founded.

CONCLUSION

The powerful phenomenon demonstrated in the minimal group studies is not in doubt (although the strong and even dominant tendency towards fairness is often neglected). Indeed, not only have the intriguing effects that Tajfel and his colleagues uncovered in their pioneering research been reproduced by several generations of researchers – they also have had a captivating effect upon them. However, while the phenomenon of minimal ingroup bias has proved to be very robust, there has been much less clarity about the precise mechanisms that underlie the effects that the studies produce. *Why exactly* does the process of assigning someone to a hitherto meaningless group lead them to want to act in ways that advantage another unknown member of that group over someone in another group – to the extent that they are happier for the person in their group to receive a smaller reward than they might otherwise if it means that the person in the other group receives even less?

Happily, after four decades of research there is now compelling evidence that allows us to conclude that several distinct processes are implicated in this phenomenon, and hence that it is multiply determined. In the first instance, although the question of when and why norms for discrimination outweigh norms for fairness is hard to answer, the role of normative factors cannot be ruled out completely. Eliminating the role of self-interest has also proven much more difficult than originally thought, partly because people expect to receive rewards from the ingroup, and take this into account when allocating rewards among ingroup and outgroup members. The precise reasons for this are not fully established, but it seems there are plausible evolutionary reasons for people to put more trust in ingroups than outgroups and hence to act in terms of bounded reciprocity. At the same time, it appears that minimal ingroup bias can arise from the tendency to use the self as an anchor and to project self-interests onto the ingroup. And finally, substantial evidence has also accumulated for more group-level explanations of Tajfel and colleagues' findings. These suggest that discrimination serves not only to enhance a positive sense of (collective) self but also to create positive group distinctiveness.

In conclusion, it is clear, as we noted at the start, that solving the riddle of the minimal group studies has involved researchers in a lot of forensic scientific detective work, and hence has had many of the hallmarks of an Agatha Christie whodunit. Moreover, in the end, it appears that the final verdict is similar to that in the case of the *Murder on the Orient Express* – *all* the key suspects had a hand on the dagger that did the outgroup down.

FURTHER READING

Tajfel, H. (1970) 'Experiments in intergroup discrimination', *Scientific American*, 223: 96–102.

This article provides an easy introduction to the minimal group studies. The paper is essential reading and also very accessible.

Tajfel, H., Flament, C., Billig, M.G. and Bundy, R.F. (1971) 'Social categorization and intergroup behaviour', *European Journal of Social Psychology*, 1: 149–77.

It is well worth reading the original account of the minimal group studies.

Bourhis, R.Y., Sachdev, I. and Gagnon, A. (1994) 'Intergroup research with the Tajfel matrices: Methodological notes', in M.P. Zanna and J.M. Olson (eds), *The Social Psychology of Prejudice: The Ontario Symposium*, Vol. 7. Hillsdale, NJ: Erlbaum. pp. 209–32.

Bourhis and colleagues provide further details on the Tajfel matrices and how the pull scores measuring the different reward strategies are computed.

Diehl, M. (1990) 'The minimal group paradigm: Theoretical explanations and empirical findings', *European Review of Social Psychology*, 1: 263–92.

Diehl provides an overview of research addressing some of the early alternative explanations.

Rubin, M. and Hewstone, M. (1998) 'Social identity theory's self-esteem hypothesis: A review and some suggestions for clarification', *Personality and Social Psychology Review*, 2: 40–62.

Rubin and Hewstone review evidence for the self-esteem hypothesis.

Gaertner, L. and Insko, C.A. (2000) 'Intergroup discrimination in the minimal group paradigm: Categorization, reciprocation or fear?', *Journal of Personality and Social Psychology*, 79: 77–94.

Gaertner and Insko make a case for reciprocity and interdependence as an explanation of minimal ingroup bias.

Cadinu, M. and Rothbart, M. (1996) 'Self-anchoring and differentiation processes in the minimal group setting', *Journal of Personality and Social Psychology*, 70(4): 661–77.

Cadinu and Rothbart provide the rationale and some evidence for the self-anchoring explanation.

Spears, R., Jetten, J., Scheepers, D. and Cihangir, S. (2009) 'Creative distinctiveness: Explaining in-group bias in minimal groups', in S. Otten, T. Kessler and K. Sassenberg (eds), *Intergroup Relations: The Role of Motivation and Emotion; A Festschrift in Honor of Amélie Mummendey*. New York: Psychology Press. pp. 23–40.

Spears and colleagues provide the rationale and some evidence for the group distinctiveness explanation.

REFERENCES

Billig, M.G. and Tajfel, H. (1973) 'Social categorization and similarity in intergroup behaviour', *European Journal of Social Psychology*, 3: 27–52.

Bourhis, R.Y., Sachdev, I. and Gagnon, A. (1994) 'Intergroup research with the Tajfel matrices: Methodological notes', in M.P. Zanna and J.M. Olson (eds), *The Social Psychology of Prejudice: The Ontario Symposium*, Vol. 7. Hillsdale, NJ: Erlbaum. pp. 209–32.

Bourhis, R.Y., Turner, J.C. and Gagnon, A. (1997) 'Interdependence, social identity and discrimination', in R. Spears, P.J. Oakes, N. Ellemers and S.A. Haslam (eds), *The Social Psychology of Stereotyping and Group Life*. Oxford: Blackwell. pp. 273–95.

Brewer, M.B. (1999) 'The psychology of prejudice: In-group love or out-group hate?', *Journal of Social Issues*, 55: 429–44.

Cadinu, M. and Rothbart, M. (1996) 'Self-anchoring and differentiation processes in the minimal group setting', *Journal of Personality and Social Psychology*, 70(4): 661–77.

Diehl, M. (1989) 'Justice and discrimination between minimal groups: The limits of equity', *British Journal of Social Psychology*, 28: 227–38.

Diehl, M. (1990) 'The minimal group paradigm: Theoretical explanations and empirical findings', *European Review of Social Psychology*, 1: 263–92.

Dunbar, R., Barrett, K. and Lycett, J. (2005) *Evolutionary Psychology*. Oxford: One World.

Gaertner, L. and Insko, C.A. (2000) 'Intergroup discrimination in the minimal group paradigm: Categorization, reciprocation or fear?', *Journal of Personality and Social Psychology*, 79: 77–94.

Hewstone, M., Rubin, M. and Willis, H. (2002) 'Intergroup bias', *Annual Review of Psychology*, 53: 575–604.

Hunter, J.A., Platow, M.J., Howard M.L. and Stringer, M. (1996) 'Social identity and intergroup evaluative bias: Realistic categories and domain-specific self-esteem in a conflict setting', *European Journal of Social Psychology*, 26: 631–47.

Jetten, J., Spears, R. and Manstead, A.S.R. (1996) 'Intergroup norms and intergroup discrimination: Distinctive self-categorization and social identity effects', *Journal of Personality and Social Psychology*, 71: 1222–33.

Jost, J.T. and Banaji, M.R. (1994) 'The role of stereotyping in system-justification and the production of false consciousness', *British Journal of Social Psychology*, 33: 1–27.

Long, K. and Spears, R. (1997) 'The self-esteem hypothesis revisited: Differentiation and the disaffected', in R. Spears, P.J. Oakes, N. Ellemers and S.A. Haslam (eds), *The Social Psychology of Stereotyping and Group Life*. Oxford: Blackwell. pp. 296–317.

Mummendey, A. and Otten, S. (1998) 'Positive-negative asymmetry in social discrimination', *European Review of Social Psychology*, 9: 107–43.

Oakes, P.J. and Turner, J.C. (1980) 'Social categorization and intergroup behaviour: Does minimal intergroup discrimination make social identity more positive?', *European Journal of Social Psychology*, 10: 295–301.

Otten, S. and Wentura, D. (2001) 'Self-anchoring and in-group favoritism: An individual profiles analysis', *Journal of Experimental Social Psychology*, 37: 525–32.

Rabbie, J.M., Schot, J.C. and Visser, L. (1989) 'Social identity theory: A conceptual and empirical critique from the perspective of a behavioural interaction model', *European Journal of Social Psychology*, 19: 171–202.

Robbins, J.M. and Krueger, J.I. (2005) 'Social projection to ingroups and outgroups: A review and meta-analysis', *Personality and Social Psychology Review*, 9: 32–47.

Rokeach, M. (1969) *Beliefs, Attitudes and Values*. San Francisco, CA: Jossey-Bass.

Rubin, M. and Hewstone, M. (1998) 'Social identity theory's self-esteem hypothesis: A review and some suggestions for clarification', *Personality and Social Psychology Review*, 2: 40–62.

Scheepers, D., Spears, R., Doosje, B. and Manstead, A.S.R. (2002) 'Integrating identity and instrumental approaches to intergroup differentiation: Different contexts, different motives', *Personality and Social Psychology Bulletin*, 28: 1455–67.

Sherif, M. (1967) *Group Conflict and Co-operation: Their Social Psychology*. London: Routledge and Kegan Paul.

Sidanius, J. and Pratto, F. (1999) *Social Dominance: An Intergroup Theory of Social Hierarchy and Oppression*. New York: Cambridge University Press.

Sidanius, J., Pratto, F. and Mitchell, M. (1994) 'In-group identification, social dominance orientation, and differential intergroup social allocation', *Journal of Social Psychology*, 134: 151–67.

Spears, R., Jetten, J. and Scheepers, D. (2002) 'Distinctiveness and the definition of collective self: A tripartite model', in A. Tesser, J.V. Wood and D.A. Stapel (eds), *Self and Motivation: Emerging Psychological Perspectives*. Lexington, KY: APA. pp. 147–71.

Spears, R., Jetten, J., Scheepers, D. and Cihangir, S. (2009) 'Creative distinctiveness: Explaining in-group bias in minimal groups', in S. Otten, T. Kessler and K. Sassenberg (eds), *Intergroup Relations: The Role of Motivation and Emotion; A Festschrift in Honor of Amélie Mummendey*. New York: Psychology Press. pp. 23–40.

St Claire, L. and Turner, J.C. (1982) 'The role of demand characteristics in the social categorization paradigm', *European Journal of Social Psychology,* 12: 307–14.

Stroebe, K.E., Lodewijkx, H.F.M. and Spears, R. (2005) 'Do unto others as they do unto you: Reciprocity and social identification as determinants of in-group favoritism', *Personality and Social Psychology Bulletin,* 31: 831–46.

Tajfel, H. (1969) 'Cognitive aspects of prejudice', *Journal of Social Issues,* 25: 79–97.

Tajfel, H. (1972) 'La catégorisation sociale (social categorization)', in S. Moscovici (ed.), *Introduction à la Psychologie Sociale*. Paris: Larouse. pp. 272–302.

Tajfel, H. (1974) 'Social identity and intergroup behaviour', *Social Science Information,* 13: 65–93.

Tajfel, H. (1978) 'Social categorization, social identity and social comparison', in H. Tajfel (ed.), *Differentiation Between Social Groups*. London: Academic Press. pp. 61–76.

Tajfel, H. (1982) 'Social psychology of intergroup relations', *Annual Review of Psychology,* 33: 1–39.

Tajfel, H. and Turner, J.C. (1979) 'An integrative theory of intergroup conflict', in W.G. Austin and S. Worchel (eds), *The Social Psychology of Intergroup Relations*. Monterey, CA: Brooks/Cole. pp. 33–48.

Tajfel, H., Flament, C., Billig, M.G. and Bundy, R.F. (1971) 'Social categorization and intergroup behaviour', *European Journal of Social Psychology,* 1: 149–77.

Turner, J.C. (1975) 'Social comparison and social identity: Some prospects for intergroup behaviour', *European Journal of Social Psychology*, 5: 5–34.

Wetherell, M. (1979) 'Social categorization in children and the role of cultural context', *New Zealand Psychologist,* 8: 51.

Yamagishi, T., Kikuchi, M. and Kosugi, M. (1999) 'Trust, gullibility, and social intelligence', *Asian Journal of Social Psychology,* 2: 145–61.

Yamagishi, T. and Kiyonari, T. (2000) 'The group as container of generalized reciprocity', *Social Psychology Quarterly*, 62: 116–32.

Yuki, M. and Yokota, K. (2009) 'The primal warrior: Outgroup threat priming enhances intergroup discrimination in men but not women', *Journal of Experimental Social Psychology,* 45: 271–4.

11

Group Decision-Making

Revisiting Janis' groupthink studies

Dominic J. Packer and Nick D. Ungson

BACKGROUND

On 17 April, 1961, more than 1400 Cuban exiles landed at the Bay of Pigs in an attempt to invade Cuba and overthrow Fidel Castro's communist government. The invasion, largely planned by the CIA and approved by US President John F. Kennedy, was a colossal failure. Within two days of their arrival at the Bay of Pigs, the paramilitaries were surrounded by a Cuban Army force that outnumbered them ten times over. The brigade was captured and subjected to public interrogations and incarceration in Cuban prisons. President Kennedy, sworn into office earlier that year, came under heavy criticism for his decision to move forward with the ill-fated plan. Importantly, however, President Kennedy did not make this decision alone; he was advised by a small, tightly knit advisory group, including Secretary of Defense Robert McNamara, Secretary of State Dean Rusk, and the president's own brother, Attorney General Robert Kennedy. The Joint Chiefs of Staff, as well as the director and deputy director of the CIA, were also aware of the plan's details. The question was obvious: how could this group of highly intelligent people fail so comprehensively?

Irving L. Janis,[1] a psychologist at Yale University, set out to answer this question. Having researched military morale in the US Army during the Second World War, Janis' early career was focused on attitude and habit change, especially in the domains of smoking and dieting. After reading an account of the Bay of Pigs fiasco, he was inspired to pivot from investigating individual-level processes to those underlying group decision-making. As Janis (1982) writes, he found himself talking

---

[1]Irving Janis lived, to cite his obituary (Smith and Mann, 1992), 'an extraordinarily productive life in ... unusually planful but unusually creative style'. He made substantive contributions to a broad array of research topics, and maintained a lifelong love of art. He was nearly expelled at 16 for skipping school to spend time at the art museum in Buffalo, NY. Many years later, having received a terminal diagnosis of cancer, he spent his last months writing a book about the psychology of art enjoyment with his wife and children.

Figure 11.1 US troops captured after the ill-fated Bay of Pigs invasion

about his ideas in a seminar on group psychology at Yale. These ideas were eventually sharpened and presented in full in his highly influential books *Victims of Groupthink* (1972) and *Groupthink: Psychological Studies of Policy Decisions and Fiascoes* (1982). In these books, Janis' purpose was to account for how 'bright, shrewd men like John F. Kennedy and his advisors [were] taken in by the CIA's stupid, patchwork plan' (Janis, 1972: iii). Although Janis concluded that the CIA's faulty planning and lack of effective communication was partially at fault for the Bay of Pigs fiasco, he diagnosed the primary problem as stemming from social psychological processes operating within the president's core advisory group.

At the time, theory and research on group and organizational decision-making were dominated by individualistic subjective utility theory (Kramer, 1998), according to which a single person's subjective evaluations of risk and reward affect their decision-making processes. However, Janis argued that individual errors were not solely to blame for the Bay of Pigs and other high-level governmental fiascoes (e.g., escalation of the North Korean War, unpreparedness for the attack on Pearl Harbor, escalation of the Vietnam War). Rather, he stressed the *group dynamics* underlying these decisions. In particular, he theorized that the cohesiveness of groups could motivate their members to prioritize group harmony and unanimity over careful deliberation when making decisions. Unlike the laboratory studies that characterize many of the classic studies in this book, Janis utilized a case-study approach. As such, he garnered evidence for his ideas mainly using secondary sources – memoirs, minutes of meetings, diaries, letters, prepared statements, and the like. As Janis trawled through these sources, critical questions guided his search for evidence of his hypotheses. Was the fiasco truly a result of group decision-making? Was the decision-making group characterized by an extreme motivation to maintain cohesion? What other antecedent conditions appeared to be present? Was the fiasco avoidable (i.e., if the group had engaged in better decision-making)? Janis' case-study approach exemplifies the diversity with which social psychologists have, over the years, attempted to study group processes, and it provided him with rich and real-life material with which to explore his ideas. Ultimately, Janis was constrained by the documents available at the time and, as we will see, as new material has entered the historical record, conceptions of these events have changed. However, on the basis of the information available to him, Janis presented 'a set of beautifully argued briefs, skillfully weaving together the extant qualitative evidence with contemporary social psychological theory' (Kramer, 1998: 240) to describe a constellation of antecedent conditions that he believed would produce poor collective decision-making, identifying a phenomenon that he termed 'groupthink'.

JANIS' GROUPTHINK MODEL:
ANTECEDENTS, SYMPTOMS AND REMEDIES

> 'Groupthink' [is] a quick and easy way to refer to a mode of thinking that people engage in when they are deeply involved in a cohesive in-group, when the members' striving for unanimity overrides their motivation to realistically appraise alternative courses of action. (Janis, 1972: 9)

At the heart of Janis' groupthink model is the idea that a specific set of antecedent conditions can lead the members of a group to *seek consensus* with one another instead of engaging in careful and deliberative decision-making. In doing so, they will tend to converge around common perspectives, exhibiting *internalization* of beliefs, such that they share a uniform point of view, both publicly and privately. The groupthink model specifies (a) the *antecedent conditions* expected to produce this consensus-seeking psychology, (b) a set of observable *symptoms* that should arise from it, which in turn result in (c) a set of *defective decision-making processes*. As summarized in Figure 11.2, the model[2] suggests that these defective processes tend, much of the time, to produce suboptimal collective decisions.

Among the antecedent conditions leading to groupthink, Janis identified highly directive (e.g., charismatic or authoritarian) leaders, limited information search, and insulation of the group from outsiders with the necessary expertise to make sound decisions. However, two antecedent conditions were predicted to be especially important: a strong sense of group cohesion (i.e., a strong collective bond of some sort) and a context of high stress or crisis, especially likely when confronting a complex and consequential decision. These in particular – evidenced strongly among Kennedy's inner circle during the Bay of Pigs deliberations – were expected to produce consensus-seeking motives.

---

[2]Janis (1971, 1982), in addition to many researchers since his original publication (see References), tended to use the terms 'hypothesis' and 'theory' interchangeably when referring to groupthink. To simplify our discussion of groupthink, we opt for the term 'model' because Janis' original conception outlines a set of antecedent conditions that are expected to produce a set of defective decision-making processes by way of a set of psychological groupthink symptoms. Consequently, we only use the term 'hypothesis' when referring to a specific prediction which might be derived from the overall model (e.g., group cohesiveness will decrease reappraisal of solution options).

Symptoms

Over-estimation of group worth
1. Illusion of invulnerability
2. Belief in morality of ingroup
Closed-mindedness
3. Collective rationalization
4. Stereotypic views of outgroups
Pressures towards uniformity
5. Self-censorship
6. Illusion of unanimity
7. Pressure placed on deviants
8. Mindguarding

Antecedents

1. High cohesiveness
2. Structural factors
   a) Insulated group
   b) Partisan leadership
   c) No procedural protocols
   d) Ideological homogeneity
3. Contextual factors
   a) External pressure
   b) Members under stress
   c) Lack of optimism
   d) Low self-esteem

Groupthink

Excessive concurrence-seeking behaviour

Decision-making characteristics

1. Limited consideration of options
2. Limited consideration of goals
3. Limited cost–benefit appraisal
4. Limited use of expert knowledge
5. Undue attention to facts that support ingroup choice
6. Limited reappraisal of options
7. Lack of contingency plans

Remedial interventions

1. Encourage critical evaluation
2. Higher administration takes impartial policy stance
3. Appoint independent groups and advisors
4. Group members seek feedback from their external constituents
5. Encourage criticism from outside experts
6. Appoint devil's advocate
7. Careful evaluation of outgroup warnings
8. Have periodic division into sub-groups
9. Have 'second-chance' meetings

Figure 11.2 Janis' groupthink model

Sources: Janis (1971); Janis and Mann (1977: 132)

Janis posited that, in turn, these antecedent conditions produce eight observable groupthink symptoms. He was a bit vague as to whether all antecedent conditions were necessary to produce all symptoms (something we discuss further below). Collectively, however, these symptoms describe a group that is (a) overly confident with regard to its morality and strengths (illusion of invulnerability, collective rationalization, perception of inherent morality), (b) derogating and simplistic about outgroups (stereotyping), and (c) exerting strong internal pressures on members to conform to shared opinions (illusion of unanimity, pressuring dissenters, mindguards, self-censorship).

Finally, these symptoms are expected to elicit various defective decision-making processes characterized by insufficient examination of preferred options and their alternatives, biased information search, and scarce attention to how things might go wrong. As such, decision-making objectives are inadequately discussed, only a few alternative solutions are entertained, originally preferred solutions are not critically examined, initially discarded solutions are not re-examined, experts are not consulted, advice is solicited in a selective and biased fashion, and the group fails to develop contingency plans.

As we will see, groupthink has led two, often quite separate, lives. As an aptly named *idea* about the power of dysfunctional group dynamics, it has had – and retains – substantial intuitive and popular appeal. As a set of specific, testable empirical *hypotheses*, it has enjoyed less success. This is due, at least in part, to imprecision on Janis' part regarding exactly how and which antecedent conditions combine to produce which symptoms.

Importantly, Janis also drew on his model to formulate recommendations, devoting the final portion of *Victims of Groupthink* to a discussion of how to prevent groupthink in all sorts of decision-making collectives (see Figure 11.2). Janis argued, for example, that group leaders should encourage all group members to be 'critical evaluators' such that they are able to freely express doubts or objections. Additionally, group leaders should avoid stating their initial preferences at the onset of any decision-making venture so that other members will not immediately feel pressured to conform. Janis advocated for the creation of several independent groups, each with their own leader, to solve the same problem. This would remove any decision from the hands of one group. Janis also argued that group members' opinions should be frequently challenged, either by allowing different external experts to attend meetings, or by designating select members to serve as temporary 'devil's advocates.' In the case of decisions that involve intergroup competition or conflict, the group should devote time to interpreting warning signs from outgroups, as well as constructing multiple scenarios regarding outgroups' possible intentions. Finally, Janis stressed the importance of 'second-chance' meetings in which group decisions could be reconsidered one last time before being settled or made public.

IMPACT OF THE GROUPTHINK IDEA

Almost 50 years have passed since Janis (1972) first presented his model, and groupthink has received a great deal of attention within academia, as well as among policymakers and in popular media. The model is discussed in introductory texts in a number of disciplines, including business and management, political science, communications, and of course psychology (Esser, 1998). As an index of its continued prominence in undergraduate curricula, examination of internet search trends reveals that searches for 'groupthink' peak twice a year – in late fall and early spring – which, not coincidentally, also show peak searches for 'psychology test'. Indeed, the correlation between weekly searches for these two terms is about .55.[3]

How can we explain the popularity of the groupthink model, both at its inception and into the 21st century? One explanation is that Janis' model represented an

_____
[3]Data from GoogleTrends, May 2016.

intuitively appealing integration of familiar social psychological phenomena such as conformity (e.g., Asch, 1956; see Chapter 5) and obedience (e.g., Milgram, 1963; see Chapter 7) with the cognitive psychology of decision-making (e.g., choice, risk aversion, information search; Simon, 1959). Additionally, the model situated itself against the backdrop of vivid and emotionally evocative case examples including the Bay of Pigs disaster and the earlier attack on Pearl Harbor. Indeed, by seeking to explain real-world failures, the groupthink model was instrumental in demonstrating the power and importance of group dynamics to audiences outside of academia.

Groupthink also benefited from broad practical appeal, representing one of the first efforts at applying small-groups psychological analysis to improving governmental decision-making (Hart, 1998). The model was attractive to academics and non-academics alike because Janis' approach suggested practical solutions to prevent potentially disastrous group decisions. Janis argued that effective, successful group decision-making is based on careful analysis, rational deliberation, and critical evaluation of all possible solutions and their consequences. These claims were bolstered by select case studies in which he demonstrated how an absence of groupthink antecedents and symptoms led to effective group decisions (e.g., during the Cuban Missile Crisis and in creating the Marshall Plan; Janis, 1972, 1982).

Over the years, the groupthink model has been presented to student and popular audiences in broadly the same form as when it was originally conceived (Fuller and Aldag, 1998). Although this may speak to the longevity and enduring nature of the model, some researchers argue that the unchanging presentation of groupthink obscures challenges to the groupthink model that have emerged since its inception (Fuller and Aldag, 1998) – which brings us to the question of how Janis' original formulation has withstood empirical investigation since 1972.

TESTING THE GROUPTHINK MODEL

Broadly speaking, there have been two approaches to testing the groupthink model. Following from Janis' original work, some researchers have revisited old case studies or examined new examples for evidence of groupthink in real-life events. Other researchers have taken to the laboratory to seek more causal evidence for Janis' predictions about how specific antecedents (e.g., cohesion) produce groupthink symptoms.

CASE STUDIES

Janis' (1972) analyses relied heavily on the private memoirs and observer accounts of private conversations that were available when originally formulating the groupthink model. Taking advantage of the passage of time and new documents that had been previously unavailable to Janis, Philip Tetlock (1979) analysed public statements made by key members of decision-making groups that Janis (1971) previously identified as exhibiting groupthink (e.g., those involved in the invasion of North Korea, the Bay of Pigs, and the Vietnam War escalation) vs. not exhibiting groupthink (i.e., those involved in the Marshall Plan and the Cuban Missile Crisis). Consistent with the groupthink model, public statements in groupthink cases were more simplistic and tended to make more ingroup-favouring references than public statements in non-groupthink cases. However, inconsistent with the model, public statements in groupthink cases were no more likely to make negative references to outgroups.

Clark McCauley (1989) also re-examined Janis' (1982) groupthink cases. Recall that Janis argued that consensus-seeking would generally lead to internalization of beliefs such that group members truly come to share a common perspective. McCauley (1989) found that three of these cases (i.e., North Korea, Pearl Harbor, Watergate) indeed appeared to involve group members internalizing collective beliefs (i.e., privately agreeing with group decisions). However, he concluded that the Bay of Pigs invasion and Vietnam War escalation were better characterized as involving *compliance* – that is, members publicly expressed agreement with group positions without privately accepting them, presumably due to social pressures to conform.

In one of the most exhaustive analyses to date, Tetlock and his colleagues (1992) examined group dynamics in Janis' original groupthink cases, as well three new potential candidates (e.g., President Ford's Mayaguez rescue attempt, President Carter's Iran hostage rescue attempt). These researchers used a Q-sort methodology in which multiple sorters sorted 100 bipolar descriptive statements to form a unique profile of each decision-making group. For example, a sorter would decide if the group dynamics of a group were better described by the statement 'The group leader is insulated from criticism' or 'The group leader is exposed to a wide range of views and arguments'. Taken together, each group's Q-sort profile sheds light on group dynamics such as cohesiveness, leadership style, concurrence seeking, as well as organizational and procedural faults. The authors found some evidence consistent with the groupthink model: structural and procedural faults (e.g., directive leadership, decision-making procedures) predicted groupthink symptoms. However, in contrast to Janis' original formulation, group cohesiveness and high stress conditions did not emerge as key antecedents to groupthink symptoms.

Other case studies have provided even more mixed support for specific hypotheses derived from the overall groupthink model. In particular, Peterson and colleagues (1998) conducted another large Q-sort study and found support for the idea that decision-making styles and procedures have important implications for the success and failures of real corporations. However, there were some caveats. First, the 'unsuccessful groups' identified by Peterson and colleagues did not resemble the sorts of groups likely to be plagued by groupthink as characterized by Janis; rather, they tended to have weaker leaders and less cohesion. In contrast, 'successful groups' were characterized by stronger leaders, greater willingness to take risks, and more optimism.

LABORATORY STUDIES

Laboratory studies have generally focused on manipulating groupthink antecedents (e.g., cohesion, decision-making procedures) to examine their effects on groupthink symptoms and decision quality. Many lab studies have focused on group cohesion, reflecting Janis' (1972, 1982) emphasis on cohesion as a primary antecedent to groupthink. Cohesion has been manipulated in a variety of ways: giving false feedback regarding the compatibility of group members' attitudes, offering rewards to successful groups, forming groups from friends vs. strangers, or highlighting shared group membership among individuals (for a review, see Esser, 1998: 127–133). Collectively, these laboratory studies have not found a consistent causal relationship between group cohesion and groupthink symptoms. However, as we discuss further below, the inconsistency of these results may have much to do with inconsistency in the way cohesion has been defined and operationalized.

James Esser's (1998) review notes that antecedents other than cohesion may more reliably predict groupthink symptoms. For example, Matie Flowers (1977) examined leadership style and found that groups with directive leaders suggested fewer potential solutions and used less available information when making decisions. Decision-making procedures were also shown to be sometimes predictive of groupthink symptoms. For example, when decision-making processes were limited (e.g., by allowing majority decisions rather than insisting they be unanimous), decision quality suffered (Kameda and Sugimori, 1993).

Taken together, although there are empirical observations that some of Janis' (1972, 1982) antecedents may produce certain groupthink symptoms, it seems fair to say that there is little or no evidence from either case or lab studies for a strict model in which all of Janis' (1972, 1982) antecedents must be present to elicit the symptoms of groupthink, or in which all groupthink symptoms necessarily co-occur. There is also little evidence for an additive model in which the accumulation of antecedents produces more or stronger symptoms (see Turner and Pratkanis, 1998b). This decidedly mixed pattern of evidence has naturally led to a variety of conceptual critiques of the original groupthink model.

CONCEPTUAL CRITIQUES OF GROUPTHINK

Although Janis' original model of groupthink is intuitively appealing to both academics and non-academics, the model has often been criticized for the vagueness with which Janis defined the antecedents and symptoms in his model. There are also questions about the psychological processes underlying groupthink. For example, Janis (1972, 1982) emphasized that group cohesion should produce consensus-seeking among its members, causing them to internalize a common set of collective beliefs. However, as noted above, there is mixed evidence for the influence of cohesion, and it appears that compliance may be more prevalent than internalization in at least some cases of groupthink (McCauley, 1998).

Still others have criticized Janis for assuming that the only goal of decision-making groups is to engage in measured deliberation to make accurate and logical decisions. Groups may have other goals in mind, such as gaining 'satisfaction with and commitment to the decision,' 'improved implementation by group members', or even 'diffused responsibility for poor decisions' (McCauley, 1998: 148). Alternatively, it might be the case that groups hold the goal of making deliberative and accurate decisions, but in a wider context than that considered by outside observers (including researchers). Once again drawing on a wider set of documents than were available to Janis, Roderick Kramer (1998) suggested that at least some of Janis' case examples are better understood as flawed decisions arising from *politicothink* rather than groupthink. Speaking to this point, archival material suggests that when President Kennedy and his advisors approved the Bay of Pigs invasion, they engaged in extensive deliberation and sought to make accurate decisions regarding what was the best political decision (e.g., would be popular domestically) to the detriment of making the best possible military decision. In other words, careful appraisal of choices (i.e., non-groupthink symptoms) in one domain may produce apparent groupthink in another.

In one of the more scathing critiques of the groupthink model, Sally Fuller and Ramon Aldag (1998) argue that the easy popularity of the model has distracted social psychologists. They claim that researchers have focused on testing the original parameters of the groupthink model at the expense of asking broader questions about group decision-making. There is a tendency in the literature to frame results in terms of how they support groupthink, with the consequence that other interesting or important effects may be ignored because they do not seem to fit the groupthink framework. Indeed, in these terms, they observe that – ironically – some of the best evidence for the groupthink model emerges from examination of the way in which groupthink research has itself been conducted. Fuller and Aldag (1998) do concede, however, that groupthink research has been instrumental in heightening awareness of the role that group dynamics can play in shaping decision-making in governmental and organizational contexts.

BEYOND THE GROUPTHINK IDEA

Not content just to critique, psychologists over the years have attempted to formulate improved models of groupthink that better fit the empirical data and observed realities of faulty group decision-making. The crux of these endeavours is to better specify crucial antecedent conditions, as well as the cognitive processes and psychological motives that may underlie groupthink (or groupthink-like) phenomena.

Social identity maintenance

Sticking fairly closely to the spirit of Janis' original approach, Marlene Turner and Anthony Pratkanis proposed a social identity maintenance model. Their model retained consensus-seeking at the heart of groupthink, but emphasized consensus of a particular type – namely, consensus around 'a shared positive view of the functioning of the group' (1998a: 212). They posited that the desire to achieve this type of consensus arises from two interactive (not additive) factors: (a) cohesion and (b) collective threat, which in combination induce behaviours that do a better job of protecting the group's self-image than ensuring sound decisions.

Importantly, although they continued to use Janis' term 'cohesion', Turner and Pratkanis (1998a) drew on social identity and self-categorization theories (Abrams and Hogg, 1988; Hornsey, 2008; Tajfel and Turner, 1979) to offer a particular definition of cohesion. Specifically, they suggest that cohesion arises when members identify with their group, such that membership in the group represents an important part of their self-concept. Thus identified, individuals seek to maintain a positive image of their group and are more reactive to potential threats to that image. Image-threatening events, which can include complex and consequential tasks (particularly when they are subject to public scrutiny) shift group members' goals towards image maintenance and away from other ends (e.g., deliberative, systematic decision-making). To the degree that image maintenance is supported by groupthink symptoms (e.g., beliefs in inherent morality, collective rationalization, stereotyping of outgroups), decision quality by the group tends to deteriorate.

A number of studies have supported the social identity maintenance approach by highlighting the role that image threat plays in groupthink-like phenomena (e.g., Turner et al., 1992). Of practical importance, decreasing image threat – for example, by providing potential excuses for poor group performance – reduces groupthink symptoms. Relatedly, Turner and Pratkanis (1998a) note that interventions intended to ameliorate groupthink should perhaps be evaluated for their potential to increase or decrease image threat. This is because some of Janis' original recommendations – such as bringing in outside experts – could pose image threats of their own, ironically thereby making groupthink-inducing situations worse.

UNCERTAINTY REDUCTION VS. THE DISCOMFORT OF FRANK APPRAISAL

Turner and Pratkanis (1998a) open-mindedly allowed that there are likely to be multiple routes to groupthink, and McCauley (1998) highlighted two other possibilities. The first, uncertainty reduction, is largely consistent with Janis' (1972, 1982) original formulation. In this case, groups may come to premature consensus on a decision due to a desire to avoid the collective 'discomfort of uncertainty about an important issue' (McCauley, 1998: 153). Faced with complex and consequential (i.e., stressful) decisions, group members seek refuge in a shared reality, often in the form of premature consensus.

Alternatively, McCauley (1998) suggested that groupthink could be produced by 'a desire to avoid the discomfort of frank appraisal of ideas that have individuals attached to them' (1998: 153). In this case, disagreement among peers is awkward and may be socially costly. Importantly, although both routes – uncertainty reduction and social discomfort – might produce groupthink-like symptoms, the underlying mechanisms likely differ. Whereas the desire to reduce uncertainty by embracing a shared social reality might produce internalization of the group's perspectives (i.e., believing it oneself), the desire to avoid awkwardness and social sanctions should simply produce compliance.

McCauley (1998) believed that evidence supporting the social discomfort account was stronger than that for uncertainty reduction. First, he noted, if uncertainty reduction is indeed the putative mechanism, several classic examples of groupthink would need to be removed from the canon: specifically, cases in which groups did not (yet) know they were confronting difficult, uncertain decisions and yet still exhibited groupthink-like symptoms. These include the Nixon administration during the early days following the Watergate break-in and the United States Navy top brass prior to the Japanese attack on Pearl Harbor.

More substantively, McCauley (1998) suggested that the social discomfort mechanism allows for a prediction about the type of group or consensus that should give rise to groupthink. Specifically, groups founded on friendly relations and cohesion based on personal attractiveness should be most likely to create a situation in which individual members are motivated to remain on good terms with their peers. McCauley drew on laboratory evidence to support his hypothesis, most notably an old experiment by Back (1951) in which high (vs. low) levels of cohesion were manipulated in a variety of ways. In particular, researchers generated high cohesion by leading pairs of participants meeting for the first time to expect that they were similar and would like one another. Participants in this condition exhibited the strongest evidence for groupthink symptoms. A subsequent meta-analysis of similar lab studies further indicated that manipulations of cohesion based on personal attractiveness (but not cohesion based on task commitment or group pride) were associated with worse group decisions (Mullen et al., 1994).

In summary, then, McCauley argued that

> evaluating a suggestion or an argument is unavoidably an evaluation of the individual behind it. High cohesion based on personal attractiveness leads group members to expect mutual respect and support, but frank criticism of individuals' ideas is inconsistent with maintaining friendly relations. (1989: 151)

In other words, one key cause of groupthink is the desire to avoid criticizing one's friends in ways that are uncomfortable to both them and you.

DISAGREEMENT OVER THE NATURE OF COHESION

Both the social identity maintenance (Turner and Pratkanis, 1998a) and the social discomfort approach (McCauley, 1998) include cohesion as a primary antecedent to groupthink, but these models are not on the same page as to the nature of that cohesion. On the one hand, Turner and Pratkanis (1998a) adopt a social identity approach and define cohesion in terms of members' identification/self-categorization with a group. McCauley (1998), on the other hand, posits that a sense of commitment or group pride is less important than cohesion grounded in agreeable personal relations among members.

There is only one study that, to our knowledge, has directly attempted to compare the effects of distinct forms of cohesion on groupthink, at least within the same dataset. In this study, Michael Hogg and Sarah Hains (1998) manipulated types of cohesion in laboratory groups, varying whether it was based on personal attractiveness (i.e., prior friendship) or social attractiveness (i.e., grounded in a shared group identity). They also measured friendship and group identification. Their findings were mixed, but the overall pattern suggested – contrary to McCauley (1998) – that cohesion grounded in personal relations was associated with fewer/weaker groupthink-like symptoms, whereas cohesion grounded in collective identity was associated with more/stronger symptoms (see also Haslam et al., 2006). Hogg and Hains also noted that these findings are consistent with what is known more broadly about distinct forms of attraction:

> In the absence of a group culture encouraging optimal decision-making procedures, identification and concomitant social attraction will relatively automatically generate cognitions, perceptions and behaviors ... that resemble, or underpin, the symptoms of groupthink. In contrast, friendship and personal attraction are more likely to allow people to differentiate themselves from others, act as individuals, disagree with one another ... since personal identity and mutual positive regard are not threatened by such behaviors. (1998: 327)

How, then, might we account for the findings of Back (1951) and others, which appear to show the opposite? We suspect it is important that the laboratory studies cited by McCauley (1998) tended to manipulate cohesion based on personal attractiveness by creating expectations of mutual liking between people meeting for the first time. In these circumstances, the desire to *establish* friendly relations – to get off on the right foot – may indeed produce consensus-seeking behaviours. In contrast, Hogg and Hains (1998) examined personal attraction among groups of existing friends. Once friendly relations exist and can, at least to some extent, be taken for granted, disagreement and divergence may become more permissible (see also McKelvey and Kerr, 1988).

GROUPTHINK IS UBIQUITOUS

To the extent that groupthink arises during high-stress, complex and consequential decision-making, it might be considered a model that is most applicable to elite groups. Indeed, Janis' (1972, 1982) case studies described group dynamics at the highest levels of government or administration. Challenging this idea, however, Robert Baron (2005) argued that groupthink-like dynamics, including conformity, suppression of dissent, polarization, self-censorship, illusions of consensus and intergroup bias are actually commonplace – meaning that they are ubiquitous to pretty much any meaningful group. Baron (2005) further argued that failures to find strong or consistent evidence for the antecedent conditions of groupthink may actually reflect the fact that it is so common. In other words, there is little variation to detect because most groups exhibit groupthink-like symptoms and defective decision-making processes. Indeed, he argued that it is its everyday nature that gives groupthink deep intuitive appeal. Few of us have found ourselves in the Cabinet or Situation Room, yet most of us will have had experiences in groups that resonate with the notion of groupthink.

As such, Baron (2005) proposed a ubiquity model of groupthink, arguing that many of the symptoms identified by Janis (1972, 1982) are common in groups and arise from three interactive (again, not additive) antecedent factors. First, at least a minimal degree of social identification (defined in social identity/self-categorization-like terms) is required. Identification with the group matters, in part, because it tends to increase *both* normative social influence (i.e., compliance), as well as informational social influence (i.e., internalization). Following from this, for social influence to occur and for identification to produce groupthink-like symptoms, the group must have a clear norm or set of norms for individuals to follow. Finally, social influence is more likely to the degree that individual group members possess low self-efficacy or confidence regarding their abilities to understand or uniquely contribute to decision-making. Unsure of themselves, group members are more likely to turn to others and strive for consensus rather than voice divergent views.

Because the ubiquity approach is based on factors that are known to produce groupthink-like phenomena (e.g., conformity, illusion of consensus, group polarization), it is capable of incorporating Janis' original antecedent conditions, in addition to other group-relevant factors. Importantly, however, the influence of additional conditions should be mediated through one or more of the three factors described above: identification, clear norms, or low self-efficacy. For example, highly directive leadership might increase groupthink insofar as this leadership style effectively establishes clear norms for group members.

IT'S ABOUT GOALS: AN OVERARCHING FRAMEWORK

Where are we today? Given the diversity of approaches to groupthink, we think it sensible to embrace Turner and Pratkanis' (1998a) proposition that there are multiple routes to groupthink symptoms. We further suggest that many of these routes can be subsumed within, or are at least consistent with, a goal-focused interpretation of Janis' original formulation.

Recall that Janis originally defined groupthink as: 'A mode of thinking that people engage in when they are deeply involved in a cohesive in-group, when the members' *strivings for unanimity* override their *motivation to realistically appraise alternative courses of action*' (1982: 9; italics added). This definition explicitly points to a conflict between two goals: concurrence/consensus-seeking vs. accurate/deliberative decision-making. This original formulation can be retained but significantly expanded if we allow for the possibility of additional, more nuanced, goal states.

Adding nuance to Janis' posited goal states, Turner and Pratkanis (1998a) and McCauley (1998) point out that the goal of achieving consensus can serve different functions – for example, protecting a social identity or regaining a sense of certainty. In some instances (e.g., under collective threat), the goal of achieving consensus may be associated with specific content: that is, group members may want to reach consensus around a particular conclusion (e.g., a positive group image). In other cases (e.g., under deep uncertainty), any consensus at all might be acceptable, making groups willing to accept negative self-perceptions so long as they are convergent (e.g., see system justification theory; Jost and Banaji, 1994).

In addition, a desire for consensus is not the only type of goal that could come into conflict with accurate and deliberative decision-making. Although certainly not an exhaustive list, other potential goals could include:

- a desire for the group to engage in effective collective action (for which consensus is perhaps a means to an end);

- a desire for the group to reach a decision quickly (heightened perhaps in crisis situations, and reminiscent of speed/accuracy tradeoffs endemic to human cognition; e.g., Tversky and Kahneman, 1974);

- a desire for the group to reach a decision with little effort (heightened when the group is overburdened with many complex issues);

- a more individual set of desires to be positively regarded and to retain one's position in the group (as per McCauley's (1998) social discomfort hypothesis).

Finally, as noted above, groups may also hold the goal of making deliberative and accurate decisions, but in a domain that is different from that considered by external critics. Kramer's (1998) suggestion that at least some apparent cases of groupthink are better understood as politicothink makes this point. Extensive and careful deliberation about the domestic implications of a foreign policy decision, for example, might produce what appears to be bad foreign policy (but perhaps good politics).

Pursuit of group-related goals – whatever they are – is stronger to the extent that members identify with their groups (Abrams and Hogg, 1988). Strongly identified group members seek to be regarded as loyal and to make decisions that serve the interests of the group. What is understood to be in the interest of the group, however, is variable and dependent on circumstances. As a result, which of the above goals are active and serving to animate members' behaviour are shaped by context, including, in all probability, the antecedent conditions identified by Janis (1972, 1982) but also others. In many instances, the type of goal a group is pursuing may itself serve as a social norm, and members look to each other to understand 'what we are trying to do here'. The key point is that any one of the goals that conflict with accuracy and deliberation could produce groupthink-type symptoms, although, as pointed out by McCauley (1998), the underlying mechanisms and precise manifestations could differ as a function of the goal in question (e.g., some producing internalization, some compliance).

Critically, however, a goal-based formulation leaves room for individual agency. Identified group members are not automatons, blind pursuers of group norms even unto disaster. Rather, they engage in critical evaluation of their groups' behaviour, at least on occasion. And if they come to believe that group norms are harmful to group interests, they are frequently willing to articulate dissenting views; indeed, they are more likely to do so than weakly identified members who are less invested in group interests (Packer, 2008; Packer and Chasteen, 2010). Put differently, each identified member of a group is capable of confronting *for themselves* the sorts of goal conflicts identified above, navigating between the desire for accurate, sound decisions and desires for other things (e.g., positive image, effective action, liking and acceptance). Even if the group as a whole has settled on a particular goal, an individual member may, on their own assessment of the situation, choose to pursue an alternate collectively oriented goal. To the degree that this entails the expression of divergent and dissenting views, it will tend to reduce many of the symptoms of groupthink.

In line with this model, recent research has identified several factors that facilitate group members' critical evaluation of group norms and promote expressions of dissent. Some of these relate to individual differences. For example, dissent is greater among individuals who are both highly open to experience (i.e., more open to countervailing perspectives) and conscientious (i.e., motivated to act on information; Packer and Chasteen, 2010). There are also situational effects. Perhaps most notable of these is an effect of abstraction such that identified and conscientious group members who are induced to think more abstractly (e.g., by adopting longer time perspectives) are also more likely to dissent from group norms (Packer, Fujita and Chasteen, 2013; Packer, Fujita and Herman, 2013).

Ultimately, it is perceptions of the group's interests that shape identified members' behaviour. In two studies, for example, we examined political party supporters' willingness to challenge normative views within their party in a highly contested and competitive intergroup environment (Dupuis et al., 2016). In one case, we examined expressions of dissent regarding the US Republican Party's position on the Affordable Care Act ('Obamacare') at the height of a political standoff in which the Republican-controlled Congress had effectively shut down the Federal government over the issue. This was precisely the sort of complex and consequential type of situation that might, as per Janis' formulation, be likely to produce groupthink-like symptoms. And it did. Among identified Republicans who personally disagreed with their party's position, we observed evidence of compliance – an unwillingness to publicly articulate their dissenting views. Critically, however, this was not a uniform response. A specific subset of identified Republicans, who disagreed with their party's position *and* who believed that this position threatened their party's future health and viability, exhibited the opposite response – heightened dissent.

CONCLUSION

The groupthink model is appropriately recognized as a classic in social psychology. When groupthink was introduced, the decision-making literature was largely focused on utility theory as it applied to individuals' decisions. Janis' emphasis on dysfunctional group dynamics dovetailed with new cognitive theories that explained how systematic biases in judgment could nudge people away from 'rational' choices (e.g., Tversky and Kahneman, 1974). Janis' (1972, 1982) rich case studies were also integral in bringing established social psychological phenomena (e.g., conformity, obedience) to public consciousness. What's more, situating the groupthink model within emotionally evocative examples like the Bay of Pigs disaster invited everyone, academics and non-academics alike, to reflect on how group dynamics can affect decision-making in all sorts of groups, from the highest levels of government to the humblest committee or social club.

Janis (1972, 1982) advanced a theoretical model in which certain antecedent conditions would – by increasing consensus-seeking – produce groupthink symptoms and, ultimately, defective decision-making processes. As reviewed here, empirical evidence has provided little support for a strict interpretation of Janis' model. At the same time, though, there is definitely clear evidence that group dynamics contribute to the quality of collective decision-making. In attempts to do justice to this evidence, researchers have, over the years, proposed multiple reformulations or re-framings of Janis' original model. We find that many of these are useful and endorse the notion that there are likely multiple routes to groupthink-like dynamics. To this end, we advance an overarching goal-based formulation, which posits that groupthink is more or less likely to emerge as a function of how group members seek an ideal balance between different personal and collective goals (e.g., the collective goal to make accurate decisions vs. the personal goal to be accepted by the group).

Although approaches to groupthink continue to evolve, Janis' model contains an inescapable truth at its core: group decision-making is not simply the sum of individuals' decisions, but rather is the result of complex social dynamics that emerge when people seek to coordinate in groups. Continuing the quest to better understand these dynamics is crucial to explaining social behaviour and improving collective decision-making.

FURTHER READING

Baron, R.S. (2005) 'So right it's wrong: Groupthink and the ubiquitous nature of polarized group decision-making', *Advances in Experimental Social Psychology*, 37: 219–53.

This article presents a model of groupthink in which a revised set of antecedent conditions explains why groupthink is ubiquitous in all sorts of groups.

Esser, J.K. (1998) 'Alive and well after 25 years: A review of groupthink research', *Organizational Behavior and Human Decision Processes*, 73: 116–41.

This review article summarizes many of the case and experimental studies that have attempted to test the groupthink model.

Hogg, M.A. and Hains, S.C. (1998) 'Friendship and group identification: A new look at the role of cohesiveness in groupthink', *European Journal of Social Psychology*, 28(3): 323–41.

This article contrasts distinct forms of cohesion and suggests that cohesiveness grounded in group identification uniquely predicts groupthink symptoms.

Janis, I.L. (1982) *Groupthink: Psychological Studies of Policy Decisions and Fiascoes*. Boston: Houghton Mifflin.

Janis' original writing provides a compelling and rich introduction to the ideas surrounding groupthink, especially as they apply to vivid and consequential decisions in American history.

Kramer, R.M. (1998) 'Revisiting the Bay of Pigs and Vietnam decisions 25 years later: How well was the groupthink hypothesis stood the test of time?', *Organizational Behavior and Human Decision Processes*, 73: 236–71.

This reanalysis of Janis' groupthink cases takes advantage of new archival resources to argue that several are better characterized by 'politicothink' than groupthink.

Turner, M.E. and Pratkanis, A.R. (1998) 'A social identity maintenance model of groupthink', *Organizational Behavior and Human Decision Processes*, 73: 210–35.

This article presents a social-identity maintenance perspective to explain how stressful contexts may promote groupthink symptoms by increasing image protection motives.

REFERENCES

Abrams, D. and Hogg, M.A. (1988) *Social Identifications: A Social Psychology of Intergroup Relations and Group Processes*. London: Routledge.

Asch, S.E. (1956) 'Studies of independence and conformity', *Psychological Monographs*, 70: 1–70.

Back, K. (1951) 'Influence through social communications', *Journal of Abnormal and Social Psychology*, 46: 9–23.

Baron, R.S. (2005) 'So right it's wrong: Groupthink and the ubiquitous nature of polarized group decision-making', *Advances in Experimental Social Psychology*, 37: 219–253.

Dupuis, D.R., Wohl, M.J.A., Packer, D.J. and Tabri, N. (2016) 'To dissent and protect: Stronger collective identification increases willingness to dissent when group norms evoke collective angst', *Group Processes & Intergroup Relations*, 19: 1–17.

Esser, J.K. (1998) 'Alive and well after 25 years: A review of groupthink research', *Organizational Behavior and Human Decision Processes*, 73: 116–41.

Flowers, M.L. (1977) 'A laboratory test of some implications of Janis' groupthink hypothesis', *Journal of Personality and Social Psychology*, 35: 888–96.

Fuller, S.R. and Aldag, R.J. (1998) 'Organizational Tonypandy: Lessons from a quarter century of the groupthink phenomenon', *Organizational Behavior and Human Decision Processes*, 73: 163–84.

Hart, P.'t. (1998) 'Preventing groupthink revisited: Evaluating and reforming groups in government', *Organizational Behavior and Human Decision Processes*, 73: 306–26.

Haslam, S.A., Ryan, M.K., Postmes, T., Spears, R., Jetten, J. and Webley, P. (2006) 'Sticking to our guns: Social identity as a basis for the maintenance of commitment to faltering organizational projects', *Journal of Organizational Behavior*, 27: 607–28.

Hogg, M.A. and Hains, S.C. (1998) 'Friendship and group identification: A new look at the role of cohesiveness in groupthink', *European Journal of Social Psychology*, 28: 323–41.

Hornsey, M.J. (2008) 'Social identity theory and self-categorization theory: A historical review', *Social and Personality Psychology Compass*, 2: 204–22.

Janis, I.L. (1971) 'Groupthink', *Psychology Today*, November, 43–6: 74–6.

Janis, I.L. (1972) *Victims of Groupthink*. Boston: Houghton Mifflin.

Janis, I.L. (1982) *Groupthink: Psychological Studies of Policy Decisions and Fiascoes*. Boston: Houghton Mifflin.

Janis, I.L. and Mann, L. (1977) *Decision Making: A Psychological Analysis of Conflict, Choice, and Commitment*. New York: Free Press.

Jost, J.T. and Banaji, M.R. (1994) 'The role of stereotyping in system-justification and the production of false consciousness', *British Journal of Social Psychology*, 33: 1–27.

Kameda, T. and Sugimori, S. (1993) 'Psychological entrapment in group decision making: An assigned decision rule and a groupthink phenomenon', *Journal of Personality and Social Psychology*, 65: 282–92.

Kramer, R.M. (1998) 'Revisiting the Bay of Pigs and Vietnam decisions 25 years later: How well has the groupthink hypothesis stood the test of time?', *Organizational Behavior and Human Decision Processes*, 73: 236–71.

McCauley, C. (1989) 'The nature of social influence in groupthink: Compliance and internalization', *Journal of Personality and Social Psychology*, 57: 250–60.

McCauley, C. (1998) 'Group dynamics in Janis' theory of groupthink: Backward and forward', *Organizational Behavior and Human Decision Processes*, 73: 146–62.

McKelvey, M. and Kerr, N.H. (1988) 'Differences in conformity among friends and strangers', *Psychological Reports*, 62: 759–62.

Milgram, S. (1963) 'Behavioral study of obedience', *Journal of Abnormal and Social Psychology*, 67: 371–78.

Mullen, B., Anthony, T., Salas, E. and Driskell, J.E. (1994) 'Group cohesiveness and quality of decision making: An integration of tests of the groupthink hypothesis', *Small Group Research*, 25: 189–204.

Packer, D.J. (2008) 'On being both with us and against us: A normative conflict model of dissent in social groups', *Personality and Social Psychology Review*, 12: 50–72.

Packer, D.J. and Chasteen, A.L. (2010) 'Loyal deviance: Testing the normative conflict model of dissent in social groups', *Personality and Social Psychology Bulletin*, 36: 5–18.

Packer, D.J., Fujita, K. and Chasteen, A.L. (2013) 'The motivational dynamics of dissent decision: A goal-conflict approach', *Social Psychological and Personality Science*, 5: 27–34.

Packer, D.J., Fujita, K. and Herman, S. (2013) 'Rebels with a cause: A goal conflict approach to understanding when conscientious people dissent', *Journal of Experimental Social Psychology*, 49: 927–32.

Peterson, R.S., Owens, P.D., Tetlock, P.E., Fan, E.T. and Martorana, P. (1998) 'Group dynamics in top management teams: Groupthink, vigilance, and alternative models of organizational failure and success', *Organizational Behavior and Human Decision Processes*, 73: 272–305.

Simon, H.A. (1959) 'Theories of decision-making in economics and behavioral science', *American Economic Review*, 49: 253–83.

Smith, M.B. and Mann, L. (1992) 'Irving L. Janis (1918–1990): Obituary', *American Psychologist*, 47: 812–13.

Tajfel, H. and Turner, J. (1979) 'An integrative theory of intergroup conflict', in W.G. Austin and S. Worchel (eds), *The Psychology of Intergroup Relations*. Monterey, CA: Brooks-Cole. pp. 33–47.

Tetlock, P.E. (1979) 'Identifying victims of groupthink', *Journal of Personality and Social Psychology*, 37: 1314–24.

Tetlock, P.E., Peterson, R.S., McGuire, C., Chang, S. and Feld, P. (1992) 'Assessing political group dynamics: A test of the groupthink model', *Journal of Personality and Social Psychology*, 63: 403–25.

Turner, M.E. and Pratkanis, A.R. (1998a) 'A social identity maintenance model of groupthink', *Organizational Behavior and Human Decision Processes*, 73: 210–35.

Turner, M.E. and Pratkanis, A.R. (1998b) 'Twenty-five years of groupthink theory and research: Lessons from the evaluation of a theory', *Organizational Behavior and Human Decision Processes*, 73: 105–15.

Turner, M.E., Pratkanis, A.R., Probasco, P. and Leve, C. (1992) 'Threat, cohesion, and group effectiveness: Testing a social identity maintenance perspective on groupthink', *Journal of Personality and Social Psychology*, 63: 781–96.

Tversky, A. and Kahneman, D. (1974) 'Judgment under uncertainty: Heuristics and biases', *Science*, 185: 1124–3.

12 | Helping in Emergencies

Revisiting Latané and Darley's bystander studies

Mark Levine

BACKGROUND

On 13 March 1964, at about 3:30 am, in the Kew Gardens district of New York City, Kitty Genovese was stabbed, then raped and murdered by Winston Moseley. This murder was one of 9,360 killings in the United States that year and, despite the horror of this apparently random attack, the story merited but a few short paragraphs on page 12 of the *New York Times* the following day. Surprising as it may seem, the murder had very little impact on public consciousness at first. It wasn't until ten days later, and a casual lunchtime conversation between Police Commissioner Michael J. Murphy and *New York Times* editor A.M. Rosenthal, that the picture began to change. The two men were discussing the arrest of Moseley for the attack on Genovese (and several other women) when Murphy berated the Kew Gardens residents for their failure to act. He suggested the police had the names of 38 witnesses who had refused to intervene.

Rosenthal returned to his office and gave one of his journalists, Martin Gansberg, the task of following up this lead. Four days later, on 27 March, the *New York Times* published a front-page article which had a profound impact on the way we think about helping behaviour in social psychology today. Gansberg's article claimed that:

> For more than half an hour 38 respectable, law-abiding citizens in Queens watched a killer stalk and stab a woman in three separate attacks in Kew Gardens. Twice the sound of their voices and the sudden glow of their bedroom lights interrupted him and frightened him off. Each time he returned, sought her out and stabbed her again.... Not one person telephoned the police during the assault; one witness called after the woman was dead. (Gansberg, 1964: 1)

Gansberg's three main claims seemed to touch a nerve. The idea that 38 ordinary men and women could watch in a kind of morbid fascination while a fellow human being was raped and murdered, and not lift a finger to help, was profoundly shocking.

A huge public debate (and associated media circus) followed publication of the article, with commentators and correspondents bemoaning the breakdown of moral and social values. A key theme of this debate was that the rise of the city (and its associated living conditions) had divided people from each other and undermined their capacity to empathize with, or feel responsible for, the lives of others. As the social psychologist John Darley observed:

> A great many articles were written on the dehumanization of man, and there was the suggestion that we needed to think about a new kind of man, 'homo urbanis', the city dweller, who cared only for himself. There was a focus on speculating on the personality flaws of people who could stand and watch while others died. It was almost as if we were reverting to the kinds of explanations used in the sixteenth century, that people were possessed by devils to do such cruel things. (Darley, in Evans, 1980: 216)

The young Darley had recently completed his PhD and, as he described some time later (Evans, 1980), one evening over dinner he began discussing the Genovese case with another young colleague, Bibb Latané. The two researchers were unconvinced by the claims that bystander behaviour in the Kitty Genovese case reflected modern processes of social breakdown. Instead they argued that more generic social psychological factors may be at work:

> Firstly, social psychologists ask not how people are different or why are the people who failed to respond monsters, but how are all people the same and how might anybody in that situation be influenced not to respond. Second we asked: What influences reach the person from the group? We argued for a several step model in which a person first had to define a situation. Emergencies don't come with a sign saying 'I am an emergency'. In defining the event as an emergency one looks at other people to see their reactions to the situation and interpret the meaning that lies behind their actions. Third, when multiple people are present, the responsibility to intervene does not focus clearly on any one person ... You feel a diffusion of responsibility in that situation and you're less likely yourself to take responsibility. We argued that these two processes, definition and diffusion, working together, might well account for a good deal of what happened. (Darley, in Evans, 1980: 216–17)

THE BYSTANDER STUDIES

To test these ideas Darley and Latané devised some of the most innovative and influential experiments in the history of social psychology. Taking the presence of others in an emergency situation as their key causal variable, they set out to examine the effect that the number of other people present in an emergency situation has on the willingness of an individual to respond to that emergency. With this in mind, the researchers conducted a number of beautifully choreographed experiments, in which participants were exposed to what they believed were real-life emergencies in the presence of varying numbers of others, and then measured the occurrence of actual helping behaviours.

1 THE 'SEIZURE' EXPERIMENT

In one such study (Darley and Latané, 1968), 72 New York University undergraduate psychology students were invited to take part in discussions about personal problems that students might have while at university. When the participants arrived for the experiment they found themselves in a long corridor with doors opening off it to several small rooms. An experimental assistant met them, took them to one of the rooms, and seated them at a table. After filling out a background information form, the participant was given a pair of headphones with an attached microphone and was told to listen for instructions. Over the intercom, the experimenter explained that he was interested in learning about the kinds of personal problems faced by normal college students in a high-pressure, urban environment. He said that to avoid possible embarrassment about discussing personal problems with strangers, several precautions had been taken. First, participants would remain anonymous, which was why they had been placed in individual rooms rather than face-to-face. Second, since the discussion might be inhibited by the presence of outside listeners, the experimenter would not listen to the initial discussion, but would examine the participants' contributions later, by questionnaire. This was to ensure that, when the emergency happened, participants would not assume that the experimenter would take charge. Participants were then told that since the experimenter was not present, it was necessary to impose some organization. Each person would talk in turn, presenting their problems to the group. Next, each person in turn would comment on what the others had said, and finally, there would be a free discussion. This discussion sequence would be automatically controlled and each participant's microphone would be turned on for about two minutes. While any microphone was on, all other microphones would be off. Only one participant, therefore, could be heard over the network at any given time.

In fact, the contributions to this discussion (apart from the participant's own) were all recordings. This allowed Darley and Latané to vary the number of people that the participant believed to be present but to keep the discussion content consistent across conditions. Depending on the experimental condition, participants were then led to believe that they were engaging in conversation with one other, two others, or six others. In the discussion, the future victim spoke first, saying that he found it difficult to adjust to New York City and to his studies. Very hesitantly, and with obvious embarrassment, he mentioned that he was prone to seizures, particularly when studying hard or taking exams. The other people took their turns (with numbers of contributions depending on the experimental condition). The naïve participant talked last in the series. When it was again the victim's turn to talk, he made a few relatively calm comments, and then began to experience medical difficulties. Expressing audible distress, he then collapsed:

> I-er-um-I think I-I need-er-if-if could-er-er somebody er-er-er-er-er-er give me a little-er-give me a little help here because-er-I-er-I'm-er-h-h-having a-a-a real problem-er right now and I-er-if somebody could help me out it would-it would er-er-er s-s-sure be good ... because-er-there-er-ag cause I er-I-uh-I've got one of

the-er-sei-er-er-things coming on and-and-and I could really use some help so if somebody would-er give me a little h-help-uh-er-er-er-er c-ould somebody-er er-help-er-uh-uh-uh [choking sounds] ... I'm gonna die-er-er ... help-er-er-seizure [chokes, then quiet]. (Darley and Latané, 1968: 95–6)

This was followed by silence.

Darley and Latané measured the percentage of participants in each condition who helped the student in trouble (helping was defined as leaving the cubicle and notifying the experimenter of the problem). They also measured the amount of time it took participants to respond to the emergency and try to help. Participants were given four minutes to respond, after which the experiment was terminated.

Latané and Darley found that likelihood of intervention, and the time taken to intervene, both varied as a function of the number of other people believed to be present. When participants believed they were the only person who had heard the emergency they were significantly more likely to intervene and also reacted far quicker to the emergency. As the data in Table 12.1 indicate, response rates were lower and reaction times slower when participants believed there was one bystander present rather than none. And they were even lower and slower when they were led to believe there were four bystanders.

Table 12.1 Effect of number of bystanders on likelihood of helping and speed of response (based on Darley and Latané, 1968)

Bystanders	N	% helping	Time to call for help (in seconds)
No bystanders	13	85	52
One bystander	26	62	96
Four bystanders	13	31	166

2 THE 'WHITE SMOKE' EXPERIMENT

In a second experiment Darley and Latané (1968) examined participants' reaction to an emergency that unfolded as they sat in a room filling in a questionnaire. Participants were all male Columbia University undergraduates who had been recruited to take part in a study on 'problems involved in life at an urban university'. When they arrived they were directed to a waiting room and asked to complete a preliminary questionnaire. However, as they were doing this, the room began to fill with a visible (but harmless) white smoke. The researchers then noted whether participants left the room to report the smoke, and measured the length of time that it took them to do so. The experiment was terminated after six minutes if participants had still failed to raise the alarm.

In different experimental conditions, participants were either on their own in the room or there with two others. Moreover, sometimes the others were naïve participants and sometimes they were confederates who had been instructed to ignore the smoke and remain passive. The results indicated that when people were on their own most of them (75%) raised the alarm, but that when they were with others only 38% did so. As well as this, they responded much more quickly in the former condition. For example, after two minutes, 55% of the subjects in the alone condition had reported the smoke but only 12% of the three-person groups had done so. After four minutes, 75% of the subjects in the alone condition had reported the smoke but the reporting rate in the four-person groups was still at 12% (the reporting rate for three-person groups went to 38% in the final two minutes). Moreover, when the other people in the room were confederates who remained passive throughout the unfolding drama, then participants were also likely to be passive with only 10% raising the alarm in this condition (a small minority helped immediately while the rest remained passive throughout).

On the basis of such findings, Latané and Darley identified two processes that they suggested served to inhibit intervention in emergency situations: *diffusion of responsibility* and *pluralistic ignorance*. Diffusion of responsibility refers to the idea that as the number of other people present in a given situation increases, the responsibility that a given individual feels for responding to that situation is correspondingly diminished. Pluralistic ignorance refers to the idea that the presence of other people who remain inactive or seem unconcerned during an event can dissuade or discourage an individual from intervention, even though they might have felt concerned by the situation (a process which has also been identified as a basis for behaviour in Asch's line-judgment studies; see Chapter 5).

Formalizing these insights, the researchers went on to propose a five-step model of the cognitive decision-making processes associated with emergency intervention (Latané and Darley, 1970). The steps that this identified were as follows:

Step 1: Notice that something is happening.

Step 2: Interpret the event as an emergency.

Step 3: Take responsibility for providing help.

Step 4: Decide how to act.

Step 5: Provide help.

Latané and Darley argued that failure to intervene in an emergency in the presence of others could result from diffusion of responsibility and pluralistic ignorance at different stages of this sequence. For example, pluralistic ignorance might reduce the likelihood of interpreting an event as an emergency (Step 2) if bystanders look to others for information about how to act and assume that they are not responding because they do not see the situation as problematic. On the other hand, diffusion of responsibility might disrupt intervention at the point of taking responsibility (Step 3) if a person is surrounded by other bystanders who could also take responsibility for action (but do not).

Since this model was proposed, different aspects of it have been tested in hundreds of experiments. In a meta-analysis of these, Latané and Nida (1981) concluded that the 'bystander effect' – whereby the presence of others reduces the likelihood of helping – was one of the most robust and reliable findings in social psychology.

Given this expression of confidence, one might have expected that this would be the end of the matter. Yet as Latané and Nida also point out, despite the wealth of accumulated empirical evidence, the bystander effect seems to lack utility. This is because (somewhat ironically) discovery of the effect has done little to help promote helping behaviour:

> To our knowledge, the research has not contributed to the development of practical strategies for increasing bystander intervention ... none of us has been able to mobilise the increasing store of social psychological understanding accumulated over the last decade to ensure that future Kitty Genoveses will receive help. (Latané and Nida, 1981: 322)

QUESTIONING THE BYSTANDER EFFECT

Latané and Nida's analysis raises the important and intriguing question as to why the apparently robust five-step model fails to provide researchers with any clues about how to increase the likelihood of bystander interventions in violent emergencies. One answer may be found in the Kitty Genovese case itself – or rather, in what we have come to know about it.

THE PROBLEM OF CULTURALLY EMBEDDED THEORIZING

In this regard, Frances Cherry (1995) offers a fascinating analysis of the way in which the Genovese murder was translated into experimental analogues. She points out that there were a number of important features of the attack, only some of which were identified as key events worthy of experimental analysis. Of course, the failure of the bystanders to act was a remarkable feature. However, what was equally remarkable was that this was a violent and unprovoked attack by a man on a woman.

Cherry suggests that this gendered aspect of the event and of the violence was almost invisible to researchers at the time. She attributes this to the fact that the event occurred at a time before feminist scholars had sensitized society to the social problem of male violence towards women. We are now very familiar with the concept of domestic violence – and with concerns about male violence towards women in both public and private spaces. However, in the early 1960s, these were social concerns that had yet to be identified. As a consequence, the experimental analogues of the Kitty Genovese case were shaped by what Cherry calls 'culturally embedded theorizing'. That is, subsequent experiments ignored issues of violence and gender because these topics were culturally unavailable to researchers – who focused instead on the dangers of the anonymous group because this chimed with contemporary social anxieties.

In the handful of studies that do examine the role of violence and/or gender (Borofsky et al., 1971; Shotland and Straw, 1976; and more recently Fischer et al.,

2006; Levine and Crowther, 2008), a far more nuanced story emerges. In these studies the psychological relationships between perpetrator and victim, or between bystander and victim, emerge as key predictors of intervention rather than just information about the presence or absence of others. For example, bystanders are more likely to intervene if they think the perpetrator and victim are strangers rather than intimates (Shotland and Straw, 1976) or when they share group membership with the victim (Levine and Crowther, 2008).

THE POSSIBILITY OF ALTERNATIVE NARRATIVES

At the same time that culturally embedded theorizing was producing implicit absences in the research agenda, there were some deliberate absences too. In the Genovese case Winston Moseley was a black man who attacked a white woman in a predominantly white borough in New York. Rosenthal, the *New York Times* Metropolitan editor, is on record as saying that had this been an attack by a black man on a black woman in Harlem, it would never have been reported in his paper at all (Rosenthal, 1964/1999). Moreover, Rosenthal deliberately withheld the race of the attacker in the newspaper report. This was because he judged that, given the political and social tensions of the time – for example, just a few months later there were three nights of 'race riots' in Harlem after a policeman killed a black youth – it would have been potentially inflammatory to do so.

The point here is not that skin colour is relevant to the attack (it is clearly not) but that there are a variety of ways that the story of the Genovese murder could have been told and might have developed. The number of bystanders provided the basis for one such narrative, but several others were equally as compelling. Accordingly, it may be the case that the limited utility of bystander research can be attributed to researchers' failure to explore these alternative narratives.

THE FACTS OF THE GENOVESE CASE

More recently, Rachel Manning and colleagues (2007) have revisited the evidence available about the night of the Genovese murder. Using the court transcripts from Moseley's trial, and a range of other evidence, they have shown that the three main claims in Gansberg's *New York Times* article – that 38 people watched the murder, that they watched events unfold for half an hour, and that nobody intervened – are not supported by this evidence. At the trial, only five witnesses from the apartments overlooking Austin Street were called (Robert Mozer, Andre Picq, Irene Frost, Samuel Koshkin, and Sophie Farrar). Of these, only three actually saw Genovese and Moseley together. It is of course possible that there were other eyewitnesses who refused to come forward or to testify, or whom the prosecution declined to call (though it is likely that the prosecution would call those witnesses with the best and most complete views of the incident). Charles Skoller, the Assistant District Attorney at the time of the murder, stated: 'we only found about half a dozen that saw what was going on, that we could use' (quoted in Rasenberger, 2004: 14). In other words, evidence suggests that there were in fact far fewer eyewitnesses than the 38 referred to in the *New York Times* article, and no list of the 38 has ever been made available.

There is also no evidence that witnesses watched for half an hour in awe and fascination. In large part, this is because Kitty Genovese was the victim of two separate attacks rather than one prolonged one. The first attack brought several witnesses to the window – none of whom was in time to see the stabbing. Indeed, witnesses were unsure about what had happened but their shouting (clear evidence of intervention) seemed to drive Moseley away. He said at his trial that he was fearful of being identified and so went to move his car – although he did say he felt sure that those who shouted would not intervene directly. When Moseley left, witnesses describe Genovese as getting to her feet and walking (slowly and unsteadily) around the corner of the building (see Figure 12.1). It appears she was trying to make her way to the entrance of her apartment, which was at the back of the two-storey Tudor Building where she lived. In doing so, she went out of sight of the eyewitnesses in the Mowbray and West Virginia Apartments who had no line of sight to the back of the building.

When Moseley returned, the second and final attack took place *inside* the building in the stairwell of 92–96 Austin Street, where none of the trial witnesses could see. The spatial arrangement of the buildings in which witnesses were located, and the site of the first and then the second (and fatal) attack, make it impossible for all but one of the known witnesses (Carl Ross, see Takooshian et al., 2005) to have observed the attack unfold or witnessed the sexual assault and the murder itself in the stairwell. Here again, the image created by the newspaper report that

Figure 12.1 The two-storey Tudor Building in which Kitty Genovese lived and where she was attacked and murdered on 13 March 1964. The first attack took place in Austin Street to the left of the building; the second (fatal) attack took place in a stairwell at the back of the building. Permission: Joseph De May, Jr., Kew Gardens, NY.

witnesses stood in their windows and watched the murder happen before their eyes is not supported by the evidence.

Finally, there is evidence that, far from observing passively, bystanders made several attempts to intervene. We have already seen that the shouts of witnesses seemed to disrupt Moseley's first attack. In addition, a sworn affidavit by a former NYPD police officer (a 15-year-old eyewitness at the time) claims that his father did make a call to the police station after the first attack (Hoffman, 2003). Similar claims have been made on behalf of other residents. For example, a cluster of newspaper reports accompanying Moseley's unsuccessful application for a retrial in 1995 report Kew Gardens residents' claims that calls were made to the police. These reports also make the point that calls were made despite the difficulties of contacting the police at the time. There was no 911 system in place in 1964 and calls to the local police station were reportedly not always welcomed by officers who would often give callers 'the bitter edge of their tongues' (Rosenthal, 1964: 67).

THE GENOVESE MYTH AS AN ENDURING PARABLE FOR THE DANGER OF GROUPS

Reflecting on these inconsistencies between the facts of the Genovese case and those reported in the press, Manning and colleagues (2007) observe that there have been several attempts to correct the record over the years. However, the myth of the 38 witnesses still persists. In particular, it appears in almost every undergraduate social psychology textbook as an introduction to the topic of bystander (non-)intervention, and it has been the inspiration for cultural products as disparate as films (*The Boondock Saints,* 1999), popular TV shows (*Girls,* 2016, Episode 49: 'Hello Kitty'), novels (Jahn, 2009), musical theatre (Simpatico and Todd, 2005/2010), and comics (Moore and Gibbons, 1986). Speculating as to why this is the case, Manning and colleagues suggest that the story is resistant to change because it functions as a kind of modern parable – exemplifying the shortcomings and dangers of the group.

As several other chapters in this volume observe, in the time leading up to Darley and Latané's research, society in general and social psychologists in particular tended to represent the presence of others as dangerous because it promotes behavioural 'excitation' and thereby clouds judgment (e.g., see Chapters 5 and 8). In this way, traditional work on collective behaviour (e.g., Le Bon, 1895; Zimbardo, 1969) suggested that the presence of others creates the conditions for an outpouring of atavistic anti-social behaviour. In particular, this is because being surrounded by others was argued to create conditions of anonymity that in turn undermine personal controls on behaviour – leading to 'mob violence' or 'mass hysteria'. At the time, then, this was the default understanding of group processes (and of their attendant dangers).

Moreover, the development of thinking about bystander non-intervention added to this picture by seeming to indicate that the presence of others can also lead to behavioural 'inhibition'. Indeed, by suggesting that the presence of others can suppress action and inhibit the impulse to help, the bystander effect completes the circle in describing the dangers that groups bring to social situations. For groups could now be accused of producing the perfect storm of negative consequences – in simultaneously both unleashing anti-social behaviour and suppressing pro-social behaviour.

Manning and colleagues argue that this negative image of the group continues to populate the imaginations both of researchers and of students to the present day. Thus, when people reflect on the problem of bystander behaviour, they tend automatically to think that the problem is one of how to overcome the shortcomings of the group. It is this idea, the researchers suggest, that lies at the heart of the failure for bystander research to prove practically useful.

BEYOND THE BYSTANDER EFFECT

It is important to be clear at this point that the debunking of the Genovese myth in no way invalidates the canon of bystander research. The argument advanced here is not that the hundreds of studies that find evidence for the effect of the presence of others on helping are somehow mistaken just because the newspaper story that launched the research was inaccurate. Instead, the claim is that, as we have come to understand it, the bystander effect provides a partial rather than a complete story. Thus, when we come to think about behaviour in emergencies, the story of the 38 witnesses populates the psychological imagination to such an extent that we fail to conceive of other ways of thinking about the impact of the group. More specifically, researchers have assumed that the influence of groups is likely to be negative and that the aim of any remedial action should be to mitigate this impact. And as a consequence, there is very little research that attempts to explore the potential for the group to have a positive impact by promoting bystander intervention.

SHARED SOCIAL IDENTITY AS A BASIS FOR HELPING

Nevertheless, in the last ten years, new ways of thinking about groups and group processes have begun to work their way into bystander research. In particular, this has involved researchers drawing on insights from _social identity theory_ (Tajfel, 1978; Tajfel and Turner, 1979) and _self-categorization theory_ (Turner et al., 1987) – theories that together can be referred to as constituting the social identity approach (e.g., Haslam, 2004). This approach rejects the idea that groups have a negative impact on psychological functioning. Instead it argues that just as an individual's personal identity can help to shape their behaviour, so too can their membership of social groups (or social identity). Moreover, the approach also rejects the idea that the presence of others creates the conditions for undermining controls on an individual's behaviour. Instead it argues that when people define themselves as a member of a particular social group (as will often happen when they are in the presence of others), then the norms and the values that are associated with that social identity determine how the individual will behave.

Research in this tradition has shown that the presence of others is not something that leads automatically to anti-social behaviour. Instead, behaviour in collective settings can be pro-social or anti-social depending on what kind of identity is salient, and what the content of that identity actually is (Postmes and Spears, 1998). To know how individuals will behave in the presence of others, one therefore needs to know (a) whether a personal or a social identity is salient; (b) the extent to which the salient identity is shared by those who are present; and (c) the norms and values associated with the salient identity.

An interesting example of how the way in which shared social identity can increase the likelihood of bystander intervention in emergencies is provided by the work of Levine and colleagues (2005). These researchers conducted experiments that used identities associated with support for football clubs to show how the salience of social identities shapes helping behaviour. One such study recruited supporters of Manchester United football club as participants and then exposed them to an emergency situation. The participants came to the psychology department to take part in a study of football fans and were shown to a small cubicle where they wrote an essay and answered some questions that served to remind them of how much they loved Manchester United. Having had the salience of this Manchester United social identity thoroughly primed, they were then asked to walk (on their own) to another building to watch a video. While they were walking, an accident was staged in front of them. A male confederate came running across their path, tripped and fell, and cried out in pain while holding on to his ankle. Sometimes the confederate was wearing a Manchester United football shirt, sometimes he was wearing a Liverpool football shirt (Liverpool being the arch rivals of Manchester United), and sometimes he was wearing an ordinary, unbranded sports shirt.

What the study revealed was that participants almost always helped the stranger when he was wearing the Manchester United shirt (92% did so in this condition) but that they were much less likely to help when he wore the Liverpool or plain shirt (in these conditions, only 30% and 33% of participants offered help, respectively). This seems to provide a clear demonstration of a preference for helping strangers when we can see some signs of shared group membership. However, Levine and colleagues then conducted a second study. Once again the Manchester United fans came to the psychology department – but this time they answered questions and wrote an essay about how much they loved being a football fan. In other words, although they supported Manchester United, they were primed to think about themselves as part of a broader and more inclusive social identity – that of a football fan. They were then exposed to exactly the same accident as the first study. Now, however, the study's results indicated that they were equally likely to help the stranger when he wore the Liverpool shirt and the Manchester United shirt (70% and 80% of participants offered help in these conditions, respectively), but they were far less likely to offer help when he wore the plain shirt (only 22% did so here).

Thus, by changing the nature of the social identity that was made salient – and including more people within the boundaries of this shared identity – it became possible to increase the extent of helping behaviour. When Manchester United fans shifted from thinking about themselves in terms of an exclusive team identity, to embrace a more inclusive football fan identity, they become more willing to help strangers who might otherwise be seen as outsiders or enemies. Of course, this strategy of re-categorization doesn't mean that everybody will be helped. When the victim wore a shirt that gave no indication of an interest in football, helping rates remained stubbornly low.

SHARED SOCIAL IDENTITY AS A BASIS FOR
BYSTANDER INTERVENTION

While the research discussed in the previous section reveals the potential for a sense of shared social identity to promote helping in emergencies, it is not yet a demonstration of the utility of the social identity approach as a basis for rethinking the bystander effect itself. In light of the original Kitty Genovese case, the key test for the approach would involve exploring the role played by social identities in emergencies that involve both gender and violence (see Cherry, 1995).

To investigate this issue, Mark Levine and Simon Crowther (2008) conducted two interrelated experiments that manipulated both the salience of social identities and the number of bystanders who witnessed an attack by a man on a woman. Male and female participants were recruited to take part in a study about gender and violence. When they arrived at the psychology department they were directed down a corridor and past an office in which a female confederate was seen to be working. They then entered the room next door where they met a male experimenter. He directed participants to sit in front of a television screen and informed them that, as this was a study about gender and violence, they would be watching a clip taken by a closed-circuit television (CCTV) camera of a violent incident in which a man attacks a woman on a city street. The experimenter then asked them to watch the clip – which lasted approximately two minutes and involved escalating aggression by the male protagonist.

In what followed, the CCTV clip then stopped on the brink of what looked like a sustained physical attack by the man on the woman. Participants were then asked to fill in a questionnaire asking about their willingness to intervene in this incident. Importantly, participants watch the CCTV clip on their own or in groups of three. And in the group condition, participants sit either in male-only groups, in female-only groups, in groups with a majority of males, or in groups with a majority of females.

Contrary to the traditional bystander effect whereby the presence of others should inhibit intervention, questionnaire responses indicated that women were more likely to say they would intervene when they sat in a group of three women than when they sat on their own. However, women indicated that they would be much less likely to intervene when they were in the presence of two men. This is consistent with the traditional bystander effect, as the presence of others seems to inhibit helping. Yet what is clear from these findings is that the presence of others has a differential effect depending on the salience of particular social identities for participants and their relationship to other bystanders. Specifically, women feel more able to intervene when they have other women around them, but are less inclined to do so when the other bystanders are men.

The data for male participants was equally interesting. Men are most likely to say they will intervene when they are the minority in a group – that is, when they are in the presence of two women. When men are in a group with other men they are not inhibited from intervening, but when they are surrounded by women the likelihood of intervention seems to be enhanced. The results of this study thus suggest that the relationship between group size and identity is a nuanced one. Sometimes the presence of others can lead to inhibition of helping, sometimes it has no effect on helping, and sometimes it enhances willingness to help.

However, it is important to acknowledge that participants in this study are only expressing a willingness to intervene. They are not engaging in actual helping behaviour and – as the research reviewed in Chapter 2 suggests – there may be a significant gap between word and deed. With that in mind, Levine and Crowther (2008) incorporated a second part to this study. As the CCTV experiment came to a close, the female confederate that participants had seen on their arrival enters the room and asks if anybody would be prepared to help her with her experiment. At this point the male experimenter is rude and verbally aggressive towards her – accusing her of interrupting his experiment – and she withdraws quickly, looking upset. Participants are then thanked and paid for their participation. But as they go back up the corridor to leave the building, they pass the office to which the female confederate has returned. She is stood in such a way that they can see her shoulder in the doorway, but not her face.

As one might imagine, the variable that the researchers were interested in measuring was whether participants stopped to offer the woman help. What they found was that results on this behavioural measure mirrored those of the CCTV study. When female participants sat in groups of three women, the first woman to leave the room offered to help 75% of the time. When they were on their own, they offered to help 38% of the time. When they were in a minority with two men, they helped only 27% of the time. For the men, sitting on their own or with other men produced low levels of helping (only 33% and 17% offering help respectively), but when they were a minority with two women 77% now offered help. Once again, then, there was a clear interaction between group size and identity – such that the presence of more bystanders inhibited helping under some conditions, but facilitated it in others.

CONCLUSION

Latané and Darley's bystander effect appears to be one of the most robust and reliable findings in social psychology. And yet for all its robustness, it has seemed to lack any practical utility – appearing simply to point to the inevitably negative impact that groups have on individual behaviour. Indeed, in line with this perspective, Zimbardo (2004) could find no place for the bystander effect in his catalogue of positive contributions that psychology has made to improving social life.

This chapter has argued that this failure can be traced, in part, to the way in which the original research questions were framed. The focus on group size (following the misleading report about the inaction of 38 witnesses to the Kitty Genovese murder) meant that researchers tended to focus on the group as the source of the problem of bystander non-intervention. As a consequence, until very recently, researchers have failed to explore the conditions under which the group can promote bystander intervention – and therefore be part of the solution. We therefore know much about the inhibiting effect of group size, but know much less about when the presence of others promotes helping.

However, over the last decade, new ways of thinking about the influence of the group on the individual have begun to appear in bystander research. Drawing on insights from the social identity approach, evidence has emerged which reveals a much more subtle relationship between social identity, group size and bystander behaviour. When bystanders fail to share a psychological relationship – that is, when they encounter each other as strangers – then the bystander effect seems robust. However, when bystanders share a salient social identity, then their behaviour is structured by the norms and the values of that social identity. Sometimes this can inhibit helping, but sometimes it can facilitate bystander intervention. Going forward, we thus need to know more about how to ensure that pro-social social identities can be made salient, and how to draw on the strength of group processes to promote bystander intervention. Moreover, in so far as it allows us to understand and to unlock the power of the group to promote pro-social behaviour, it appears that such research will, for the first time, prove to have very positive practical consequences.

FURTHER READING

Latané, B. and Darley, J.M. (1970) *The Unresponsive Bystander: Why Doesn't He Help?* New York: Meredith Corporation.

Latané and Darley's book describes early work that developed the 'bystander effect' paradigm, and provides a clear statement of the five-step cognitive decision-making model of bystander behaviour.

Latané, B. and Nida, S. (1981) 'Ten years of research on group size and helping', *Psychological Bulletin*, 89: 308–24.

Latané and Nida's meta-analysis is a good place to find a robust statement of the classic bystander effect – supported by ten years' worth of studies examining the relationship between group size and helping.

Cherry, F. (1995) *The 'Stubborn Particulars' of Social Psychology*. London: Routledge.

Frances Cherry's chapter on Kitty Genovese and culturally embedded theorizing in this excellent book opens up alternative ways of thinking about the Kitty Genovese case. Cherry makes an impassioned plea for exploring the historical, political and social meanings of intervention and of the failure to intervene.

Manning, R., Levine, M. and Collins, A. (2007) 'The Kitty Genovese murder and the social psychology of helping: The parable of the 38 witnesses', *American Psychologist*, 62: 555–62.

This article revisits the evidence surrounding the Kitty Genovese case and shows how the story we think we know is not supported by the evidence. The authors argue that the myth of the 38 witnesses populates the psychological imagination in such a way that we have neglected to look for ways in which the group can promote bystander intervention.

Levine, M. and Crowther, S. (2008) 'The responsive bystander: How social group membership and group size can encourage as well as inhibit bystander intervention', *Journal of Personality and Social Psychology*, 95: 1429–39.

Finally, Levine and Crowther conduct social identity and bystander intervention experiments in the spirit of the original bystander research. Using CCTV images of violence, and behavioural measures of responses to aggression, they show how gender identities and group size can interact to promote (as well as inhibit) intervention in violent events where a man attacks a woman.

REFERENCES

The Boondock Saints (1999) [Film] Written and directed by T. Duffy. Canada/United States: Cinema Club.

Borofsky, G.L., Stollak, G.E. and Messe, L.A. (1971) 'Sex differences in bystander reactions to physical assault', *Journal of Experimental Social Psychology*, 7: 313–18.

Cherry, F. (1995) *The 'Stubborn Particulars' of Social Psychology*. London: Routledge.

Darley, J. and Latané, B. (1968) 'Group inhibition of bystander intervention in emergencies', *Journal of Personality and Social Psychology*, 10: 215–21.

Evans, R.I. (1980) *The Making of Social Psychology*. New York: Gardner Press.

Fischer, P., Greitemeyer, T., Pollozek, F. and Frey, D. (2006) 'The unresponsive bystander: Are bystanders more responsive in dangerous emergencies?', *European Journal of Social Psychology*, 36: 267–78.

Gansberg, M. (1964) '37 who saw murder didn't call the police', *New York Times*, 27 March: 1.

Girls: Hello Kitty (2016) [TV Show] Written by S. Heyward and directed by R. Shephard. HBO.

Haslam, S.A. (2004) *Psychology in Organizations: The Social Identity Approach*, 2nd edn. Thousand Oaks, CA: Sage Publications.

Hoffman, M. (2003) Affidavit. State of Florida.

Jahn, R.D. (2009) *Acts of Violence*. Macmillan.

Latané, B. and Darley, J.M. (1970) *The Unresponsive Bystander: Why Doesn't He Help?* New York: Meredith Corporation.

Latané, B. and Nida, S. (1981) 'Ten years of research on group size and helping', *Psychological Bulletin*, 89: 308–24.

Le Bon, G. (1895, translated 1947) *The Crowd: A Study of the Popular Mind*. London: Ernest Benn.

Levine, M. and Crowther, S. (2008) 'The responsive bystander: How social group membership and group size can encourage as well as inhibit bystander intervention', *Journal of Personality and Social Psychology*, 95: 1429–39.

Levine, M., Prosser, A., Evans, D. and Reicher, S. (2005) 'Identity and emergency intervention: How social group membership and inclusiveness of group boundaries shape helping behaviour', *Personality and Social Psychology Bulletin*, 31: 443–53.

Manning, R., Levine, M. and Collins, A. (2007) 'The Kitty Genovese murder and the social psychology of helping: The parable of the 38 witnesses', *American Psychologist*, 62: 555–62.

Moore, A. and Gibbons, D. (1986) *Watchmen*. New York: DC Comics.

Postmes, T. and Spears, R. (1998) 'Deindividuation and anti-normative behaviour: A meta-analysis', *Psychological Bulletin*, 123: 238–59.

Rasenberger, J. (2004) 'Kitty, 40 years later', *New York Times*, 8 February: 14.

Rosenthal, A.M. (1964/1999) *Thirty-Eight Witnesses*. Berkeley, CA: University of California Press.

Shotland, R.L. and Straw, M.G. (1976) 'Bystander response to an assault: When a man attacks a woman', *Journal of Applied Social Psychology*, 101: 510–27.

Simpatico, D. and Todd, W. (2005/2010) *The Screams of Kitty Genovese*. Public Theatre, New York; The Merchants' Hall, Edinburgh.

Tajfel, H. (ed.) (1978) *Differentiation Between Social Groups: Studies in the Social Psychology of Intergroup Relations*. London: Academic Press.

Tajfel, H. and Turner, J.C. (1979) 'An integrative theory of intergroup conflict', in W.G. Austin and S. Worchel (eds), *The Social Psychology of Intergroup Relations*. Monterey, CA: Brooks/Cole. pp. 33–48.

Takooshian, H., Bedrosian, D., Cecero, J., Chancer, L., Karmen, A., Rasenberger, J. et al. (2005) 'Remembering Catherine "Kitty" Genovese: A public forum', *Journal of Social Distress and the Homeless*, 14: 63–77.

Turner, J.C., Hogg, M.A., Oakes, P.J., Reicher, S.D. and Wetherell, M.C. (1987) *Rediscovering the Social Group: A Self-Categorization Theory*. New York: Blackwell.

Zimbardo, P.G. (1969) 'The human choice: Individuation, reason, and order versus deindividuation, impulse, and chaos', *Nebraska Symposium on Motivation*, 17: 237–307.

Zimbardo, P.G. (2004) 'Does psychology make a significant difference in our lives?', *American Psychologist*, 59: 339–51.

13

Promoting Positive Intergroup Relations

Revisiting Aronson et al.'s jigsaw classroom

John F. Dovidio

BACKGROUND

S tudies can achieve the status of 'classic' for many reasons. Some can be theoretically groundbreaking, such as Leon Festinger's foundational work on cognitive dissonance theory (see Chapter 3) or the seminal studies by Henri Tajfel leading to social identity theory (see Chapter 10). Others achieve this recognition through counterintuitive empirical results, such as Solomon Asch's conformity studies (see Chapter 5) or Stanley Milgram's findings on obedience (see Chapter 7). The work on the jigsaw classroom, which was an intervention designed by Elliot Aronson and his colleagues (1978) to increase educational attainment and improve intergroup relations, is recognized as classic research for a different reason – because it so successfully addressed pressing practical issues in the field and in society. It was an innovation born of necessity.

CRISES IN THE FIELD AND IN SOCIETY

In the 1970s, the field of social psychology, many argued, was in a state of crisis. Many critics questioned the generalizability of social psychological findings and, ultimately, the practical relevance not only of its findings but also of the field itself. Leonard Berkowitz observed that 'social psychology is now in a "crisis stage".... We seem to be somewhat at a loss for important problems to investigate' (as quoted by Smith, 1972: 86). Muzafer Sherif further noted 'the skyrocketing volume of research which yields but little of substance' (1977: 368).

America was also in crisis. In 1954, the landmark Brown v. Board of Education US Supreme Court case no longer allowed 'separate but equal' racial segregation in the schools. In the mid-1960s, the United States adopted sweeping civil rights legislation. In the aftermath, the decade of the 1970s was a period of experimentation with concrete policies to implement these principles. School busing, in which African American and White students were transported to predominantly White or African American schools respectively, was one way that public (state) schools

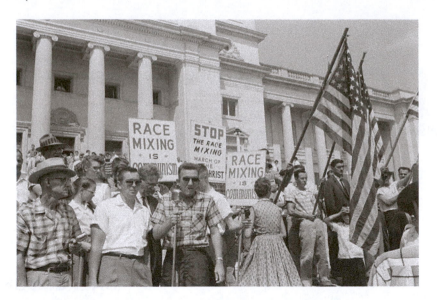

Figure 13.1   Opposition to busing in Little Rock, Arkansas, in 1959

Source: US Library of Congress

were racially desegregated. Busing to achieve desegregation, though, was highly contested politically and often opposed by communities (see Figure 13.1). Moreover, these efforts were challenged in terms both of the seemingly more limited academic achievement of African American and White students in newly desegregated schools and the social friction that busing caused in these schools. It was in the context of this national controversy and unrest that Elliot Aronson and his students initiated their work on the jigsaw classroom.

The jigsaw classroom research achieved its classic status because of the way it addressed academic and social crises. This research reoriented the field of social psychology toward issues of immediate relevance, and it provided an effective remedy to the social tensions fomenting in public schools. The jigsaw classroom research demonstrated, both inside the field of social psychology and to the general public and policy-makers, the unique practical value of social psychological insight. Aronson (Jigsaw Classroom, www.jigsaw.org) recounts:

> The jigsaw classroom was first used in Austin, Texas. My graduate student and I had invented the strategy that year, as a matter of absolute necessity to help defuse an explosive situation. The city's schools had recently been desegregated, and because Austin had always been racially segregated, White youngsters, African American youngsters, and Hispanic youngsters found themselves in the same classrooms for the first time. Within a few weeks, long-standing suspicion, fear, and distrust between groups produced an atmosphere of turmoil and hostility. Fist-fights erupted in corridors and schoolyards across the city. The school superintendent called me in to see if we could do anything to help students get along with one another ... We realized that we needed to shift the emphasis from a relentlessly competitive atmosphere to a more cooperative one.

The jigsaw classroom was not an abstract social psychological framework developed to explain intergroup relations but rather a strategy developed in response to an immediate need for social intervention.

JIGSAW GROUPS AND THE DESEGREGATED CLASSROOM

The research on jigsaw groups, summarized by Aronson et al. (1978), reflected the convergence of many streams of work in social psychology at the time. One line that it built on was the already convincing body of evidence concerning intergroup contact. The contact hypothesis identified how intergroup interaction can reduce prejudice and improve intergroup relations (Allport, 1954; Pettigrew and Tropp, 2011). But, critically, Gordon Allport specified four conditions that needed to be met for successful contact: equal status between the groups within the contact situation, intergroup cooperation, common goals, and the support of authorities, law, or custom. However, these conditions were not met in the desegregated Austin schools, because: (a) African American and Hispanic/Latino students in the Austin school district often came from economically or educationally disadvantaged backgrounds, they were lower in status than the White students in the school; (b) relations among students from different racial and ethnic groups were primarily competitive in the classroom, rather than cooperative; (c) the education system promoted the achievement of individual goals (i.e., individual academic success), rather than common goals; and (d) public controversy about busing to achieve desegregation created an uncertain atmosphere of support from authorities. Thus, the mix of conditions in desegregated schools was unlikely to produce the positive outcomes desired.

A second line of scholarly work that was critical in the development of Aronson et al.'s (1978) studies of jigsaw groups in the classroom was the Boys' Camp studies by Muzafer Sherif and colleagues (1961), particularly the Robbers Cave research (see Chapter 9). Sherif and his colleagues had conducted a field study on intergroup conflict in which 12-year-old boys attending summer camp were randomly assigned to two groups (who subsequently named themselves Eagles and Rattlers). When the groups engaged in a series of competitive activities (tug-of-war, baseball and touch (American) football games), intergroup bias and conflict quickly developed. Group members regularly exchanged verbal insults (e.g., 'sissies,' 'stinkers', 'pigs', 'bums' and 'cheaters'), and each group conducted raids on the other's cabins that resulted in the destruction and theft of property. Later, Sherif and his colleagues arranged intergroup contact under neutral, noncompetitive conditions. However, mere intergroup contact was not sufficient to change the nature of the relations between the groups. In fact, the boys took advantage of this contact to escalate hostilities (e.g., communal meals promptly descended into food fights; see Chapter 9).

It was only after the investigators altered the functional relations between the groups by introducing a series of superordinate goals – goals that could not be achieved without the full cooperation of both groups and which were successfully achieved – that the relations between the two groups became more harmonious, and intergroup bias was greatly reduced. Although the boys continued to acknowledge their separate group identities (Rattlers and Eagles), they regularly referred to members of both groups as 'we' after achieving these superordinate goals. For instance, Sherif and colleagues reported that after cooperatively pulling a stalled truck back toward camp, the boys celebrated: 'Allen [a Rattler] shouted: "We won the tug-of-war against the truck!" Bryan [an Eagle] repeated, "Yeah! We won the tug-of-war against the truck." This cry was echoed with satisfaction by others from both groups' (1961: 171).

A third line of research that formed the conceptual basis for the jigsaw classroom was one for which Aronson was already widely recognized[1] – cognitive dissonance. Cognitive dissonance theory posits that individuals strive to be consistent in their attitudes, beliefs, and behaviours (see Chapter 3). Perceived inconsistency among these elements is thought to elicit an unpleasant emotional state, cognitive dissonance, which motivates individuals to change one or more of the elements to re-achieve consistency. A major finding from research on cognitive dissonance theory, including Aronson's own research in areas of attitudes outside of intergroup relations, was that changing the ways that people behaved could change their attitudes. Because behaviour is public and thus difficult to deny, attitudes, which are often privately held and not always salient, would be more susceptible to change to achieve consistency in orientations. In the case of the desegregated classroom, the relevant implication was that changing the atmosphere from competitive (a negative orientation) to cooperative (a positive orientation) would improve the intergroup climate and, eventually, increase academic performance and esteem. The practical challenge was how to create this cooperative classroom atmosphere in an ecologically valid way. This is what the jigsaw classroom studies set out to do.

THE JIGSAW CLASSROOM STUDIES

In the jigsaw classroom (see www.jigsaw.org), as in a jigsaw puzzle, the information that each student uniquely possesses is essential for completing an academic task and achieving a full understanding of the final product. Students are first divided into small (five- or six-student) groups that are diverse in terms of gender, ethnicity, race, and academic achievement. One student is selected as leader. The day's lesson is then divided into five or six discrete segments (e.g., in learning about a famous person; segmenting the person's life into early years, education, professional life). Each student is assigned a segment to learn and is given the opportunity to become knowledgeable about the segment by working with students from other groups assigned the same segment of

---

[1]Interestingly, Eliot Aronson is the only psychologist to have won the highest award of the American Psychological Association in all three major academic categories: Distinguished Writing (1973), Distinguished Teaching (1980), and Distinguished Research (1999). In 2002, he was named one of the 100 most eminent psychologists of the 20th century.

the lesson. Students then return to their own jigsaw group and present the segment to the others. At the end of the session, they are quizzed to ensure they have mastery of the material.

According to Aronson and Bridgeman in this jigsaw technique:

> Children gradually learn that the old competitive behavior is no longer appropriate. Rather, in order to learn all of the material (and thus perform well on the quiz), each child must begin to listen to others, ask appropriate questions, and in other ways contribute to the group. The process makes it possible for children to pay attention to one another and begin to appreciate each other as potentially valuable resources. It is important to emphasize that the motivation of students is not necessarily altruistic; rather, it is primarily self-interest, which, in this case, happens also to produce outcomes that are beneficial to others. (2004: 427)

The first experiment to investigate the effects of the jigsaw classroom was conducted by Nancy Blaney and colleagues (1977) in elementary school classrooms in Austin. White, African American, and Hispanic/Latino students participated in jigsaw groups for 45 minutes per day, three days a week for six weeks. Importantly, at the end of this time, they showed an increase in liking for the members of their group, both within and across racial and ethnic group lines, and they exhibited greater increases in self-esteem than students in a control condition who received 'education as usual' that involved traditional, competitive teaching methods. In addition, children in the experimental group perceived the classroom environment as less competitive and were more likely to rate their peers as a positive learning source than children in the control group.

Additional research within the Austin elementary schools (Lucker et al., 1977) demonstrated changes in academic achievement in a unit on American history. Moreover, compared with students in traditional control classrooms, African American and Hispanic/Latino students in the jigsaw classroom performed significantly better on a standardized test, whereas White students performed

Table 13.1 Changes in classroom-related outcomes for experimental and control group students in a jigsaw classroom (adapted from Blaney et al., 1977)

	Experimental Group		Control Group	
	Pre-test	Post-test	Pre-test	Post-test
Liking for group-mates	4.04	4.26		
Liking for other classmates	4.16	4.22		
Self-esteem	5.16	5.50	5.47	5.37
Competitiveness	3.30	3.12	2.88	3.48
Perception of peers as learning source	4.68	5.14	4.73	4.32
Perception of being liked by others	4.57	4.74	4.56	5.31

Note: Liking scores only collected for the experimental group.

equivalently well. Indeed, the jigsaw classroom closed the achievement gap between the White and the racial/ethnic minority by almost half – to 10 percentage points from the 17 percentage points in the traditional classrooms.

IMPACT OF THE JIGSAW CLASSROOM STUDIES

Over the past four decades, research on the jigsaw classroom has continued to yield positive results in terms of enhanced academic performance and esteem, particularly among students from economically or educationally disadvantaged backgrounds, as well as improved intergroup relations within the classroom and the school (Johnson et al., 2000; Tomcho and Foels, 2012). It has been applied successfully to diverse topical areas such as English as a second language (ESL; Ghaith and El-Malak, 2004) and physics classes (Hänze and Berger, 2007), and positive results have been replicated internationally (Walker and Crogan, 1998).

In summary, within a short but critical period, work on the jigsaw classroom had significant academic and social impact. It demonstrated the applicability of social psychological principles to an immediate problem of public concern. The research on jigsaw groups in desegregated classrooms vividly illustrated the practical relevance of social psychological theory outside of the field and helped to ameliorate the 'relevance crisis' in social psychology among critics within the field. This research further showed how scholars who built their reputation on laboratory-based research can pivot, when needed, to test extensions of their academic work to field settings. Indeed, stimulated in part by the attention that the jigsaw classroom attracted, there was a new wave of field research in social psychology in the 1970s and the early 1980s that helped demonstrate the generalizability and practical value of social psychological research, while expanding the scope of social psychology theoretically. For instance, beyond the topic of intergroup relations, work on attitudes and persuasion bridged theory and application in innovative and impactful ways. During this period Robert Cialdini initiated an influential set of studies on social influence that drew on observations of strategies used by individuals, such as salespeople, in applied settings, identified underlying psychological principles, and tested these ideas in field settings (Cialdini, 2009). Also, basic research on attitudes and behaviour, such as the work of Ajzen and Fishbein's (1980) theory of reasoned action (see Chapter 2), significantly guided the development of effective interventions to change sexual practices and promote medical adherence to help curb the emerging international AIDS epidemic (Albarracin et al., 2001).

The jigsaw classroom research also expanded perspectives on intergroup relations research. Whereas the considerable attention devoted to intergroup contact theory focused primarily on improving intergroup attitudes, with cooperative learning – as captured by the jigsaw classroom – one of the few prejudice reduction techniques to have evidence for its efficacy in the laboratory and the field

(Paluck and Green, 2009), work on the jigsaw classroom demonstrated the capacity for impact on a broader array of outcomes. In particular, the jigsaw classroom intervention enhanced classroom achievement and increased the esteem of minority-group students in desegregated classrooms, as well as improving social relations between members of different racial and ethnic groups during a period of racial tension locally and nationally. Indeed, the earliest publications on the jigsaw classroom – also known as cooperative learning – were published in education journals rather than social psychological journals.

BEYOND THE JIGSAW CLASSROOM

One of the main strengths of research on the jigsaw classroom – its immediate and effective application in the context of desegregated schools – may have also limited its long-term, direct influence. Empirically, within the field of education, it spawned a new generation of cooperative learning interventions that were constructed to be effective in a wider range of classroom situations, not just under the specific circumstances associated with recently desegregated schools. Thus, these newer cooperation-based interventions, some directly inspired by the work of Aronson and colleagues (1978), were more generally effective educationally. So it was that when David Johnson and colleagues (2000) ranked eight commonly used cooperation-based teaching methods in terms of their effectiveness the jigsaw classroom was only ranked sixth in terms of impact on educational achievement. Nevertheless, the fact that, by the early 1990s, 79% of US elementary schools used cooperative learning methods (Puma et al., 1993) attests to the influence of the jigsaw classroom on policy implementation.

Within social psychology, the theoretical contribution of the jigsaw strategy was limited because of difficulty in clarifying the underlying mechanisms that accounted for the effects obtained. In this regard, Aronson and colleagues (1978) had certainly speculated about a variety of mechanisms. They suggested, for example, that reduced intergroup anxiety likely facilitates greater active participation in learning activities, which in turn promotes learning. However, the research that followed from the classic jigsaw classroom studies focused more on evaluating the breadth of its effectiveness in improving education-related outcomes than in delineating precisely what the underlying psychological processes were. Indeed, moving into the contemporary era, this focus on outcomes rather than process limited the kind of theory development that was becoming critically important for publication within social psychology. Indeed, it is salutary to note that the phrase 'jigsaw classroom' has not appeared in the title of an article published in a leading social psychology journal, such as the *Journal of Personality and Social Psychology*, *Personality and Social Psychology Bulletin*, the *Journal of Experimental Social Psychology*, and the *European Journal of Social Psychology*, since 1980.

This is not to say that the research on the jigsaw classroom has been ignored within psychology. On the contrary, it has been very influential. According to

Google Scholar, the Aronson et al. (1978) book presenting the early studies has been cited over three thousand times and the jigsaw strategy, generally, has been referred to in many thousands more articles. However, the influence of the studies on the field has been more indirect than direct. Beginning with research in the 1930s but catalysed by Allport's (1954) classic book *The Nature of Prejudice*, the contact hypothesis had represented the state-of-the art intervention for improving intergroup relations (see Dovidio et al., 2003). Aronson et al.'s research on jigsaw groups highlighted the particular importance of the element of cooperative inter-dependence, just one of the various conditions specified in the contact hypothesis, for improving intergroup attitudes *and* functioning under conditions of intergroup tension and conflict. The attention drawn to the Aronson et al. (1978) report of the success of the jigsaw classroom, which drew heavily on Sherif et al.'s (1961) con-cept of superordinate goals in the Robbers Cave study, helped to revitalize interest in the *way* intergroup contact can improve intergroup relations. And although it may seem that the jigsaw classroom was somewhat neglected by social psycholo-gists, this is certainly not the case today. In a recent review of the effectiveness of prejudice reduction strategies, Betsy Paluck and Donald Green noted that 'coopera-tive learning is the most outstanding example of theoretically driven programmatic laboratory and field research' (2009: 358). This impact, however, is due in no small part to the incorporation of theoretical insights from other research to understand *why* the jigsaw classroom produces such positive results.

UNDERSTANDING WHY THE JIGSAW CLASSROOM WORKS

CATEGORIZATION AND IDENTITY

It was the development of two other contemporaneous frameworks – social cog-nition and social identity – that ultimately provided the essential insights into the underlying processes (e.g., after Fiske and Taylor, 1984; Tajfel and Turner, 1979). From the perspective of social cognition, intergroup biases are conceptualized as outcomes of normal cognitive processes associated with simplifying and storing the overwhelming quantity and complexity of information that people encounter daily. One fundamental aspect of this process is the tendency to categorize indi-viduals as members of social groups based on distinguishing characteristics, often socially constructed as essential qualities.

Social categorization has important psychological and social consequences (see Chapter 10). When people are categorized, into groups, differences among mem-bers within a group tend to be minimized, and distinctions between members of different categories tend to be exaggerated. Moreover, because of the evolutionary significance of group life, people automatically distinguish between others who are members of one's own group, the ingroup, and others who are members of another group, an outgroup (but see Chapter 10 for an alternative interpretation of categorization effects).

This distinction has profound effects, resulting in a number of ingroup/out-group biases (see Dovidio and Gaertner, 2010; see also Chapter 10). Among other things, people (a) process information more deeply for ingroup than outgroup members, (b) favour ingroup over outgroup members in evaluations, (c) are more generous and forgiving in their behavioural attributions of ingroup versus outgroup members, (d) exhibit a physical readiness to approach ingroup members and avoid outgroup members, (e) are more helpful toward ingroup versus outgroup members, (f) are more cooperative toward and trustful of ingroup than outgroup members, and (g) exercise more personal restraint when using endangered resources with ingroup versus outgroup members. All of these elements could contribute to the success of jigsaw classroom interventions.

According to *social identity theory* (Tajfel and Turner, 1979; see also Abrams and Hogg, 2010), the other important development around the time of Aronson and colleagues' (1978) original work on the jigsaw strategy, a person's experience of identity varies along a continuum that ranges at one extreme from the self as a separate individual with personal motives, goals, and achievements, to another extreme in which the self is the embodiment of a social collective or group. At the individual level, one's personal welfare and goals are most salient and important. At the group level, the goals and achievements of the group are merged with one's own, and the group's welfare is paramount. As shown in the work of both Sherif and Tajfel (see Chapters 9 and 10), intergroup relations begin when people think about themselves as group members rather than solely as distinct individuals.

In social identity theory, Tajfel and Turner (1979) further proposed that a person's need for positive identity may be satisfied by membership in prestigious social groups. The basic human drive here is for self-esteem – the desire to feel good about ourselves. One way to achieve this end is to join social groups that are socially valued; another is to increase the perceived worth of the social groups to which one already belongs. To the extent that people are motivated to regard themselves positively, they will also be motivated to differentiate themselves from outsiders by perceiving as much difference as possible between their ingroup and those groups to which they do not belong (Tajfel and Turner, 1979). This need for positive distinctiveness also motivates social comparisons that favourably differentiate ingroup from outgroup members, particularly when self-esteem has been challenged. In these terms, successful intergroup bias is thus presumed to restore, enhance, or elevate one's self-esteem.

A key premise of social identity theory, which is particularly relevant to Aronson and colleagues' (1978) classic jigsaw classroom research, is that social identities are malleable. People tend to activate social identities that are most important in a given context. Thus, whereas racial and ethnic identities may be generally important socially, within the classroom, students' identities as members of a specific jigsaw group is of immediate significance. By shifting the relevant social identity from one based on race and ethnicity to one tied to learning in the classroom, Aronson and colleagues' intervention reduced racial and ethnic tension that interfered with students' opportunities to learn, and created a sense of social belonging within the classroom that is particularly critical to the educational achievement of members of traditionally marginalized groups, such as racial and ethnic minorities (Walton and Cohen, 2011).

BUILDING A COMMON INGROUP IDENTITY

Importantly, though, as Sherif's Boys' Camp studies showed, understanding the processes that promote intergroup competition and conflict can also provide insight into ways to facilitate cooperation, improve intergroup relations, and promote motivations to work effectively with others for the common welfare. These are key elements in the successful impact of Aronson et al.'s jigsaw strategy in desegregated classrooms. They are also aspects of primary interest in the *common ingroup identity model* (Gaertner and Dovidio, 2000; Gaertner et al., 2016), a framework that can help illuminate the psychological processes activated by the jigsaw intervention.

Building on social categorization and social identity principles, the key idea of the common ingroup identity model is that factors that induce members of different groups to recategorize themselves as members of the same, more inclusive group can reduce intergroup bias and promote cooperation through cognitive and motivational processes involving ingroup favouritism. Thus, the more positive beliefs, feelings, and behaviours usually reserved for ingroup members are extended or redirected to former outgroup members because of their recategorized ingroup status. Consequently, recategorization dynamically changes the conceptual representations of the different groups from an 'us' versus 'them' orientation to a more inclusive, superordinate connection: 'we' (Turner, Hogg, Oakes, Reicher and Wetherell, 1987).

A sense of common identity between members of different groups can be created by either emphasizing existing identities, such as shared national identity between White Americans and African Americans, or by creating a new superordinate identity more locally through cooperative interdependence and interaction. Once common identity is salient, the ways members of different racial- and ethnic-group members sharing that identity are perceived and responded to are transformed (see Gaertner et al., 2016). Common identity reduces anxiety, promotes trust and cooperation, and increases acceptance of innovations introduced by individuals formerly seen as a member of another group.

These affective and cognitive processes are also conducive to effective learning. Additionally, people are more responsive emotionally, experiencing greater empathy, when becoming aware of the needs of former outgroup members who are now perceived within a common ingroup identity across a range of situations. They are more responsive behaviourally too, acting more prosocially in everyday interactions and in emergency situations. The main objective of the jigsaw classroom was to change the climate of the classroom from one of competition – both between individuals and between racial and ethnic groups – to one of interpersonal and intergroup cooperation.

Indeed, introducing cooperative interdependence, as in jigsaw interventions, produces more favourable and mutually beneficial relations between members of different groups – including facilitating even more cooperation – largely because this interdependence creates a sense of common identity (Gaertner et al., 1990). In jigsaw classrooms, in part because they share a sense of common identity with students from other racial and ethnic backgrounds in their work group, students develop mutual respect for one another and feel responsible for the achievement of other members of their team. They thus become sensitive and responsive to the needs of other members of their jigsaw group and engage in reciprocal helping. In the process, they learn more about each other personally, which undermines negative racial and ethnic stereotypes, and they form new friendships, which can create social networks that promote more positive and more frequent intergroup contact, which in turn improves intergroup attitudes more generally. Therefore cooperative interaction, which is central to jigsaw groups and creates a new common group identity that supersedes racial and ethnic differences, has cascading positive educational, personal, and social benefits.

Addressing limits to a jigsaw approach

In addition to the advances the field has made, in terms of understanding the mechanisms by which jigsaw strategies can have beneficial effects on educational outcomes and intergroup relations, more recent research also cautions about the limitations of the impact of the intervention. That is, because the link binding members of jigsaw groups (typically of size five or six) is specific and task-oriented, the influence of these experiences may be limited educationally and socially. For instance, Hänze and Berger (2007) found that the effects of the jigsaw experience were stronger for measures directly related to the group activities than to academic performance more generally.

The longer-term effects of the jigsaw strategy on intergroup relations are also not well documented (Paluck and Green, 2009). On the one hand, such positive and successful interactions can form the foundation of more enduring intergroup friendships – as forming an intergroup friendship is certainly one of the most potent influences for improving intergroup attitudes generally and for facilitating greater intergroup contact with others in the future (Davies et al., 2011). On the other hand, though, task-oriented interaction is less effective for improving inter-group attitudes than is socially oriented interaction, in which individuals exchange personalizing information that undermines group stereotypes. In addition, to the extent that people focus only on their shared identity around a specific task in a way that reduces the acknowledgement and salience of their different racial- or ethnic-group memberships, they sever the associative links between the positive jigsaw-group contact and the racial or ethnic groups as a whole. As a consequence, their positive interactions within their group may be limited in their capacity to generalize in ways that produce more positive attitudes and orientations to other racial- or ethnic-group members (see Brown and Hewstone, 2005).

CONCLUSION

The work on the jigsaw classroom originally described by Aronson et al. (1978) was extremely important and timely. Within the field, it helped address the crisis that social psychology was experiencing as scholars and the public questioned the generalizability and relevance of the research within the discipline. Practically, the jigsaw intervention provided an immediate remedy within the context of schools that were experiencing tensions that were interfering with the education of majority- and minority-group students and escalating into conflict between students. Despite the Court's efforts to create a more equal society, left unattended, the psychological dynamics of intergroup relations were increasing the racial and ethnic divide, educationally and socially. In this regard, the jigsaw intervention developed by Elliot Aronson and his students at the request of the Superintendent of the schools in Austin, Texas, was transformative. It provided a blueprint of the way to structure instruction in desegregated schools to help realize the promise of legislation to create a more just society with greater educational opportunity for all.

Yet despite its direct success in addressing a growing problem for schools in Austin and across the United States during a period of expanding school desegregation, the longer-term impact of this specific technique has been limited. While a catalyst for cooperative learning interventions generally, other interventions eventually proved to be even more effective at promoting educational performance. Within psychology, the work on the jigsaw classroom, because it focused – understandably given the circumstances – on immediate outcome more than process, by itself had limited influence on new conceptual understandings of intergroup relations. Nevertheless, it helped galvanize interest in the importance of studying intergroup relations at a time when social cognitive and social identity frameworks were rapidly developing in theory, method, and application. It also helped reorient the field of social psychology from the laboratory to the field, and to bridge social psychology with theory and practice in education.

Warranting its 'classic' status, Aronson and colleagues' (1978) research has thus had an indelible influence on both the discipline of social psychology and society at large. Indeed, by helping to bring science and society together, its role in promoting positive change has been felt well beyond the specific contexts in which the intervention has been delivered.

FURTHER READING

Pettigrew, T.F. and Tropp, L.R. (2011) *When Groups Meet: The Dynamics of Intergroup Contact*. New York: Psychology Press.

This book reviews the history of intergroup contact theory as well as current research on factors that moderate, and mechanisms that mediate, the effects of positive intergroup contact on intergroup relations and outcomes.

Tomcho, T.J. and Foels, R. (2012) 'Meta-analysis of group learning activities: Empirically-based teaching recommendations', *Teaching of Psychology*, 39: 159–69.

This article describes, reviews, and evaluates a range of interventions to promote learning generally in racially and ethnically diverse classrooms.

www.jigsaw.org

This website is devoted to work on the jigsaw classroom. It describes the history of the intervention, presents the latest recommendations for implementing the intervention, and directs readers to relevant literature on the jigsaw classroom as well as testimony of its impact.

REFERENCES

Abrams, D. and Hogg, M.A. (2010) 'Social identity and self-categorization', in J.F. Dovidio, M. Hewstone, P. Glick, and V.M. Esses (eds), *SAGE handbook of prejudice, stereotyping, and discrimination*. London: Sage. pp. 179–94.

Ajzen, I. and Fishbein, M. (1980) *Understanding Attitudes and Predicting Social Behavior: Attitudes, Intentions, and Perceived Behavioral Control*. Englewood Cliffs, NJ: Prentice Hall.

Albarracin, D., Johnson, B.T., Fishbein, M. and Muellerleile, P.A. (2001) 'Theories of reasoned action and planned behavior as models of condom use: A meta-analysis'. *Psychological Bulletin*, 127: 142–61.

Allport, G.W. (1954) *The Nature of Prejudice*. New York: Addison-Wesley.

Aronson, E. and Bridgeman, D. (2004) 'Jigsaw groups and the desegregated classroom: In pursuit of common goals', in E. Aronson (ed.), *Readings about the Social Animal* (9th edn). New York: Worth. pp. 423–34.

Aronson, E., Stephan, C., Sikes, J., Blaney, N. and Snapp, M. (1978) *The Jigsaw Classroom*. Beverly Hills, CA: Sage.

Blaney, N.T., Stephan, C., Rosenfield, D., Aronson, E. and Sikes, J. (1977) 'Interdependence in the classroom: A field study', *Journal of Educational Psychology*, 69: 139–46.

Brown, R. and Hewstone, M. (2005) 'An integrative theory of intergroup contact', *Advances in Experimental Social Psychology*, 37: 255–343.

Cialdini, R.B. (2009) *Influence: Science and Practice* (5th edn). New York: Pearson.

Davies, K., Tropp, L.R., Aron, A., Pettigrew, T.F. and Wright, S.C. (2011) 'Cross-group friendships and intergroup attitudes: A meta-analytic review', *Personality and Social Psychology Review*, 15: 332–51.

Dovidio, J.F. and Gaertner, S.L. (2010) 'Intergroup bias', in S.T. Fiske, D. Gilbert and G. Lindzey (eds), *Handbook of Social Psychology*, Vol. 2 (5th edn). New York: Wiley. pp. 1084–121.

Dovidio, J.F., Gaertner, S.L. and Kawakami, K. (2003) 'The Contact Hypothesis: The past, present, and the future', *Group Processes and Intergroup Relations*, 6: 5–21.

Fiske, S.T. and Taylor, S.E. (1984) *Social Cognition*. Cambridge, MA: Addison-Wesley.

Gaertner, S.L. and Dovidio, J.F. (2000) *Reducing Intergroup Bias: The Common Ingroup Identity Model*. Philadelphia, PA: Psychology Press.

Gaertner, S.L., Mann, J.A., Dovidio, J.F., Murrell, A.J. and Pomare, M. (1990) 'How does cooperation reduce intergroup bias?', *Journal of Personality and Social Psychology*, 59: 692–704.

Gaertner, S.L., Dovidio, J.F., Guerra, R., Hehman, E. and Saguy, T. (2016) 'A common ingroup identity: A categorization-based approach for reducing intergroup bias', in T. Nelson (ed.), *Handbook of Prejudice, Discrimination, and Stereotyping* (2nd edn). New York: Psychology Press. pp. 433–54.

Ghaith, G. and El-Malak, M.A. (2004) 'Effect of Jigsaw II on literal and higher-order EFL reading comprehension', *Educational Research and Evaluation*, 10: 105–55.

Hänze, M. and Berger, R. (2007) 'Cooperative learning, motivational effects, and student characteristics: An experimental study comparing cooperative learning and direct instruction in 12th grade physics classes', *Learning and Instruction*, 17: 29–41.

Johnson, D., Johnson, R.T. and Stanne, M.B. (2000) 'Cooperative learning methods: A meta-analysis', retrieved from http://s3.amazonaws.com/academia.edu.documents/33787421/Cooperative_Learning_Methods_A_Meta-Analysis.pdf?AWSAccessKeyId=AKIAJ56TQJRTWSMTNPEA&Expires=1480208990&Signature=YfXQR0R7Cp%2Bk4qs6Vjf4NsZZJKM%3D&response-content-disposition=inline%3B%20filename%3DCooperative_Learning_Methods_A_Meta-Anal.pdf

Lucker, G.W., Rosenfield, D., Sikes, J. and Aronson, E. (1977) 'Performance in the interdependent classroom: A field study', *American Education Research Journal*, 13: 115–23.

Paluck, E.L. and Green, D.P. (2009), 'Prejudice reduction: What works? A review and assessment of research and practice', *Annual Review of Psychology*, 60: 339–67.

Pettigrew, T.F. and Tropp, L.R. (2011) *When Groups Meet: The Dynamics of Intergroup Contact*. New York: Psychology Press.

Puma M.J., Jones C.C., Rock D. and Fernandez, R. (1993) 'Prospects: The congressionally mandated study of educational growth and opportunity', *Interim Report*. Bethesda, MD: Abt Associates.

Sherif, M. (1977) 'Crisis in social psychology: Some remarks towards breaking through the crisis', *Personality and Social Psychology Bulletin*, 3: 368–82.

Sherif, M., Harvey, O.J., White, B.J., Hood, W.R. and Sherif, C.W. (1961) *Intergroup Conflict and Cooperation: The Robbers Cave Experiment*. Norman, OK: University of Oklahoma Book Exchange.

Smith, M.B. (1972) 'Is experimental social psychology advancing?', *Journal of Experimental Social Psychology*, 8: 86–96.

Tajfel, H. and Turner, J.C. (1979) 'An integrative theory of intergroup conflict', in W.G. Austin and S. Worchel (eds), *The Social Psychology of Intergroup Relations*. Monterey, CA: Brooks/Cole. pp. 33–48.

Tomcho, T.J. and Foels, R. (2012) 'Meta-analysis of group learning activities: Empirically-based teaching recommendations', *Teaching of Psychology*, 39: 159–69.

Turner, J.C., Hogg, M.A., Oakes, P.J., Reicher, S. and Wetherell, M.S. (1987) *Rediscovering The Social Group: A Self-Categorization Theory*. Oxford: Basil Blackwell.

Walker, I. and Crogan, M. (1998) 'Academic performance, prejudice, and the jigsaw classroom: New pieces to the puzzle', *Journal of Community & Applied Social Psychology*, 8: 381–93.

Walton, G.M. and Cohen, G.L. (2011) 'A brief social-belonging intervention improves academic and health outcomes of minority students', *Science*, 331: 1447–51.

14

Stereotype Formation

Revisiting Hamilton and Gifford's
illusory correlation studies

Craig McGarty

BACKGROUND

Social psychology in the 1970s developed a powerful new cognitive paradigm. Studies of social influence, attitude change and group dynamics had dominated the field for the preceding 20 years (as illustrated by the studies discussed in Chapters 3 to 13). Even though social psychology had always studied mental life, and had avoided the behaviourist domination of experimental psychology that had seen the near banishment of the study of mental phenomena from the psychological laboratory, in the late 1960s and early 1970s a new approach that became known as 'cognitive psychology' was starting to dominate psychology. Many cognitive psychologists were armed with the metaphor of the person as a faulty information-processing device and this idea was imported into social psychology in the 1970s. This metaphor implied that as people processed information about the world around them, they made a series of errors (in particular, because they had limited processing capacity) and these had a range of unintended and unfortunate consequences.

In this colonization of the sub-discipline of social psychology by the proponents of the information-processing metaphor there was intense enthusiasm for cognitive accounts of social phenomena. As it became permissible to explain mental life in terms of events within the mind it also seemed possible to explain many of the outcomes of mental life, including social relations and social structure, in terms of these mental phenomena.

It is difficult to overstate the appeal of this approach for many psychologists. Society is composed of relationships between people and these people are thinking beings. Given this, it was compelling to ask whether it is possible to explain the relationships between people in terms of the mental states that these people experience. If this were possible then it would be enormously convenient for social psychology, because it would mean that, in our scientific accounts of the social world, we would be able to dispense with a lot of other ideas. If we could explain social structure by reducing it to the aggregate effect of the ways that individuals think, then we might be able to explain important social phenomena – such as stereotyping and prejudice – without the need to consider competing and complicating explanations provided by other accounts (e.g., those in sociology and political science that relied on concepts such as groups, class and culture). Indeed, it was believed that by focusing exclusively on cognitive factors, social psychology might make the kind of breakthrough that physics and chemistry were able to achieve with the theory of the atom and that biology was able to achieve with the discovery of the structure of DNA.

If there was one good place to try to explain social structure in cognitive terms then stereotyping was that place. Among social psychologists at the time, there was near unanimous agreement that stereotypes were intensely problematic. They were widely held to be negative, rigid and false beliefs that created social barriers and led to prejudice and discrimination. Nowhere could this be clearer than in the case of stereotypes of minority groups. It seems obvious that negative and false stereotypes would help to maintain the disadvantage of such groups, and yet social psychology had no systematic account of where these stereotypes came from.

Why, for example, do so many people have negative views of ethnic minorities? And why do so many different people share the same negative view of these groups? Could it be that different people come to the same conclusion because their minds work in the same way? These are the tantalizing questions that Hamilton and Gifford sought to answer in 1976 when they explained the formation of social stereotypes in terms of an *illusory correlation*.

THE ILLUSORY CORRELATION STUDIES

The idea of illusory correlation was introduced into the general psychological literature by Loren and Jean Chapman in a 1967 article that appeared in the *Journal of Abnormal Psychology*. These researchers used the term to refer to the way that clinical concepts that were actually unrelated to each other could come to be seen as related because they were expected or made sense in some way. In the mid-1970s this line of thinking was extended by David Hamilton and Robert Gifford – two social psychologists who hypothesized that negative stereotypes of minorities might also form as a result of people's tendency to make faulty associations. In particular, they postulated that there were cognitive factors that tended to lead people to make erroneous associations between small groups and negative behaviour.

As noted above, these cognitive factors relate to the metaphor of people as defective information processors. In particular, this metaphor built on an earlier suggestion by the journalist Walter Lippmann that humans' information-processing power is limited by virtue of the fact that the social world is far too complex to make sense of in detail. In his 1922 book *Public Opinion*, Lippmann suggested that in order to avoid information overload, people are forced to summarize and be selective, and to use generalizations to form impressions of groups rather than of individuals – that is, to rely on *stereotypes*.

In line with arguments by other influential cognitive social psychologists such as Susan Fiske and Shelley Taylor, Hamilton and Gifford reasoned that one consequence of this need to simplify the world is that people pay attention only to those things that demand attention. The things that are most likely to grab attention are the things that stand out or are distinctive, and the most distinctive things of all are not those that are old and common (and that have thus been seen before) but rather those that stand out by virtue of being novel and rare. When we think of groups whose members are encountered infrequently, for most people, those are minority groups. And if this is the case, then, as they go about their lives, those people should pay extra attention to minority group members.

If it is true that minorities are distinctive, then one might also ask whether there are any types of social behaviour that are equally distinctive. Hamilton and Gifford argued that because it is socially desirable to behave positively, negative behaviour should be less common and hence it too should attract more attention. Yet this still does not explain why minority groups should be seen particularly negatively. It does, however, once Hamilton and Gifford made the additional assumption that rare – i.e., undesirable – behaviours performed by minority members would be *doubly distinctive* and once they argued that as a consequence of this they will be *particularly* attention-grabbing and hence *particularly* likely to be processed with care and stored in memory. Indeed, this idea that the co-occurrence of distinctive groups and distinctive acts was a potent basis for stereotype formation was the core premise of their illusory correlation model.

The attraction of this model is that it suggests that cognitive factors alone might explain the pervasiveness of negative stereotypes of minorities (except among the minority group itself where there may be frequent exposure to other minorities). The model could explain why so many people misperceive the world in the same way without needing to draw on accounts of social structure that are not based on cognitive factors.

METHOD

It was this model, with these potential implications, that Hamilton and Gifford tested in groundbreaking studies that were published in the *Journal of Experimental Social Psychology* in 1976.[1]

Hamilton and Gifford (1976) reported two experiments that used a common method. In the first of these, participants were presented with 39 statements that described either positive or negative behaviors undertaken by a member of one of

---

[1]An extended distinctiveness account was also subsequently developed by McConnell and colleagues (1994) nearly 20 years later. This account retained the idea of paired distinctiveness but emphasized the importance of the reinterpretation of stimuli in the local context in which they were presented. In effect, stimuli could be distinctive (and hence attention-grabbing) by virtue of standing out during presentation in a local sequence of stimuli. This local distinctiveness was expected to affect the interpretation of the stimuli after presentation but prior to judgment.

Table 14.1 The distribution of desirable and undesirable behaviours across the two groups in Hamilton and Gifford's original stimulus set (1976, Study 1)

	Group A	Group B
Desirable	18	9
Undesirable	8	4

Note: The important feature of this set of stimulus statements is that the ratio of positive to negative statements is the same for both groups (i.e., 9:4).

two (unnamed) groups: Group A or Group B. These statements were of the form: 'John, a member of Group A, is not always honest about small sums of money.'

The important feature of the set of descriptions presented to participants was that they were not distributed evenly across the two groups or the two types of behaviour. The experiment's cover story informed participants that 'in the real world population, Group B is smaller than Group A. Consequently statements about Group B occur less frequently'. In line with this, of the 39 statements, 26 were about Group A and 13 were about Group B. Similarly, 27 statements described behaviours that had previously been judged to be positive and 12 described behaviours that had previously been judged to be negative. Positive and negative behaviours were ascribed to members of both the large group (A) and the small group (B). Importantly, though, as can be seen from Table 11.1, the *ratio* of positive to negative behaviours was the same for the two groups.

In light of these design features, there would be no apparent reason for participants to see one group more positively than the other. Moreover, because the groups are unnamed (and there are therefore no cues about the groups they might correspond to in society) there is no reason for the participants to have expectations about one group or the other. The key empirical question, then, was whether participants would see the two groups to be equally good, or whether they would judge one more positively than the other. In particular, would they tend to favour the majority over the minority?

RESULTS

Hamilton and Gifford tested for the existence of an illusory correlation on three measures. The first was an *assignment* measure that examined participants' recognition of the statements. In this, participants were presented with the 39 behaviours and asked to remember the group membership of the person who had exhibited each of the behaviours. Here, if the doubly distinctive behaviours (negative behaviours performed by Group B) were overrepresented in memory then one would expect negative behaviours attributed to the small group to be less likely to be forgotten and hence to be overestimated. The second measure involved *frequency estimation*. This asked participants to indicate the number of negative behaviours performed by members of the two groups. Again one would expect that if doubly distinctive behaviours are more likely to attract attention and be stored in memory, then participants would tend to overestimate the negative behaviours performed by the minority group.

On both these measures, the existence of illusory correlation can be measured by a special correlation coefficient called phi that is used for calculating associations in contingency tables. On both measures in Hamilton and Gifford's study, this statistic revealed a highly significant departure from the value of 0 that would be expected if participants saw no correlation between group membership and behaviour. As the example pattern in Table 11.2 illustrates, this derived from the fact that, as predicted, they overestimated the number of undesirable behaviours performed by members of the minority group (B).

These two measures are interesting measures of cognitive processes but they are not without their problems. Paired distinctiveness implies improved memory rather than the creation of false or distorted memories, and we would therefore expect that any effect on measures of memory would be rather muted. In this regard, the third of Hamilton and Gifford's (1976) measures is particularly interesting because this required participants to make *trait ratings* rather than perform a memory task. Specifically, it involved rating the two groups on a range of evaluative dimensions (e.g., indicating how popular, sociable, industrious and intelligent they were). This last measure has captured less subsequent attention but in some ways it is more intriguing because it involves responses that are close to the everyday conception of stereotypes. In other words, it could show that paired distinctiveness impacts on actual judgments of groups – and indeed this is precisely what happened, with participants here rating Group A much more positively than Group B.

The study was followed up with a second study in which the majority of behaviours were negative rather than positive. This study again showed the effect on all three measures – two of memory, one of stereotypical judgment. However, as the notion of paired distinctiveness would predict, in this case it demonstrated an association between the small group and *positive* behaviours. This second study was important because it appears to rule out the possibility that the effect could be caused by a bias against small groups or something as simple as a preference for the label 'Group A' vs. 'Group B'.

Table 14.2 Typical frequency estimates of the distribution of desirable and undesirable behaviours from a standard illusory correlation study (after Hamilton and Gifford, 1976, Experiment 1)

	Group A	Group B
Desirable	17	7
Undesirable	9	6

Note: The important feature of this pattern of responses is that participants overestimate the number of undesirable Group B statements (recalling 6 when the actual number was 4).

IMPACT OF THE ILLUSORY CORRELATION STUDIES

The paper by Hamilton and Gifford had immediate impact as a key example of the social cognitive approach to the study of stereotyping and social psychology more generally. The paper has been cited in the scientific literature over 400 times on Web of Science but, more strikingly, it has provided the benchmark answer to the critical question of 'how do stereotypes form?' for generations of authors of textbooks that have been used by millions of psychology students over the last 40 years. This process can be seen as early as 1980 in Richard Eiser's *Cognitive Social Psychology* and almost 30 years after that in the 3rd edition of Eliot Smith and Diane Mackie's *Social Psychology* (2007). These two texts, which bracket the period after the original studies, were written by authors who have contributed to key insights into the social cognitive aspects of categorization including illusory correlation itself (for details see Smith, 1991; Spears et al., 1985, 1986). It is fair to say these texts do offer some commentary and qualification of the implications of the effect for stereotype formation, but innumerable other texts – many by equally distinguished authors whose primary expertise relates to other topics– have tightened and consolidated the intellectual connection between illusory correlation and stereotype formation. It might seem fair to say that no discussion of stereotype formation remains complete without a discussion of the illusory correlation effect and in particular the paper by Hamilton and Gifford (1976), but in fact that is actually a gross understatement. It would be fairer to say that many discussions of stereotype formation extend little further than a discussion of distinctiveness-based illusory correlation as initiated by Hamilton and Gifford.

There are, of course, other situations where a social psychological experimental result has come close to being seen as the perfect expression of a complex social psychological phenomenon (e.g., as demonstrated by numerous other chapters in this volume such as Tajfel's minimal group studies, or Zimbardo's Stanford Prison Experiment; see Chapters 10 and 8). In the case of the illusory correlation effect, however, the effect is located at the core of the explanation of a social psychological phenomenon that is so common in everyday life that it is scarcely possible to imagine that we could understand human social relations without an account of it.

So, why was illusory correlation research so attractive and impactful? As suggested earlier, part of the attraction for many social psychologists must be that it allows us to avoid explanatory principles drawn from other disciplines such as sociology, political science, and history. This is not to say that this is what Hamilton and Gifford set out to sell, but nevertheless there were many buyers for this idea (just as a generation earlier there had been a receptive audience for the idea that fascism was the product of a personality type that stemmed from child-rearing practices in particular cultures; after Adorno et al., 1950). In the case of stereotype formation, in the 1970s social psychology was ready for a cognitive revolution that would cut through the complexity of alternative accounts that were framed in terms of social structure and ongoing social relations.

Importantly too, research into the illusory correlation effect was also most certainly aided by the robustness of the effect – that is, the ease with which it could be reproduced. This robustness was confirmed in a meta-analysis by Brian Mullen and Craig Johnson (1990) that showed that the effect was significant but of small size. The key point, then, is that as well as appearing to explain an important social phenomenon, this is a seemingly simple effect, which can be easily explained and understood, and which can be easily reproduced in the laboratory or classroom. In short, the study has all the ingredients of a classic study.

BEYOND THE ILLUSORY CORRELATION STUDIES

COGNITIVE ACCOUNTS OF ILLUSORY CORRELATION

Despite the impact of Hamilton and Gifford's work, there were good reasons to be circumspect about distinctiveness-based illusory correlation as an account of stereotype formation. These started to emerge around 15 years after the original publication. In particular, papers by Klaus Fiedler and Eliot Smith (both published in 1991) proposed two new accounts of illusory correlation. The important aspect of these new accounts was that neither model afforded any special importance to paired or doubly distinctive information.

A common feature of the two models was that they explained the illusory correlation effect as a natural consequence of asking people to process skewed distributions of information. In effect, the new models were explanations of the illusory correlation effect rather than of stereotype formation, and these new papers heralded a move from engagement with the phenomenon of stereotyping (so apparent in the original work of Hamilton and colleagues) to a very detailed engagement in the study of cognitive processes (also seen in later work; e.g., Berndsen et al., 1998; McConnell et al., 1994; Sherman et al., 2009).

Fiedler's model focused on information loss (the model was developed further in 1996 so some of the treatment here reflects these later refinements rather than the specifics of the 1991 paper). The core argument is that if perceivers encounter a complex distribution of information such as the 39 behavioural statements in an illusory correlation study then it is likely that much of that information will be lost (in fact such information loss is inevitable for almost all of us). The information may be 'lost' because it was never processed (perhaps people were not paying attention) or because the perceivers forgot what they saw, or because they cannot retrieve what they saw from memory. Regardless of whether the information loss is a result of perceptual or memory processes (or both), the effect of the information loss is expected to take a particular form providing that this information loss is random. If the information loss is random then on average the same amount of information loss will tend to do more damage to the impression of the smaller group. In the standard illusory correlation paradigm the balance of information about both groups is very positive. It follows that if perceivers had the full set of information they would form positive impressions of both groups. If a proportion of that information is lost about both groups then there may still be enough information to retain a positive impression about the large group, but the positive impression of the small group may decay.

An attractive feature of Fiedler's account is that its broad nature means that it is almost certainly true some of the time. It seems very plausible that there would be some random information loss in the perception, storage, and retrieval of complex sets of stimuli. If there is, and the remaining information is aggregated, then it is almost inevitable that the statistical principles described by Fiedler will yield the outcome he describes (simply because of the wide applicability of the statistical principle widely known as the law of large numbers). What is more difficult to judge is whether these processes are likely to yield effects that are big enough and rapid enough to explain the illusory correlation effect. It is also the case that the model should predict a rapid decay in the illusory correlation effect when the small group is large (e.g., when Group A has 52 stimuli and Group B 26). The available evidence, however, is very limited on this point.

Smith arrived at a similar conclusion to Fiedler independently in the same year but he did so by positing the existence of an information-processing architecture derived from work on connectionist modelling. Smith argued that if we assume that perceivers possess a cognitive system which, in an illusory correlation study, is forming and storing impressions of the two groups, then it is very plausible that the impression of the larger group will be more positive than that of the smaller group due simply to properties of the information set to which they are exposed. This is because, in the case of the larger group there are ten more positive pieces of information than there are negative pieces, while in the case of the smaller group this difference is just five pieces of information. In short, if the positivity of impressions stems from the balance of positive and negative information then it is difficult to see how small groups could be seen as positively as the large group. Despite the fact that this particular information-processing model is plausible it is worth noting that the model rests on a specific cognitive architecture that may not actually exist. It is also the case that the model is sensitive to sample size in similar ways to Fiedler's proposal.

MEANING-BASED ACCOUNTS OF ILLUSORY CORRELATION

In 1993 my colleagues and I built on the ideas of Fiedler and Smith, but also departed from them in a number of ways. In particular, we asked whether the illusory correlation effect was more than a byproduct of passive information processing but might instead reflect an *active* process of trying to *make sense* of the stimuli. In other words, we were interested in the question of whether there were ways of interpreting the information presented to participants such that the so-called illusory correlation was actually not a distortion of reality but a fair response to the information presented to participants.

We reasoned that when presented with two groups about which nothing was known prior to the experiment, participants would presume that there must be some difference between those groups and that they would be motivated to discover what that difference was. That is, in the absence of prior information that there was no difference between the groups, we expected the participants to search for a meaningful way to see the groups as in some way different.

Our approach was informed by an alternative social cognitive approach to stereotyping that was inspired by the social identity approach, and in particular self-categorization theory (Turner et al., 1994). This alternative approach was also underpinned by an argument – first made by Jerome Bruner in 1957 – that social perceivers are not hampered by too much information about the social world but by too little. As we have noted, like Lippmann (1922), but also after William James who famously wrote about the world as a 'blooming buzzing confusion' (1890: 488), many psychologists believe that social perceivers are challenged by a confrontingly complex world and that, as a result, they need to shut some of this confusion out (even at the risk of oversimplifying it). We believed that social perceivers instead seek to add to their stock of knowledge; that they seek out subtleties and concealed insights.

This approach also assumed that stereotypes were not rigid, simplifying, and negative distortions of reality but in fact were impressions of groups that would tend to be as flexible, complex, positive, and accurate as they needed to be, in order to reflect the requirement of the perceivers who formed them to adapt to and interact with the environment they confront. For example, during the Second World War we might expect Jews to have a rigid, straightforward, and negative view of members of the SS (just as the SS had similar views about Jews), but that does not mean that the views of Jews about the SS were inaccurate *simply because* they were stereotypes (see Oakes et al., 1994). In particular, the stereotype of the SS as being homogeneously and constantly evil was an accurate and functional view for Jews to have about the members of the SS at that time. Cognitions, behaviours and stereotypes, however, also need to be able to change because, unless they can, people could never respond to a changing world and could never reach consensus (McGarty, 1999). And without these things meaningful social behaviour would be impossible (because, among other things, it would rule out the possibility of social cooperation and social change).

The purpose of this digression is to underscore the importance we attached to reconnecting the phenomenon of illusory correlation to the process of stereotype formation. In effect, we argued that both things resulted from processes of searching for what McGarty and Turner (1992) referred to as *differentiated meaning*: the meaning that reflects an understanding that one thing or set of things is different from some other set of things. And if we assume that in an illusory correlation study the perceivers are motivated to discover how Group A and Group B are different (something it is reasonable to assume since the experimenter has given them different labels), then this leads to the question of why they tend to see one group as better than the other.

Importantly, McGarty and colleagues (1993) proposed that people could derive differentiated meaning in the illusory correlation paradigm from the process of interpreting the stimulus information in ways that did not rely on notions of distinctiveness. In particular, there were two ways in which they could do this. One of these closely aligns to the arguments of Fiedler (1991) and Smith (1991): if perceivers entertained the hypothesis that Group A is more positive than negative, then they have ten pieces of evidence that support this hypothesis (i.e., 18 – 8) but only five pieces of evidence (i.e., 9 – 4) that support the alternative hypothesis that Group B is more positive than negative. It is not unreasonable therefore (in line with Smith's model) that participants would have formed a strong favourable impression of Group A but remain undecided about Group B.

However, our approach went beyond Fiedler and Smith to argue that rather than simply encoding (or losing) this information, perceivers go beyond the information given in order to refine and sharpen the contrast between the two groups. Our first proposal for testing this rested on the logic that if people were expecting that the groups they were viewing were different, then their task was to search for plausible ways to differentiate between the groups. Intriguingly, if this were the case then we should expect to find differentiation when there were expectations even if there was no stimulus information at all.

We tested this rather unusual idea in an initial study. The logic here was that if the illusory correlation effect involves reinforcing expectations rather than detecting distinctiveness in the stimulus information, then we should expect to find the effect if participants are provided with the standard instructions and some key expectations about the stimuli, but are then asked to complete the tasks without actually receiving the stimulus information. We tested this idea simply by telling participants (a) that there were twice as many statements about Group A as about Group B and (b) that there were twice as many positive statements as negative ones. When they responded by indicating how they *expected* group members to behave, there was evidence of significant levels of illusory correlation (such that Group B was represented more negatively than Group A) in five of six tests.

Study 2 involved a similar procedure, but prior to measuring the illusory correlation effect we actually provided the statements, unattributed to the groups, to the participants (i.e., so that they read 39 statements of the form 'AC, a member of Group X, tries not to take sides when two of his friends have an argument'). Here we found that the illusory correlation effect was powerfully present in all conditions.

Arguably, this evidence of illusory correlation in the presence of minimal stimulus information is a clear instantiation of the importance of information loss as argued by Fiedler. The key difference here is that it was not so much that information was lost as that it was never acquired in the first place.

This logic was subsequently followed up in research by Haslam and colleagues (1996). We reasoned that if the illusory correlation effect was produced by reinforcing initial expectations that there should be differences between the two groups, then we should be able to eliminate the effect by reducing the motivation to detect such differences. To examine this idea, we replicated Hamilton and Gifford's first study, but told the participants that the large group (A) was composed of right-handed people and the small group (B) was composed of left-handed people. As predicted, participants' subsequent responses revealed no evidence of perceived difference between the two groups (i.e., no evidence of illusory correlation) – presumably because they were not looking for differences.

Taking these various ideas further, Mariette Berndsen and colleagues also conducted a raft of important studies on this topic. One of the most important of these demonstrated that in a standard illusory correlation study, the statements about the two groups are reinterpreted over the course of the experiment (Berndsen et al., 1998). That is, rather than the desirability and undesirability of the various statements being a constant, positive behaviours performed by the larger group come to be seen more positively, and negative behaviours performed by the minority come to be seen less positively. This is powerful evidence that searching for differences between groups can transform not just the perceptions of those groups but also the very information that those perceptions are based on. If this is the case, then information processing must involve more than just aggregating and storing traces of fixed stimuli, because the evaluation of those stimuli changes over time. It is difficult to overstate the importance of this uncommonly noted finding for our understanding of social cognition and social judgment more generally.

Another very important contribution of Berndsen and colleagues' (2001) work involved tracking the cognitive processes of participants in an illusory correlation study using a 'thinking aloud' procedure. By this means they were able to confirm that most of the naïve participants who were viewing the stimuli were engaged in a process of hypothesis-testing and a search for differentiated meaning. Again, this work confirms suggestions that the processes that underpin the effects first observed by Hamilton and Gifford are based not on a passive concern to simplify information, but on an active, effortful search after meaning. Importantly too, this search is not blind to reality, but highly responsive to it.

CONCLUSION

In 2009 Jeff Sherman and colleagues developed a new distinctiveness model whose core insight is that stimuli can be distinctive not by virtue of their novelty or statistical rarity but in terms of their capacity to distinguish between groups (Sherman et al., 2009). Among many other things, the model instantiates the differentiated-meaning account described in the preceding section. From this it is apparent that the concept of stimulus distinctiveness as defined in terms of statistical infrequency is almost certainly unnecessary to explain either the illusory correlation effect or stereotype formation. This is not to say that statistical infrequency is never important or meaningful, but rather that it is not consistently, basically, and essentially meaningful in a way that helps us explain the structure and nature of intergroup relations. If we were to ask, then, how far we can push the cognitive approach in order to explain social phenomena like stereotyping, the answer would seem to be 'not that far'. Stereotypes are cognitive phenomena; they form through cognitive processes, and the work inspired by Hamilton and Gifford's paper almost certainly articulates some of the cognitive processes that are involved in forming impressions of groups of people. However, there are strong reasons for doubting whether they allow us to isolate a unique and universal process that could be said to be *the* account of stereotype formation.

Yes, it is true that minority groups may often be reviled by majority groups but there are so many small groups that are not reviled, and so many large groups that are, that any correlation between group size and negativity of stereotypes may itself be an illusion.

The illusory correlation effect is a useful phenomenon for understanding aspects of category learning. Yet if there is one point that we could derive from the differentiated-meaning account that has broad relevance to social psychology, it is that learning about categories of people is not a cold process of aggregating traces of unchanging stimulus information. Rather, it is a motivated process of deriving meaning – and those meanings can change. Accordingly, it is essential to admit to the study of cognitive processes, perhaps especially to the study of cognitions about people, a realization that perceivers are influenced by the quest for social meaning – much as Bruner (1957) argued long ago. Psychological experiments are themselves social psychological interactions between experimenters and participants, and people strive to make sense of these situations in terms of the logic of that situation and their own knowledge. These situations are still explicable in psychological terms and experiments are still of considerable value, but in order to understand and learn from them, we need to see participants not as passive vessels but as motivated agents who are always seeking to do much more than merely process information.

FURTHER READING

Bruner, J.S. (1957) 'On perceptual readiness', *Psychological Review*, 64: 123–52.

If you are interested in social cognitive processes then you need to read (or re-read) Bruner's treatment of the motivated nature of perception.

Hamilton, D.L. and Gifford, R.K. (1976) 'Illusory correlation in intergroup perception: A cognitive basis of stereotypic judgments', *Journal of Experimental Social Psychology*, 12: 392–407.

When it comes to illusory correlation, there is no substitute for reading Hamilton and Gifford's groundbreaking investigation.

Fiedler, K. (1996) 'Explaining and simulating judgment biases as an aggregation phenomenon in probabilistic, multiple-cue environments', *Psychological Review*, 103: 193–214.

Fiedler's elaboration and generalization of ideas contains notions that are both ingenious and at times infuriating.

Sherman, J.W., Kruschke, J.K., Sherman, S.J., Percy, E.T., Petrocelli, J.V. and Conrey, F.R. (2009) 'Attentional processes in stereotype formation: A common model for category accentuation and illusory correlation', *Journal of Personality and Social Psychology*, 96: 305–23.

This article presents a statement of a widely applicable model that accounts for a range of category accentuation and illusory correlation effects.

Berndsen, M., Spears, R., McGarty, C. and van der Pligt, J. (1998) 'Dynamics of differentiation: Similarity as the precursor and product of stereotype formation', *Journal of Personality and Social Psychology*, 74: 1451–63.

Berndsen and colleagues' paper presents the most sophisticated empirical presentation of the differentiated meaning approach.

McGarty, C., Yzerbyt, V.Y. and Spears, R. (eds) (2002) *Stereotypes as Explanations: The Formation of Meaningful Beliefs about Social Groups*. Cambridge: Cambridge University Press.

This edited book brings together the different aspects of an international collaboration on stereotype formation involving Australian and European researchers.

REFERENCES

Adorno, T.W., Frenkel-Brunswik, E., Levinson, D.J. and Sanford, R.N. (1950) *The Authoritarian Personality*. New York: Harper.

Berndsen, M., McGarty, C., van der Pligt, J. and Spears, R. (2001) 'Meaning-seeking in the illusory correlation paradigm: The active role of participants in the categorization process', *British Journal of Social Psychology,* 40: 209–34.

Berndsen, M., Spears, R., McGarty, C. and van der Pligt, J. (1998) 'Dynamics of differentiation: Similarity as the precursor and product of stereotype formation', *Journal of Personality and Social Psychology*, 74: 1451–63.

Bruner, J.S. (1957) 'On perceptual readiness', *Psychological Review*, 64: 123–52.

Chapman, L.J. and Chapman, J.P. (1967) 'Genesis of popular but erroneous psychodiagnostic signs', *Journal of Abnormal Psychology*, 72: 193–204.

Eiser, J.R. (1980) *Cognitive Social Psychology*. London: McGraw-Hill.

Fiedler, K. (1991) 'The tricky nature of skewed frequency tables: An information loss account of distinctiveness-based illusory correlations', *Journal of Personality and Social Psychology*, 60: 24–36.

Hamilton, D.L. and Gifford, R.K. (1976) 'Illusory correlation in intergroup perception: A cognitive basis of stereotypic judgments', *Journal of Experimental Social Psychology*, 12: 392–407.

Haslam, S.A., McGarty, C. and Brown, P. (1996) 'The search for differentiated meaning is a precursor to illusory correlation', *Personality and Social Psychology Bulletin*, 22: 611–19.

James, W. (1890) *Principles of Psychology*. New York: Henry Holt & Co.

Lippmann, W. (1922) *Public Opinion*. New York: Harcourt Brace.

McConnell, A.R., Sherman, S.J. and Hamilton, D.L. (1994) 'Illusory correlation in the perception of groups: An extension of the distinctiveness-based account', *Journal of Personality and Social Psychology*, 67: 414–29.

McGarty, C. (1999) *Categorization in Social Psychology*. London: Sage.

McGarty, C. and Turner, J.C. (1992) 'The effects of categorization on social judgment', *British Journal of Social Psychology*, 31: 253–68.

McGarty, C., Haslam, S.A., Turner, J.C. and Oakes, P.J. (1993) 'Illusory correlation as accentuation of actual intercategory difference: Evidence for the effect with minimal stimulus information', *European Journal of Social Psychology*, 23: 391–410.

Mullen, B. and Johnson, C. (1990) 'Distinctiveness-based illusory correlations and stereotyping: A meta-analytic integration', *British Journal of Social Psychology*, 29: 11–28.

Oakes, P.J., Haslam, S.A. and Turner, J.C. (1994) *Stereotyping and Social Reality*. Oxford: Blackwell.

Sherman, J.W., Kruschke, J.K., Sherman, S.J., Percy, E.T., Petrocelli, J.V. and Conrey, F.R. (2009) 'Attentional processes in stereotype formation: A common model for category accentuation and illusory correlation', *Journal of Personality and Social Psychology*, 96: 305–23.

Smith, E.R. (1991) 'Illusory correlation in a simulated exemplar-based memory', *Journal of Experimental Social Psychology*, 27: 107–23.

Smith, E.R. and Mackie, D. (2007) *Social Psychology*, 3rd edn. Philadelphia, PA: Psychology Press.

Spears, R., van der Pligt, J. and Eiser, J.R. (1985) 'Illusory correlation in the perception of group attitudes', *Journal of Personality and Social Psychology*, 48: 863–75.

Spears, R., van der Pligt, J. and Eiser, J.R. (1986) 'Generalizing the illusory correlation effect', *Journal of Personality and Social Psychology*, 51: 1127–34.

Turner, J.C., Oakes, P.J., Haslam, S.A. and McGarty, C. (1994) 'Self and collective: Cognition and social context', *Personality and Social Psychology Bulletin,* 20: 454–63.

15 | Stereotypes and Performance

Revisiting Steele and Aronson's
stereotype threat experiments

Toni Schmader and Chad Forbes

BACKGROUND

Social psychology is a discipline that has always sought to understand societal problems through the lens of sound theory and empiricism. One issue that stimulated a great deal of discussion in the 1990s was racial gaps in academic achievement and test scores that persisted despite legal and social efforts to dismantle institutionalized barriers to educational advancement (Kao and Thompson, 2003). In popular media and academic circles, explanations ranged from stark differences in educational quality in what were (and still are) racially segregated schools (Kozol, 2012) to controversial claims of inherent genetic differences in intelligence based on race (Herrnstein and Murray, 1994). It was in the context of this broader national debate about the racial gap in performance that Claude Steele and Joshua Aronson introduced a ground-breaking set of studies that have become a modern classic in the field (Devine and Brodish, 2003; Fiske, 2003).

Steele and Aronson's work on what they called *stereotype threat* was informed in various ways by other social psychological theories of the day. In particular, in the 1980s, social psychology had developed influential theories about the role of social identities in self-definition (Tajfel and Turner, 1979), motives to preserve self-integrity (Steele, 1988), consensually shared and automatically triggered social stereotypes (Devine, 1989), and the consequences of social stigma for those who are targeted by it (Crocker and Major, 1989). Drawing from these theories and with an interest in understanding racial differences in performance, Steele and Aronson's central idea was that situational reminders of negative racial stereotypes that exist and threaten to impugn the intellectual abilities of African Americans might impair Black students' ability to perform well academically.

In this chapter, we revisit the four experiments published by Steele and Aronson in 1995. We will review the theoretical and practical impact of these studies, but, in keeping with the format of other chapters in this volume, we will also consider the critiques that have been raised against this literature – particularly in the context of current concerns about the replicability of psychological findings (e.g., after Pashler and Wagenmakers, 2012). Finally, we will offer our own view of the legacy of Steele and Aronson and the remaining questions that await future investigation.

THE STEREOTYPE THREAT STUDIES

The four studies reported in Steele and Aronson's seminal paper tested the idea that when, '[Black] students perform an explicitly scholastic or intellectual task, they face the threat of confirming or being judged by a negative societal stereotype – a suspicion – about their group's intellectual ability and competence' (1995: 797). They hypothesized that because this self-threat is not experienced by people who are not stereotyped in this manner (e.g., White students), simply knowing that one's intellectual abilities are being assessed and compared across racial groups might impair performance for Black relative to White students. Although they cited much earlier evidence for this hypothesis by Katz (Katz et al., 1964; Katz et al., 1965), Steele and Aronson ignited new interest in the phenomenon with their series of elegant experiments.

Start by putting yourself in the shoes of some of the students who participated in this research. Imagine you are a Black student who has made it into one of the best universities in the world. You are unequivocally intelligent. But you suspect that some people might question whether you really deserve to be here, given broader stereotypes about your race. And now you are in a psychology experiment and asked to put your intellectual merit on the line with a test that can identify strengths and weaknesses in your verbal ability. How would you feel in this situation? Nervous? Cognizant of racial stereotypes? Motivated to disprove those stereotypes? And more importantly, would all these thoughts and feelings converge to ultimately interfere with your performance or would these concerns be irrelevant? This is the experience that Steele and Aronson sought to capture in their studies.

Study 1 tested their stereotype threat hypothesis by having 117 Black and White university students (both male and female) spend 30 minutes completing a verbal test consisting of 30 difficult items from the Graduate Record Exam – a standardized test that is a requirement for admission to most graduate schools in the United States – along with three anagram problems. However, before they performed this test, participants were randomly assigned to hear one of three frames for the task. The condition theorized to induce stereotype threat was modelled after a typical testing context where performance is assumed to be diagnostic of ability. In this *diagnostic test* (DT) *condition*, participants learned that the study concerned 'various personal factors involved in performance on problems requiring reading and verbal reasoning abilities' (p. 799). Feedback would be provided that 'may be helpful to you by familiarizing you with some of your strengths and weaknesses' (p. 799) in verbal problem solving. Test difficulty was justified as a means of providing 'a genuine test of your verbal abilities and limitations so that we might better understand the factors involved in both' (p. 799). The assumption underpinning this condition is that any reminder of intellectual testing would trigger reminders of the racial stereotypes about intellectual ability among Black participants that would undermine their performance.

Two non-diagnostic test (ND) conditions were designed to neutralize these processes by framing the purpose of the study as a way to better understand the 'psychological factors involved in solving verbal problems' (p. 799). Feedback would be provided to familiarize participants 'with the kinds of problems that appear on tests [they] may encounter in the future' (p. 799). The challenging nature of the problems was justified in terms of a research focus on difficult verbal problems in the *non-diagnostic only* condition and on giving 'highly verbal people ... a mental challenge' (p. 799) in the *non-diagnostic challenge* (NDC) condition.

How did these instructions affect students' performance on the task? Analyses of participants' test performance, controlling for self-reported verbal SAT, revealed only preliminary evidence in support of the theory. Focused analyses just of Black participants' performance suggested that after controlling for SAT scores, Black students performed significantly worse on the test in the diagnostic condition than in either of the two non-diagnostic conditions. In comparison, performance for White students was relatively unaffected by the way the task was described. However, the critical statistical test of the race by test description interaction was not significant, $p < .19$.

Results of Study 1 were provocative but by no means convincing on their own. Study 2 therefore sought to replicate the effect and examine the role of anxiety in explaining these performance impairments. Twenty Black and 20 White female participants were assigned to the same non-diagnostic and diagnostic test frame conditions used in Study 1 and spent 25 minutes solving the same 30-item GRE test used in the prior study. Participants also self-reported their anxiety levels. In this study, the predicted interaction was significant: controlling for verbal SAT scores, Black participants in the diagnostic test frame condition solved fewer items correctly, were less accurate on the questions they completed, completed fewer problems, and tended to be slower than participants in all other conditions (see Figure 15.1). There were no differences between conditions in anxiety, however.

Studies 1 and 2 thus provided evidence that framing a test as diagnostic of ability can undermine performance for Black but not for White students. Study 3 was designed to test three implications of the theory: that Black students taking a diagnostic (vs. non-diagnostic) test would (a) show increased activation of negative racial stereotypes and self-doubt, (b) distance themselves from Black stereotypes, and (c) show a tendency to self-handicap by making pre-emptive excuses for poor performance.

In Study 3, 35 Black and 33 White students were randomly assigned to a diagnostic test frame, a non-diagnostic test frame, or a control condition where participants completed the critical dependent measures without expecting to take a test of any sort. Although participants in the two test conditions were told they would ostensibly be completing a verbal test and were given examples of the types

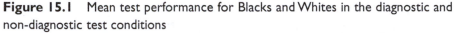

Figure 15.1 Mean test performance for Blacks and Whites in the diagnostic and non-diagnostic test conditions

Source: Steele and Aronson (1995, Study 2)

of difficult problems they would face, in this study the focus was actually on psychological measures, and test performance was not assessed. Specifically, participants completed a word-completion task to measure whether thoughts about racial stereotypes and self-doubt were automatically activated by the test instructions. Stereotype avoidance was assessed by having participants rate a series of activities and personality traits, some of which were related to Black stereotypes (e.g., 'How much do you enjoy being a lazy couch potato?', 'How much do you enjoy rap?'). Self-handicapping was assessed by having participants rate items (e.g., sleep, lack of focus, stress, unfair test) that could offer plausible attributions for poor performance that were not related to ability.

Results from this study provided evidence that anticipating performance on a diagnostic test had a host of psychological implications for Black but not for White students. Controlling for verbal SAT scores, Black participants anticipating a diagnostic test were more likely than Blacks in the other conditions (and more likely than Whites in the diagnostic condition) to complete word fragments (e.g., _ _ A C K and D U _ _) with race-related (i.e., BLACK) and self-doubt-related (i.e., DUMB) words. They were also significantly more likely to avoid endorsing stereotypic activities and traits. They were even less likely to indicate their race before the supposed test, and self-handicapped more by suggesting that they had experienced less sleep and might have less ability to focus on the coming test.

These first three studies in the paper all induced stereotype threat by describing a task as diagnostic of students' abilities. The paper's final study examined a more subtle manipulation of stereotype threat. Guided by the observation that 75% of Black students in the diagnostic condition of Study 3 had refused to mark their race before the test, Steele and Aronson posited that explicit reminders of race in an academic performance context might be sufficient to induce stereotype threat. Accordingly, in Study 4, the same verbal test from Study 2 was described to 22 Black and 22 White participants as being non-diagnostic of ability. However, prior to taking the test half of the participants were required to indicate their race while the other half were not. As in Studies 1 and 2, test performance on the 30 GRE items was the primary dependent measure.

Results revealed that Black participants in the race prime condition answered significantly fewer items correctly than those in all other conditions (again controlling for prior SAT score). They also seemed to approach the questions more methodically in the race prime condition – completing fewer items, avoiding guesses, but still performing somewhat less accurately. There were no differences found for reported effort and performance estimates, but a follow-up study reported in the discussion section suggested that priming race might have elevated anxiety for Black compared with White participants.

In sum, the four experiments together provided compelling evidence that subtle situational reminders of negative stereotypes – the description of a test, the request to mark one's race – can impair the intellectual performance of African American university students. The fact that these are students from an elite university suggests that even those who are intellectually capable can fall prey to these effects. Although the exact mechanism remained unclear in these studies, the effects on other measures suggested that students in these conditions of stereotype threat do not expend less effort on their performance. Instead, having their abilities tested reminds Black students of negative racial stereotypes and motivates them to distance themselves from them. They might be plagued by greater feelings of self-doubt (and perhaps anxiety) and seek to self-handicap for potentially poor performance. As a suite of findings, these effects in broad strokes sketched the outline for what was to become one of social psychology's most fascinating effects.

IMPACT OF THE STEREOTYPE THREAT STUDIES

The impact of Steele and Aronson's paper was immediate but has also been enduring. Of course, one way to assess impact is in the sheer quantity of research an article has inspired. As of November 2016, the article has been cited close to 2000 times in PsycINFO and over 5800 times in Google Scholar. As we next review, the research has been extraordinarily generative with follow-up studies aiming to establish a number of key questions about generalizability, moderators, mediators, and applications.

ESTABLISHING THE GENERALIZABILITY OF STEREOTYPE THREAT

The 'first wave' of research building upon Steele and Aronson's (1995) article demonstrated the generalizability of the stereotype threat effect to different domains and different groups. Researchers from many different labs began reporting evidence for the notion that essentially any group, given the right context, could feel threatened by a negative stereotype in ways that might undermine performance. In addition to the original effects among African Americans taking a verbal ability test, stereotype threat effects have been documented among Latinos, individuals of low socioeconomic status (SES), and psychology majors (compared with science majors) taking a challenging test of intellectual ability (Gonzales et al., 2002; Croizet et al., 1998, 2004). Other studies of cognitive performance have shown that stereotype threat can affect elderly individuals completing a memory assessment, individuals with a history of mental illness taking an intellectual test (Quinn et al., 2004), or head trauma patients taking a neurological test (Kit et al., 2008). Considerable follow-up research has applied the theory to understand the often-found gender gap in mathematical testing (Logel et al., 2012; Spencer et al., 1999).

Beyond effects on intellectual or cognitive performance, stereotype threat has also been shown to impair other kinds of behaviours. Stereotype threat can affect Whites completing what was assumed to be a test of athletic ability (Stone et al., 1999), women engaging in negotiations with men (Kray et al., 2001), and women completing driving simulations (Yeung and von Hippel, 2008). In more social contexts, stereotype threat can lead Whites concerned with appearing racist to experience mental load in interracial interactions (Richeson and Shelton, 2003) or exhibit greater activation of bias on an implicit association test (Frantz et al., 2004). Stereotype threat can lead men to underperform on measures of social sensitivity (Koenig and Eagly, 2005) and elevate anxiety among gay men led to believe they would be interacting with children (Bosson et al., 2004). In all of these studies, priming negatively stereotyped individuals with their group membership in an evaluative setting led to effects on performance or other outcomes consistent with the theory. The breadth of these effects and the reliability of evidence across so many different groups and domains, and as demonstrated by many different researchers, gives greater credence to the scope of the theory and to the impact stereotype threat can have on human behaviour.

Part of the process of generalizing effects to different groups stigmatized in different domains has been to understand what kinds of events can trigger stereotype threat. The original studies suggested that stereotype threat can be cued for Black college students by how a task is described or whether one's group identity is made salient. Along with our colleague Michael Johns, we proposed that stereotype threat is triggered when a situation simultaneously primes three incongruent cognitions: _I am a member of Group X, Group X is thought to do poorly in this domain, I care about doing well in this domain_ (Schmader et al., 2008). From this perspective, stereotype threat can occur whenever these three unbalanced elements of self, group, and domain are activated. Cues to subtle sexism, such as a cartoon demeaning women's math performance on a lab wall, can for example impair women's math performance (Adams et al., 2006; Oswald and Harvey, 2000). But simply being outnumbered by men in a math or science context can also trigger a concern among women that they might not belong or perform well in the setting (Inzlicht and Ben-Zeev, 2000; Murphy, Steele and Gross, 2007).

Importantly, individuals often need to feel personally invested in doing well, as individual anonymity often reduces effects (Jamieson and Harkins, 2010; Wout et al., 2008; Zhang et al., 2013).

IDENTIFYING MODERATORS OF STEREOTYPE THREAT

The 'second wave' of stereotype threat research has been largely concerned with identifying the moderators and mediators that help to illuminate the 'who, when, and why?' of the phenomenon. Regarding who is susceptible to the effects, theoretically any individual who feels targeted by a negative stereotype can experience stereotype threat. For example, White men (a group that is not often understood to be stigmatized) have shown performance decrements when they believe their math performance will be compared with that of Asian men (Aronson et al., 1999). That said, some groups are subjected to more frequent and chronic reminders of negative stereotypes. Women might encounter negative stereotypes about their math ability relative to men more frequently than White men encounter negative stereotypes about their math ability relative to Asians. Furthermore, because negative stereotypes about ethnic minorities are more uniformly negative and often span multiple domains, Blacks, Latino-Americans, and Native Americans might face more chronic experiences of stereotype threat than do women (Logel et al., 2012).

Within a given stigmatized group, some individuals are also more susceptible to experiencing stereotype threat than others. A key assumption of the theory is that to experience stereotype threat, one must have knowledge of a negative stereotype about one's group in relevant domains (Forbes and Schmader, 2010; Keifer and Sekaquaptewa, 2007; McKown and Weinstein, 2003). Although believing the stereotype is true is not necessary to experience effects, suspicions that the stereotype might be accurate can magnify performance impairments (Schmader et al., 2004). Likewise, individuals are more susceptible to stereotype threat effects when they are more stigma conscious, or attuned to these negative stereotypes (Brown and Lee, 2005; Brown and Pinel, 2003). The core assumption of stereotype awareness might shed light on cross-national variation in performance gaps. For example, gender gaps in performance are non-existent in countries where there is no evidence of a strong math = male association or where there is greater evidence of gender equality in the culture as a whole (Else-Quest et al., 2010; Nosek et al., 2009). Although correlational, this variability might suggest that women in these more gender egalitarian cultures experience less stereotype threat.

Even in cultures where stereotypes are prevalent, not all members of a stigmatized group will be vulnerable to effects. As Steele's (1997) vanguard hypothesis posits, individuals who are most invested in performing well might ironically show the largest performance impairments because the stereotypes themselves pose a greater threat to their identity (Lawrence et al., 2010; Nguyen and Ryan, 2008). Such effects could help explain why among one sample of students, racial minorities who initially placed a high value on academic pursuits were later the most likely to drop out of high school (Osborne and Walker, 2006). Just as identification with the domain raises the stakes for one's performance, so too does the identification with the stigmatized groups to which one belongs (Davis et al., 2006; Ployhart et al., 2003; Schmader, 2002). Those who are highly group identified perform poorly when scores will be used to compare groups, even if their personal performance is anonymous (Wout et al., 2008). Finally, other kinds of individual difference variables make it easier for some to cope with the experience of stereotype threat. Effects are weaker among those who are less concerned with maintaining a positive self-image or high status (Inzlicht, et al., 2006; Josephs et al., 2003; von Hippel et al., 2005).

IDENTIFYING MEDIATORS OF STEREOTYPE THREAT

Alongside this work identifying moderators of stereotype threat has been research identifying the sequence of variables that mediate or explain the *why* of the effect. In contrast with early efforts to identify the single variable that can explain why stereotype threat occurs, we proposed an integrated process model of stereotype threat whereby priming stereotype threat elicits a cascade of stress-based physiological, negative appraisal, self-regulatory and performance-monitoring processes as people try to make sense of and cope with this threat to their identity (Schmader et al., 2008). The problem is that some of these activated processes rely on the same working-memory resources needed for performance on complex cognitive tasks, like the GRE test used in Steele and Aronson's original research.

Multiple studies have supported this process model. Manipulations of stereotype threat impair working memory (Schmader and Johns, 2003), impair performance on working-memory-intensive tasks (Beilock et al., 2007), and have their strongest effects on those with lower working-memory capacity (Régner et al., 2010). Furthermore, although the original studies did not find clear evidence of increased anxiety under stereotype threat, subsequent research has established that it increases physiological biomarkers of stress including higher blood pressure (Blascovich, et al., 2001) and skin conductance (Osborne, 2006, 2007). This autonomic stress response is coupled with negative appraisal processes as stereotype-threatened individuals sometimes report heightened levels of explicit (Spencer et al., 1999) and implicit anxiety (Johns et al., 2008; Bosson et al., 2004), negative expectations (Sekaquaptewa et al., 2007; Stangor et al., 1998), feelings of dejection (Keller and Dauenheimer, 2003), and task-related worries (Beilock et al., 2007; Cadinu et al., 2005).

Although these negative thoughts and worries might directly mediate the performance-decrements observed (Cadinu et al., 2005; Keller and Dauenheimer, 2003), another possibility is that individuals' increased vigilance to threatening cues and active attempts to suppress negative thoughts and feelings hijack the working-memory resources needed for optimal performance. For example, evidence of enhanced vigilance under stereotype threat can be found in neurological indices of error detection (Forbes et al., 2008) and increased attention to even subliminally presented threat-related cues (Kaiser et al., 2006). This vigilance also translates into enhanced memory encoding of negative feedback and other cues to threat that can undermine one's identification with the domain

(Forbes et al., 2015; Forbes et al., 2016; Murphy et al., 2007). Conscious attention to performance cued by stereotype threat can be especially debilitating for tasks that are better performed through well-practised automated processes, such as putting for expert golfers (Beilock et al., 2006).

In addition to these vigilance processes, stereotype threat also increases emotion regulation efforts as the person attempts to push negative thoughts and feelings out of mind (Johns et al., 2008; Logel et al., 2009; Schmader et al., 2009; Wraga et al., 2007). If individuals' experience of anxiety is normalized so that it is not interpreted as a sign of failure, this tendency to suppress anxiety under stereotype threat is reduced and performance improves (Johns et al., 2005; Johns et al., 2008). Even those chronically good at reappraising their negative emotions show lower susceptibility to stereotype threat effects (Schmader et al., 2009). One of the reasons explicit measures of anxiety, like those used in the original research, sometimes fail to capture stereotype threat could be that individuals are motivated to deny or suppress these feelings.

In addition to these cognitive and affective processes involved in explaining why stereotype threat impairs performance by impairing working memory, it is important not to lose sight of an important motivational dimension to these effects. Steele and Aronson originally found that Blacks under threat avoid endorsing stereotypic traits and activities, indicative of an increased motivation to disconfirm the stereotypes people might have of their group (or at least how those stereotypes are applied to oneself). More recent research suggests that this increased motivation spurs greater conscious effort to perform the task in ways that activate prepotent response styles and strategies that can sometimes be counterproductive for performance (Jamieson and Harkins, 2007, 2009).

TRANSLATING STEREOTYPE THREAT THEORY INTO EFFECTIVE INTERVENTIONS

Finally, a 'third wave' of stereotype threat research has utilized tenets of the theory to combat the deleterious consequences of these effects in the lab and the real world. The contextualized frame that stereotype threat gives to performance gaps allows researchers to create 'identity safe' environments that avoid cuing stereotype threat. In the original laboratory studies, this was done by framing the task in a non-diagnostic way. Later studies created identity safety by directly communicating an expectation that groups would perform equally well (Good et al., 2008; Spencer et al., 1999) or by retraining implicit stereotypes (Forbes and Schmader, 2010). Because these methods of creating identity-safe environments are not always practical to implement in field settings, researchers have sought to test other interventions to reduce naturalistic experiences of stereotype threat.

For example, moving demographic questions to the end of an Advanced Placement exam boosted women's performance on a calculus test, though the size and significance of these effects has been debated (i.e., the manipulation did not improve performance for minorities; Danaher and Crandall, 2008; Stricker and Ward, 2004). Positive role models are also effective in both the lab and the field in combatting stereotype threat, changing implicit stereotypes, and increasing students' self-efficacy (Dasgupta and Asgari, 2004; Marx and Goff, 2005; McIntyre et al., 2003, 2005).

When the context itself is not so easily changed, researchers have employed interventions that equip stigmatized students with useful coping strategies. For example, in both the lab and the field, prompting students to affirm important values improves stigmatized students' performance by mitigating stereotype threat (Martens et al., 2006). In a remarkable field study at an elite university, minority students who completed brief self-affirmation exercises in their first semester in school showed improved grades up to two years later compared with those in a no-affirmation control condition (Cohen et al., 2006; Cohen et al., 2009; see also Miyake et al., 2010, and Sherman et al., 2013, for similar studies with women in physics and middle-school students, respectively). These effects seem to work by cuing a sense of social belonging that motivates other adaptive behaviours that recursively improve performance.

Other interventions in the field have boosted performance by changing students' mindsets about their stress and performance. Walton and Cohen (2011) helped African-American students reframe social adversity as commonplace but transitory, and found that this simple intervention effectively cut the achievement gap between African Americans and Whites in half. Finally, studies have found success in boosting female and minority performance in the field by manipulating a sense that intelligence is malleable rather than fixed or that performance situations are a challenge rather than a threat (Alter et al., 2010; Good et al., 2003).

In sum, stereotype threat was originally a theoretical perspective developed to understand the role of social stereotypes in reinforcing and recreating group differences in performance. Its impact has been shown to extend far beyond the experience of ethnic minority college students at an elite university. Collectively, in light of the sheer magnitude of research spawned by the original article and topic itself, it would be difficult to find a more stimulating, worthwhile theory. But even more importantly, the theory has come to have positive ramifications for stigmatized individuals. The Educational Testing Service recently agreed to ask demographic information at the end of testing sessions after being lobbied to make this change from social psychologists. The body of research on stereotype threat was cited in at least two separate expert reports, called amici curiae (2012, 2014), that were submitted to the United States Supreme Court for Fisher v. University of Texas. The Supreme Court's ruling, informed in part by this evidence, upheld a university's use of holistic-admissions policies that take race into account to ensure a diverse student body. By these various measures of policy change, the impact of this research has been profound.

BEYOND THE STEREOTYPE THREAT STUDIES

Yet research on stereotype threat, beginning with the original paper by Steele and Aronson (1995), has not been without critique. One aspect of that critique relates to how the original research has been described in media outlets, textbooks, and by scientists directly. In their studies, Steele and Aronson covaried out participants' prior performance on high-stakes standardized tests as assessed with their self-reported SAT scores. This covariate analysis increases the power to detect the effect of a manipulation in the context of individual variation. However, critics have argued that this statistical caveat is too often lost in the retelling of the findings, leading people to report that the threat-free environment eliminates the racial gap in test performance (Sackett et al., 2004; Wicherts, 2005). The problem with this conclusion is that by controlling for SAT, the authors have removed a portion of group performance differences and we simply do not know if stereotype threat or other factors led to this gap in the first place. A similar critique was lodged against Spencer et al.'s (1999) research demonstrating stereotype threat impairments on highly identified women's math performance (Stoet and Geary, 2012).

The concern raised by those who question these covariate analyses is that the effect of stereotype threat on performance has been overhyped. This, it is argued, has led to an impression, not that stereotype threat merely contributes to racial and gender gaps in performance, but that it is the largest contributor to these gaps. These concerns have been amplified by the relatively low rate of replicability of research findings in social psychology (Open Science Collaboration, 2015), which has led many researchers to take a closer look at the field's treasured classics (e.g., those reported in other chapters of this book). Through the current lens of replicability, readers are increasingly sceptical of findings based on small sample sizes and effects that might seem to rely on the use of covariate analysis (Fraley and Vazire, 2014; Simonsohn et al., 2014).

So how does Steele and Aronson (1995) fare on closer inspection? In the current context, the sample sizes used were indeed small, often representing only 10–12 participants per condition. Such samples were quite typical 20 years ago in experimental social psychology and especially for studies with select populations. However, in recent years, a greater understanding of the unreliability of estimates leading to false positives has led to changing norms for larger samples based on power analyses and combined with clear rules for when to stop data collection. For the purposes of this review, we obtained the original data from the authors and have combined the datasets to provide an aggregate analysis of the effects of cues to stereotype threat on test performance in this seminal paper. Recall that the key manipulation in Studies 1 and 2 of Steele and Aronson's original paper involved describing the task as diagnostic of ability or not, whereas the key manipulation in Study 4 was to prime race (or not) prior to a task that was otherwise described in neutral terms. Study 3 did not assess performance.

This combined analysis of 160 participants (40 per cell) yields a significant race X threat cues interaction regardless of whether SAT is or is not a covariate in the model (see Figure 15.2). We can compare the size of the stereotype threat effect for Black and White participants using Cohen's (1988) d, a way to quantify the size of some manipulation on behaviour ($d = .20$ is a small effect, $d = .50$ is a medium effect, and $d = .80$ is considered a large effect). Even without

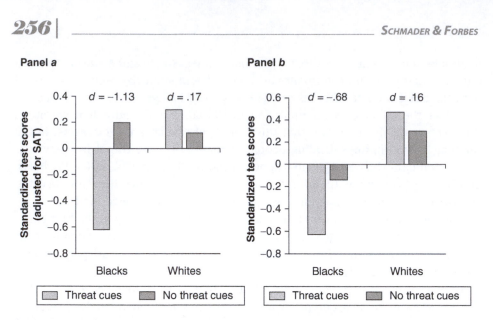

Figure 15.2 Reanalysis of original data combining performance data from Studies 1, 2, and 4 and analysing effects both with (panel a) and without SAT as a covariate (panel b)

Note: N = 40 per cell. In both analyses, the race by threat cues interaction is significant: panel a: $F(1, 155) = 18.45, p < .001$; panel b: $F(1, 156) = 5.38, p = .022$. The d scores at the top represent the size of the effect that the manipulation had on test performance for Black and White participants in each analysis.

controlling for prior test performance, the manipulation of stereotype threat had a sizable effect on reducing Black students' performance ($d = -.68$) whereas Whites were relatively unaffected ($d = .16$).[1] In other words, the overall finding from the original paper is not contingent on covarying out prior test performance, although it is strengthened by removing this source of variation in the sample.

Those who critique the way that stereotype threat research has been described contend that the original studies do not show evidence that a threat-free context eliminates a race difference in performance (Jussim et al., 2016). But such a claim is not made in the original article. Rather, the authors state:

_____

[1]It is interesting to note that in Steele and Aronson's (1995) studies there was a failure of random assignment that worked against the hypothesis. A nearly significant race X condition interaction on prior SAT scores, $F(1, 156) = 3.77, p = .054$, reflected the fact that Blacks in the non-threatening condition ($M = 577.25, SD = 64.73$) had significantly lower SAT scores than Blacks in the threat condition ($M = 616.88, SD = 57.39$) or Whites in either condition ($M_{threat} = 638.50, SD = 68.52; M_{no\ threat} = 638.75, SD = 68.43$). The implication is that Black students randomly assigned to the threat condition came into the studies with a history of performing two-thirds of an SD higher than Blacks assigned to the no-threat condition, but as a result of stereotype threat performed two-thirds of an SD lower than these peers.

An important implication of this research is that stereotype threat is an underappreciated source of classic deficits in standardized test performance (e.g., IQ) suffered by Blacks and other stereotype-threatened groups such as those of lower socioeconomic status and women in mathematics (Herrnstein, 1973; Jensen, 1969, 1980; Spencer and Steele, 1994). In addition to whatever environmental or genetic endowments a person brings to the testing situation, this research shows that this situation is not group-neutral. (Steele and Aronson, 1995: 810)

Nonetheless, these critiques raise an important point about how consumers of science can simplify, distort, and magnify effects in the retelling of them, a problem identified in other chapters reviewing the classic work on obedience (Chapter 7), tyranny (Chapter 8), and bystander intervention (Chapter 12). Another aspect of the critique against research on stereotype threat is that it is a phenomenon created in a laboratory but not one that occurs naturalistically. The difficulty here is that there is no clear barometer to measure the 'threat in the air.' When group differences are assessed on a given high-stakes test, what percentage, if any, of that gap is due to stereotype threat? As summarized above, researchers have sought to create 'identity-safe' environments that level the psychological playing field for racial and gender groups. Interventions that affirm core values, normalize the stress of transition, or encourage an incremental mindset have all been shown to narrow racial and gender gaps in performance, and point to the real-world applicability of the theory. A meta-analysis of such field studies suggests that promoting an identity-safe environment for women in math and minorities in academics can reveal the latent ability that those students have (Walton and Spencer, 2009). All of these findings suggest that stereotype threat is not only experienced in contrived laboratory experiments.

Finally, the replicability of stereotype threat effects on performance has also been questioned because these original studies relied on small samples that might yield unreliable estimates of population parameters. There have now been numerous meta-analyses aiming to estimate a more reliable effect size for different groups or domains where the effect has been studied. Even though the effect should theoretically be moderated by a host of different contextual and person variables (and indeed all of these meta-analyses suggest considerable heterogeneity across studies), the findings are extraordinarily consistent. Meta-analytic data generally suggest that situational reminders of being negatively stereotyped lead members of stigmatized groups to perform a quarter to a half a standard deviation lower than they would in a more threat-free context (see Table 15.1). The meta-analysis that focuses specifically on the detrimental effect that stereotype threat can have for racial and ethnic minority students suggests a medium but reliable effect ($d = -.52$, Nadler and Clark, 2011). In other words, subsequent studies have established that the effect first isolated by Steele and Aronson has now been replicated by many, many independent labs. That said, evidence of publication bias endemic to science as a whole might still mean that these overall effect sizes overestimate the true effect (Flore and Wicherts, 2015).

Table 15.1 Summary of meta-analyses of overall stereotype threat effects among different groups and domains

	Stereotyped group	Stereotyped domain	Effect size[1]	k
Walton and Cohen (2003)	Several groups	Several domains	−.29	43
Nguyen and Ryan (2008)	Women and devalued minorities	Maths and intellectual testing	−.26	116
Walton and Spencer (2009)	Several groups	Several domains	−.48	39
Nadler and Clark (2011)	African Americans and Hispanic Americans	Intellectual testing	−.52	23
Stoet and Geary (2012)[2]	Women	Maths	−.61/−.17	10/10
Picho, Rodriguez and Finnie (2013)	Women	Maths	−.24	103
Flore and Wicherts (2015)	Girls (age 6–18)	Maths	−.22	47
Lamont, Swift and Abrams (2015)	Older adults	Cognitive performance	−.28	82
Appel, Weber and Kronberger (2015)	Negatively stereotyped immigrants	Intellectual performance	−.63	19

Notes: 1 All effect sizes have been converted so negative values reflect lower performance in stereotype threat compared with control conditions; they are Cohen's *d* except for Flore and Wicherts, which is Hedges' *g*. 2 No overall effect size was reported; but separate effects are given for studies that did/did not use a prior performance covariate.

CONCLUSION

Steele and Aronson's studies on stereotype threat were groundbreaking and they dovetailed with a growing appreciation at the time for understanding the unique psychological predicament faced by those who are socially stigmatized (Crocker et al., 1998). The empirical evidence that subtle situational cues can activate a host of psychological processes that might impair (and sometimes boost) performance has laid the groundwork for broader theoretical development. In particular, later conceptualizations of *social identity threat* have articulated how environments communicate which groups are socially devalued and the implications of these identity contingencies beyond just performance (Steele et al., 2002).

As a result, even before people become identified with a domain, the stereotypes of values, activities, and people in that setting serve to attract or repel them from those domains (Cheryan et al., 2009; Diekman et al., 2010; Haslam et al., 2012; Walton and Cohen, 2007). For example, the under-representation of women in the physical, computing, and engineering sciences is partly a function of stereotype threat that might undermine their performance (Spencer et al., 1999), but it also results from social identity threat that erodes women's sense of belonging (Cohen and Garcia, 2008). In contrast, when STEM fields are framed as facilitating more communal values or as requiring less stereotypically masculine preferences, women increase their interest in these careers (Diekman et al., 2011). Thus, a deeper understanding of contextualized sources of identity threat has paved the way for new theoretical models seeking to understand why those who are socially devalued self-segregate out of domains that can be pathways to greater success (Schmader and Sedikides, 2016).

Perhaps the greatest testament to the strength and breadth of the theoretical insights provided by Steele and Aronson is the fact that over two decades later there are still clear avenues for greater inquiry. In the context of current concerns about replicability, there is a need for new research that aims to replicate key findings with larger samples and pre-registered designs. Importantly, such studies might not always be direct replications of prior procedures, but they need to be mindful of the necessary preconditions for stereotype threat. For example, people must know the stereotype to be threatened by the possibility of confirming it, but this requirement means that results might not always replicate with groups that are recent immigrants to a new culture (e.g., Deaux et al., 2007), children or adolescents (McKown and Strambler, 2009; Shelvin et al., 2014), and in cultural contexts where stereotypes are weaker (Nosek et al., 2009).

Furthermore, because stereotype threat is, by definition, most damaging to those who are marginalized, there is a greater need for multi-site investigations that can recruit larger numbers of minority participants than one lab might be able to do alone. This practical hurdle is likely a key reason why fewer follow-up studies have sought to examine replication or extensions of the effects with African American or other devalued ethnic minority groups, in comparison with more easily obtainable samples of undergraduate women who contend with gender stereotypes about mathematical performance.[2] Larger samples are particularly critical if we are to understand the role of intersectionality of social identities in amplifying or mitigating effects (Shih et al., 2007).

From a theoretical perspective, there are still interesting open questions about when contextual cues to one's devalued status trigger avoidance motivation, disidentification, and exit from the domain, and when they trigger approach-related effort aimed at doubling one's effort to disconfirm the stereotype. Despite many studies pointing to important moderating variables, there is not a consensus picture of which individuals are susceptible to stereotype threat and which become resilient to these effects. However, more recent theoretical developments from a multi-threat framework suggest that key moderating variables are likely to vary across group and stereotyped domain (Shapiro and Neuberg, 2007; Shapiro et al., 2013). More research is therefore needed to understand how stereotype threat is experienced similarly or differently across various stereotyped groups.

---

[2] A Google search in July of 2016 of peer-reviewed studies including 'stereotype threat' and 'race or ethnicity or black or African* or Hispanic' yielded 165 articles in comparison to 312 articles when 'stereotype threat' was combined with 'gender or sex or female or woman or women'.

Finally, an extremely fruitful area of inquiry over the last decade has been the application of elements from the broader theoretical perspective to design targeted interventions that boost performance for those who are socially devalued. The early evidence reveals that when contexts are identity safe or devalued groups are given less threatening mindsets, long-standing gaps in interest, achievement, and/or self-confidence gaps begin to narrow. These changes can also compound over time in ways that are only beginning to be understood (Powers et al., 2016). Although stereotype threat is not the only contributor to group differences in performance, the contextualized nature of the theory provides us with the opportunity to structure environments in ways most likely to maximize human potential.

In sum, the theory itself, and the studies that provided the foundation of evidence, have themselves achieved something that very few empirical articles can claim: a legacy of scientific inquiry that has expanded our understanding of the human condition and provided clear tools to facilitate greater social equality.

ACKNOWLEDGMENTS

The authors thank Claude Steele, Joshua Aronson, Greg Walton, and Steven Spencer for their input and access to the original datasets for reanalysis. This work was partially supported by the Social Sciences and Humanities Research Council under Grant 435-2013-1587 awarded to Toni Schmader, and National Science Foundation grants #1329281 and 1535414 awarded to Chad Forbes.

FURTHER READING

Steele, C.M. and Aronson, J. (1995) 'Stereotype threat and the intellectual test performance of African-Americans', *Journal of Personality and Social Psychology*, 69: 797–811.

Steele, C.M. (1997) 'A threat in the air: How stereotypes shape intellectual identity and performance', *American Psychologist*, 52: 613–29.

Steele, C.M. (2010) *Whistling Vivaldi and Other Clues to How Stereotypes Affect Us*. New York: W.W. Norton & Company.

The original ground-breaking studies are reported in detail in Steele and Aronson's (1995) journal article, but Steele provided a broader view of his theoretical approach in the 1997 paper. In 2010, he published *Whistling Vivaldi*, an engaging book that summarizes not only the research findings on stereotype threat but also his personal experiences as an African American scholar and scientist building a successful career in the academy.

Spencer, S.J., Logel, C. and Davies, P.G. (2016) 'Stereotype threat', *Annual Review of Psychology*, 67: 415–37.

This paper provides the most recent scholarly review of research on stereotype threat.

Schmader, T., Johns, M. and Forbes, C. (2008) 'An integrated process model of stereotype threat effects on performance', *Psychological Review*, 115: 336–56.

Schmader and colleagues provide a more focused review of the mechanisms that mediate stereotype threat effects.

Shapiro, J.R. and Neuberg, S.L. (2007) 'From stereotype threat to stereotype threats: Implications of a multi-threat framework for causes, moderators, mediators, consequences, and interventions', *Personality and Social Psychology Review*, 11: 107–30.

In this paper, Shapiro and Neuberg provide an important model of the different forms that stereotype threat can take.

Walton, G.M. and Spencer, S.J. (2009) 'Latent ability grades and test scores systematically underestimate the intellectual ability of negatively stereotyped students', *Psychological Science,* 20: 1132–9.

In this paper, the authors meta-analysed several intervention studies to estimate the degree to which stereotype threat can mask latent ability for women and minorities.

Inzlicht, M. and Schmader, T. (eds) (2012) *Stereotype Threat: Theory, Process, and Application*. New York: Oxford University Press.

Finally, reviews of stereotype effects for different groups and across a variety of domains can be found in this edited volume.

REFERENCES

Adams, G., Garcia, D.M., Purdie-Vaughns, V. and Steele, C.M. (2006) 'The detrimental effects of a suggestion of sexism in an instruction situation', *Journal of Experimental Social Psychology*, 42: 602–15.

Alter, A.L., Aronson, J., Darley, J.M., Rodriguez, C. and Ruble, D.N. (2010) 'Rising to the threat: Reducing stereotype threat by reframing the threat as a challenge', *Journal of Experimental Social Psychology*, 46: 166–71.

Amicus Brief of Experimental Psychologists to the United States Supreme Court. Fisher v. University of Texas, August 13, 2012 (No. 01-1015).

Amicus Brief of Social Psychologists to the United States District Court. NAACP v. Horne, March 10, 2014 (No. 2:13-cv-01079-PHX-DGC).

Appel, M., Weber, S. and Kronberger, N. (2015) 'The influence of stereotype threat on immigrants: review and meta-analysis', *Frontiers in Psychology*, 6: 900.

Aronson, J., Fried, C.B. and Good, C. (2002) 'Reducing the effects of stereotype threat on African American college students by shaping theories of intelligence', *Journal of Experimental Social Psychology*, 38: 113–25.

Aronson, J., Lustina, M.J., Good, C., Keough, K., Steele, C.M. and Brown, J. (1999) 'When white men can't do math: Necessary and sufficient factors in stereotype threat', *Journal of Experimental Social Psychology*, 35: 29–46.

Beilock, S.L., Jellison, W.A., Rydell, R.J., McConnell, A.R. and Carr, T.H. (2006) 'On the causal mechanisms of stereotype threat: Can skills that don't rely heavily on working memory still be threatened?', *Personality and Social Psychology Bulletin*, 32: 1059–71.

Beilock, S.L., Rydell, R.J. and McConnell, A.R. (2007) 'Stereotype threat and working memory: Mechanisms, alleviation, and spillover', *Journal of Experimental Psychology: General*, 136(2): 256–76.

Blascovich, J., Spencer, S.J., Quinn, D. and Steele, C. (2001) 'African Americans and high blood pressure: The role of stereotype threat', *Psychological Science*, 12: 225–9.

Bosson, J.K., Haymovitz, E.L. and Pinel, E.C. (2004) 'When saying and doing diverge: The effects of stereotype threat on self-reported versus non-verbal anxiety', *Journal of Experimental Social Psychology*, 40: 247–55.

Brown, R.P. and Lee, M.N. (2005) 'Stigma consciousness and the race gap in college academic achievement', *Self and Identity*, 4: 149–57.

Brown, R.P. and Pinel, E.C. (2003) 'Stigma on my mind: Individual differences in the experience of stereotype threat', *Journal of Experimental Social Psychology*, 39: 626–33.

Cadinu, M., Maass, A., Rosabianca, A. and Kiesner, J. (2005) 'Why do women under-perform under stereotype threat?', *Psychological Science*, 16: 572–8.

Cheryan, S., Plaut, V.C., Davies, P.G. and Steele, C.M. (2009) 'Ambient belonging: How stereotypical cues impact gender participation in computer science', *Journal of Personality and Social Psychology*, 97: 1045–60.

Cohen, G.L. and Garcia, J. (2008) 'Identity, belonging, and achievement: A model, intervention, implications', *Current Directions in Psychological Science,* 17: 365-9.

Cohen, G.L., Garcia, J., Apfel, N. and Master, A. (2006) 'Reducing the racial achieve-ment gap: A social-psychological intervention', *Science*, 313: 1307–10.

Cohen, G.L., Garcia, J., Purdie-Vaughns, V., Apfel, N. and Brzustoski, P. (2009) 'Recursive processes in self-affirmation: Intervening to close the minority achievement gap', *Science*, 324: 400–3.

Crocker, J. and Major, B. (1989) 'Social stigma and self-esteem: The self-protective properties of stigma', *Psychological Review*, 96: 608–30.

Crocker, J., Major, B. and Steele, C.M. (1998) 'Social stigma', in D.T. Gilbert, S.T. Fiske and G. Lindzey (eds), *The Handbook of Social Psychology* (Vol. 2). Boston: McGraw-Hill. pp. 504–53.

Croizet, J. and Claire, T. (1998) 'Extending the concept of stereotype threat to social class: The intellectual underperformance of students from low socioeconomic back-grounds', *Personality and Social Psychology Bulletin*, 24: 588–94.

Croizet, J., Després, G., Gauzins, M., Huguet, P., Leyens, J. and Méot, A. (2004) 'Stereotype threat undermines intellectual performance by triggering a disruptive mental load', *Personality and Social Psychology Bulletin*, 30: 721–31.

Danaher, K. and Crandall, C.S. (2008) 'Stereotype threat in applied settings re-examined', *Journal of Applied Social Psychology*, 38: 1639–55.

Dasgupta, N. and Asgari, S. (2004) 'Seeing is believing: Exposure to counterstereo-typic women leaders and its effect on the malleability of automatic gender stereotyping', *Journal of Experimental Social Psychology*, 40: 642–58.

Davis, C.I., Aronson, J. and Salinas, M. (2006) 'Shades of threat: Racial identity as a moderator of stereotype threat', *Journal of Black Psychology*, 32: 399–417.

Deaux, K., Bikmen, N., Gilkes, A., Ventuneac, A., Joseph, Y., Payne, Y.A. and Steele, C.M. (2007) 'Becoming American: Stereotype threat effects in Afro-Caribbean immi-grant groups', *Social Psychology Quarterly*, 70(4): 384–404.

Devine, P.G. (1989) 'Stereotypes and prejudice: Their automatic and controlled com-ponents', *Journal of Personality and Social Psychology*, 56: 5–18.

Devine, P.G. and Brodish, A.B. (2003) 'Modern classics in social psychology', *Psychological Inquiry*, 14: 196–202.

Diekman, A.B., Brown, E.R., Johnston, A.M. and Clark, E.K. (2010) 'Seeking congruity between goals and roles: A new look at why women opt out of science, technology, engineering, and mathematics careers', *Psychological Science*, 21: 1051–7.

Diekman, A.B., Clark, E.K., Johnston, A.M., Brown, E.R. and Steinberg, M. (2011) 'Malleability in communal goals and beliefs influences attraction to stem careers: Evidence for a goal congruity perspective', *Journal of Personality and Social Psychology*, 101: 902–18.

Else-Quest, N.M., Hyde, J.S. and Linn, M.C. (2010) 'Cross-national patterns of gender differences in mathematics: a meta-analysis', *Psychological Bulletin*, 136(1): 103–27.

Fiske, S.T. (2003) 'The discomfort index: How to spot a really good idea whose time has come', *Psychological Inquiry*, 14: 203–8.

Flore, P.C. and Wicherts, J.M. (2015) 'Does stereotype threat influence performance of girls in stereotyped domains? A meta-analysis', *Journal of School Psychology*, 53(1): 25–44.

Forbes, C.E., Amey, R., Magerman, A.B., Duran, K. and Liu, M. (2016) 'Stereotype-based stressors facilitate emotional memory neural network connectivity and encoding of negative information to degrade math self-perceptions among women', unpublished manuscript.

Forbes, C.E., Duran, K.A., Leitner, J.B. and Magerman, A. (2015) 'Stereotype-threatening contexts enhance encoding of negative feedback to engender underperformance and anxiety', *Social Cognition*, 33: 605–25.

Forbes, C.E. and Schmader, T. (2010) 'Retraining attitudes and stereotypes to affect motivation and cognitive capacity under stereotype threat', *Journal of Personality and Social Psychology*, 99: 740–54.

Forbes, C.E., Schmader, T. and Allen, J.J.B. (2008) 'The role of devaluing and discounting in performance monitoring: A neurophysiological study of minorities under threat', *Social Cognitive and Affective Neuroscience*, 3: 253–61.

Fraley, R.C. and Vazire, S. (2014) 'The N-pact factor: Evaluating the quality of empirical journals with respect to sample size and statistical power', *PLoS ONE*, 9: e109019.

Frantz, C.M., Cuddy, A.J.C., Burnett, M., Ray, H. and Hart, A. (2004) 'A threat in the computer: The race implicit association test as a stereotype threat experience', *Personality and Social Psychology Bulletin*, 30: 1611–24.

Gonzales, P.M., Blanton, H. and Williams, K.J. (2002) 'The effects of stereotype threat and double-minority status on the test performance of Latino women', *Personality and Social Psychology Bulletin*, 28: 659–70.

Good, C., Aronson, J. and Harder, J.A. (2008) 'Problems in the pipeline: Stereotype threat and women's achievement in high-level math courses', *Journal of Applied Developmental Psychology*, 29(1): 17–28.

Good, C., Aronson, J. and Inzlicht, M. (2003) 'Improving adolescents' standardized test performance: An intervention to reduce the effects of stereotype threat', *Journal of Applied Developmental Psychology*, 24(6): 645–62.

Haslam, C., Morton, T.A., Haslam, S.A., Varnes, L., Graham, R. and Gamaz, L. (2012) '"When the age is in, the wit is out": Age-related self-categorization and deficit expectations reduce performance on clinical tests used in dementia assessment', *Psychology and Aging*, 27: 778–84.

Herrnstein, R.J. (1973) *IQ in the Meritocracy*. Little, Brown.

Herrnstein, R. and Murray, C. (1994) *The Bell Curve.* New York: Free Press.

Inzlicht, M., Aronson, J., Good, C. and McKay, L. (2006) 'A particular resiliency to threatening environments', *Journal of Experimental Social Psychology,* 42: 323–36.

Inzlicht, M. and Ben-Zeev, T. (2000) 'A threatening intellectual environment: Why females are susceptible to experiencing problem-solving deficits in the presence of males', *Psychological Science,* 11: 365–71.

Inzlicht, M. and Schmader, T. (eds) (2012) *Stereotype Threat: Theory, Process, and Application.* New York: Oxford University Press.

Jamieson, J.P. and Harkins, S.G. (2007) 'Mere effort and stereotype threat performance effects', *Journal of Personality and Social Psychology,* 93: 544–64.

Jamieson, J.P. and Harkins, S.G. (2009) 'The effect of stereotype threat on the solving of quantitative GRE problems: A mere effort interpretation', *Personality and Social Psychology Bulletin,* 35(10): 1301–14.

Jamieson, J.P. and Harkins, S.G. (2010) 'Evaluation is necessary to produce stereotype threat performance effects', *Social Influence,* 5: 75–86.

Jensen, A.R. (1969) 'How much can we boost IQ and scholastic achievement?', *Harvard Educational Review,* 39: 1–123.

Jensen, A.R. (1980) *Bias in Mental Testing.* New York: Free Press.

Johns, M., Inzlicht, M. and Schmader, T. (2008) 'Stereotype threat and executive resource depletion: Examining the influence of emotion regulation', *Journal of Experimental Psychology: General,* 137: 691–705.

Johns, M., Schmader, T. and Martens, A. (2005) 'Knowing is half the battle: Teaching stereotype threat as a means of improving women's math performance', *Psychological Science,* 16: 175–79.

Josephs, R.A., Newman, M.L., Brown, R.P. and Beer, J.M. (2003) 'Status, testosterone, and human intellectual performance: Stereotype threat as a status concern', *Psychological Science,* 14: 158–63.

Jussim, L., Crawford, J.T., Stevens, S.T., Anglin, S.M. and Duarte, J.L. (2016) 'Can high moral purposes undermine scientific integrity?', in J. Forgas, P. van Lange and L. Jussim (eds), *The Social Psychology of Morality.* New York: Psychology Press. pp. 173–95.

Kaiser, C.R., Vick, S.B. and Major, B. (2006) 'Prejudice expectations moderate preconscious attention to cues that are threatening to social identity', *Psychological Science,* 17: 332–38.

Kao, G. and Thompson, J.S. (2003) 'Racial and ethnic stratification in educational achievement and attainment', *Annual Review of Sociology,* 29: 417–42.

Katz, I., Epps, E.G. and Axelson, L.J. (1964) 'Effect upon negro digit-symbol performance of anticipated comparison with whites and with other negroes', *Journal of Abnormal and Social Psychology,* 69(1): 77–83.

Katz, I., Roberts, S.O. and Robinson, J.M. (1965) 'Effects of task difficulty, race of administrator, and instructions on digit-symbol performance of Negroes', *Journal of Personality and Social Psychology,* 2: 53–59.

Keifer, A.K. and Sekaquaptewa, D. (2007) 'Implicit stereotypes and women's math performance: How implicit gender–math stereotypes influence women's susceptibility to stereotype threat', *Journal of Experimental Social Psychology,* 43: 825–32.

Keller, J. and Dauenheimer, D. (2003) 'Stereotype threat in the classroom: Dejection mediates the disrupting threat effect on women's math performance', *Personality and Social Psychology Bulletin,* 29: 371–81.

Kit, K.A., Tuokko, H.A. and Mateer, C.A. (2008) 'A review of the stereotype threat literature and its application in a neurological population', *Neuropsychology Review*, 18: 132–48.

Koenig, A.M. and Eagly, A.H. (2005) 'Stereotype threat in men on a test of social sensitivity', *Sex Roles*, 52: 489–96.

Kozol, J. (2012) *Savage Inequalities: Children in America's Schools*. New York: Broadway Books.

Kray, L.J., Thompson, L. and Galinsky, A. (2001) 'Battle of the sexes: Gender stereotype confirmation and reactance in negotiations', *Journal of Personality and Social Psychology*, 80: 942–58.

Lamont, R.A., Swift, H.J. and Abrams, D. (2015) 'A review and meta-analysis of age-based stereotype threat: Negative stereotypes, not facts, do the damage', *Psychology and Aging*, 30: 180–93.

Lawrence, J.S., Marks, B.T. and Jackson, J.S. (2010) 'Domain identification predicts black students' underperformance on moderately-difficult tests', *Motivation and Emotion*, 34(2): 105–9.

Logel, C., Walton, G.M., Spencer, S.J., Iserman, E.C., von Hippel, W. and Bell, A.E. (2009) 'Interacting with sexist men triggers social identity threat among female engineers', *Journal of Personality and Social Psychology*, 96: 1089–113.

Logel, C.R., Walton, G.M., Spencer, S.J., Peach, J. and Mark, Z.P. (2012) 'Unleashing latent ability: Implications of stereotype threat for college admissions', *Educational Psychologist*, 47: 42–50.

Martens, A., Johns, M., Greenberg, J. and Schimel, J. (2006) 'Combating stereotype threat: The effect of self-affirmation on women's intellectual performance', *Journal of Experimental Social Psychology*, 42: 236–43.

Marx, D.M. and Goff, P.A. (2005) 'Clearing the air: The effect of experimenter race on target's test performance and subjective experience', *British Journal of Social Psychology*, 44(4): 645–57.

McIntyre, R.B., Lord, C.G., Gresky, D.M., Ten Eyck, L.L., Frye, G.D.J. and Bond Jr., C.F. (2005) 'A social impact trend in the effects of role models on alleviating women's mathematics stereotype threat', *Current Research in Social Psychology*, 10: 116–36.

McIntyre, R.B., Paulson, R. and Lord, C. (2003) 'Alleviating women's mathematics stereotype threat through salience of group achievements', *Journal of Experimental Social Psychology*, 39: 83–90.

McKown, C. and Strambler, M.J. (2009) 'Developmental antecedents and social and academic consequences of stereotype-consciousness in middle childhood', *Child Development*, 80: 1643–59.

McKown, C. and Weinstein, R.S. (2003) 'The development and consequences of stereotype consciousness in middle childhood', *Child Development*, 74: 498–515.

Miyake, A., Kost-Smith, L.E., Finkelstein, N.D., Pollock, S.J., Cohen, G.L. and Ito, T.A. (2010) 'Reducing the gender achievement gap in college science: A classroom study of values affirmation', *Science*, 330: 1234–7.

Murphy, M.C., Steele, C.M. and Gross, J.J. (2007) 'Signaling threat: How situational cues affect women in math, science, and engineering settings', *Psychological Science*, 18: 879–85.

Nadler, J.T. and Clark, M.H. (2011) 'Stereotype threat: A meta-analysis comparing African Americans to Hispanic Americans', *Journal of Applied Social Psychology*, 41: 872–90.

Nguyen, H.-H.D. and Ryan, A.M. (2008) 'Does stereotype threat affect test performance of minorities and women? A meta-analysis of experimental evidence', *Journal of Applied Psychology*, 93: 1314–34.

Nosek, B.A., Smyth, F.L., Sriram, N., Lindner, N.M., Devos, T., Ayala, A. ... and Kesebir, S. (2009) 'National differences in gender–science stereotypes predict national sex differences in science and math achievement', *Proceedings of the National Academy of Sciences*, 106(26): 10593–7.

Open Science Collaboration (2015) 'Estimating the reproducibility of psychological science', *Science*, 349(6251): aac4716.

Osborne, J.W. (2006) 'Gender, stereotype threat and anxiety: Psychophysiological and cognitive evidence', *Journal of Research in Educational Psychology*, 8: 109–38.

Osborne, J.W. (2007) 'Linking stereotype threat and anxiety', *Educational Psychology*, 27: 135–54.

Osborne, J.W. and Walker, C. (2006) 'Stereotype threat, identification with academics, and withdrawal from school: Why the most successful students of colour might be the most likely to withdraw', *Educational Psychology*, 26: 563–77.

Oswald, D.L. and Harvey, R.D. (2000) 'Hostile environments, stereotype threat, and math performance among undergraduate women', *Current Psychology: Developmental, Learning, Personality, Social*, 19: 338–56.

Pashler, H. and Wagenmakers, E.-J. (2012) 'Editors' introduction to the special section on replicability in psychological science: A crisis of confidence?', *Perspectives on Psychological Science*, 7: 528–30.

Picho, K., Rodriguez, A. and Finnie, L. (2013) 'Exploring the moderating role of context on the mathematics performance of females under stereotype threat: A meta-analysis', *Journal of Social Psychology*, 153: 299–333.

Ployhart, R.E., Ziegert, J.C. and McFarland, L.A. (2003) 'Understanding racial differences on cognitive ability tests in selection contexts: An integration of stereotype threat and applicant reactions research', *Human Performance*, 16: 231–59.

Powers, J.T., Cook, J.E., Purdie-Vaughns, V., Garcia, J., Apfel, N. and Cohen, G.L. (2016) 'Changing environments by changing individuals: The emergent effects of psychological intervention', *Psychological Science*, 27: 150–60.

Quinn, D.M., Kahng, S.K. and Crocker, J. (2004) 'Discreditable: Stigma effects of revealing a mental illness history on test performance', *Personality and Social Psychology Bulletin*, 30: 803–15.

Régner, I., Smeding, A., Gimmig, D., Thinus-Blanc, C., Monteil, J. and Huguet, P. (2010) 'Individual differences in working memory moderate stereotype-threat effects', *Psychological Science*, 21: 1646–8.

Richeson, J.A. and Shelton, J.N. (2003) 'When prejudice does not pay: Effects of interracial contact on executive function', *Psychological Science*, 14: 287–90.

Sackett, P.R., Hardison, C.M. and Cullen, M.J. (2004) 'On interpreting stereotype threat as accounting for African American–White differences on cognitive tests', *American Psychologist*, 59: 7–13.

Schmader, T. (2002) 'Gender identification moderates stereotype threat effects on women's math performance', *Journal of Experimental Social Psychology*, 38: 194–201.

Schmader, T., Forbes, C.E., Zhang, S. and Mendes, W.B. (2009) 'A metacognitive perspective on the cognitive deficits experienced in intellectually threatening environments', *Personality and Social Psychology Bulletin*, 35: 584–96.

Schmader, T. and Johns, M. (2003) 'Converging evidence that stereotype threat reduces working memory capacity', *Journal of Personality and Social Psychology*, 85: 440–52.

Schmader, T., Johns, M. and Barquissau, M. (2004) 'The costs of accepting gender differences: The role of stereotype endorsement in women's experience in the math domain', *Sex Roles*, 50: 835–50.

Schmader, T., Johns, M. and Forbes, C. (2008) 'An integrated process model of stereotype threat effects on performance', *Psychological Review*, 115: 336–56.

Schmader, T. and Sedikides, C. (2016) 'Situated inauthenticity as fit to environment (SAFE): How social identity threat disrupts being, doing, and belonging', unpublished manuscript. Vancouver, BC.

Sekaquaptewa, D., Waldman, A. and Thompson, M. (2007) 'Solo status and self-construal: Being distinctive influences racial self-construal and performance apprehension in African American women', *Cultural Diversity and Ethnic Minority Psychology*, 13: 321–7.

Shapiro, J.R. and Neuberg, S.L. (2007) 'From stereotype threat to stereotype threats: Implications of a multi-threat framework for causes, moderators, mediators, consequences, and interventions', *Personality and Social Psychology Review*, 11: 107–30.

Shapiro, J.R., Williams, A.M. and Hambarchyan, M. (2013) 'Are all interventions created equal? A multi-threat approach to tailoring stereotype threat interventions', *Journal of Personality and Social Psychology*, 104: 277–88.

Shelvin, K.H., Rivadeneyra, R. and Zimmerman, C. (2014) 'Stereotype threat in African American children: The role of Black identity and stereotype awareness', *Revue Internationale de Psychologie Sociale*, 27: 175–204.

Sherman, D.K., Hartson, K.A., Binning, K.R., Purdie-Vaughns, V., Garcia, J., Taborsky-Barba, S. … and Cohen, G.L. (2013) 'Deflecting the trajectory and changing the narrative: How self-affirmation affects academic performance and motivation under identity threat', *Journal of Personality and Social Psychology*, 104: 591–618.

Shih, M., Bonam, C., Sanchez, D. and Peck, C. (2007) 'The social construction of race: Biracial identity and vulnerability to stereotypes', *Cultural Diversity and Ethnic Minority Psychology*, 13(2): 125–33.

Simonsohn, U., Nelson, L.D. and Simmons, J.P. (2014) 'p-Curve and effect size correcting for publication bias using only significant results', *Perspectives on Psychological Science*, 9(6): 666–81.

Spencer, S.J., Logel, C. and Davies, P.G. (2016) 'Stereotype threat', *Annual Review of Psychology*, 67: 415–37.

Spencer, S.J., Steele, C.M. and Quinn, D.M. (1999) 'Stereotype threat and women's math performance', *Journal of Experimental Social Psychology*, 35: 4–28.

Stangor, C., Carr, C. and Kiang, L. (1998) 'Activating stereotypes undermines task performance expectations', *Journal of Personality and Social Psychology*, 75: 1191–7.

Steele, C.M. (1988) 'The psychology of self-affirmation: Sustaining the integrity of the self', *Advances in Experimental Social Psychology*, 21: 261–302.

Steele, C.M. (1997) 'A threat in the air: How stereotypes shape intellectual identity and performance', *American Psychologist*, 52: 613–29.

Steele, C.M. (2010) *Whistling Vivaldi: And Other Clues to How Stereotypes Affect Us*. New York: W.W. Norton & Company.

Steele, C.M. and Aronson, J. (1995) 'Stereotype threat and the intellectual test performance of African-Americans', *Journal of Personality and Social Psychology*, 69: 797–811.

Steele, C.M., Spencer, S.J. and Aronson, J. (2002) 'Contending with group image: The psychology of stereotype and social identity threat', *Advances in Experimental Social Psychology*, 34: 379–440.

Stoet, G. and Geary, D.C. (2012) 'Can stereotype threat explain the gender gap in mathematics performance and achievement?', *Review of General Psychology*, 16: 93–102.

Stone, J., Lynch, C.I., Sjomeling, M. and Darley, J.M. (1999) 'Stereotype threat effects on Black and White athletic performance', *Journal of Personality and Social Psychology*, 77: 1213–27.

Stricker, L.J. and Ward, W.C. (2004) 'Stereotype threat, inquiring about test takers' ethnicity and gender, and standardized test performance', *Journal of Applied Social Psychology*, 34: 665–93.

Tajfel, H. and Turner, J.C. (1979) 'An integrative theory of intergroup conflict', in W.G. Austin and S. Worchel (eds), *The Social Psychology of Intergroup Relations*. Monterey, CA: Brooks-Cole. pp. 33–48.

von Hippel, W., von Hippel, C., Conway, L., Preacher, K.J., Schooler, J.W. and Radvansky, G.A. (2005) 'Coping with stereotype threat: Denial as an impression management strategy', *Journal of Personality and Social Psychology*, 89: 22–35.

Walton, G.M. and Cohen, G.L. (2003) 'Stereotype lift', *Journal of Experimental Social Psychology*, 39: 456–67.

Walton, G.M. and Cohen, G.L. (2007) 'A question of belonging: Race, social fit, and achievement', *Journal of Personality and Social Psychology*, 92(1): 82–96.

Walton, G.M. and Cohen, G.L. (2011) 'A brief social-belonging intervention improves academic and health outcomes of minority students', *Science*, 331: 1447–51.

Walton, G.M. and Spencer, S.J. (2009) 'Latent ability grades and test scores systematically underestimate the intellectual ability of negatively stereotyped students', *Psychological Science*, 20: 1132–39.

Wicherts, J.M. (2005) 'Stereotype threat research and the assumptions underlying analysis of covariance', *American Psychologist*, 60(3): 267–69.

Wout, D., Danso, H., Jackson, J. and Spencer, S. (2008) 'The many faces of stereotype threat: Group- and self-threat', *Journal of Experimental Social Psychology*, 44: 792–99.

Wraga, M., Helt, M., Jacobs, E. and Sullivan, K. (2007) 'Neural basis of stereotype-induced shifts in women's mental rotation performance', *Social Cognitive and Affective Neuroscience*, 2: 12–19.

Yeung, N.C.J. and von Hippel, C. (2008) 'Stereotype threat increases the likelihood that female drivers in a simulator run over jaywalkers', *Accident Analysis and Prevention*, 40: 667–74.

Zhang, S., Schmader, T. and Hall, W.M. (2013) 'L'eggo my ego: Reducing the gender gap in math by unlinking the self from performance', *Self and Identity*, 12: 400–12.

Author Index

Aberson, C.L., 156
Abrams, D., 58–76, 81, 191, 195, 225, 258
Adams, G., 250
Adams, H.F., 59
Adams, W.G., 145
Adorno, T.W., 236
Aiello, J.R., 22
Ajzen, I., 32–4, 38, 222
Albarracin, D., 32, 229
Aldag, R.J., 187, 190
Alexander, C.N. Jr., 66–7
Allen, J.J.B., 263
Allport, F.H., 22, 23, 59, 63, 154
Allport, G.W., 219, 224
Alter, A.L., 254
Alvaro, E.M., 100
Amey, R., 263
Anastasio, P.A., 161
Andrade, M.G., 82
Anglin, S.M., 264
Anthony, T., 199
Antley, A., 129
Apfel, N., 262
Appel, M., 258
Arendt, H., 108–9, 111, 118, 119, 122–3
Argote, L., 75
Armitage, C.J., 32
Aron, A., 229
Aronson, E., 53, 54–5, 217–30
Aronson, J., 245–68
Asch, S.E., 1, 9, 59, 68, 77–92, 108, 186
Asgari, S., 254
Axelson, L.J., 264
Ayala, A., 266

Bachman, B.A., 161
Back, K., 192, 193

Banaji, M.R., 41, 172, 195
Banker, B.S., 161
Banks, C., 133
Banuazizi, A., 139
Banyard, P., 139
Barker, C., 129
Baron, R.S., 74, 100, 193–4
Baron, S.H., 76
Barquissau, M., 267
Barrett, K., 180
Bar-Tal, D., 70
Baumeister, R.F., 3, 4, 5
Baumrind, D., 119
Beauvois, J., 54
Becker, A.H., 25
Bedeian, A.G., 34
Bedrosian, D., 216
Beer, J.M., 264
Beilock, S.L., 252, 253
Bell, A.E., 265
Ben-Zeev, T., 250
Berger, R., 222, 227
Berndsen, M., 237, 241
Biddle, S.J.H., 41
Bierbrauer, G., 91
Bikmen, N., 262
Billig, M.G., 156, 173
Binning, K.R., 267
Birney, M., 120
Blaney, N., 221
Blanton, H., 263
Blascovich, J., 262
Blass, T., 109–10, 113, 118–9, 122
Bochario, P., 126
Bogart, L.M., 74
Bonam, C., 267
Bond, C.F., 11, 22

Bond Jr., C.F., 265
Bond, R., 82
Borofsky, G.L., 206
Bosson, J.K., 250, 252
Bourhis, R.Y., 167, 173
Bovard, E.W. Jr., 65
Braden, M., 47–8
Braly, K., 30
Brannigan, A., 119, 155
Brewer, M.B., 101, 156, 157, 175
Bridgman, D., 229
Brindley, S.G., 96
Brodish, A.B., 2, 4, 5, 245
Brody, C.L., 73, 75
Brown, E.R., 263
Brown, J., 261
Brown, P., 243
Brown, R., 227
Brown, R.J., 148, 156, 157
Brown, R.P., 251
Browning, C., 137, 140
Bruner, J.S., 239, 242
Brzustoski, P., 262
Bundy, R.F., 178
Burger, J., 121–2, 125
Burnett, M., 263
Byrka, K., 41

Cacioppo, J.T., 54
Cadinu, M., 175–6, 252
Campbell, D.T., 67–8
Cantril, H., 158
Carlsmith, J.M., 3, 9, 48–54
Carnahan, T., 140
Carr, C., 267
Carr, T.H., 261
Cecero, J.J., 216
Cesarani, D., 108, 123
Chaiken, S., 34, 36
Chancer, L., 216
Chang, S., 200
Chapanis, A., 53
Chapanis, N.P., 53
Chapman, J.P., 232
Chapman, L.J., 232
Chasteen, A.L., 196
Chatzisarantis, N.L.D., 41
Cherry, F., 119, 156, 206, 212
Cheryan, S., 258
Choi, H.-S., 74
Cialdini, R.B., 222
Cihangir, S., 181
Claire, T., 262
Clark, E.K., 263
Clark, M.H., 257–8
Clemens, M., 138
Cochrane, S., 73, 91

Cohen, G.L., 225, 254–5, 258–9
Collins, A., 216
Condor, S., 161
Conner, M., 32
Conrey, F.R., 244
Conway, L., 268
Cook, J.E., 266
Cooper, J., 43–57
Cottrell, N.B., 23
Crandall, C.S., 37, 83, 253
Crano, W., 100
Crawford, J.T., 264
Crocker, J., 245, 258
Crogan, M., 222
Croizet, J., 250
Crowther, S., 207, 212, 213
Croyle, R., 54
Crutchfield, R., 86
Cuddy, A.J.C., 263
Cullen, M.J., 266

Danaher, K., 253
Danso, H., 268
Darley, J., 118, 201–16, 261
Darroch, R.K., 40
Dasgupta, N., 254
Dashiell, J., 23
Dauenheimer, D., 252
Davidson, A.R., 33
Davies, K., 227
Davies, P.G., 262
Davis, C.I., 252
Davis, S.F., 12, 13, 23
Davison, A., 129
Deaux, K., 69, 259
DeChurch, L.A., 70
Despres, G., 262
Deutsch, M., 68, 81
Deutscher, I., 31
Devine, P.G., 2, 4, 5, 245
Devos, T., 266
Diehl, M., 170, 173
Diener, E., 3
Diekman, A.B., 258, 259
Dimow, J., 122
Dion, K.L., 157
Dockery, T.M., 34
Doms, M., 101
Donnellan, M.B., 138
Doosje, B., 180
Douthitt, E.A., 22
Dovidio, J.F., 158, 217–30
Drenan, S., 91
Driskell, J.E., 199
Duarte, J.L., 264
Duckitt, J., 155
Duffy, T., 209

Dunbar, R., 172
Dunton, B.C., 41
Dupuis, D.R., 196
Duran, K., 263
Durkheim, E., 58, 63

Eagly, A.H., 265
Echterhoff, G., 70
Eiser, J.R., 236
El-Malak, M.A., 222
Ellemers, N., 10
Elms, A.C., 121, 124
Else-Quest, N.M., 251
Epps, E.G., 264
Eshleman, A., 40
Esser, J.K., 187, 189
Evans, D., 216
Evans, R.I., 202

Fan, E.T., 199
Fazio, R.H., 54
Feld, P., 200
Fernandez, R., 230
Festinger, L., 3, 9, 43–57
Fiedler, K., 238–40
Fine, G.A., 156
Finkelstein, N.D., 265
Finnie, L., 258
Fischer, P., 206
Fishbein, M., 222
Fiske, S.T., 224, 245
Flament, C., 167
Flore, P.C., 257–8
Flowers, M.L., 189
Foddy, M., 161
Foels, R., 222
Forbes, C.E., 245–68
Frantz, C.M., 250
Fraley, R.C., 144, 255
Fraser, C., 10
Frenkel-Brunswik, E., 243
Freud, S., 63
Frey, D., 215
Fried, C.B., 261
Frye, G.D., 265
Fujita, K., 199
Fuller, S.R., 187, 190
Funder, D.C., 9

Gaertner, L., 174
Gaertner, S.L., 158, 222, 226
Gaffney, A.M., 156
Gagnon, A., 179
Galinsky, A., 265
Gamaz, L., 263
Gansberg, M., 215
Garcia, D.M., 261

Garcia, J., 258–9
Gardikiotis, A., 107
Gauzins, M., 262
Gawronski, B., 41
Geary, D.C., 255, 258
Geen, R.G., 11, 23
Gerard, H., 68, 81
Ghaith, G., 222
Gibbons, D., 209
Gifford, R.K., 155, 231–44
Gilbert, S.J., 120
Gilbert Cote, N., 38
Gilkes, A., 262
Gimmig, D., 266
Girgis, Z.M., 125
Goethals, G.R., 12
Goff, P.A., 265
Goldberg, S.C., 65
Goldhagen, D., 123
Gonzales, P.M., 250
Good, C., 253, 254
Grace, D.M., 161
Graham, R., 263
Grandberg, D., 155
Graveline, C., 138
Graves, J., 26
Greenberg, J., 127, 265
Green, D.P., 223, 224, 227
Greenwald, A.G., 37, 38–9
Greitemeyer, T., 215
Gresky, D.M., 265
Gross, J.J., 265
Gschwendner, T., 41
Guerin, B., 23
Guerra, R., 229
Guger, C., 129

Hagger, M.S., 32
Haines, H., 22
Hains, S.C., 192–3
Hall, W.M., 268
Hambarchyan, M., 267
Hamilton, D.L., 155, 231–44
Haney, C., 132, 133, 134, 137, 139, 140
Hanze, M., 222, 227
Harder, J.A., 263
Hardin, C.D., 70
Hardison, C.M., 266
Hardyck, J.A., 47–8
Harkins, S.G., 251, 253
Harmon-Jones, E., 53
Hart, A., 263
Hart, P.'t., 187
Hartig, T., 41
Hartson, K.A., 267
Harvey, O.J., 67, 160, 230
Harvey, R.D., 250

Haslam, C., 259
Haslam, N., 125
Haslam, S.A., 1–10, 87, 108–45, 154, 157, 158,
    193, 210, 240, 259
Hatfield, B., 22
Haymovitz, E.L., 262
Hehman, E., 229
Helt, M., 268
Herman, S., 199
Herrnstein, R.J., 245, 257
Hewstone, M., 93–107, 171, 227
Higgins, E.T., 70
Hoffman, E.L., 64
Hoffman, M., 209
Hoffman, S., 91
Hofmann, W., 37
Hogg, M.A., 26, 38, 70, 86, 162, 191, 192–3, 195,
    216, 225, 226
Hollander, M.M., 124
Hood, W.R., 160, 162, 230
Hornik, J.A., 40
Hornsey, M.J., 77–92, 191
Hothersall, D., 12
Houlette, M., 161
Hovland, C.I., 69
Howard M.L., 180
Hull, C.L., 23
Hunter, J.A., 146–163, 171
Hunyadi, O., 69
Huguet, P., 262
Huss, M.T., 25
Hyde, J.S., 263

Ingham, A.G., 23
Insko, C.A., 65, 81, 174
Inzlicht, M., 250, 252
Iserman, E.C., 265
Iso-Ahola, S.E., 22
Ito, T.A., 265

Jaccard, J.J., 33
Jackson, J., 268
Jackson, J.R., 41
Jackson, J.S., 265
Jacobs, E., 268
Jacobs, R.C., 67–8
Jahn, R.D., 209
Jahoda, M., 86–87
Jamieson, J.P., 251, 253
James, W., 239
Janis, I.L., 182–200
Jarrett, C., 1, 6
Jaspars, J.M.F., 10
Jellison, W.A., 261
Jensen, A.R., 257
Jetten, J., 77–92, 122, 174, 199
Johns, M., 250, 252–3

Johnson, B.T., 229
Johnson, C., 237
Johnson, D., 222, 223
Johnson, K.M., 161
Johnson, R.T., 230
Johnston, A.M., 263
Jones, E.E., 57
Jones, C.C., 230
Joseph, Y., 262
Josephs, R.A., 252
Jost, J.T., 69, 172, 195
Joule, R.V., 54
Jovchelovitch, S., 69
Jussim, L., 256

Kahnernan, D., 195, 197
Kahng, S.K., 266
Kaimen, I.P., 65
Kaiser, C.R., 252
Kaiser, F.G., 36
Kameda, T., 189
Kao, G., 245
Karau, S.J., 11–26
Karmen, A., 216
Katz, D., 30, 246
Kawakami, K., 229
Keifer, A.K., 251
Keller, J., 252
Kelman, H.C., 65
Keough, K., 261
Kerr, N., 106
Kerr, N.H., 193
Kershaw, I., 125
Kiesner, J., 262
Kikuchi, M., 181
King, G., 107
Kit, K.A., 250
Kiyonari, T., 174
Koenig, A.M., 265
Konečni, V.J., 138
Kosloff, S., 127
Kost-Smith, L.E., 265
Kozol, J., 245
Kosugi, M., 181
Kramer, R.M., 183, 184, 190, 195
Kronberger, N., 258
Kravitz, D.A., 12
Kray, L.J., 250
Krishnan, R., 75
Krueger, J.I., 71, 176
Krueger, R.F., 144
Kruschke, J.K., 244
Kuhn, T., 4
Kutner, B., 31

Lage, E., 107
LaLancette, M.-F., 82

Lamont, R.A., 258
Landau, M.J., 127
LaPiere, R.T., 3, 9, 27–42
Latané, B., 201–16
Laurens, S., 102, 103
Lawrence, J.S., 251
Le, H., 41
Lea, M., 75
LeBon, G., 12, 13, 83, 209
Lee, M.N., 251
Leitner, J.B., 264
Leo, G., 107
Lepper, M., 26
Leve, C., 199
Levine, J.M., 58–76
Levine, M., 201–16
Levinger, G., 26
Levinson, D.J., 243
Levy, J., 59
Leyens, J., 262
Linder, D.E., 53, 54
Lindner, N.M., 266
Linn, M.C., 263
Lippmann, W., 232, 239
Liu, M., 263
Lodewijkx, H.F.M., 181
Logel, C., 250, 251, 253
Long, K., 171
Lord, C.G., 265
Losch, M.E., 54
Loughnan, S., 120
Lozowick, Y., 123
Lovibond, S.H., 139
Lucker, G.W., 221
Lustina, M.J., 261
Lycett, J., 180
Lynch, C., 268

Maass, A., 262
Mackie, D., 236
MacNeil, M.K., 68
Magerman, A.B., 263
Majkut, L., 91
Major, B., 245
Malinowski, B., 63
Mann, J.A., 229
Mann, L., 182
Manning, C.C., 125
Manning, R., 207, 209–10
Manstead, A.S.R., 180
Mantell, D.M., 118
Mark, Z.R., 265
Marks, B.T., 265
Martens, A., 120, 254
Master, A., 262
Martin, B., 12
Martin, P.Y., 107

Martin, R., 93–107
Martorana, P., 199
Marx, D.M., 254
Mateer, C.A., 265
Mathews, A., 161
Maynard, D.W., 124
McCauley, C., 188–9, 191–5
McConnell, A.R., 233, 237, 261
McDonald, R., 127
McDougall, W., 1
McFarland, L.A., 266
McFarland, S., 144
McGarty, C., 3, 4, 5, 231–68
McGhee, D.E., 41
McGlynn, E.A., 161
McGuire, C., 200
McIntyre, R.B., 254
McKay, L., 264
McKelvey, M., 193
McKimmie, B.M., 91
McKown, C., 251, 259
Mead, M., 63
Meeus, W.H.J., 120, 122
Mendes, W.B., 266
Meot, A., 262
Mesmer-Magnus, J.R., 70
Messe, L.A., 215
Milgram, A., 110
Milgram, S., 3, 4, 9, 59, 108–29, 186
Millard, K., 4, 112, 117, 121
Miller, A.G., 118
Miller, N., 106
Mills, J., 53
Mitchell, M., 180
Mithiran, X., 145
Modigliani, A., 121–4
Montell, J., 266
Montgomery, R.L., 66–7
Miyake, A., 265
Mols, F., 122
Moore, A., 209
Moreland, R.L., 70
Morselli, D., 122
Morton, T.A., 259
Moscovici, S., 2, 9, 69, 83, 87, 93–107
Movahedi, S., 139
Muellerleile, P.A., 229
Mullen, B., 192, 237
Mummendey, A., 175
Murphy, M.C., 250, 253
Murray, C., 245
Murrell, A.J., 229

Nadler, J.T., 257–8
Naffrechoux, M., 107
Navarick, D.J., 120
Nelson, L.D., 267

Neuberg, S.L., 259
New York Times 147
Newman, M.L., 264
Nguyen, H.H.D., 251, 258
Nicholson, I., 119
Nida, S., 205–6
Nosek, B.A., 37, 251, 259
Novick, P., 111

Oakes, P.J., 1, 158, 171, 216, 226, 239
O'Brien, L.T., 40
Open Science Collaboration 255
Osborne, J.W., 252
Oswald, D.L., 250
Otten, S., 164–81
Overy, R., 123
Owens, P.D., 199

Packer, D.J., 116, 120, 182–200
Paluck, E.L., 223, 224, 227
Panzarella, R., 118
Pashler, H., 6, 246
Passini, S., 122
Paulson, R., 265
Payne, Y.A., 262
Peach, J., 265
Peck, C., 267
Peckham, V., 26
Percy, E.T., 244
Perrin, S., 82
Perry, G., 120
Personnaz, B., 93–107
Personnaz, M., 106
Peterson, R.S., 188
Petrocelli, J.V., 244
Pettigrew, T.F., 156, 219
Philogene, G., 69
Piaget, J., 62, 71
Picho, K., 258
Pinel, E.C., 251
Platow, M.J., 127, 146–63, 180
Platt, J.R., 18
Plaut, V.C., 262
Ployhart, R.E., 252
Poehlman, A.T., 41
Pollis, N.P., 66–7
Pollock, S.J., 265
Pollozek, F., 215
Pomare, M., 229
Postmes, T., 71, 199, 211
Powers, J.T., 260
Pratkanis, A.R., 189, 190–1, 192, 194, 200
Pratto, F., 172
Preacher, K., 268
Prescott, C., 134, 139–40
Probasco, P., 200
Prosser, A., 216

Puma, M.J., 223
Purdie-Vaughns, V., 261

Quinn, D., 250

Raaijmakers, Q.A., 120, 122
Rabbie, J.M., 157, 173
Radvansky, G.A., 268
Rasenberger, J., 207
Ray, H., 263
Regner, I., 252
Reicher, S.D., 87, 108–45, 161, 216, 226
Reynolds, K.J., 158
Richeson, J.A., 250
Riecken, H.W., 45
Rivadeneyra, R., 267
Rivers, W.H.R., 63
Robbins, J.M., 71, 176
Roberts, S.O., 264
Robinson, J.M., 264
Rochat, F., 113, 121–4
Rock, D., 230
Rodriguez, A., 258
Rodriguez, C., 261
Rohrer, J.H., 64
Rokeach, M., 173
Rosabianca, A., 262
Rosenberg, M.J., 53
Rosenfield, D., 229
Rosenthal, A.M., 201, 207, 209
Ross, L., 18, 85
Ross, L.D., 118
Rothbart, M., 175–6
Rozin, P., 3, 5
Rubin, M., 171
Ruble, D.N., 261
Russell, N.J.C., 112
Rust, M.C., 161
Ryan, A.M., 251, 258
Ryan, M.K., 199
Rydell, R.J., 261

Sachdev, I., 179
Sackett, P.R., 255
Saguy, T., 161, 229
Salas, E., 199
Salinas, M., 262
Sampson, E.E., 65
Sanchez, D., 267
Sanford, R.N., 243
Sarup, G., 155
Savin, H.B., 137
Schachter, S., 45
Scheepers, D., 177
Scher, S.J., 57
Schimel, J., 254
Schmader, T., 127, 245–68

Schmitt, M., 41
Schooler, J.W., 268
Schot, J.C., 180
Schwartz, J.L.K., 33
Schwartz, S.H., 157
Sedikides, C., 259
Sekaquaptewa, D., 252
Shapiro, J.R., 259
Sheeran, P., 32
Shelton, J.N., 250
Shelvin, K.H., 259
Sherif, C.W., 69, 147–50, 152, 155, 230
Sherif, M., 58–76, 146–63, 170, 177, 217, 219–20, 224, 225–6
Sherman, D.K., 254
Sherman, J.W., 237, 241
Sherman, S.J., 243
Shih, M., 259
Shotland, R.L., 206–7
Sibley, C.G., 155
Sidanius, J., 172, 174
Sikes, J., 229
Simmons, J.R., 267
Simon, H.A., 187
Simonsohn, U., 255
Simpatico, D., 209
Sjomeling, M., 268
Slater, M., 121
Smeding, A., 266
Smith, E.R., 236–8, 240
Smith, J.R., 1–10, 27–42, 117
Smith M.B., 182, 217
Smith, P., 82
Smith, R., 91
Smith, T.G., 75
Smyth, F.L., 266
Snapp, M., 229
Solomon, M.R., 91
Sorrentino, R.M., 102,103
Spears, R., 75, 89, 164–81, 199, 211, 236
Spence, K.W., 23
Spencer, C., 82
Spencer, S.J., 250, 252, 253, 255, 257
Sriram, N., 266
St Claire, L., 169, 170
Standing, L., 82
Stangneth, B., 123
Stangor, C., 252
Stanne, M.B., 230
Steele, C.M., 55, 245–68
Steinberg, M., 263
Stephan, C., 229
Stephan, C.W., 156
Stephan, W., 156
Stevens, S.T., 264
Stoet, G., 255, 258
Stollak, G.E., 215

Stone, J., 55, 250
Strambler, M.J., 259
Straw, M.G., 206–7
Stricker, L.J., 253
Stringer, M., 180
Stroebe, K.E., 174
Struch, N., 157
Sugimori, S., 189
Sullivan, K., 268
Swander, D.V., 74
Swapp, D., 129
Swift, H.J., 258

Taborsky-Barba, S., 267
Tabri, N., 198
Tajfel, H., 5, 9, 68–9, 141, 158, 164–81, 191, 210, 217, 224, 225, 245
Takooshian, H., 111, 208
Taves, P.A., 57
Taylor, S.E., 224
Ten Eyck, L.L., 265
Terry, D.J., 27–42, 91
Tetlock, P.E., 187, 188
Time 130
Titus, T.J., 11, 22
Thinus-Blanc, C., 266
Thompson, J.S., 245
Thompson, L., 265
Thompson, M., 267
Todd, W., 209
Tomcho, T.J., 222
Triplett, N., 11–26
Tropp, L., 219
Tuokko, H.A., 265
Turner, J.C., 1, 70, 86, 88, 141, 156, 158, 169, 170, 171, 191, 210, 217, 224, 225, 226, 239, 245
Tversky, A., 195, 197
Twenge, J.M., 122

Uhlmann, E.L., 41
Ungson, N.D., 182–200
US Supreme Court 254

van Avermaet, E., 101
van der Pligt, J., 243
Varnes, I., 263
Vaughan, G.M., 22
Vazire, S., 255
Ventuneac, A., 262
Vetlesen, A.J., 123
Vick, S.B., 264
Vidulich, R.N., 65
Visser, L., 180
Vohs, K.D., 9
von Hippel, C., 250
von Hippel, W., 252

Wade, G., 161
Wade, T.J., 91
Wagenmakers, E.J., 6, 246
Waldman, A., 267
Walker, C., 252
Walker, I., 3, 222
Walker, M.B., 82
Walton, G.M., 225, 254, 257–8, 260
Weber, S., 258
Webley, P., 199
Ward, A., 28
Ward, W.C., 253
Weil, A.M., 71
Weinstein, R.S., 251
Wentura, D., 176
Wetherell, M.S., 73, 91, 163, 170, 216, 226
White, B.J., 160, 230
Wicherts, J.M., 257–8
Wicker, A.W., 31–3, 38
Wilkins, C., 41
Williams, A.M., 267
Williams, C.J., 41
Williams, J.A., 161

Williams, K.D., 11–26
Williams, K.J., 263
Willis, H., 180
Wohl, M., 198
Worchel, S., 54
Wout, D., 252
Wraga, M., 253
Wright, S.C., 229

Yamagishi, T., 174
Yarrow, P.R., 41
Yeung, N.C.J., 250
Yuki, M., 174
Yzerbyt, V.Y., 243

Zajonc, R.B., 11, 21, 23
Zanna, M.P., 54
Zdaniuk, B., 74
Zhang, S., 251
Ziegart, J.C., 266
Zimbardo, P.G., 126, 130–45, 209, 214
Zimmerman, C., 267
Zucker, L.G.,73, 75

Subject Index

accountability 13
agentic state 118–19
aggression 139–41
altruism 140, 173
ambiguity 59–72
anonymity 71, 166
after-image effects 93–107
archival analysis 13–15, 18
arousal 23, 24, 38, 43, 54
Asch line-judgment studies 76–90
attitudes 3
— change 70
— implicit, explicit 36–9
attitude–behaviour relationship 27–42
attraction (and liking) 173
attribution (and attributional biases) 224–5, 248
attribution 54, 156, 225, 248
authoritarian personality 132, 133, 140, 142
authority 3, 5, 77–8, 108–29, 130–43
autokinetic effect 58–76

banality of evil 109, 118, 122
behaviour
— change 45, 49
— helping 201–16
— symbolic 28–9
beliefs 184, 188–9, 191
bias, cognitive; see cognitive biases
biology 232
bystander intervention; see behavior, helping

categorization 63, 69, 70–1, 158
— social 166, 168–79
cognition (and cognitive constructs)
— social; see social cognition
cognitive biases 182–200
cognitive consistency 44–5
cognitive dissonance 3, 43–57

cognitive psychology 231
collective behaviour; see intergroup behaviour
communication 71–2
compatibility
— principle of competition 33–4
— intergroup 150, 151–3, 156–9
— realistic 170
— social 170
compliance 48–53, 125, 181, 189, 191, 196
— induced 48–53
confederates 98, 101
conflict, social 69, 147, 153, 155, 156–7, 158, 159–60
— realistic 175, 177
— symbolic 156, 170
conformity 65, 68, 76–90, 93–5
conformity bias 93–4
consensus, social 93, 94
contact, social and intergroup 151, 153, 155
context, social; see social context
control
— behavioural 32–3
— perceived 32–3
cooperation 63, 69
coping 254
culture 59, 63–4

debriefing 35
decision-making 182–200
determinism 138 147
deindividuation 13, 71
deviance 80–1, 94–6, 185
differentiation 150
diffusion of responsibility 197, 200–1
discrimination 37, 148, 150–2, 155, 156–7, 159, 164–181
disobedience 116–9
dispositionalism 132–3, 137–8

dissent 135, 185, 193, 196
dissonance 3, 43–57
— arousal of 43, 54
— reduction of 43–57
— theory (see also cognitive dissonance) 48–9
distinctiveness
— group 165, 170–8

emotion 13, 44, 170, 187, 197, 220
ethics 132
European social psychology; see social
    psychology, European approach to
evaluative priming 69, 82, 93
evolution 172, 174, 178
evolutionary psychology 172–8
expectancies 50, 66–7, 70, 101, 169, 173–4,
    234, 252
experimental social psychology 69, 82, 93

fairness 63, 168–70, 173, 178
Festinger's cognitive dissonance studies 43–57
followers 45
frame of reference 59, 60–1, 62–4, 69–70, 71

gender 21, 174, 201–2, 207
Gestalt psychology 58
goals
— group 72, 142, 148–51, 153–4
— superordinate 156–7, 160
group(s)
— formation 117, 124, 148, 150, 152
— norms 58–72
— size 12, 193, 208, 209
— structure 58–72
group cohesion 86
group dynamics 231
group processes 61, 69, 72

Hamilton and Gifford's illusory correlation
    studies 231–44
health 27, 196
helping behaviour 201–16
historical case studies 121
Holocaust, the 2, 6, 108, 109, 111
homogeneity, group 185

identity
— national 226
— personal 206
— salience 71, 206–8
— social; see social identity
ideology 69, 147
identification, social 177
illusory correlation 231–44
Implicit Association Test (IAT) 37–39
impression formation 232, 237–8, 240–2
individualism 59, 72, 82
induced compliance paradigm 48–52

independence 87–9
ingroup bias 164, 166–78
ingroup formation — see group formation
influence
— informational 70–1, 81
— latent 95–101, 103–4
— majority 95–6
— manifest 95–101, 103–4
— minority 63, 69, 93–107
— normative 81, 83
— peer 78-90
initiation 53
interaction, social 12, 70
interactionism 142–3
intention 32–4
interdependence
— approach 69, 151, 158
intergroup
— attitudes 148, 150–2, 155, 156–7, 159,
    164–181
— behaviour 146–63
— contact 151, 153, 155
— competition 150, 151–3, 156–9, 165
— differentiation 150
— hostility 151–5, 157
— perspective 148–57
— relations 150, 151–3, 156–9, 165
interpersonal relations 147
intragroup
— attitudes 147, 176
— behaviour 150, 156
— processes 12, 72, 146, 152, 154–5, 158
involvement 118
isolation 140

justice 197

knowledge 157, 185

LaPiere's hospitality study 27–42
language 124, 222
Latané and Darley's bystander studies 201–16
latitude of acceptance 68–9
leadership 141–2, 150, 152
learning 48
levels of analysis; see social psychology
limited information processing capacity 231,
    238, 241

meaning 170, 177, 239–241
memory 250–3
message processing 44, 46
Milgram's obedience studies 3, 108–29
minimal groups 165, 166–7, 170, 175
minimal ingroup bias 164, 166–78
minorities (and minority groups) 93,
    232–3, 259
minority influence 63, 69, 93–107

Moscovici's blue–green afterimage studies 93–107
motivation 22–4, 53, 183–4

negative emotion 253
nonconformity 77–92
norms
    formation of 58–76
    group 67–72
    social 59, 63, 69, 72
    subjective 32–3

obedience 123–5
observational research 13, 36
organization 147–56

perceived behavioural control 32–3
perception
    — self- 195
personality 65, 69
persuasion 63
philosophy of science 4
political psychology 63
power 136, 139, 255
prejudice 37, 165
prestige 117
private
    — attitudes 51, 79, 95–6, 103
    — behaviour 83
prison 140–2
proximity 118
public
    — attitudes 34–5, 45, 84, 93, 95–7, 103
    — behaviour 34–5

reality testing 58–72
reciprocity
    — bounded 174–5, 175–6, 178
reductionism 59, 69, 72
rejection 95
resistance 81, 83–4, 86–9
roles 115, 119, 122, 134–5, 140–2

self
    — anchoring 170, 175–6, 178
    — enhancement 171
    — similarity 176
    — standards 55
self-categorization
    — theory 70, 158
self-concept 55, 132, 148, 170
self-efficacy 194, 254
self-esteem 119, 171, 186, 221, 225
self-interest 166, 167, 170, 173, 175, 176, 178
shared reality 70
Sherif's autokinetic studies 58–76
Sherif's Boys Camp studies 146–63, 165
shock generator 112–13

situationism 132–3, 137, 138, 140
social approval 93, 94
social change 88–9
social cognition 55, 69, 182–200
social comparison 43, 170
social context 143, 149, 161
social construction 58
social dominance 172
social facilitation 11–25
social identity
    — approach 72, 137–8, 159, 192, 210, 212–14, 239
    — theory 145, 157, 164
social impact 222
social influence 93–4, 100, 105, 131, 147
social interaction 12, 70
social loafing 11–26
social perception 69
social problems 6, 159
social psychology
    — applications of 223, 249, 260
    — definition of 1
    — European approach to 69, 82, 93
    — history of 1–11
    — importance and relevance of 1–11
social reality 70, 176
social representations 2
social structure 59, 64, 69, 233
social support 47, 48
social validation 89
society 29, 39
sociology 1
sports psychology 12, 22
status 63–5
stereotype(s)
    — formations 231–43
stereotyping 30, 245–68
stress 67, 88, 119–20, 184, 188, 252
surveys 30
system justification theory 69

Tajfel matrices 167–9, 171
Tajfel's minimal group studies 164–81
theory development 223
theory of planned behavior 32–3
theory of reasoned action 32–3
Triplett's competition studies 11–26
tyranny 142–3

uncertainty 62–72

value(s) 62
virtual reality 121

World War I 9, 28
World War II 64, 108, 121, 182, 239

Zimbardo's Stanford Prison study 130–45